Romantic Environmental Sensibility

Edinburgh Critical Studies in Romanticism
Series Editors: Ian Duncan and Penny Fielding

Available Titles

A Feminine Enlightenment: British Women Writers and the Philosophy of Progress, 1759–1820
JoEllen DeLucia

Reinventing Liberty: Nation, Commerce and the Historical Novel from Walpole to Scott
Fiona Price

The Politics of Romanticism: The Social Contract and Literature
Zoe Beenstock

Radical Romantics: Prophets, Pirates, and the Space Beyond Nation
Talissa J. Ford

Literature and Medicine in the Nineteenth-Century Periodical Press: Blackwood's Edinburgh Magazine, *1817–1858*
Megan Coyer

Discovering the Footsteps of Time: Geological Travel Writing in Scotland, 1700–1820
Tom Furniss

The Dissolution of Character in Late Romanticism
Jonas Cope

Commemorating Peterloo: Violence, Resilience, and Claim-making during the Romantic Era
Michael Demson and Regina Hewitt

Dialectics of Improvement: Scottish Romanticism, 1786–1831
Gerard Lee McKeever

Literary Manuscript Culture in Romantic Britain
Michelle Levy

Scottish Romanticism and Collective Memory in the British Atlantic
Kenneth McNeil

Romantic Periodicals in the Twenty-First Century: Eleven Case Studies from Blackwood's Edinburgh Magazine
Nicholas Mason and Tom Mole

Godwin and the Book: Imagining Media, 1783–1836
J. Louise McCray

Thomas De Quincey: Romanticism in Translation
Brecht de Groote

Romantic Environmental Sensibility: Nature, Class and Empire
Ve-Yin Tee

Forthcoming Titles

Romantic Pasts: History, Fiction and Feeling in Britain and Ireland, 1790–1850
Porscha Fermanis

Romantic Networks in Europe: Transnational Encounters, 1786–1850
Carmen Casaliggi

Romanticism and Consciousness
Richard Sha and Joel Faflak

Death, Blackwood's Edinburgh Magazine *and Authoring Romantic Scotland*
Sarah Sharp

Visit our website at: www.edinburghuniversitypress.com/series/ECSR

Romantic Environmental Sensibility

Nature, Class and Empire

Edited by Ve-Yin Tee

EDINBURGH
University Press

Edinburgh University Press is one of the leading university presses in the UK. We publish academic books and journals in our selected subject areas across the humanities and social sciences, combining cutting-edge scholarship with high editorial and production values to produce academic works of lasting importance. For more information visit our website: edinburghuniversitypress.com

© editorial matter and organisation Ve-Yin Tee, 2022
© the chapters their several authors, 2022

Edinburgh University Press Ltd
The Tun – Holyrood Road, 12(2f) Jackson's Entry, Edinburgh EH8 8PJ

Typeset in 10.5/13pt Sabon LT Pro
by Cheshire Typesetting Ltd, Cuddington, Cheshire

A CIP record for this book is available from the British Library

ISBN 978 1 4744 5647 0 (hardback)
ISBN 978 1 4744 5649 4 (webready PDF)
ISBN 978 1 4744 5650 0 (epub)

The right of Ve-Yin Tee to be identified as the editor of this work has been asserted in accordance with the Copyright, Designs and Patents Act 1988, and the Copyright and Related Rights Regulations 2003 (SI No. 2498).

Contents

List of Illustrations   vii
Acknowledgements   ix
Notes on Contributors   xi

    Introduction: Environmentalism, Class and Nature   1
    Ve-Yin Tee

Part I: Green Imperialism

1. The Environmental Aesthetics of the Chinese Garden   17
   Kuri Katsuyama

2. Orientalising the British Class System: Exploring the 'Chinese' Landscapes of Sir William Chambers, 1740–1775   34
   Laurence Williams

3. Ecogothic Chinatown   60
   Li-hsin Hsu

4. Climate Change, Inequality and Romantic Catastrophe   78
   David Higgins

5. Governing from the Country House: Landscape and the Aesthetics of Colonial Rule in India, 1780–1830   93
   Rosie Dias

6. On the Prowl: Tigers and the Tea Planter in British India   113
   Romita Ray

Part II: Land and Creature Ethics

7. William Cowper and Suburban Environmental Aesthetics   141
   Kaz Oishi

8. Exclusionary Landscapes: Shenstone and the Development of a Romantic Aesthetics of Enclosure   157
   Ve-Yin Tee

9. A World of Fire and Drought: Ecosocialism, Improvement and Apocalypse in James Woodhouse's *Crispinus Scriblerus*   172
   Adam Bridgen

10. Clifton Walks: Milkmaids Real and Imaginary   195
    Yuko Otagaki

11. Blake and the Pastoral-Georgic Tradition   211
    Steve Clark

12. Untidying the Landscape: Romantic Poetics, Class and Non-Human Nature   230
    Simon J. White

13. Sensing the Population Debate: Poverty, Ecology and the Senses in Malthus and his Critics   249
    Peter Denney

    Afterword: 'A tear to Nature's tawny sons is due': Alexander Wilson's *The Foresters* and Romantic Period Uprootings   272
    Bridget Keegan

Index   280

List of Illustrations

Figure 1   Mei Leng, *Bishu Shanzhuang* [Mountain Resort to Escape the Heat], 1713. © The Palace Museum, Beijing.   130

Figure 2   Giuseppe Castiglione (aka Shining Lang), *Xieqiqu Nanmian* [South Façade of the Palace of Delightful Harmony], 1785. Copper engraving. © The National Information Study Institute Digital Archive, Toyo Bunko, Tokyo.   130

Figure 3   Cantonese merchant's house from William Chambers, *Designs of Chinese Buildings* (London: printed for the author, 1757), plate ix. Engraving by Edward Rooker. Public domain.   131

Figure 4   William Marlow, *View of the Wilderness at Kew*, 1763. Watercolour. © Metropolitan Museum of Art, 25.19.43.   131

Figure 5   William Hodges, *View of Warren Hastings' House at Alipur and Two Figures in the Foreground*, c. 1781–3. Drawing and watercolour. Yale Center for British Art, Paul Mellon Collection.   132

Figure 6   William Hodges, *Natives Drawing Water from a Pond with Warren Hastings' House at Alipur in the Distance*, c. 1781. Oil on canvas. Private collection.   132

Figure 7   Richard Wilson, *Dinas Bran from Llangollen*, 1770–1. Oil on canvas. Yale Center for British Art, Paul Mellon Collection.   133

Figure 8   William Hodges, *View of an Indian Village with a Man Seated in the Foreground*, c. 1781–3. Gray wash, pen and black ink and graphite on laid paper. Yale Center for British Art, Paul Mellon Collection.   133

Figure 9   James Baillie Fraser, 'A View of the Botanic Garden

viii   List of Illustrations

	House and Reach', from *Views of Calcutta and Its Environs* (London: Smith, Elder & Co, 1826). Coloured aquatint. © The British Library Board, X644(4).	134
Figure 10	John Young Porter, *Palladian Garden House in a Wooded Park*, 1811. Watercolour on paper. © The British Library Board, WD4417.	134
Figure 11	John Closterman, *Maurice Ashley-Cooper and Antony Ashley-Cooper, 3rd Earl of Shaftesbury*, c. 1700–1. Oil on canvas. © National Portrait Gallery, London.	135
Figure 12	Jacket cover illustration, A. R. Ramsden, *Assam Planter: Tea Planting and Hunting in the Assam Jungle* (London: John Gifford, 1945). Author's private collection.	135
Figure 13	Frank Nicholls with Tigress shot at Borgang River, Assam, 1936. Reproduced in Frank Nicholls, *Assam Shikari: A Tea Planter's Story of Hunting and High Adventure in the Jungles of North East India* (Auckland: Tonson, 1970), figure 16. Author's private collection.	136
Figure 14	Map of The Leasowes from Robert Dodsley's 'A Description of the Leasowes', *The Works in Verse and Prose of William Shenstone*, 3 vols (London: Dodsley, 1764–9), II: facing page 333. Engraving. Author's private collection.	136
Figure 15	'Wolverhampton from the Penn Road', from William West, *Picturesque Views in Staffordshire* (Birmingham: Emans, 1834), plate v. Engraving by T. Radclyffe after Frederick Calvert's drawing. © The Bodleian Library.	137
Figure 16	*A Survey of the Estate of Sandleford in the County of Berkshire belonging to Mrs Montagu*, 1781. © Berkshire Record Office, BRO:D/ELM/T19/2/13.	137

Acknowledgements

It is with great pleasure that I can finally thank David Higgins for our discussions over the summer of 2011, when I decided to commit to an environmental direction in my work. I am also grateful to Kaz Oishi for his advice and help in putting together the application for government funding, which I received for a project on Romantic Environmental Aesthetics from April 2013 to March 2016 under the Grant-in-Aid for Scientific Research (C) scheme. It is this study that I pursued together with David, Kaz, Rosie Dias, Simon J. White, Kuri Katsuyama and Yuko Otagaki which laid the foundations of this essay collection. I would also like to mention the people with Edinburgh University Press: the encouragement I received from Michelle Houston, who commissioned this book, the responsiveness of the series editors Ian Duncan and Penny Fielding, and the support given by Ersev Ersoy, Susannah Butler and Caitlin Murphy.

In memory of David Mayer, SVD, colleague, friend and author of *Komagane Poems* (1999). He was the only person I knew who loved insects more than I did.

Notes on Contributors

Adam Bridgen is Fleeman Research Fellow in Eighteenth-Century Literature and Culture at the University of St. Andrews. His research concerns the impact of social class and religion on writing about slavery, empire, and the natural world during the long eighteenth century. He has previously published on James Woodhouse, and has essays forthcoming on Hannah More as well as the animal ethicists Thomas Tryon and Humphry Primatt. He is currently completing a monograph on labouring-class writing and colonial slavery for Oxford University Press.

Steve Clark is Visiting Professor at the Graduate School of Humanities and Sociology at the University of Tokyo, Japan. Previous publications include *Historicising Blake* (1994), *Blake in the 90s* (1999) and *Blake, Nation and Empire* (2006), all co-edited with David Worrall; *Blake in the Orient* (2006), co-edited with Masashi Suzuki; *Blake, Modernity and Popular Culture* (2007), co-edited with Jason Whittaker; *Blake 2.0: William Blake in 20th Century Art, Music and Culture* (2012), co-edited with Tristanne Connolly and Jason Whittaker. His most recent publication is *British Romanticism in European Perspective* (2015), co-edited with Tristanne Connolly.

Peter Denney is a Senior Lecturer in History at Griffith University, Australia. He has recently co-edited *Sound, Space and Civility in the British World, 1700–1850* (2019); *Politics and Emotions in Romantic Periodicals* (2019); and *Transcultural Ecocriticism: Global, Romantic and Decolonial Perspectives* (2021). His research on British literature and culture in the long eighteenth century focuses on rural life, poverty, the senses and political radicalism. He is currently completing a book on landscape and soundscape in Britain from Defoe to Cobbett.

Rosie Dias is Reader in the History of Art at the University of Warwick. She works on late eighteenth- and nineteenth-century British art, particularly in relation to issues of national identity and colonial encounter. She is the author of *Exhibiting Englishness: John Boydell's Shakespeare Gallery and the Formation of a National Aesthetic* (2013) and co-editor (with Kate Smith) of *British Women and Cultural Practices of Empire, 1770–1940* (2019).

David Higgins is Professor of Environmental Humanities at the University of Leeds. His most recent book is *British Romanticism, Climate Change, and the Anthropocene: Writing Tambora* (2017). His current research focuses on two areas: the history of British nature writing, and the philosophical roots of Anglo-American climate change discourse.

Li-hsin Hsu is Associate Professor of English at National Chengchi University, Taiwan. She has published in international journals such as the *Emily Dickinson Journal*, *Symbiosis*, *Cowrie* and *Romanticism*. Her research interests include Emily Dickinson studies, Romanticism, Transatlantic studies, Transpacific studies, Orientalism and Ecocriticism. She has been serving on the Emily Dickinson International Society board and is editor-in-chief of *The Wenshan Review*, an international academic journal devoted to the promotion of interdisciplinary and multidisciplinary approaches to literary and cultural studies. Her current project involves Ecogothic in Romantic writings and modern Taiwan poetry.

Kuri Katsuyama is Professor of English at Kyoto University of the Arts, Japan. Her publications include 'Coleridge and the Orient: The Transformation of a Discourse of Otherness', in *Voyages of Conception* (2005); 'Coleridge and the Chinese Garden', in *Essays in English Romanticism* 29/30 (2006); '"Kubla Khan" and British Chinoiserie: The Geopolitics of the Chinese Garden', in *Coleridge, Romanticism, and the Orient* (2013); and 'Organic Life: Dynamism in Coleridge's "Theory of Life"', in *Coleridge's Romanticism* (2020).

Bridget Keegan is Professor of English and Dean of Arts and Sciences at Creighton University, USA. She is the author of *British Labouring-Class Nature Poetry, 1730–1837* (2008) and editor with John Goodridge of *A History of British Working-Class Literature* (2017). Her work as a scholar and editor has focused on eighteenth- and nineteenth-century British labouring-class poetry, Romantic period environmental writing and John Clare. She is currently at work on a study of occupation-based writing in the long eighteenth century.

Kaz Oishi finished his DPhil at Oxford, taught at the Open University of Japan, Nagoya University, and is Professor at the University of Tokyo. His publications include *Coleridge, Romanticism, and the Orient: Cultural Negotiations* (2013), co-edited with David Vallins and Seamus Perry; a journal special issue of *Cross-Cultural Negotiations: Romanticism, Mobility and the Orient* (2011), co-edited with Felicity James; and published chapters in *Coleridge and Contemplation* (2017), edited by Peter Cheyne; *The Reception of Blake in the Orient* (2006), edited by Steve Clark and Masashi Suzuki; and *British Romanticism in European Perspective: Into the Eurozone* (2015), edited by Steve Clark and Tristanne Connolly. He has been working on English Romanticism and cultural negotiations, the reception/regeneration of English Romanticism in the early twentieth century, and the idea of philanthropy in the Romantic period.

Yuko Otagaki is Professor of English at the University of Hyogo, Japan. She is also a member of the Association for the Study of Literature and Environment in Japan (ASLE-Japan). Primarily interested in walking literature and travel writing, her recent publications include 'Reconsideration of Wordsworth's *Guide to the Lakes*', in *Poole Gakuin University Journal* (2015); 'Isabella Bird's Perspective: Her Writings on the Far East', in *Minzokugaku* (2015); and 'Milkmaid Songs Freighted with Class, Gender and Nationality Bias', in *Literature and Environment: The Journal of the Association for the Study of Literature and Environment in Japan* (2018).

Romita Ray is associate professor of art history at Syracuse University, USA, where she teaches European and Indian art. Her area of research is the art and architecture of the British empire in India, on which she has published widely. The author of *Under the Banyan Tree: Relocating the Picturesque in British India* (2013), Ray is currently working on a book manuscript about the visual cultures of tea in India, tentatively titled *Leafy Wonders: Art, Aesthetics, and the Science of Tea in India*. Together with Dr Jos Hackforth-Jones, she is also editing a multi-volume project for Routledge on art, architecture, material culture and early cinema in the British empire.

Ve-Yin Tee is Assistant Professor in the Department of British and American Studies, Nanzan University, Japan. He is the author of *Coleridge, Revision and Romanticism* (2009) as well as the teen novel *On Donuts and Telekinesis* (2014). He has published book chapters and journal articles on British painting, British nature poetry and Singaporean war history.

Simon J. White is a Reader in Romantic and Nineteenth-Century Literature at Oxford Brookes University. He is the author of *Robert Bloomfield, Romanticism and the Poetry of Community* (2007) and *Romanticism and the Rural Community* (2013), and is currently completing a book on magical belief and practice in nineteenth- and early twentieth-century regional fiction for Palgrave Historical Studies in Witchcraft and Magic. Dr White is also beginning a major project on human discourse and the representation of non-human animals.

Laurence Williams is Associate Professor in the Department of English Studies at Sophia University, Tokyo, Japan. His research centres on British travel writing on Japan and China, particularly examining the ways in which broader patterns of trade flows, diplomatic relations and cultural exchange are represented in eighteenth- and nineteenth-century literature and popular culture. He has co-edited (with Steve Clark) a journal special issue of *Studies in Travel Writing* on Isabella Bird (2017) and (with Alex Watson) the essay collection *British Romanticism in Asia: The Reception, Translation, and Transformation of Romantic Literature in India and East Asia* (2019). He has also published articles in the *Journal for Eighteenth-Century Studies* and the essay volume *New Directions in Travel Writing Studies*, edited by Paul Smethurst and Julia Kuehn (2015).

Introduction: Environmentalism, Class and Nature

Ve-Yin Tee

As the environmental historian Frederik Albritton Jonsson has neatly summarised, the standard narrative on the rise of green consciousness 'runs from the romantic critique of industrialization in Britain and the United States to the creation of the first national parks in these countries'.[1] There are other competing accounts, and while Jonsson investigates the forgotten legacy of the Scottish Enlightenment, the main alternative is actually represented by the line of scholarship that looks to colonisation by Britain and France (and the environmental degradation that resulted) as the trigger. What is not in dispute, however, is the importance of the eighteenth and early nineteenth century to the development of modern environmentalism, except that where the first account concentrates on the evolution of a poetic 'green language',[2] the second concentrates on a scientific language of conservation.[3] But whether it is nature poetry or colonial knowledge production being attended to, what is almost invariably communicated is an elite perspective. It should come as no surprise then that an environmentalism which traces its origins to the socially elevated (poets, scientists and, with Jonsson, the Scottish agricultural improvers) continues to accrue to itself the aspersions of elitism that it does in British mainstream society,[4] or a misconception as unfortunate as American political economist Lester Thurow's that 'environmentalism is an interest of the upper middle class. Poor countries and poor individuals simply aren't interested.'[5]

Indeed, having surveyed the work of environmental historians on tree activism in India[6] and postcolonial scholars on environmental justice,[7] I am certain that many individuals from a background economically less well-off than mine were far more committed to the protection of the air, water and soil than I – an upper-middle-class Singaporean living in Nagoya – could ever be. The Himalayan villagers of the Chipko movement fought even harder, with more imagination and with greater success against deforestation in the 1970s than the American radical environmental activists of the Earth Liberation Front have ever done in the twenty-first century.[8] As far as I am aware, not a single one of the 212 land and environment activists murdered in 2019 was American or British.[9] Poorer individuals from poorer countries have risked and lost far more for environmental causes, and there is every likelihood that they will continue to do so given their situation of greater vulnerability to environmental degradation. Almost all the buildings in the city of Nagoya are earthquake-resistant. The river embankments and sea walls of Tokai are ubiquitous and raised high, and even if this region of Japan in which I have dwelt for sixteen years were to experience a disaster comparable to the ongoing nuclear catastrophe up north in Tohoku, I would have the option of relocating to a different country altogether if I so chose without being a refugee.

The fundamental problem with the idea of climate change as an emergency for all, so passionately conveyed by the Swedish activist Greta Thunberg,[10] is that it overlooks entirely the uneven distributive effects of the crisis. Due to the legacy of colonial exploitation, the people of the Global South are disproportionately vulnerable. As feminist philosopher Nancy Tuana puts it, 'To say that all lives are precarious, that we are all vulnerable, is the kind of truism that covers over, obscures, and, wilfully or not, flattens the complexities of oppressions.'[11] And it's not only the circumstance of poorer countries and poorer individuals being more exposed, but also the case that harsher environments drive those who are already privileged to further 'enhance their privilege at the expense of those whose inequalities are made even more severe'.[12] This is a thread that is taken up by David Higgins (Chapter 4) in his analysis of Mary Shelley's novel *The Last Man* (1826), which chronicles the ravages of an infectious disease sweeping across the globe in the twenty-first century. Alert to the topicality of his subject (this essay collection being put together during the Covid-19 pandemic) as much as the recidivist tendency of ecocritics on the Anthropocene to elide race and class, David not only shows how 'the privileged characters have places to take refuge away from large groups of people', but – looking across Percy Shelley's eschatological drama *Prometheus Unbound* (1820) and Byron's eco-disaster poem 'Darkness' (1816) – presents in no uncertain terms also how 'apocalypticism, techno-utopianism, and pure denialism [are] products of privilege'. (For this introduction, the first name of the contributors to this volume is used in order to distinguish them from the other experts that I refer to.)

'In academia', according to the leading postcolonialist critic in Britain, Priyamvada Gopal, 'a retrograde strain of making the so-called case for colonialism is now resurgent.'[13] It is much to be regretted that

Insurgent Empire: Anticolonial Resistance and British Dissent (2019), her fierce, meticulously researched account of how the 'freedom' of the metropole (Britain) originated in the 'resistance' of the periphery (Britain's colonial possessions), does not deal with anti-colonial environmental activism. After all, the idea of being environmental has very similar race and class inflections to that of being free. (For example, the criticism Tuana levels at the idea of climate change as an emergency for all would do just as well as a riposte to the supporters of All Lives Matter.) Gopal's omission is perhaps indicative that the fairly recent rapprochement between environmentalism and postcolonialism is still uneasy. Even the editors of *Postcolonial Ecologies* (2011), one of the two foundational texts of this détente, have warned: 'the discourse of nature is a universalizing one, and thus ecocriticism is particularly vulnerable to naturalizing dominant forms of environmental discourse, particularly those that do not fundamentally engage with questions of difference, power, and privilege'.[14] The arguments of biocentrists prioritising non-humans grate on the ear of decolonialists who have their eye on the 'intensified and sustained exploitation of the majority of humans and non-humans . . . by a cartel [of] European/north American elites'.[15] While the authors of *Postcolonial Ecocriticism* (2010), the other foundational text, insist that 'it would be a mistake to see ecocriticism as being more concerned with inhabiting the world than with changing it',[16] the 'retrograde strain' deplored by Gopal is nonetheless detectable. In his foreword to *Eco-Cultural Networks and the British Empire* (2015), John M. MacKenzie mentions Marxism as one of the scholarly frameworks in decline or discredited by 'increasing complexity[, which] has become the order of the day'.[17] In the 1960s, 70s and 80s, Raymond Williams, E. P. Thompson and John Barrell had shown the very different lifeworlds of labouring- and working-class peoples. In the 1990s, the implications of class and locality were advocated for with uncommon elan by David Harvey, Donna Haraway, William Cronon and other American ecosocialists. But despite the impact of the environmental justice movement on so-called second-wave ecocriticism during the first decade of the twenty-first century,[18] which 'took all "deep" eco-critical positions to task',[19] attention has shifted away from human relations towards relations between species to such an extent that the class angle has dropped off the radar of ecocriticism. Shocking to relate, but Greg Garrard's 600-page *Oxford Handbook of Ecocriticism* (2014) does not have a single article considering class differences.

Ironically, this ecologicalisation of green discourse has been effected by Timothy Morton's influential *Ecology without Nature* (2007) as a way towards a more egalitarian and socially grounded ecocriticism:

> To write about ecology is to write about society, and not simply in the weak sense that our ideas of ecology are social constructions. Historical conditions have abolished an extra-social nature to which theories of society can appeal, while at the same time making the beings that fell under this heading impinge ever more urgently upon society.[20]

Nature has too much historical baggage,[21] the idea of it so freighted with an obfuscating Romantic preoccupation with wildness and beauty that it now has become a debilitating delusion in our era of environmental catastrophe:[22] 'we need to smash the aestheticization: in case of ecological emergency, break glass'.[23] As the Marxist theorist Raymond Williams famously wrote in *Culture and Materialism* (1980), 'the idea of nature contains ... an extraordinary amount of human history',[24] which he conceded in *Keywords* (1983) to be 'perhaps the most complex word in the language'.[25] Be that as it may, I do not quite understand why the move away from the history of nature to the science of ecology would necessarily mark an improvement. The latter is no more proof than the former against retrograde tendencies, as the life work of Donna Haraway attests.[26] It is not my intention here at all to oppose an ecological approach, much less that of scientific study as a whole, but rather my sense that scholars in literature and art history need reminding of the fact that our strength lies in the realm of representation. As far as this 'nature' is an issue of representation, it is historical rather than scientific observation that should take precedence for ecocritics who ask themselves whose 'nature' is being represented, for whom it is being represented, and to what end. The abiding impression I had of Williams's revisionist account of the history of English literature in *The Country and the City* (1973) was how class-bound the representations he deals with were. Marxism is allied with postcolonialism in being deeply invested in 'questions of difference, power, and privilege', except that the former focuses on class and the latter on race. To keep such questions in the mind of the reader, every contributor in this volume of essays connects the eighteenth- and nineteenth-century representations they deal with of the land, and of the plants, animals and people who live on that land, with social class.

Focusing on the first-hand accounts of Han and Qing imperial gardens by the upper-, middle- and working-class members of the 1792–3 British embassy to China, Kuri Katsuyama reminds us that our 'aesthetics [are] never ... abstracted from the social and political contexts in which all of us are embedded' (Chapter 1). I deploy a similar approach but on the metropole itself in juxtaposing the landscape poetry of William Shenstone on The Leasowes, Samuel Taylor Coleridge's on 'almost anywhere ... or nowhere in particular', and James Woodhouse, the 'Poetical Shoemaker' whom Shenstone granted access to his estate (Chapter 8). Instead of trying to escape an aesthetic representation of reality, which is probably impossible, attending to different class perspectives allows us to suggest why the 'nature' of one person might be more enlightened (or at least less oppressive) than another's, politically and ecologically. The advantage of paying attention to class over race is that 'questions of difference, power, and privilege' can be investigated not only between peoples, but also within peoples of multicultural societies and within countries that are less multiracial than America or Britain.

Furthermore, as far as the realm of representation is our sphere of expertise, it might be to the advantage of those of us sympathetic to Marxism to move away from a rigidly economic conception of class towards a broader consideration of its hybrid, discursive aspects. British society conventionally defines three broad class groups. First, an upper class with vast holdings of land, who held the greatest power economically, politically and culturally in the eighteenth and nineteenth centuries. I do not believe that ecocriticism has fully taken into account the implications of the existence of a social group that has consciously manipulated the entire ecological fabric of Britain since Anglo-Saxon times.[27] I am referring to their part in husbandry and landscape gardening, as well as their position as originators and disseminators of entire structures of knowledge. For example, even with as innocuous an opening assertion as Peter Heyman's 'that the Romantics' aesthetic perception of animality both influenced and was influenced by their ethical, scientific and religious understanding of species',[28] one only needs to pay attention to the social status of the philosophers, scientists and religious leaders who established the framework to reveal how much Romantic ways of seeing drew from the upper class. The cautionary note sounded by postcolonial ecocritics against 'environmental orientalism',[29] that is, the reification in mainstream environmentalism of Indigenous peoples, where 'continuous occupation [of the land] [has] established a powerful entitlement',[30] receives added force if it is borne in mind that the most privileged and powerful group in the metropole (who still exist) can make the claim on very similar grounds. The middle class, the largest group in British society now, was much smaller with their growth in numbers and influence being the outstanding demographic feature of the eighteenth century.[31] From schoolteachers, lawyers and other members of the professions to the industrialists and East India Company merchants, they could be as highly educated as the upper class, even as wealthy, except that they worked for a living. The people who laboured with their hands as the servants and workers of the upper and middle classes, as well as the highly skilled artisans, craftsmen, midwives and milkwomen, were the most numerous by far of the three classes. This third group, the working or labouring class, who had a strong sense of identity through communal work or through being engaged in work done by family members over several generations, is greatly diminished now and should be distinguished from the underclass of people who have emerged in the twentieth and twenty-first centuries without work, or without work regular enough or sufficiently remunerative for them to survive on a day-to-day basis.[32]

Laurence Williams (Chapter 2) and Rosie Dias (Chapter 5) are exemplary in showing how these class divisions were bridged through landscape writing, painting and gardening, as well as how the relationship between human beings and the natural world was reconfigured in the process. William Chambers, 'the son of a Scottish expatriate merchant, born in Sweden and educated at a grammar school in Ripon', cashed in on time spent overseas, aristocratic patronage and his Swedish connections to gain respectability as the bona fide possessor of a Swedish knighthood (Chapter 2). His stint in Bengal and Canton as an employee of the Swedish East India Company, and training as an architect in Paris, were strategically employed to win elite acceptance as a China expert. Laurence demonstrates how, on achieving the position of Royal Architect and chief designer of Kew Gardens, he insinuated into this most rarefied yet programmatic of landscape gardens a more ordinary mercantile perspective. Where Laurence unpacks the landscape thinking of a mercantile individual, Rosie reveals the environmental legacy of the class: the evolution of a corporate discourse of sustainability and the practice of greenwashing. Through the East India Company, an early prototype of the multinational corporation, mere employees could govern whole peoples and territories. Rosie's subject is the British expatriate to India in the advent of the Bengal famine of 1770, which resulted in the loss of millions of lives. Analysing landscape paintings of the colonial country house, she communicates how these colonial administrators repurposed a stewardship ideal of landlordship to portray themselves as responsible managers living in harmony with the local people and local environment.

Class is less fixed as a category than the feudalistic stratification of rank or the traditional one of caste in the societies of the Global South. Nevertheless, people refashion themselves to bridge these boundaries, a process which applies doubly to their ideas. Sensitising ourselves to the modification of ideas of nature as they are deployed under different socio-historical contexts would help us perceive not just the tensions and the alliances but also the power differentials between aristocratic, mercantile and labouring interests. Partly to explore the diverse responses to the environment that arose in the politically and aesthetically revolutionary Romantic period, and partly out of a desire to oppose the pernicious trend in ecocriticism of levelling differentials in the human condition,[33] every contributor has pursued one or more of the following strategies in addition to attending to class:

1. Consider the environmental implications of Romantic period land aesthetics and land management practices.
2. Recover an alternative, or marginal, or suppressed land ethics from the Romantic period.
3. Engage with residual and emergent strands in environmental discourse of the present day.

I will now briefly discuss these three aspects.

Considering the rapid loss of land and marine biodiversity, as well as the prodigious number of suffering beings under factory farming systems, the greening of Romantic literary studies is a welcome development. Nevertheless, Kate Rigby's warning in 2004 that 'aspects of romanticism might . . . be part of the problem . . . rather than its hoped-for solution' is prescient.[34] The Romantic turn to nature could well have fostered the very catastrophe that we are facing today. Indeed, the degree to which the aestheticisation of nature is inherited from the Romantic period and the negative environmental outcome this has facilitated is the general tenor of this volume. It is the line of argument my chapter adopts, a preoccupation that also features in the contributions by Kuri Katsuyama (Chapter 1), Li-hsin Hsu (Chapter 3), Rosie Dias (Chapter 5), Romita Ray (Chapter 6), Adam J. Bridgen (Chapter 9), Yuko Otagaki (Chapter 10) and Simon J. White (Chapter 11).

Though the causes fingered and the consequences foregrounded vary from contributor to contributor, for many of us it is an inescapable fact that the Romantic period coincided with the wave of parliamentary enclosure acts that legalised the massive appropriation of land by upper-class landowners. It was perhaps the largest land grab in British history, which turfed out millions of labouring people,[35] as well as being a time of unprecedented deforestation.[36] Having already commented on my own work, Kuri's and Rosie's, and as I intend to address Adam's, Yuko's and Simon's on the next point, let me focus here on the contributions of Romita and Li-hsin. Comprising a mere 0.16 per cent of the total land surface of the earth, the malign human and ecological outcomes witnessed in Britain would be a mere footnote in world history were it not for colonisation and the tremendous soft power of the world's leading nation. Focusing on the development of the tea industry in Assam, where tiger hunting was keenly pursued by the British plantation managers, Romita is in accord with Rosie on India as a site for the social elevation of these ambitious men: 'While planters were neither royals nor members of the landed elite, in the eyes of their staff and labourers, their stewardship of acres of land and their position on top of the plantation hierarchy made them all-powerful figures.' Through them, the upper-class appropriation of the land – 'improvement', in the regular parlance of the day – received a distinctly mercantile twist abroad. 'If the tea industry had brought a civilising touch to the jungle, then it had done so by transforming forest into landscape, natives into disciplined workers and tigers into personal memorabilia' (Chapter 6). The land regime brought deforestation and wildlife depletion as it had done at home, but on a canvas ten times larger. Before India, the crown jewel of the British empire had of course been America. Despite its having broken free of British rule in the Romantic period, British ideas and British culture were still tremendously influential there. One of the key contributions of postcolonial literary studies is the revelation that unequal relations between coloniser and colonised persist long after colonisation. In America, three times the size of India, vast swathes of land also came to be enclosed and the pre-European settlers of the land forcibly removed to create the landscape that would be indelibly ingrained in the minds of its new masters as beautiful: wilderness.[37] Whether or not William Wordsworth originated the idea of national parks, as it is sometimes claimed,[38] his numinous depictions of upland Cumbria did foster among his middle-class admirers a yearning for wilderness that has had negative environmental outcomes. As Li-Hsin's analysis of representations of Chinatown in the 1870s shows, the reification of wilderness engenders a hostility not only towards urban areas but also to the human and biological diversity found there, which it codes as unnatural. In the eyes of middle-class Americans, 'Chinatown was ... a perverted Romantic landscape ... unsettling of the social and environmental order,' with the city gardening and obsessive recycling of the Chinese labourer placing him as an 'ecological other' from a degraded foreign land, rather than the product of inhumane economic exploitation and racially discriminatory laws (Chapter 3).

No less eminent a naturalist than Aldo Leopold had himself taken aim at the craving of fellow Americans 'to get back to nature'.[39] As the concluding section of *A Sand County Almanac* (1949) lays out in no uncertain terms, when this is a pursuit taken up by millions of people on motorised transport, the result is ecological devastation. The best thing most people can do for wilderness is simply to stay away: 'The weeds in a city lot convey the same lesson as the redwoods.'[40] Nature is everywhere. As Walt Whitman observed in 1855, it is 'every atom belonging to me as good as you', common to all things man-made or otherwise, all of it beautiful: 'Not an inch nor a particle of an inch is vile.'[41] According to Emily Dickinson, possibly the world's first hikikomori, the mundane is still the same 'Nature', just 'like Us ... sometimes caught / Without her Diadem'.[42] But the legacy of Romantic nature poetry has been such that it all seems ink spilt in vain: how many people can take pleasure in crowded urban places as Whitman could? Or have the interest in the nature of everyday life, as Dickinson did, to put a name to 'weeds in a city lot'? Wordsworth is not to blame for this: he wrote many good poems, for which he is duly admired, but there are many more he did not write offering a different perspective that has unjustly been left by the wayside. In terms of alternative ways of seeing the land, as well as alternative representations of the plants, animals and people who live on the land, the work done on Romantic labouring-class nature poetry by Bridget Keegan, John Goodridge, Simon J. White and Simon Kövesi has been nothing short of a revelation.[43]

Lacking the geographical mobility of middle- and upper-class people, these poets concentrate by necessity on the places and nature of their localities. For William Blake it was the environs of London, where he lived most of his life.[44] *Milton*, which Blake 'started writing in 1804 after his residence at Felpham in Sussex, the only time he ever lived outside London', is set in his cottage garden (Chapter 11). As I will be highlighting Steve Clark's contribution in connection with the final point, let me address instead Yuko Otagaki's work on Ann Yearsley (Chapter 10), Simon J. White's on John Clare (Chapter 12) and Adam J. Bridgen's on James Woodhouse (Chapter 9), all of whom demonstrated the same situatedness and who valorised the mundane and small in nature. Every single scene in 'Clifton Hill' is drawn from 'Yearsley['s] ... own locale', in which she not only attends to the farm animals of her working life as a milkmaid, but also to the relationships between the people of her village and the local wildlife: a suffering robin on the doorstep of a cottager, 'the rabbit seeking shelter, the mole, the woodland rat, the long-nosed mouse, snail, caterpillar and viper' on pasture woodland (Chapter 10). The great poet of natural history is of course John Clare, the farm labourer who went 'on hands and knees ... to observe the smaller mammals and invertebrates' of his neighbourhood, and through whom Simon makes a compelling appeal for socially conscious rewilding. Less well-known than Clare or Yearsley is the 'Staffordshire-born shoemaker-poet James Woodhouse' (Chapter 9). Under Adam's reading, Woodhouse's 28,013-line poetic autobiography *The Life and Lucubrations of Crispinus Scriblerus* – published in its entirety by his grandson in 1896 – is revealed as an extraordinary work of ecosocialism, where 'the return to nature' is implicated in the same extractive and destructive capitalism underlying agricultural 'improvement'.

I also look at James Woodhouse (in Chapter 8), and Kuri (Chapter 1) the travelogue of Samuel Holmes, in which he is advertised as 'a worthy, sensible, but unlearned man'. But whatever the social class, all the writers and artists examined in this volume beautify in some way the nature they render. For a specialist of literature or art history to eschew the aestheticisation altogether, as Morton recommends, would be a case of throwing out the baby with the bathwater. Moreover, for those of us who take into account multiple class perspectives, it is clear there are certain representations of nature which are more ecological than others. As to the third aim of this essay collection, it is, like the second, a strategy to encourage diversity. There has been a greening of theology as well, and Kaz Oishi (Chapter 7) and Steve Clark's (Chapter 11) analysis of William Cowper and Blake's poetry acknowledge religious perspectives on nature. According to Sea Shepherd founder Paul Watson, 'What we need if we are to survive is a new story, a new myth, a new religion. We need to replace anthropocentrism with biocentrism. We need to construct a religion that incorporates all species and establishes nature as sacred and deserving of respect.'[45] But these recuperative elements already exist in the faiths of today, even in one with as bad an environmental reputation as Christianity.[46] As Kaz shows, it was the stewardship tradition that fostered in Cowper a sense of the sacredness of nature and his deep sympathy for 'other members of the biotic community'. Similarly, Steve highlights Blake's use of Lucretius to create a non-anthropocentric Christian universe in which human beings are 'eminently dispensable'. Many faiths have a long history and the soul-searching prompted by the environmental crisis has been profound. Rather than inventing a new religion altogether, biodiversity and heritage conservationists across Asia have chosen instead to re-examine the diverse traditions of the religion they know and love for positive environmental outcomes.[47]

Religious environmentalism is ascendant, but in Asia it seems particularly susceptible to nationalism. It is sobering to see Chipko Andolan, the Indian forest conservation movement that was such an inspiration in the 1990s, co-opted by the ruling Bharatiya Janata Party as an exemplar of Hinduism's contribution to the environment. Thomas Malthus, on the other hand, with whom Peter Denney engages (Chapter 13), is a residual presence in environmental discourse. Inspired by Fairfield Osborn's *Our Plundered Planet* (1948) and William Vogt's *Road to Survival* (1948), Malthusians 'argu[ed] that the sheer proliferation of human beings on the planet would lead to the breakdown of the ecological systems on which life on earth was predicated'.[48] Though no longer the force it was during the 1960s and 1970s,[49] Malthusianism continues to survive in the idea that the earth has a maximum carrying capacity to which we are either very close, or have already exceeded.[50] Peter exposes the repressive ideology underpinning Malthus's *Theory of Population* (1798), which was rightfully attacked not only by progressive liberals like William Hazlitt, but also writers occupying a more politically centrist position like Robert Southey. Famine was the spectre haunting Malthus's society; the onus he placed on controlling the fertility and consumption of labouring people is as unfair as the emphasis now placed on countries of the Global South to curtail their birth rate and economic development by Malthusians haunted by environmental collapse (Chapter 13). China is the country in which population control has been taken the most seriously, and its recent history with the one-child policy, as well as the population control it is enforcing on Muslim peoples, should hopefully be enough to put this oppressive ideology to bed.

Finally, I would like to acknowledge Richard Grove and Aldo Leopold, on whose shoulders I stand. This book is divided into two sections, the first named after the former's seminal work and the second inspired by the latter's call to develop 'a land ethic'. By placing essays reflecting the diversity of Romantic environmentalism at home and abroad beside each other, it is my fervent hope to put the spirit of these two very different people in conversation.

Notes

1. Fredrik Albritton Jonsson, *Enlightenment's Frontier: The Scottish Highlands and the Origins of Environmentalism* (New Haven, CT: Yale University Press, 2013), p. 7.
2. An evocative term first coined by Raymond Williams to describe the nature poetry of Wordsworth and Clare; see *The Country and the City* (Oxford: Oxford University Press, [1973] 1975), pp. 127–41.
3. The seminal work here is Richard Grove's *Green Imperialism: Colonial Expansion, Tropical Island Edens and the Origins of Environmentalism, 1600–1860* (Cambridge: Cambridge University Press, 1996). Paul Warde's *The Invention of Sustainability: Nature and Destiny, c. 1500–1870* (Cambridge: Cambridge University Press, 2018) is an important addition to Grove's original thesis.
4. 'At the last UK climate march people of colour like myself were poorly represented, if not invisible,' opines Suzanne Dhaliwal in 'Why are Britain's green movements an all-white affair?' (*The Guardian*, 28 September 2015).

Or, according to Catherine Happer, a sociologist with Glasgow University, 'The environmental movement has always had a middle class aura to it and, in spite of attempts to use the language of inclusivity, it has never quite lost this tag' (*The Conversation*, 16 September 2019).
5. Lester C. Thurow, *The Zero-Sum Society: Distribution and the Possibilities for Change*, first published by Basic Books (New York: Penguin, [1980] 2008), p. 104.
6. For the Chipko movement, refer to Ramachandra Guha, *The Unquiet Woods: Ecological Change and Peasant Resistance in the Himalaya* (Berkeley: University of California Press, 2001).
7. Exemplary in this respect is Rob Nixon's *Slow Violence and the Environmentalism of the Poor* (Cambridge, MA: Harvard University Press, 2011).
8. Ve-Yin Tee, 'The Dark Side of Romantic Dendrophilia', in Stuart Cooke and Peter Denney (eds), *Transcultural Ecocriticism: Global, Romantic and Decolonial Perspectives* (London: Bloomsbury, 2021).
9. Patrick Greenfield and Jonathan Watts, 'Record 212 land and environment activists killed last year', *The Guardian*, 29 July 2020, <https://www.theguardian.com/environment/2020/jul/29/record-212-land-and-environment-activists-killed-last-year> (accessed 29 August 2020).
10. Greta Thunberg, Address to the European Parliament, 16 April 2019, <https://www.youtube.com/watch?v=14w8WC1I3S4> (accessed 31 August 2020).
11. Nancy Tuana, 'Climate Apartheid: The Forgetting of Race in the Anthropocene', *Critical Philosophy of Race* 7, no. 1 (2019): 19.
12. Ibid. p. 10.
13. Priyamvada Gopal, *Insurgent Empire: Anticolonial Resistance and British Dissent* (London: Verso, 2019), p. 17. Many thanks to Seng Puay Ong for drawing my attention to Gopal's book.
14. Elizabeth DeLoughrey and George B. Hanley (eds), *Postcolonial Ecologies: Literatures of the Environment* (Oxford: Oxford University Press, 2011), p. 14.
15. Upamanyu Pablo Mukherjee, *Postcolonial Environments: Nature, Culture and the Contemporary Indian Novel in English* (London: Palgrave, 2010), p. 5.
16. Graham Huggan and Helen Tiffin, *Postcolonial Ecocriticism: Literature, Animals, Environment* (London: Routledge, 2010), p. 13.
17. John M. MacKenzie, 'Foreword', in James Beattie, Edward Melillo and Emily O'Gorman (eds), *Eco-Cultural Networks and the British Empire: New Views on Environmental History* (London: Bloomsbury, 2015), pp. xv–xvi.
18. Greg Garrard, 'Introduction' to *The Oxford Handbook of Ecocriticism* (Oxford: Oxford University Press, 2014), pp. 1–2.
19. Mukherjee, *Postcolonial Environments*, p. 46.
20. Timothy Morton, *Ecology without Nature: Rethinking Environmental Aesthetics* (Cambridge, MA: Harvard University Press, 2007), p. 17.
21. Ibid. p. 21.
22. Ibid. pp. 115–25.
23. Ibid. p. 127.

24. Raymond Williams, *Culture and Materialism: Selected Essays* (London: Verso, [1980] 2005), p. 67.
25. Raymond Williams, *Keywords: A Vocabulary of Culture and Society*, 2nd edn (Oxford: Oxford University Press, 1983), p. 219.
26. I highly recommend Donna J. Haraway, 'Universal Donors in a Vampire Culture', in William Cronon (ed.), *Uncommon Ground: Rethinking Human Place in Nature* (New York: Norton, 1996). She has written a number of important books on the subject, including *Primate Visions: Gender, Race, and Nature in the World of Modern Science* (New York: Routledge, 1989); *Simians, Cyborgs and Women: The Reinvention of Nature* (New York: Routledge, 1991); and *Modest_Witness@Second_Millennium. FemaleMan©_Meets_OncoMouse™: Feminism and Technoscience* (New York: Routledge, 1997).
27. 'Anglo-Saxon documents make it perfectly clear that by then there was no wilderness: every inch of England had an owner'; Oliver Rackham, *Ancient Woodland: Its History, Vegetation and Uses in England* (Kirkcudbrightshire: Castlepoint Press, 2003), p. 501.
28. Peter Heymans, *Animality in British Romanticism: The Aesthetics of Species* (London: Routledge, 2012), p. 1.
29. DeLoughrey and Hanley, *Postcolonial Ecologies*, pp. 6 and 20.
30. Huggan and Tiffin, *Postcolonial Ecocriticism*, p. 53.
31. J. O. Lindsay (ed.), *The New Cambridge Modern History: Volume 7, The Old Regime, 1713–1763* (Cambridge: Cambridge University Press, [1957] 1988), p. 2.
32. Keith Hayward and Majid Yar, 'The "chav" phenomenon: Consumption, media and the construction of a new underclass', *Crime, Media, Culture: An International Journal* 2, no. 1 (2006), pp. 9–28.
33. This is clearest in the idea of the Anthropocene, whose implication of a species-wide responsibility for the enfolding climate crisis has been attacked by a number of postcolonial and Marxist critics including Nancy Tuana, to whom I have referred earlier, as well as notably Andreas Malm and Alf Hornborg, 'The geology of mankind? A critique of the Anthropocene narrative', *The Anthropocene Review* 1 (2014): 62–9. I find Dan McQuillan's perspective from the field of computer science particularly interesting; see 'The Anthropocene, Resilience and Post-Colonial Computation', *Resilience* 5, no. 2 (2017): 92–109.
34. Kate Rigby, *Topographies of the Sacred: The Poetics of Place in European Romanticism* (Charlottesville: University of Virginia Press, 2004), p. 2.
35. 'In agriculture the years between 1760 and 1820 are the years of wholesale enclosure in which, village after village, common rights are lost', E. P. Thompson, *The Making of the English Working Class* (New York: Pantheon, [1963] 1964), p. 198.
36. The period from '1770 to 1860', according to Oliver Rackham, 'was the most destructive in [forest] history'; see *Trees and Woodland in the British Landscape* (London: Dent, [1976] 1983), p. 157.
37. For this history, see Mark David Spence, *Dispossessing the Wilderness: Indian Removal and the Making of the National Parks* (Oxford: Oxford University Press, 1999).
38. For example, 'William Wordsworth and the Invention of National Parks',

the 2013 exhibition at the Harold B. Lee Library, Brigham Young University, 'traces the origin of the idea of national parks back to the leading poet of the English Romantic Movement, William Wordsworth', <exhibits.lib.byu.edu/Wordsworth//> (accessed 18 October 2020). See also 'The Future of the National Park Concept', the conclusion of Warwick Frost and C. Michael Hall (eds), *Tourism and National Parks: International Perspectives on Development, Histories and Change* (London: Routledge, 2009), p. 304.
39. Aldo Leopold, *A Sand County Almanac and Sketches Here and There* (Oxford: Oxford University Press, [1949] 1968), p. 165.
40. Ibid. p. 174.
41. Walt Whitman, *Leaves of Grass* (New York: printed for the author, 1855), pp. 13–14.
42. Emily Dickinson, 'The Sky is low – the Clouds are mean' (*c.* 1866), from Thomas H. Johnson (ed.), *The Complete Poems of Emily Dickinson* (Boston: Back Bay Books, [1955] 1976), p. 488.
43. Simon White and I were fellow students at the University of York, where he started his project on *Robert Bloomfield, Romanticism and the Poetry of Community* (Farnham: Ashgate, 2007). Though it was he who first convinced me of the value of labouring-class nature poetry, it was the corpus revealed by Bridget Keegan's *British Labouring-Class Nature Poetry, 1730–1837* (London: Palgrave, 2008) that amazed me and made me feel it was what I really wanted to work on.
44. London was much less built up than it is now, and many of the seemingly rural scenes in Blake's poetry might in fact have been metropolitan green spaces.
45. See Paul Watson, 'Biocentric Religion – A Call For', in Bron Taylor (ed.), *Encyclopedia of Religion and Nature* (New York: Continuum, 2005), pp. 176–9.
46. Steven Bouma-Prediger summarises the 'case against Christianity' in *The Greening of Theology* (Atlanta: Scholars Press, 1995), pp. 2–5. For environmentally recuperative elements in the Christian tradition, refer to Michael S. Northcott, *The Environment and Christian Ethics* (Cambridge: Cambridge University Press, 1996).
47. An important work in this respect is Bas Verschuuren and Naoya Furuta (eds), *Asian Sacred Natural Sites: Philosophy and Practice in Protected Areas and Conservation* (London: Routledge, 2016).
48. Robert J. Mayhew, in *New Perspectives on Malthus* (Cambridge: Cambridge University Press, 2016), p. 15.
49. When Paul R. Ehrlich's *The Population Bomb* (1968) sold two million copies, see Matthew Connelly, *Fatal Misconception: The Struggle to Control World Population* (Cambridge, MA: Harvard University Press, 2008), p. 259.
50. For example, see Edward O. Wilson, *The Future of Life* (New York: Knopf, 2002), pp. 33–4.

Part I
Green Imperialism

'We need, perhaps, to reconstruct an historical anthropology of global environmental awareness.'

Richard Grove, *Green Imperialism* (1995), p. 12

Chapter 1

The Environmental Aesthetics of the Chinese Garden

Kuri Katsuyama

In September 1792, Lord Macartney was sent on a mission to China to negotiate a treaty of trade and friendship. As Frances Wood has pointed out, 'Macartney's was not the first embassy ... to China'.[1] Colonel Charles Cathcart had been despatched in 1788, but the expedition had to turn back when he died of tuberculosis off Sumatra. The East India Company (EIC) had lobbied the government for the two missions in the hope of further expanding its already enormous China trade. Apart from instructions to open more ports to British merchants (who were restricted to Canton) and to establish an ambassador in Beijing, Macartney also carried with him the offer of a military alliance against France. That three ships (the *Lion*, a 64-gun warship; the 1,200-ton *Hindostan*, owned by the EIC; and the *Jackall*, a brig) were committed to the expedition, despite the impending war, was 'proof' – in Alain Peyrefitte's words – 'of its importance'.[2]

Lord Macartney had an entourage of ninety-five, including

> his secretary (and deputy ambassador) Sir George Leonard Staunton and two under-secretaries, a surgeon and a physician, several 'mechanics' or technical experts, two artists, two Chinese Jesuit interpreters, a watchmaker and a mathematical instrument maker, two botanists and five German musicians, all protected by ten dragoons, twenty artillerymen and twenty infantry. Staunton brought along his 11-year-old son and his German tutor[.][3]

The expedition lasted two years, when China, heretofore largely closed to Britain, was suddenly open to direct observation by a veritable microcosm of British society. I offer a close reading of the body of texts generated by the British embassy, focusing on the observations of Yuanming Yuan (the Garden of Perfect Brightness) in Beijing as well as of Bishu Shanzhuang (the Mountain Resort) in Chengde (Jehol), where Wanshu Yuan (the Garden of Ten Thousand Trees) is located. Things Chinese were the rage then: Chinese pagodas were erected in aristocratic estates,

Chinese ceramics decorated middle-class homes, and tea was replacing beer as the drink of choice at breakfast for the labouring classes.[4] *A Narrative of the British Embassy to China* (1795), the first book-length narrative of the expedition, was avidly consumed. It was written by Macartney's valet, Aeneas Anderson. Other books soon followed, including Staunton's consciously authoritative *An Authentic Account of an Embassy* (1797), Samuel Holmes's self-deprecatory *Journal by One of the Guard on Lord Macartney's Embassy to China* (1798) and *Travels in China* (1804) by John Barrow, who like Anderson was from the middle class. Macartney himself kept a detailed journal on the expedition,[5] which Barrow occasionally quoted from for his work.

From the middle of the eighteenth century to the Romantic period, the image of China steadily darkened from that of an enlightened monarchy to a site of despotism, of which Wordsworth's evocation in *The Prelude* of Wanshu Yuan is a notable example. 'The paradise of ten thousand trees' shows not only a vision of despotic tyranny but also tarnishes the nation as a whole. His contemporaries, including Jane Austen and Maria Edgeworth, shared the same entanglement of political and aesthetic concerns. Indeed, a negativity towards China is palpable in a number of the embassy members. When we view gardens and offer judgements as to their aesthetics, we never do so abstracted from the social and political contexts in which all of us are embedded. My rendering of the aesthetic judgements by Macartney and his entourage reveals how the progressive degradation of China might be understood in tandem with the overall democratisation of cultural discourse, from the province of upper-class patronage of the arts to middle-class market liberalism. This essay not only examines how these writers represented the gardens they saw, but also gardens they did not see or even imagined, to consider the way in which the environmental aesthetics that the Romantic poets inherited was implicated in social class, market liberalism and orientalism, whose consequences haunt British representations of China to the present day.

The Garden of Perfect Brightness

In the preface to the journal that Samuel Holmes – guard of the embassy – kept, the editor highlights its value: the diary, he says, possesses 'every mark of authenticity'; it is honest and ingenuous, 'written by a worthy, sensible, but unlearned man'; and 'as it is perfumed by the character of the writer', 'the curious reader may with confidence place it to his account of knowledge respecting that great and secluded nation, to which the inquiries of the politician and philosopher have been so long and much directed'.[6] In other words, the editor insists upon the importance of a fresh point of view offered on China by the man of the labouring class. Two trends were being taken advantage of here: the China craze and the yen for natural genius, which turned up 'uneducated' people who could write poetry such as Ann Yearsley and Robert Bloomfield. With Holmes, it is the phenomenon of an 'unlearned man' being able to write good prose on a subject as highly fashionable as China. These marvels gratified the vanity of patron, publisher and reader alike in bespeaking the liberal instincts of the person who groomed, nurtured or consumed them.

After passing 'a most charming rural prospect', writes Holmes, the embassy entered 'the celebrated city of Pekin early in the forenoon' and were set down at a country seat belonging to the emperor, six miles to the northward of the city, called Yuanming Yuan, about noon on 20 August 1793.

> This place was walled round, and might be near 2 miles in extent, and contained a vast variety of elegant little buildings; in the front of most of them was a cabal for bathing, and other useful purposes. The houses, or barracks appointed for the guard, were in the middle of a thick wood, but sufficiently open and airy, and surrounded with water; nothing, in short, could be more charming and delightful.[7]

It is a description which draws from the idea originating in landscape painting that a scene of various small and bright objects is beautiful. Since the popularisation of this aesthetics of the picturesque was connected with the growth of middle-class consumerism and tourism,[8] its deployment by a person in Holmes's position is highly questionable. Either he wasn't quite labouring class, or it was a case of editorial intervention. In either instance, it indicates the taste of contemporary readers of the genre.

Then, how did the valet to Macartney, Aeneas Anderson, record the entry to Beijing and the imperial gardens there? Anderson claims in the preface to his narrative that '[his] only business is to relate what [he] saw in the course of this embassy' and 'the merit of faithful representation is all [he has] to claim, and [all he wishes] to receive'. He describes the approach to Beijing as follows:

> Having passed through the eastern suburbs of the city, we entered into a rich and beautiful country, when a short stage of about four miles brought us to one of the Emperor's palaces named *Yuanming Yuan*, where we arrived about five o'clock in the afternoon, oppressed with fatigue from the extreme heat of the day, and the various impediments which obstructed our passage.[9]

And he continues in an entry dated 23 August 1793:

> In several courts of the palace there are artificial rocks and ruins of no contrivance, which, though not very congenial to their situation, were formed with considerable skill, and were, in themselves, very happy imitations of those objects they were designed to represent.[10]

Although he acknowledges the skill of the Chinese gardener at producing authentic-looking rocks and ruins, he focuses at once on their poor placement. Since writers promoting English landscape gardens like The Leasowes commonly remarked on how well-placed landscape features were (with words connected with naturalness, propriety, appropriateness), rather than on the quality of their manufacture, Anderson was virtually saying that while Chinese gardens are nice, they are not as good as the English ones. This condescension has affinities with that exercised on Dutch landscape painting, which were supposedly marvellous on realistic detail but lacking in imaginative conception when compared with the works of the best English painters.

John Barrow, as comptroller, was of a higher ranking than Holmes or Anderson. Unwilling to confine himself to the itinerary that was set out for them, he went on 'little excursions' by himself 'by stealth' to take a 'glance at these celebrated gardens' away from the watchful eyes of the palace eunuchs.

> The grounds of *Yuen-min-yuen* are calculated to comprehend an extent of at least ten English miles in diameter, or about sixty thousand acres, a great part of which, however, is waste and woodland. The general appearance of those parts near where we lodged, as to the natural surface of the country, broken into hill and dale, and diversified with wood and lawn, may be compared with Richmond park [in London] to which, however, they add the very great advantage of abundance of canals, rivers, and large sheets of water, whose banks, although artificial, are neither trimmed, nor shorn, nor sloped, like the glacis of a fortification, but have been thrown up with immense labour in an irregular, and as it were, fortuitous manner as to represent the free hand of nature. Bold rocky promontories are seen jutting into a lake, and retiring, some choaked with wood, others in a state of high cultivation. In particular spots where pleasure-houses, or places of rest or retirement, were erected, the views appeared to have been studied. The trees were not only placed according to their magnitudes, but the tints of their foliage seemed also to have been considered in the composition of the picture, which some of the landscapes might have been called with great propriety. But . . . they fall very short of the fanciful and extravagant descriptions that Sir William Chambers has given of Chinese gardening.[11]

Yuanming Yuan, despite being much larger in Barrow's estimate than Holmes or Anderson's, isn't as fancifully extravagant as Sir William

Chambers had claimed in his *Dissertation on Oriental Gardening* (1773).[12] Rather, according to Barrow, the Chinese garden is a model of picturesque beauty balancing elements of the beautiful with that of the sublime: the smooth, luminous lake before them is shadowed at its edges by rugged cliffs, and the land beyond a panorama of rolling hills contrasted with deep valleys, bright lawns with dark woods, the neatness and orderliness of cultivation with profuse, overgrowing nature.

Sir George Staunton described Yuanming Yuan as 'a garden laid out in serpentine walks' with 'a rivulet winding round an island, a grove of various trees interspersed with patches of grass ground, and diversified with artificial inequalities, and rocks rudely heaped upon each other'.[13] While Staunton's familiarity with landscape theory is clearly demonstrated in the terminology ('serpentine', 'rivulet', 'artificial' and so on), his *Authentic Account* is less interested in passing judgement on the Chinese garden than on Chinese imperial governance, on which he left a lengthy and critical record of its bureaucracy, and its impact on social organisation and infrastructure. He singled out for special notice the corruption and malfeasance of Chinese bureaucratic officials and lamented the lack in China of the sort of leisured, affluent class that had arisen in the more mercantile societies of Europe. Nevertheless, the work is reflective of his class biases in the high valuation he accorded to the sophisticated manners of the men and women of the upper classes, and the security that multigenerational households in China afforded.

Though Macartney's journal remained unpublished until long after the embassy, as it was partially quoted by Barrow, it was known to near contemporaries such as Wordsworth and Southey. Macartney was intoxicated by the beauty and scale of the emperor's palace of Yuanming Yuan:

> This place is truly an Imperial residence; the park is said to be eighteen miles round, and laid out in all the taste, variety, and magnificence which distinguish the rural scenery of Chinese gardening. There is no one very extensive contiguous building but several hundreds of pavilions scattered through the grounds and all connected together by close arbors, by passages apparently cut through stupendous rocks, or by fairyland galleries, emerging or receding in the perspective, and so contrived as to conceal the real design of communication and yet contribute to the general purpose and effect intended to arise from the whole. The various beauties of the spot, its lakes and the rivers, together with its superb edifices, which I saw (and yet I saw but a very small part), so strongly impressed my mind at this moment that I feel incapable of describing them.[14]

Lord Macartney was typical of the aristocracy in the keen interest he took in landscape gardening. Indeed, he paid Yuanming Yuan the very highest compliment by asserting that it was to some extent beyond description. Given the high cultural standing the Chinese gardening style enjoyed among these gardening connoisseurs, it is understandable that they generally adopted a more favourable position on China.[15]

After staying in Beijing for about a week, the embassy departed for Bishu Shanzhuang, the Qianlong Emperor's Mountain Resort at Chengde. Yuanming Yuan in the Chinese capital featured a traditional gardening style inherited from the Han Chinese, who the Manchurian Qing had subjugated. It and other gardens in Beijing had been laid out based on the Southern Han style best represented by the Suzhou gardens in Jiangsu province.[16] The Mountain Resort of Chengde in which Wanshu Yuan was located, on the other hand, was full of meaning for the Qing dynasty as its Manchurian palace. In contrast to the gardening style of Yuanming Yuan, which reflected the Qing embrace of the whole of China, Wanshu Yuan was part of a larger oeuvre to represent the Qing's nomadic origins. The Qianlong Emperor spent half his yearly retreat in Chengde and met with foreign ambassadors and other dignitaries in order to assert his Manchurian origins.

The Garden of Ten Thousand Trees

Holmes recorded that 'early on the morning of the 14th of September, the day appointed for delivering some of the presents from his Britannic Majesty to the Emperor, we all marched through Jehol ... but none, except his Excellency and the gentlemen, were suffered to enter the gates'. Though clearly disappointed at being kept from 'a sight of this favourite and famous residence of the greatest monarch on earth', he nevertheless satisfied himself with what 'gratification the outside afforded; the extent and elegance of it was beyond description', he reports, and as it 'contrasted with the adjacent mountains and precipices, the scene was great and beautiful indeed, to which the rising sun added a splendour truly magnificent'.[17] The juxtaposition of culture and nature offered by the palace and its environs formed a scene that was, in summary, perfectly picturesque.

The route from Beijing to Chengde, according to Anderson, 'was very mountainous and irregular, as well as naked, and without any other marks of cultivation but as denoted the poverty of it'.[18] The vast population of China has haunted the imagination of Europeans for centuries. If it has been conceived as an existential threat to civilisation, it has also proffered to the champions of trade liberalisation the tempting prospect of a market of hundreds of millions of consumers. How then did Anderson process the desolate expanse that lay beyond the Great Wall? His eye landed on one peasant as 'a very curious example of the natural industry of the Chinese people': he 'had a rope fastened round his middle' and by this means 'let himself down to any part of the precipice where a few square yards of ground gave him encouragement to plant his vegetables, or his corn: and in this manner he had decorated the mountain with those little cultivated spots that hung about it'.[19] Could this be a prototype for the portraits of aestheticised precarity in Romantic poetry, such as the leech gatherer in Wordsworth's 'Resolution and Independence' (1807)? The lightness of Anderson's tone suggests his position on population is closer to Arthur Young than Thomas Malthus. In other words, rather than the spectre of famine, China's great population was evocative of an advanced agriculture and an intrepid farming community.

Upon reaching the emperor's mountain resort, Anderson described it thus: 'It is a large and populous place, built without any attention whatever to regularity of design, and lies in a hollow, formed by two large mountains'.[20] Anderson, as Macartney's valet de chamber, was allowed into Bishu Shanzhuang (literally, 'the mountain villa for avoiding the heat'), from which Holmes had been barred. He writes: 'This place is built on an elevated situation, and commands an extensive view of the mountainous country that surrounds it. [It has] gardens extend[ing] for several miles, [which] are surrounded by a strong wall, about thirty feet in height. In front of the palace there is a large plain, with a considerable lake in the centre of it.'[21] It is the celebrated Double Tower Mountain, however, more than three kilometres east of the emperor's summer resort, on which the narrative climaxes – 'two rocks,' he says, 'which are among the most extraordinary objects [he has] ever seen or read of':[22]

> It is situated on the pinnacle of a large mountain, and near the verge of it: from which it rises, in an irregular manner, to the height of three hundred feet. Its base is small, but it gradually thickens toward the top; and from several of its projecting parts issue streams of the finest water.[23]

This stupendous feature (Fig. 1), he imagines, elicits in a passer-by looking up from the valley below 'an equal degree of horror and amazement'.[24] It is most significant that the gaze of Anderson is drawn to a feature that is geological (the Double-Towered mountain) rather than architectural (the summer palace itself), which bespeaks the rise of Romanticism and its focus on wildness (understood of course as 'nature').[25] Anderson would have appreciated the priority given to wildness in the painting, where the palace – off centre and diminutive – is literally a footnote to an imposing physical landscape.

Barrow, a member of the rising middle classes, was frustrated in his wish to see more of the country and its fabled gardens. Left behind in Beijing to take care of the embassy's excess baggage, Barrow couldn't go with Macartney and Staunton to Gehol. For his description of 'the Emperor's great park at Gehol, which ... seemed to be almost unrivalled for its features of beauty, sublimity, and amenity',[26] he had to rely on Macartney, 'whose taste and skill in landscape gardening are so well known' as 'a connoisseur of gardens'.[27] This reputation of Macartney rests not on books but (as was so often the case with the aristocracy) on the beauty of their estates. His father had not only restored the castle of Lissanoure, which the father acquired in 1733, but also had further improved it with thousands of trees and exotic plants from his travels. The serious problem with respect to Barrow's work was how he combined Macartney's first-hand observations of the landscape with dispositive judgements of his own disguised as Macartney's:

> Whether our style of gardening was really copied from the Chinese, or originated with ourselves, I leave for vanity to assert, and idleness to discuss[.] There is certainly a great analogy between our gardening and the Chinese, but our excellence seems to be rather in improving nature, theirs to conquer her, and yet produce the same effect. [. . .] It is indifferent to a Chinese where he makes his garden, whether on a spot favoured, or abandoned, by rural deities. His point is to change every thing from what he found it, to explode the old fashion of the creation, and introduce novelty in every corner.[28]

There is nothing like this anywhere in Macartney's journal, nor the insistence that 'it is a common effect of enormous riches to push every thing they can procure to bombast and extravagance, which are the death of taste'.[29] Where the upper-class writer typically aimed at the education of taste, the tyranny of wealth originates in middle-class Whig liberalism. It is inconceivable that Macartney, who had implemented extensive renovations on his estate at Antrim (including the renovation of the family castle), could launch the following attack on the impropriety of property:

> In other countries . . . as well as in China, I have seen some of the most boasted seats, either outgrowing their beauty from a plethora of their owner's wealth, or becoming capricious and hypocondriacal [sic] by a quackish application of it. A few fine places, even in England, might be pointed out that are labouring under these disorders; not to mention some celebrated houses where, twined stair-cases, window-glass cupolas, and embroidered chimney-pieces, convey nothing to us but the whims and dreams of sickly fancy, without an atom of grandeur, taste, or propriety.[30]

Barrow's description of a land conquered and remade by an oriental despot into an extravagant imperial garden has proven talismanic.

While the idea of the Chinese garden was already freighted in the 1770s as an expression of Tory despotism,[31] increasingly distanced from this political context of accusation of political corruption, it became instead the alleged propensity of cultures and peoples labelled as 'Oriental'. The oriental despot appears as Coleridge's 'Kubla Khan', who transforms wilderness into a pleasure garden. When Wordsworth evokes Wanshu Yuan in Book VII of *The Prelude*, he is surely influenced by Barrow.[32] Contrasted against this Eastern imperial garden, the Lake District was 'the paradise / Where [he] was reared; in Nature's primitive gift,' 'Man free, man working for himself'. It is through the dehumanising trope of Chinese despotism, still deployed in the British media, that the Occidental subject's freedom and liberty are realised.

It is particularly interesting to compare Barrow's disingenuous evaluation of Wanshu Yuan with that of Staunton, who, together with Anderson and Macartney, actually saw it first-hand. Each man's aesthetic marks his place within the social structure of England. While Barrow imagined a spectacle redolent of the capricious excesses of rank and wealth, to Staunton, who was of the landed gentry, Wanshu Yuan seemed a thing that nature had felicitously brought into being:

> It stood up an irregular surface near the base of a gentle hill, which, with a part of the vale below, was inclosed, and divided into a park and pleasure grounds, with a very pleasing effect. Trees were here thickly interspersed, but permitted a view thro them of a stream running at a little distance. Beyond it, the rising hills were some of them planted, and some left naked. The different objects seemed in their natural state . . . as if assembled here only by a fortunate chance. A Chinese gardener is the painter of nature; consulting which he contrives, without rule or science, to unite simplicity and beauty.[33]

The terms of praise Staunton lavished – in particular, on a Chinese gardener being 'the painter of nature' and of Chinese gardens uniting 'simplicity and beauty' – were also the aesthetic ideals of the picturesque. For example, to quote William Gilpin, 'It is a much easier matter to erect a temple, or a Palladian bridge, than to improve a piece of ground with simplicity and beauty, and give it an air of nature'.[34]

To Macartney, who was a member of the aristocracy, the whole region was covered with tasteful parks:

> Our journey upon the whole has been pleasant and, being divided into seven days, not at all fatiguing. At the end of every stage we have been lodged and entertained in the wings or houses adjoining to the Emperor's palaces. These palaces, which occur at short distances from each other on the road, have been built for his reception on his annual visit to Tartary. [. . .] They front the south and are usually situated on irregular ground near the bases of gentle hills which together with their adjoining valleys are enclosed by high walls

and laid out in parks and pleasure grounds with every possible attention to picturesque beauty.³⁵

This passage – indeed, all of the following passages from Macartney – are quoted and duly acknowledged by Barrow's *Travels in China*. Wanshu Yuan was shown on the instructions of the emperor, which Macartney considered 'an instance of uncommon favour':

> We rode about three miles through a very beautiful park, kept in the highest order, and much resembling the approach to Luton in Bedfordshire; the grounds gently undulated and chequered with various groups of well-contrasted trees in the offskip. As we moved onward an extensive lake appeared before us, the extremities of which seemed to lose themselves in distance and obscurity. [. . .] The shores of the lake have all the varieties of shape which the fancy of a painter can delineate, and are so indented with bays or broken with projections, that almost every stroke of the oar brought a new and unexpected object to our view; nor are islands wanting, but they are situated only where they should be, each in its proper place and having its proper character.³⁶

The accounts provided by Staunton and Anderson are positively impressionistic in comparison to Macartney, demonstrating not only the latter's superior connoisseurship but also the depth of his knowledge of landscape gardening. The lake described here was artificial, created by drawing water from the Martial River. East to west, it was as much as 750 meters across; north to south, a kilometre. The main island in the centre was called Ruyizhou, and on it stood seraglios, a constellation of palaces for the empress and her ladies. As Macartney surmised, it had all been carefully designed, the constituent parts 'situated only where they should be, each in its proper place and having its proper character'.

Wanshu Yuan was on the north side of the lake, which extended out to a flat plain planted with many trees. *Wan* ('ten thousand') when combined with a noun (in this case, *shu*: 'tree' or 'trees'), is a common figurative expression (then as now) for vastness, as in 'countless'. This was where the embassies from the Mongolian tribes and other regions were received.³⁷ Here, on the other side of the earth, at the symbolic heart of the Qing Empire, Macartney discovered what seemed to him to be no less than a home away from home:

> It would be an endless task were I to attempt a detail of all the wonders of this charming place. There is no beauty of distribution and contrast, no feature of amenity, no reach of fancy which embellishes our pleasure grounds in England, that is not to be found here. Had China been accessible to Mr. Brown or to Mr. Hamilton I should have sworn they had drawn their happiest ideas from the rich sources which I have tasted this day; for in the course of a few hours I have enjoyed such vicissitudes of rural delight, as I did not

conceive could be felt out of England, being at different moments enchanted by scenes perfectly similar to those I had known there – to the magnificence of Stowe, the soft beauties of Woburn or the fairy-land of Paine's Hill.[38]

Lancelot Brown (1716–83), nicknamed 'Capability Brown', designed more than 170 gardens and parks in England, including Stowe. Charles Hamilton (1704–87), the youngest son of the sixth Earl of Abercorn, built the landscape garden in Painshill in Surrey, which was praised by Horace Walpole and Uvedale Price. Under Macartney's aristocratic gaze, then, 'the Emperor's great park at Jehol' was revealed as being 'perfectly similar' to the great landscape gardens of England.

Was this mere hyperbole? Macartney had identified with precision the features of Yuanming Yuan that distinguished it from other gardens in Eastern China. Leaving Wanshu Yuan for 'the western garden', Macartney immediately appreciated that it was meant to create 'a strong contrast with the other [exhibiting] all the sublimer beauties of nature in as high a degree as the part which we saw before possess[ing] the attractions of softness and amenity'. In vocabulary and idiom, he fairly resonates with Walpole, Price and Gilpin, as well as William Chambers and Jean-Denis Attiret:[39]

> In many immense woods, chiefly oaks, pines and chestnuts grow upon perpendicular steeps and force their sturdy roots through every resistance of surface, and of soil, where vegetation would seem almost impossible. These woods often clamber over the loftiest pinnacles of the stony hills, or gathering on the skirts of them, descend with a rapid sweep, and bury themselves in the deepest valleys. There, at proper distances you find palaces, banqueting houses and monasteries ... sometimes with a rivulet on one hand gently stealing through the glade, at others with a cataract tumbling from above, raging with foam, and rebounding with a thousand echoes from below or silently engulfed in a gloomy pool or yawning chasm.[40]

If Macartney here seems especially reminiscent of Romantic representations of nature,[41] in prose or verse, it is a measure perhaps of the extent to which Romanticism borrows from the fascination with wildness in the picturesque and with the spectacular in chinoiserie, which were in turn parallel developments on that effect of defamiliarisation Burke distinguished as the sublime.[42]

After a tour of several hours, Macartney is brought to 'a covered pavilion, open on all sides, and situated on a summit so elevated as perfectly to command the whole surrounding country, to a vast extent.' Macartney continues:

> The radius of the horizon, I should suppose, to be at least twenty miles from the central spot where we stood, and certainly so rich, so various, so

beautiful, so sublime a prospect my eyes had never beheld. I saw everything before me as on an illuminated map, palaces, pagodas, towns, villages, farm houses, plains and valleys watered by innumerable streams, hills waving with woods and meadows covered with cattle of the most beautiful marks and colours. All seemed to be nearly at my feet and that a step would convey me within reach of them.[43]

The prospect was crucial to the evaluation of land as a landscape. On the park estate, it appealed to patrician feelings in the way it arranged the property as a glorious spectacle. Allowing Macartney to occupy the summit of the western park was to give him the opportunity of imagining himself as its owner. But while the views it offered were broad, they were not completely unobstructed. His attention was drawn to the 'vast enclosure below, which was not accessible . . . being never entered but by the Emperor, his ladies and his eunuchs'. If the emperor acknowledged Macartney's status as the highest ranked member of the embassy, it was also made manifestly clear to him that he was not the master of all he surveyed. Macartney might not be fully cognisant of imperial semiotics, but he would have known enough from existing European practices 'to read it as a landscape of power'.[44] Proceeding on to repudiate the extravagant excesses of Chinese gardening, 'which Father Attiret and Sir William Chambers have intruded upon us as realities', he insisted again on the equivalency between the landscapes of China and Britain:

> If any place in England can be said in any respect to have similar features to the western park which I have seen today it is Lowther Hall in Westmorland, which (when I knew it many years ago) from the extent of prospect, the grand surrounding objects, the noble situation, the diversity of surface, the extensive woods, and command of water I thought might be rendered by a man of sense, spirit, and taste the finest scene in the British dominions.[45]

Westmorland is a historic county in north-western England, bounded on the north and west by Cumberland, on the south-west and south-east by Lancashire, on the east by Yorkshire, and on the north-east by Durham. Part of the districts of Eden and South Lakeland in the administrative county of Cumbria, it encompasses a portion of the scenic mountains, valleys and lakes of what is now known as the Lake District.

Gardens Not Seen

The Qianlong Emperor surely tops the list in Chinese history for the number and scale of the landscape gardens he laid out. He also composed some fifty thousand poems.[46] Though Yuanming Yuan was officially completed in 1744, when a series of forty paintings was commissioned to commemorate its most scenic spots, he continued to add to it. When the British embassy stayed at Yuanming Yuan, they did not see or hear anything of Changchun Yuan (The Garden of Eternal Spring) in the east, which had European-style mansions and gardens (see Fig. 2) laid out along a 65-acre strip across its northern end.[47] By incorporating European architecture in the imperial garden, Qianlong conveyed his purview over the West. European visitors certainly appreciated Yuanming Yuan as a representation of sovereignty and power. It was actually 'composed of three distinct gardens, independent from each other but connected':[48] apart from Changchun Yuan, there was Qichun Yuan (The Garden of Elegant Spring) to the south. Due to its size and complexity, 'the European Jesuits who visited Yuanming Yuan in the eighteenth century did not hesitate to call it the "Versailles of China"'.[49]

Yuanming Yuan was however dwarfed by Bishu Shanzhuang, which had taken the emperors of the Qing Dynasty eighty-nine years to complete. With its walls enclosing an area of 5.6 square kilometres, it is the largest existing imperial garden in China, occupying almost half the city of Chengde.[50] Where water connected the various parts of Yuanming Yuan with Wanshu Yuan, 'the western garden', and the other places that Macartney toured in Bishu Shanzhuang, it was the mountainous terrain that dominated. If the Beijing residence of Yuanming Yuan signified the place of the Qing emperors as the rightful successors and guardians of Han Chinese civilisation, crossing the Great Wall to the wilder Bishu Shanzhuang allowed them to manifest their Manchurian ancestral identity. The grandfather of Qianlong, the Kangxi Emperor, had initiated the construction of Bishu Shanzhuang in 1701 after integrating a number of Mongolian tribes into the Qing Dynasty. Unlike his grandfather, who had engaged in numerous wars to dominate the Mongols, Qianlong was the cannier monarch. He developed the fields to the north of the lakes creating Wanshu Yuan to engage with them politically and diplomatically.[51] At the edge of Bishu Shanzhuang, instead of a strip of European mansions, Qianlong erected Tibetan temples. Although Macartney saw these temples and at least appreciated them as another exertion of power,[52] we who live under the culture of depoliticisation encouraged by globalisation clearly have not. This is obvious in the universalism of UNESCO, whose recognition of 'the Mountain Resort and its Outlying Temples' as World Heritage in 1994 has allowed the Chinese state to 'place Tibet firmly within the borders of the PRC'.[53]

This culture of depoliticisation is also detectable in the imposition of that regime of the land known as nature preservation. The desire for wildness, first articulated in the aesthetic of the sublime and later in Romantic representations of sparsely populated lands, was a reaction against the rapid advance of agriculture.[54] With the progress of industrialisation, it has metamorphosised into an anti-human desire for wilderness. While there is a willingness in American academic circles to trace the invention of the national park back to Wordsworth, it is probably truer to say that it is their system that has inspired the Lake District, considering it only became a national park on 9 May 1951. The anti-human nature of the desire for wilderness is apparent in the failure of the Lake District to win recognition as a natural World Heritage Site,[55] and in the way that muscular NGOs have impelled the ethos of nature preservation across many countries in Asia. 'Despite parks being thought of as foundations of conservation, they have . . . cast a shadow over the lives of the traditional inhabitants and custodians.'[56] Typically, due to the lack of integration with land uses and activities within and surrounding the protected zone, local practices are suppressed and a professional community of scientists and technicians imported in who have little connection with the specific historical, spiritual and religious circumstances of the area.[57] Unlike the travel writers and poets of the Romantic era, we can see that farming can be beautiful. But these examples are almost invariably traditional and small-scale. Looking at the land, separated by modern factory farming (understood as ugly) and by recreational nature reserves (understood as beautiful), it is clear that it will take us a long time to combine again what the travel writers and poets of the Romantic era have unwittingly separated.

Notes

1. Frances Wood (ed.), *Aeneas Anderson in China: A Narrative of the Ill-Fated Macartney Embassy 1792–94* (Hong Kong: Earnshaw Books, 2020), p. 7.
2. Alain Peyrefitte, *The Collision of Two Civilisations: The British Expedition to China 1792–4* (London: Harvill, 1993), pp. 3–4.
3. Wood, *Aeneas Anderson in China*, p. 7.
4. David Porter, in *The Chinese Taste in Eighteenth-Century England* (Cambridge: Cambridge University Press, 2010), analyses the processes by which Chinese aesthetics were assimilated into English culture. In Eugenia Zuroski Jenkins's *A Taste for China: English Subjectivity and the Prehistory of Orientalism* (Oxford: Oxford University Press, 2013), an examination of England's eighteenth-century obsession with Chinese arts and crafts, she argues that chinoiserie in literature and material culture played a key role in shaping the emergent conceptions of taste and subjectivity. Furthermore, Elizabeth Hope Chang has highlighted in *Britain's Chinese Eye: Literature, Empire, and Aesthetics in Nineteenth-Century Britain* (Stanford: Stanford

University Press, 2010) China's central impact on the British visual imagination in the nineteenth century.
5. The journal remained unpublished until the twentieth century, when it was issued as *An Embassy to China: Being the journal kept by Lord Macartney during his embassy to the Emperor Ch'ien-lung* (London: Longmans, 1962).
6. Samuel Holmes, *The Journal of Mr. Samuel Holmes: One of the Guard on Lord Macartney's Embassy to China and Tartary* (London: Bulmer and Co, 1798), p. iv.
7. Ibid. p. 135.
8. Stephen Copley and Peter Garside have provided an admirable summary of eighteenth-century ideas of the picturesque in their introduction to *The Politics of the Picturesque: Literature, Landscape and Aesthetics since 1770* (Cambridge: Cambridge University Press, 1994).
9. Aeneas Anderson, *A Narrative of the British Embassy to China, in the Years 1792, 1793, and 1794* (Basil: Tourneisen, 1795), p. 134.
10. Ibid. p. 144.
11. John Barrow, *Travels in China* (London: Cadell and Davies, 1804).
12. Porter, *The Chinese Taste in Eighteenth-Century England*, p. 50.
13. George Staunton, *An Authentic Account of an Embassy from the King of Great Britain to the Emperor of China*, 3 vols (London: Nicol, 1797), 2: 299.
14. George Macartney, *An Embassy to China*, ed. J. L. Cranmer-Byng (London: Longman, 1962), p. 95.
15. Refer to Yu Liu, *Seeds of a Different Eden: Chinese Gardening Ideas and a New English Aesthetic Ideal* (Columbia: University of South Carolina Press, 2008), pp. 1–41, and Porter, *The Chinese Taste*, pp. 37–54.
16. See Young-tsu Wong, *A Paradise Lost: The Imperial Garden Yuanming Yuan* (Honolulu: University of Hawaii Press, 2001), pp. 1–6.
17. Holmes, *Journal*, pp. 143–4.
18. Anderson, *A Narrative of the British Embassy to China*, p. 165.
19. Ibid. p. 166.
20. Ibid. p. 181.
21. Ibid. p. 185.
22. Ibid. p. 204.
23. Ibid. p. 204.
24. Ibid. p. 205.
25. As Copley and Garside highlight, critics are divided over the exact relationship between Romanticism and the picturesque. While I read the picturesque as 'an expression of contemporary liberalism', I do not quite see it – as some of them do – as an 'antithesis of Romantic mystificatory absolutism'. See Copley and Garside, *The Politics of the Picturesque*, pp. 3–5.
26. Barrow, *Travels in China*, p. 43.
27. Ibid. p. 43.
28. Ibid. p. 46.
29. Ibid. p. 47.
30. Ibid. p. 47.
31. James Watt, *British Orientalisms, 1759–1835* (Cambridge: Cambridge University Press, 2019), p. 11. See also Peter Kitson, *Forging Romantic*

China: Sino-British Cultural Exchange 1760–1840 (Cambridge: Cambridge University Press, 2013), p. 187.
32. Duncan Wu, *Wordsworth's Reading, 1800–1815* (Cambridge: Cambridge University Press, 1995), p. 13.
33. Staunton, *An Authentic Account of an Embassy*, pp. 351–2.
34. William Gilpin, *Observations on the Western Parts of England, Relative Chiefly to Picturesque Beauty* (London: Cadell and Davies, 1798), p. 174.
35. Macartney, *An Embassy to China*, p. 116; Barrow, *Travels in China*, p. 43.
36. Macartney, *An Embassy to China*, p. 125; Barrow, *Travels in China*, p. 44.
37. Miyoko Nakano, *Kenryūtei: Sonoseiji to zuzougaku* [*The Qianlong Emperor: His Politics and Iconography*] (Tokyo: Bungeishunjū, 2007), pp. 138–49.
38. Macartney, *An Embassy to China*, p. 126; Barrow, *Travels in China*, p. 45.
39. Chang, *Britain's Chinese Eye*, pp. 23–37.
40. Macartney, *An Embassy to China*, p. 132; Barrow, *Travels in China*, p. 45.
41. A number of scholars, including myself, have connected this passage and Coleridge's 'Kubla Khan', for example. See Kuri Katsuyama, '"Kubla Khan" and British Chinoiserie: The Geopolitics of the Chinese Garden', in David Vallins, Kaz Oishi and Seamus Perry (eds), *Coleridge, Romanticism and the Orient* (London: Bloomsbury, 2013), pp. 191–206. Also Nigel Leask, '*Kubla Khan* and Orientalism: The Road to Xanadu Revisited', in *Romanticism* 4 (1998): 1–21.
42. 'The sublime ... is an effect of defamiliarization,' according to David S. Miall, 'Foregrounding and the Sublime: Shelley in Chamonix', *Language and Literature* 16, no. 2 (2007): 155.
43. Macartney, *An Embassy to China*, pp. 132–3; Barrow, *Travels in China*, pp. 45–6.
44. Kitson, *Forging Romantic China*, p. 199.
45. Macartney, *An Embassy to China*, p. 133; Barrow, *Travels in China*, p. 46.
46. Guo Daiheng headed a research project on the ruins of Yuanming Yuan and presented the digital restoration in *China's Lost Imperial Gardens* (Shanghai: Shanghai Press, 2016).
47. Nakano, *Kenryūtei*, p. 194.
48. Bianca M. Rinaldi, *The Chinese Garden: Garden Types for Contemporary Landscape Architecture* (Basel: Birkhäuser, 2011), p. 28.
49. Ibid. p. 28.
50. 'Mountain Resort of Chengde and Its Outlying Temples', in Guobin Xu, Yanhui Chen and Lianhua Xu (eds), *Introduction to Chinese Culture: Cultural History, Arts, Festivals and Rituals* (Singapore: Springer Nature, 2018), p. 61.
51. Nakano, *Kenryūtei*, pp. 169–200.
52. Macartney, *An Embassy to China*, pp. 134–6.
53. James L. Hevia, 'World Heritage, National Culture and the Restoration of Chengde', *Positions: East Asia Cultures Critique* 9, no. 1 (2001): 224.
54. Keith Thomas, *Man and the Natural World: Changing Attitudes in England 1500–1800*, first published in 1983 by Allen Lane (Harmondsworth: Penguin, 1984), p. 254.
55. For more information, refer to Christina Cameron in Ken Taylor, Archer

St Clair and Nora J. Mitchell (eds), *Conserving Cultural Landscapes: Challenges and New Directions* (New York: Routledge, 2015), pp. 64–6.
56. Bas Verschuuren, 'Re-Awakening the Power of Place', in *Asian Sacred Natural Sites: Philosophy and Practice in Protected Areas and Conservation* (London: Routledge, 2016), p. 8.
57. Bas Verschuuren, 'Conclusions', in *Asian Sacred Natural Sites*, p. 300.

Chapter 2

Orientalising the British Class System: Exploring the 'Chinese' Landscapes of Sir William Chambers, 1740–1775

Laurence Williams[1]

In his preface to *The Citizen of the World* (1760–1) – a philosophical satire in the manner of Giovanni Marana's *Letters Writ by a Turkish Spy* (1684), describing the adventures of a Chinese philosopher in London – the playwright and essayist Oliver Goldsmith (1728–74) humorously describes a dream in which he foresees the critical reception of his book.[2] Standing by the side of a frozen Thames, where a 'Fashion Fair' is taking place in booths on the ice, Goldsmith watches as other authors venture out into the centre, drawing carts and sleds packed with various literary wares, and return again with their spoils. Encouraged by their success, he decides to venture onto the river with a 'small cargoe [sic] of Chinese morality', reasoning that 'The furniture, frippery and fire-works of China, have long been fashionably bought up [...] If the Chinese have contributed to vitiate our taste, I'll try how far they can help to improve our understanding.' No sooner does he reach the centre, however, when 'I fancied the ice, that had supported an hundred waggons before, cracked under me; and wheel-barrow and all went to the bottom.'[3]

Goldsmith's anxiety dream could of course be interpreted in the broader context of the cut-throat eighteenth-century London literary world, but I would like in this chapter to focus on the more specific anxieties that China, in both literary and material culture, could evoke in mid-century Britons. The idea of China as a long-fashionable but now over-familiar and even 'vitiate[d]' topic – which may still win favour with an elite audience, or may alternatively sink unread to the bottom of the Thames – seems indicative of a contemporary ambivalence towards the country. As Elizabeth Chang summarises, the middle decades of the century saw 'the waning of chinoiserie's popularity', during a 'period when the style's defiance of representational logic and multiplication of functionless ornament more disturbed than delighted'.[4] The high cultural associations that Chinese material culture had possessed in the post-Restoration period, when the style had been largely the preserve of an aristocratic elite, had gradually declined as these designs – now imported in bulk and increasingly imitated by domestic manufacturers – became accessible to a broader commercial and professional middle class. This process can of course be understood in terms of what Maxine Berg describes as the broader expansion of consumer culture, which 'directed the activity, occupied the mind, and infatuated the emotions of Britain's rapidly expanding middling classes in the eighteenth century'.[5] As Eugenia Zuroski Jenkins has argued, Chinese objects, incorporated into both physical spaces and literary narratives, became a particular marker in debates about taste, virtue, and 'cosmopolitan prestige'.[6]

The process of cultural devaluation prompted by this shift can be seen in the numerous satires appearing from the early decades of the eighteenth century which portrayed China, in opposition to the cultural prestige of neoclassicism, as a debased, eclectic and feminised taste that drained the purses of the 'middle' classes. Examples of this included the nouveau riche merchant Timothy Tallapoy in Nicholas Rowe's *The Biter* (1704), who arrives back in London spouting cod Chinese words and boasting of his acquaintance with the 'Serene *Cham*',[7] or Earl Squanderfield, the dissipate aristocrat in William Hogarth's *Marriage A-la-Mode* series (1743–5), whose living room, with its porcelain tea cups and grinning jade Buddhas, signals his disastrous adoption of the tastes of his new wife, a city merchant's daughter.[8] We see it too in the numerous eighteenth-century satires on middle-class Chinese interior and landscape designs, typically presented as a colonisation of the landscape by Chinese designs. John Brown's 1757 attack on the 'depraved' public taste and the decline of true 'Connoisseurs' in *An Estimate of Manners and Principles of the Times* (1757) singles out the taste for China as a particular symptom of decay: 'Every House of Fashion is now crowded with Porcelain Trees and Birds, Porcelain Men and Beasts, cross-legged Mandarins and Bra[h]mins[.] Every gaudy *Chinese* Crudity ... is adopted into fashionable Use, and becomes the Standard of Taste and Elegance.'[9] The social ambiguity of the Chinese object is enhanced by the tendency of the object itself to be ambiguously balanced between authenticity and kitsch imitation, possessing, as David Porter argues, 'an aura of cultural legitimacy constantly in tension with the aesthetic trivialisation set in motion by the products of its export trade'.[10]

This chapter explores the eighteenth-century tendency to imagine 'China' as an aestheticised space into which domestic debates about hierarchy, taste and social order could be transferred, reconfigured and developed: a process which might be termed the 'orientalisation of class'. This approach aligns with studies by Chi-ming Yang and Eugenia Zuroski Jenkins, which have affirmed the importance of Chinese objects in eighteenth-century debates about virtue, taste and commerce.[11] However, in contrast to these approaches, my focus is not on the shaping of national self-identity through and against China, but on uses of China within British class debates: in essence, I am interested in how visions of China could be used to place Britons in social relation to each other.

I analyse 'class' here in discursive rather than socioeconomic terms, in the awareness that Marxian categories have limited applicability in a pre-industrial age that understood itself through 'gradations of "status" or "rank"'.[12] This chapter largely omits discussions of working-class representations of China, focusing narrowly on the opposition between an emergent 'middle' class (a relatively small commercial and professional elite, diverse in religious backgrounds and political beliefs) and a traditional aristocratic class. As Nicholas Hudson argues, literary representations of this conflict during the eighteenth century usually create 'controlled tension rather than confrontation', debating questions of 'morality and national interest while implicitly underwriting the legitimacy of the traditional social hierarchy'.[13] Although class discourse could be explored across a range of fictional 'Chinese' spaces during this period – from the Oriental tale, to the comic opera, to the fictional landscapes drawn on the side of porcelain such as Josiah Spode's 'willow pattern' – this essay focuses on the unique environmental space of the landscape garden, which, uniting concepts of material culture, environmental design, and debates about land ownership and inequality, offers a particularly rich field for analysis.

My approach is influenced by other critical studies that have explored the ways in which eighteenth-century anxieties about class were transferred onto, and played out in, 'the Orient'. Saree Makdisi, building on Ann Stoler's work on the intersectionality of class and race,[14] explores how the language of civilisation and savagery, developed in colonial discourse, was transferred onto spaces and peoples within Britain understood to be 'less developed'.[15] Gerard Cohen-Vrignaud, by contrast, explores how lower- and middle-class Romantic-period radicals orientalised Britain's rulers as Eastern despots.[16] Jeng-Guo S. Chen, in an important contribution to our understanding of romantic orientalism, argues that a newly sociological and structural understanding of society, which read the situation of women and the lower classes as the measure of a country's civilisation, shaped British attitudes towards Asia, as 'the British view of Asian societies articulated in the nineteenth century relied extensively on the language and epistemes of class consciousness'.[17]

The discussion below traces a Tory, rather than radical, perspective on these debates, exploring the shifting articulations of 'China' across the career of the Anglo-Swedish architect William Chambers (1723–96). Chambers was, in both his social origins and his career, located on the fault lines between different class interpretations of China. The son of a Scottish expatriate merchant, born in Sweden and educated at grammar school in Ripon in Yorkshire, he joined the newly incorporated Swedish East India Company, making three trips to Bengal and China from 1740–9. These allowed him to accrue the financial capital to train as an architect in Paris, along with a 'small cargo' of Chinese knowledge to be tactically deployed throughout his career as a means of gaining attention and elite patronage.[18] Without wealth or noble status, he nonetheless rose in London society, publishing in 1757 his study of the *Designs of Chinese Buildings, Furniture, Dresses, Machines, and Utensils*, and becoming Royal Architect and chief designer of Kew Gardens, where he was responsible for the installation of several 'Chinese' follies, including the Great Pagoda of 1762.

Much recent scholarship on Chambers has focused on his career as a Sinologist. Peter Kitson and Yu Liu see Chambers as ambivalently balanced between Enlightenment and Romantic Sinology, emphasising the ways in which his attempts to import Chinese ideas were undermined by a predilection for exaggeration and a willingness to substitute the fantasies of other writers for his own experience.[19] Chambers's publications on Chinese gardens depicted the country in starkly different ways. The first, a short essay titled 'Of the Art of Laying Out Gardens Among the Chinese', was included at the end of the 1757 *Designs*. Although less well known than his later writings, it had an independent reception history, being serialised in publications including *The Gentleman's Magazine* in May 1757,[20] and was influential on writers including Goldsmith, who drew on it in his descriptions of the philosopher Lien Chi Altangi's gardens in *The Citizen of the World*.[21] Chambers's more famous *Dissertation on Oriental Gardening* was not published until 1772, when its provocative and polemical satires on the landscape gardens of Lancelot 'Capability' Brown (1716–83) provoked a wide response. In a perceptive reading of this latter work, Elizabeth Chang argues that it is the literary, fictive qualities of Chambers's visions of China which make him particularly influential, both as a 'synthesis of visions of the Chinese garden' and a 'major point of opposition for later writers hostile to Chinese landscape styles'.[22] David Porter, by contrast, focuses on discourses of misunderstanding and incomprehension in his work, speculating that the *Dissertation* can be understood as oblique travel writing, expressing Chambers's 'recollected experience of alienation and radical unfamiliarity in China as a young man'.[23]

The remainder of this chapter begins by exploring Chambers's experiences at Canton and the actual gardens, mostly belonging to Chinese merchants, that he saw there. Next, I discuss how these experiences are selectively drawn on and deployed in his *Designs* as well as in the garden designs at Kew, in order to create a more aristocratic and 'authentic' Chinese style distinguishable from popular rococo chinoiserie follies. Finally, I discuss the *Dissertation* as a decisive break from Chambers's early writings and as an intervention in the more polarised politics of landscape of the 1770s. Originating as an attack on the social background and garden designs of Capability Brown, this essay offers a defence of Gothic sensationalism in garden design and of the Tory ideology of landscape as the personal expression of wealth and taste. This parodic and exaggerated text associates China with an orientalised aesthetics of dispossession and appropriation that engages with contemporary debates about land ownership, as well as debates about the role of the monarch in the English constitution.

A Mercantile Perspective on Chinese Gardens: Chambers in Canton

The authenticity of Chambers's knowledge on China was questioned even by his contemporaries:[24] as Christian Hirschfeld recognised in 1779, 'he planted English ideas in a Chinese terrain so that it would give them a more striking appearance and render them more seductive'.[25] This is ironic, as in a field of knowledge largely dominated by Jesuit writers, Chambers was one of the first British travellers to provide sustained first-hand descriptions of Chinese gardens.[26] His Scottish father, a partner in the Gothenburg brokering firm Chambers and Pierson, had died during his schooling in England. Well-connected but not wealthy, he was forced to delay his ambition of becoming an architect, instead joining the Swedish East India Company (chartered in 1731) as cadet to the assistant supercargoes: a low rank, but one with the promise of future profit. Over the next ten years he made three journeys to Bengal (1740–2) and China (1742–3, 1748–9). The voyages were long and tedious, and he made use of the time to study 'modern languages, mathematics and the liberal arts, but chiefly architecture'.[27]

Canton (modern-day Guangzhou) in many ways offered an unpromising environment for Oriental study. The several thousand male European merchants resident in this walled city lived a largely comfortable but restricted life, spent mostly in the wooden European factories located close together on the banks of the Pearl River,[28] an area of Canton which contained 'only shops and warehouses'.[29] Europeans were forbidden to travel in the country, with the exception of short journeys around the vicinity of Canton, and were required to spend the off season (from February to July) at the nearby Portuguese colony in Macao.[30] Geographical marginalisation was compounded by language barriers between the two sides: the Chinese were forbidden (on pain of death) to teach their language to the English, and, as Peter Perdue writes, communication between traders took place in 'a mixture of Chinese, Malay, and English serviceable for trade, but not for the expression of high cultural ideals'.[31]

The difficulty of gathering information about Chinese culture is illustrated in a travel account by Charles Noble, an English East India Company merchant resident at Canton in 1747–8 (a period roughly overlapping with Chambers's second journey), who paid a visit to the 'Honan Joss-house' (Haizhuang temple) with a local guide. He complains that: 'Though my Chinese companion could speak English better than any [Chinese] merchant in Canton; yet he spoke it so imperfectly, especially about theological or ecclesiastical matters, that I got very little information.' Atop the temple, Noble regrets that 'alas! for want of the language, I could obtain but small information from [the priests] about the objects in view; and was therefore obliged to be contented with the bare prospect, which was indeed very agreeable'.[32]

Although Chambers published no travel narrative of his time in Canton, his experiences in the city – what Porter calls 'the primal drama of encounter' concealed within 'the naturalized, domesticated spectacle of exoticism' of his later writings – can be indirectly traced through notes and brief personal reflections in the 1757 *Designs*.[33] The authority projected by the 'survey' format of this work conceals the fact that, as the attached notes reveal, this is a selective and geographically limited perspective: for example, Chambers's notes on Chinese columns reveal that his observations were based on just four local pagodas, including 'a small Pagoda in the street where the European factories stand'.[34] Several brief remarks illustrate the racial tensions and mutual suspicion between the European and Chinese communities. Apologising for the approximations in his measurements, he states that 'it is a matter of great difficulty to measure any publick work in China with accuracy, because the populace are very troublesome to strangers, throwing stones, and offer other insults'.[35] Here he echoes Noble, who writes that he attempted to take walks outside the walls of Canton but that the 'pleasure and satisfaction we might have had in walking through this pleasant country' was ruined by the Chinese 'mob': 'Sometimes ten or twelve of us, when we have been walking in the countryside for a few miles, though armed with good sticks, have been set upon by the mob, who threw stones at us, calling out, *Aki-o, Quy-toy, Quy-lo*, and other diminutive names.'[36]

More positive memories are evoked in brief descriptions of local artisans who, deriving their business from the European market, seem to have been more open to cultural exchange. These included 'Lepqua, a celebrated Chinese painter' and '*Siou Sing Saang*, a celebrated Chinese master, whom, when I was at Canton, I employed to paint on glass all the Chinese dresses'.[37] Nevertheless, Chambers is still compelled to linguistic evasiveness in order to paper over the gaps in his knowledge. Thus, even though he admits that 'The gardens which I saw in China were very small,' he insists that 'several conversations on the subject of gardening' with Lepqua have given him 'sufficient notions of their knowledge on this head'.[38] Attempting to excuse his reliance on Canton to support conclusions about the whole of 'Chinese architecture', he is reduced to citing Jean-Baptiste Du Halde's *Description of the Empire of China* (1738), with its notoriously scanty maps, to support the idea that more observation of other cities would avail little, as 'there is such a resemblance between the cities of China, that one is almost sufficient to give an idea of all'.[39]

Chambers's knowledge of Chinese homes and gardens seems to have come mostly via one important conduit: relationships with local merchants from the *hong* guild system that monopolised export trade. These individuals had profited greatly from the European trade, building mansions along the banks of the Pearl River (particularly in Lizhiwan, in the western suburbs of Canton).[40] The Europeans seem to have recognised them as an equivalent social class:[41] Noble writes that they 'are exceeding complaisant, are sure to give you particular directions to their houses, to extol their goods, and invite you to tea with them, of which they are very liberal'.[42] Chambers describes the spacious reception halls of these houses, which were furnished with

> stands, four or five feet high, on which they set plates of citrons, and other fragrant fruits, or branches of coral in vases of porcelain, and glass-globes containing gold-fish ... On such tables as are intended for ornament only, they also place little landscapes, composed of rocks, shrubs, and a kind of lilly [sic] that grows among pebbles covered with water: sometimes too they have artificial landscapes, made of ivory, chrystal, amber, pearls, and various stones. I have seen of these that cost a thousand tael.[43]

These limestone scholar's stones, or *gongshi*, seem to have left an impression on Chambers: indeed, they are one of the few specific objects that he describes in his later essays on Chinese gardens. However, the sparse description provided here makes their intended symbolism difficult to gauge. David Porter suggests, in his speculative reading of eighteenth-century encounters with *gongshi*, that the forms may have appealed to Europeans for their 'bizarre' qualities, as a challenge to aesthetic ideas of symmetry and taste.[44] At the same time, however, their price provides a readily comprehensible marker of the socioeconomic status of the owner.

Equally suggestive, but also frustratingly brief, are Chambers's descriptions of the gardens attached to these houses. Lisa Hellman emphasises the transcultural status of mercantile gardens, in both China and Europe, as 'space[s] for manifestation of status, and important to demonstrate both sociability and domesticity'.[45] Tours were commonly provided to European guests, offering opportunities for sociability as well as a chance to showcase 'exotic plants for sale'.[46] Chambers's awareness of the cross-cultural status of these gardens is signalled in the very flatness of the language through which he describes them:

> Every apartment has before it a court; at the farther end of which is generally a pond, or cistern of water, with an artificial rock placed therein, on which grow some bambou-trees, and shrubs of different sorts; the whole forming a little landscape pretty enough: the cistern, or pond, is stocked with gold-fish, some of which are so tame, that they will come to the surface of the water, and feed out of one's hand. The sides of the court are sometimes adorned with flower-pots, and sometimes with flowering shrubs, or vines, and bambous, that form arbours. In the middle is generally placed, on a pedestal, a large porcelain vase, in which grow those beautiful flowers called Lien-Hoa; and in these little courts they frequently keep pheasants, Bantam fowls, and other curious birds.[47]

The passage, despite its apparent blandness, signals cautious approval (through words such as 'beautiful' and 'pretty enough') and works to smooth over the potential strangeness of Chinese aesthetics through the use of vocabulary such as 'arbours', 'gold-fish' (for koi carp) and 'cistern', which express what is seen in terms of traditional European garden features. By contrast, a more jarringly exotic scene is depicted in a cross-section of one of these 'merchants houses, towards the river' (11), included as Plate IX of the *Designs*.[48] It is of interest as perhaps the first visual representation of a Chinese house and garden to be produced by a British writer (Fig. 3).[49]

Transplanting Chinese Designs to English Soil: Chambers at Kew Gardens

Mid-century British anxiety about the 'Chinese' taste as something increasingly socially suspect, if not outright déclassé – signalled in the quotation from Goldsmith's *Citizen of the World*, discussed above – is crucial to understanding the trades that Chambers makes with his imported 'cargo' of Cantonese knowledge. Restoration and early eighteenth-century experiments in Chinese designs, inspired by Jesuit reports, imported material goods and illustrations in travel accounts, had largely been the preserve of an aristocratic or scholarly elite. Copperplate engravings of the imperial summer resort at Jehol (Chengde), for example, were brought by the Jesuit court painter Matteo Ripa to London in 1724, where they were shown to East India Company officials and to Richard Boyle, third Earl of Burlington (1695–1753). Yu Liu argues that Boyle drew inspiration from these designs to remodel his Chiswick gardens in irregular style, assimilating 'Chinese horticultural naturalism . . . into a subtly iconoclastic rereading of the classical European past'.[50]

The shift in the cultural value imputed to Chinese styles is connected to a shift in the class associations of the trope. David Porter notes the rapid 'dissemination across class boundaries' of Chinese goods and stylistic motifs during this period, which 'initially appeared as luxurious markers of class distinction in the drawing rooms of the social elite but soon spread to a much broader market, driven by the forces of fashion and the new merchant classes' contagious ambitions of social mobility'.[51] The expanding wealth of the English middle classes, from profits largely derived from Atlantic slavery and imperial trade, propelled a revolution not just in personal consumption but also in house and garden design. From the middle decades of the century, innovations in landscape garden design were increasingly driven by the British middle classes. These included London townhouse gardens, which (like their Hong merchant equivalents in China) combined practicality and sociability, as well as the larger-scale Quaker and merchant gardens in Bristol, which attempted a 'bourgeois reworking of aristocratic aesthetics', incorporating Whiggish motifs and often celebrating the industries and regions from which the owner's wealth derived.[52]

Middle-class enthusiasm for China precipitated a series of essays and satires, around the middle decades of the century, on the follies now proliferating in more modest gardens. By 1753, Horace Walpole was able to complain of the taste for 'paltry Chinese buildings and bridges', which had originated less than two decades earlier and grown into a 'very numerous race over the kingdom'.⁵³ The broad market for these was indicated in do-it-yourself guides such as William Halfpenny's *Rural Architecture in the Chinese Taste* (1752), aimed at rural landowners 'at a Distance from this Metropolis' who were wealthy but still budget-conscious (a guideline price for each structure is included, ranging from around £100 to £500).⁵⁴ The whimsical style of these follies had initially been seen as one of the key merits of oriental style, offering a welcome contrast to the restrained symmetry of neoclassical designs: as the Earl of Shaftesbury notes, 'Effeminacy pleases me. The Indian Figures, the Japan work, the enamel strikes my Eye. The luscious colours and glossy paint gain upon my fancy.'⁵⁵ As prevailing aristocratic tastes moved in the direction of more austere, Palladian styles, eclecticism became less frequently praised, and by the 1740s Chinese garden structures had become the object of satires, as mongrel in style, garish and cheaply constructed (their flimsy materials typically concealed under bright paint, varnish and stucco). Halfpenny's designs indeed provide some evidence for this criticism, such as his 'Garden Temple partly in the Chinese taste', with its Gothic gables, spires and foils and classical statues positioned on either side.⁵⁶

This context helps us to understand the social positioning of Chambers's first major publication on China, *Designs of Chinese buildings, furniture, dresses, machines, and utensils. Engraved by the best hands, from the originals drawn in China by Mr. Chambers, architect* (1757). This short folio volume, which gave Chambers a 'not entirely deserved career as an expert' on China, is a prestige publication aimed at an elite audience.⁵⁷ The book contains architectural descriptions of the main categories of Chinese buildings, divided into temples, towers and houses, along with a short standalone essay titled 'Of the Art of Laying Out Gardens Among the Chinese'. Twenty-one plates are attached, including architectural sketches, elevations of buildings and images of Chinese furniture, boats and costumes. It was subscribed to by 164 prominent Britons, including the Duke of Bridgewater, the Earl of Chesterfield and the Duke of Portland, alongside literary figures such as Horace Walpole and Adam Smith. A French edition, also printed in London, was produced later in the same year, suggesting that part of the aim was to drum up business in Europe.⁵⁸ It was dedicated by permission to Frederick, Prince of Wales, who had recently employed Chambers as architectural tutor. Despite these honours, Chambers's personal circumstances were still relatively straitened: he had apparently exhausted most of the capital accrued in Cantonese trade on architectural training at the École des Arts in Paris and travels in Italy. The title page advertised that the book was 'published by the author, and sold by him next door to Tom's Coffee-house, Russell-street, Covent-Garden', a down-at-heel area (one contemporary described him as living in 'a poor mean lodging up a long dark stair').[59]

Given the mockery already directed towards Chinese designs by satirists such as Hogarth, Chambers is unsurprisingly keen to differentiate himself from Halfpenny's mongrelised bourgeois styles. The preface to the *Designs* strikes a defensive tone, noting that it had originally been 'not my design to publish' the drawings, that they are offered only as curiosities, and even that 'several of my good friends have endeavoured to dissuade me from publishing this work, through a persuasion that it would hurt my reputation as an Architect'.[60] The aim, Chambers stresses, is to introduce a greater authenticity to British understandings of Chinese architecture, and thus to put 'a stop to the extravagancies that daily appear under the name of Chinese'. Avoiding the rhetoric of cultural enchantment on the one hand and the encomiums of the Jesuits on the other, Chambers aims to subject China to more judicious scrutiny: 'It is difficult to avoid praising too little or too much. The boundless panegyricks which have been lavished upon the Chinese learning, policy, and arts, shew with what power novelty attracts regard, and how naturally esteem swells into admiration.'[61]

The *Designs* aims to encourage a more sophisticated understanding of China as a coherent architectural tradition, analogous in many ways to the Western classical tradition. Chinese architecture is founded on the principles of 'singularity', 'justness', 'simplicity, and sometimes even beauty', making use of columns and fretwork, regular proportions and fundamental shapes such as the pyramid and arch.[62] Chambers's desire to relate Western and Chinese styles frequently leads to eyebrow-raising comparisons: thus the columns of Cantonese merchant houses are likened to one of Palladio's Tuscan bases, while the pagodas 'bear a great resemblance to the Attic base of the ancients'.[63] The drawings he includes even show 'swags on triumphal arches' and 'Greek key frets and friezes'.[64]

As John Harris notes, the *Designs* is groundbreaking in that 'for the first time, Chinese architecture was presented as a subject worthy of the kind of serious study previously reserved for western antiquity'.[65] Nevertheless, Chambers does not accord to China the cultural pre-eminence of Italy or France, but only an intermediate rank within a Western-dominated hierarchy. The inclusion of Chinese designs in landscape gardens is justified, tellingly, through the logic of the Enlightenment Wunderkammer: these are 'toys in architecture: and as toys are sometimes, on account of their oddity, prettyness, or neatness of workmanship, admitted into the cabinets of the curious, so may Chinese buildings be sometimes allowed a place among compositions of a nobler kind'.[66] The solution adopted to the problem of Chinese value can be compared to the approach taken in David Hume's essay 'Of the Standard of Taste' (also published in 1757), which similarly traces cross-cultural principles of taste, while also insisting that these principles have found their highest expression in Western art. Thus, while the 'peasant or Indian' is impressed by the 'coarsest daubing' and the Koran is a 'wild and absurd performance', Greek culture remains relevant across space and time: 'The same HOMER who pleased at ATHENS and ROME two thousand years ago, is still admired at PARIS and at LONDON.'[67]

Chambers translated these principles into practice in his actual designs at Kew, following his appointment in 1757 as architect to Princess Augusta. Although he included several 'oriental' structures on the grounds – including a Turkish mosque with two minarets and an 'Alhambra', vaguely modelled after the original in Granada – he seems to have had a distaste for the inauthentic Chinese follies then proliferating in English gardens. Notably, one of his first decisions at Kew was to move the rococo 'House of Confucius', designed in the 1740s for the previous owner, Frederick, Prince of Wales (1707–51), to a less prominent location.[68] In its place, he added several structures drawing directly on his own experience at Canton, including a Menagerie (built in 1760). According to Chambers's *Plans, Elevations, Sections, and Perspective Views of the Gardens and Buildings at Kew in Surry* [sic] (1763), this consisted of 'a large bason of water surrounded by a walk; and the whole is enclosed by a range of pens, or large cages, in which are kept great numbers of Chinese and Tartarian pheasants, besides many sorts of other large exotic birds'.[69] Chambers described it as an 'imitation of a Chinese open TING',[70] which we know from the *Designs* he had seen an example of 'in the middle of a small lake, in a garden at Canton'.[71] The structure thus seems balanced between royal menagerie and attempted recreation of the more modest 'little landscape pretty enough', originally seen at southern Chinese merchant houses, with their water features and 'pheasants, Bantam fowls, and other curious birds'.[72]

The more famous Great Pagoda, completed in 1762, can similarly be seen as an oblique attempt to introduce first-hand knowledge of China into European gardens. In a concession to the visual conventions of rococo chinoiserie, this octagonal ten-storey structure was painted in copper verdigris, then the brightest green available,[73] and decorated with eighty pine-carved dragons (which Chambers removed in a 1784 restoration).[74] It is notable that Chambers termed it a 'pagoda', a word then associated with travel writing about Asia, rather than ornamental follies,[75] and avoided the word 'gazebo', which had been introduced to English as a synonym for an imitation 'Chinese tower' by William Halfpenny in 1750.[76] The degree of first-hand experience embodied in this structure is open to debate: Patrick Connor argues plausibly that it was based in part on an engraving of the Porcelain Tower in Nanjing from a 1665 travel account by Johan Nieuhof.[77] Nevertheless, the structure also seems based (with some modifications) on a pagoda in the *Designs*, which was 'copied from one of those towers, that stands on the banks of the Ta-Ho, between Canton and Hoang-Pou [Huangpu]'.[78] Aldous Bertram notes the resemblance of the Great Pagoda to two structures at Canton – the Pazhou Pagoda (built 1597–1600) and the Chigang Pagoda (built 1619) – which were well-known landmarks at the entrance to the harbour, and which were both visible to Chambers from the European factory.[79] The Chigang Pagoda (also known to Europeans as the Honan Pagoda) seems the more likely contender, however, as Chambers specifically indicated having visited it.[80]

The indeterminate symbolism of the Great Pagoda, both in its architectural form and in its relationship to the surrounding heterotopic space of the landscape garden, can be related to what Vanessa Alayric-Fielding terms 'ornamental orientalism': a fundamentally ambivalent mode of cultural self-definition, relying on 'historical and cultural comparisons, reminiscences and echoes' created by the entanglement of British and Chinese cultures.[81] Although, in form and function, the Pagoda has obvious resemblances to early eighteenth-century whimsical garden follies and deeper roots in the Wunderkammer tradition, it also seems to mark a transformation of these earlier traditions of curiosity and collection into an imperial mode of epistemological authority and accumulative power (as the Mosque positioned nearby suggests, over not just East Asia but also the Middle East). It can of course be interpreted in the context of the Seven Years' War (1756–63), which had confirmed Britain's pre-eminence over France as the dominant European colonial power. More specifically, as a structure 'transplanted' from Asia into British soil, the Pagoda suggests a parallel with the establishment of the botanical gardens under William Aiton (1731–93) in 1759, which would make Kew not just a pleasure garden, but also a 'major metropolitan node in a complex network of a global botanical empire'.[82]

As a signifier of class, the Great Pagoda can most obviously be read as a statement of monarchical wealth and dominance. Towering over the chinoiserie follies in other English gardens, it inspired a series of rival aristocratic structures on the Continent.[83] William Marlow's 1763 watercolour *View of the Wilderness at Kew* (Fig. 4) captures the startling scale of the structure, which rose fifty metres in height and offered a bird's-eye view of London.[84] At the same time, however, the Pagoda's status as 'Cantonese' (rather than, like Ripa's illustrations, based on the imperial gardens northeast of Beijing) suggests a celebration of the indispensable role played by trade in imperial networks of accumulation. It can perhaps be connected to the tendency among Whig designers, in the second half of the eighteenth century, to incorporate celebrations of commerce into gardens. Examples of this include the use of 'hardened, molten copper waste' in a grotto at Warmley in the late 1760s to suggest an 'industrial sublime',[85] to Repton's recommendation that the garden of a wealthy merchant at Bristol be designed to show views of shipping on the Bristol Channel (an idea which he allowed might 'go amiss with an aristocratic client').[86] Subtly transporting the skyline of Canton, seen from the European factories, into the heart of the English royal garden, Chambers suggests the importance of the 'mercantile perspective' on China.

Aestheticising Aristocratic Power: Chambers's Essays on Chinese Gardening

The ambiguity of the 'ornamental Orientalism' in Chambers's architectural designs contrasts with the more targeted symbolism of his two essays on Chinese gardens. The first of these is placed at the end of the 1757 *Designs*, titled 'Of the Art of Laying Out Gardens Among the Chinese'. The practical value of these rather general reflections, which occupy just four pages, is limited not only by their lack of description of Chinese buildings, but also the scarcity of botanical detail. Disappointingly, the only Chinese plants mentioned are the 'Lyen Hoa' (*lianhua*, or lotus) and the weeping willow: a serious omission in a period when botanical collection, especially of Asian and tropical plants, was rapidly expanding in Britain.[87] We may suspect that the vagueness is, in part, intended to conceal Chambers's limited practical experience. Revealingly, the only point at which the essay moves into the first person is in its discussions of the scholar's rocks that Chambers has seen 'numbers of artificers constantly employed' in producing in Canton: they fetch a high price, 'insomuch that I have seen several Tael given for a bit no bigger than a man's fist'. For gardens, a larger type of stone is used, often joined with a blueish cement: 'I have seen some of these exquisitely fine, and such as discovered an uncommon elegance of taste in the contriver.'[88]

Although Chambers had subordinated Chinese architecture to the classical tradition, he positions Chinese gardening as the forerunner of the British landscape style. As Liu indicates, the idea that the Chinese had been the first to discover the art of 'naturalistic disposition of ground, water, plants, and ornamental structures' dates back to a 1685 essay by William Temple, which introduced the (supposedly) Chinese word *sharawadgi* to refer to the principle of irregular harmony.[89] If Chambers is aware of Temple's essay, it is notable that he avoids this aesthetic term, turning instead to a rather bland and generalising language of cultural confluence. He begins with the statement that, for Chinese gardeners, 'NATURE is their pattern, and their aim is to imitate her in all her beautiful irregularities': an anodyne formulation which had been deployed in similar forms by William Kent (*c.* 1686–1748), Capability Brown (*c.* 1715–83) and Humphry Repton (1752–1818) to summarise their own approach to garden design.[90] The Chinese, we are told, take as their 'first consideration ... the form of the ground, whether it be flat, sloping, hilly, or mountainous',[91] an idea which seems to echo Alexander Pope's advice in 'Epistle to Burlington' (1731) to 'Consult the Genius of the Place in all'.[92] The essay continues through a series of largely conventional reflections, imitating other gardening treatises, including the benefits of 'judicious arrangement' of 'light and shade', and the importance of creating a 'multiplicity of scenes' to complement different times of day.[93]

But Chambers also introduces the radical idea that the Chinese are ahead of the British in this art – their gardens embody 'what we have for some time past been aiming at in England, though not always with success' – to open up new imaginative and polemical possibilities, in which the Chinese garden is portrayed as a cutting-edge style for Britons to aspire to.[94] Chambers seems particularly interested in exploring uses of sublimity and terror: Chinese gardens, he tells us, are divided into 'pleasing, horrid, and enchanted' scenes, and make heavy use of 'artifices to excite surprize'.[95] This idea, apparently not found in previous writings on Chinese gardens by Temple or by Jesuit authors, suggests intriguing parallels with Edmund Burke's *Philosophical Enquiry* (which had been published in April 1757, the same month as the *Designs*). As in Burke, there is an interest in the encounter with the sublime as a moment of pleasurable horror, arising from the encounter with overwhelming power, in which the reasoning ability is suspended. Amongst the artifices that Chambers credits to China are artificial echoes and 'monstrous birds and animals',[96] which resonate with Burke's suggestion that the sublime 'comes upon us in the gloomy forest, and in the howling wilderness, in the form of the lion, the tiger, the panther, or rhinoceros'.[97] To these are added, in a bold aestheticisation of social inequality, 'impetuous cataracts' flowing through ruined and depopulated landscapes, in which a few burned buildings or 'miserable huts dispersed in the mountains serve, at once to indicate the existence and wretchedness of the inhabitants'.[98]

Although William Kent had experimented with a thatched Merlin's Cave and a Hermitage at Richmond Lodge for Queen Caroline in the early 1730s, the idea of artificial moans and lightning-blasted peasant huts unsurprisingly proved a step too far for the Prince of Wales at Kew.[99] Nevertheless, Chambers does experiment, in more limited ways, with a more controlling and artificial gardening aesthetic. Yu Liu has explored how his use of zigzagging pathways on the fringes of the estate, in contrast to Hogarth's more sinuous 'line of beauty',[100] are positioned to create 'a surprising drama of alternate revelation and concealment'.[101] Miles David Samson similarly points out that Chambers adopts an 'aggressively exotic approach to placing Chinese elements in the landscape', at odds with the developing Brownian taste for 'unnoticeable intervention'.[102]

Fifteen years pass between the publication of the *Designs* and Chambers's longer and more famous work on Chinese gardens, the *Dissertation on Oriental Gardening* (1772). This essay, which revises and substantially expands 'Of the Art of Laying Out Gardens Among the Chinese', is not a serious attempt to add to knowledge of China (indeed, the shift to 'Oriental' in the title signals that cultural precision is not the concern here) but primarily a polemical intervention into contemporary gardening debates. The main satirical target is Capability Brown, who, as Royal Gardener from 1764 and as chief designer for Princess Augusta at Richmond Gardens near Kew, had become a rival for royal favour. Indeed, the timing of the *Dissertation* may also reflect a renewed bid for royal patronage: in 1772 George III had extended his holdings at Kew by inheriting the adjoining Kew Palace and grounds, which he was planning to make his official summer residence.[103]

The opening sections of the *Dissertation*, with their ad hominem attacks on Brown (the son of a land agent and a chambermaid, who had begun his career as apprentice at Kirkhale Hall), are steeped in the language of class. In China, gardening is considered an elite profession, rather than a mere occupation: gardeners are 'men of high abilities, who join to good natural parts, most ornaments that study, travelling, and long experience can supply them with'.[104] Chambers adds that: 'It is not in China, as in Italy and France, where every petty Architect is a Gardener; neither is it as in another famous country [i.e. England], where peasants emerge from the melon grounds to take the periwig, and turn professors.'[105] The snobbery also reflects Chambers's newfound social status as founding member of the Royal Academy of Arts and recipient of the Swedish knighthood of the Polar Star, a title which he was granted exceptional permission to use in England.

This early attack on Brown is developed, over the course of the *Dissertation*, into a broader critique of dominant British gardening tastes. The unadorned Brownian landscape, with its undulating grounds leading down to gently winding streams, close-cut grass and clumps of trees, is mocked as slavish adherence to 'vulgar nature' and (in an apparent dig at the Whiggish elevation of trade) as bearing 'a great resemblance to the barge-canals of Holland'.[106] A formulaic set of aesthetic principles, Chambers argues, is endlessly replicated across Brownian gardens, regardless of the scale of the grounds or the munificence of the owner, meaning that even grand estates appear 'like the honest batchelor's feast, which consisted in nothing but a multiplication of his own dinner; three legs of mutton and turneps [sic], three roasted geese, and three buttered apple-pies'.[107] The satire here is directed not just against a supposed preference for the plain and the comfortable, but also against the bourgeois levelling instinct, which fails to understand the importance of hierarchy and gradation.

Chambers's *Dissertation* has the character of a philosophical experiment, corresponding to what Eric Hayot argues is a characteristic use of China in Western thought as a limit point showing the horizons of human possibility,[108] or as an exceptional space which 'comes through its very marginality to provide the support from the structure from which it has been removed'.[109] This fantasy of absolute despotism over nature goes far beyond anything Chambers could have seen in China, even exceeding the Jesuit Jean-Denis Attiret's glowing description of the emperor of China's lavish gardens at Beijing.[110] The visitor to Chambers's Chinese garden becomes a 'traveller', 'spectator' or 'passenger' (the words significantly connote the loss of the individual agency and freedom of movement that Brown had seen as crucial to the effect of the landscape garden),[111] who is led along a route 'where his attention is constantly to be kept up, his curiosity excited, and his mind agitated by a great variety of opposite passions'.[112] Chinese gardens are divided into 'the pleasing, the terrible, and the surprizing':[113] this is subtly different from the 'pleasing, horrid, and enchanted' tripartite aesthetic mentioned in the *Designs*, suggesting a renewed focus on violent, agitating emotions.[114] The traveller is led along a growing gradient of strangeness, from 'spotted buffaloes, shen-si sheep, and Tartarean horses'[115] to electric shocks, gibbets and 'dragons, infernal furies, and other horrid forms, which hold in their monstrous talons, mysterious, cabalistical sentences, inscribed on tables of brass'.[116] This 'veritable Disneyland of exotic devices' focuses heavily, in a similar manner to the nascent Gothic genre, on the aestheticisation of terror and the exoticism of foreign cultures.[117]

The *Dissertation*, in short, rejects Brown's suggestion that the garden designer should use the charms of unadorned nature as their standard. It also inverts Horace Walpole's suggestion in 'On Modern Gardening' (1771) that the tendency of aristocratic taste to excess and solipsism might be moderated by pulling down the walls to the garden and connecting it with the 'charms of landscape' outside.[118] By contrast, Chambers's China is one vast walled garden, extending over the face of the continent (canals and even prisons are built as decorative features), inside which the garden designer, as the representative of the owner, wields unquestioned control. Here it is impossible to ignore the broader wave of legislation in England (consolidated and accelerated by the Enclosure Act of 1773) which removed communal rights and erected hedges and fences across large swathes of the English countryside: some of the consolidated land was used to expand farms, and some merely 'annexed to estates for show, creating broad vistas and carefully designed wild areas'.[119] If working-class agrarian writers (echoed in elite literary texts such as Goldsmith's *The Deserted Village*, 1770) had protested against this change by creating a rhetoric of 'dispossession in which farmers saw themselves as refugees in their own land',[120] Chambers, by contrast, celebrates that economic dispossession as the necessary price for the creation of a Gothic landscape of sublimity and terror, in a space 'where treasures are inexhaustible, where power is unlimited, and where munificence has no bounds'.[121]

In addition, the *Dissertation* intervenes more broadly in the polarised constitutional climate of the early 1770s, drawing on the well-established use of landscape metaphors by both Whig and Tory writers. In contrast to the Whiggish, pro-American poet William Mason's *The English Garden* (1772), which celebrates the English garden (and by extension the British constitution) as a state of decentred irregularity, Chambers argues that the Chinese garden achieves greatness by channelling its unlimited central power to enforce harmony across the whole scheme. Where Mason insists that 'Great Nature scorns controul',[122] Chambers asserts that 'great diversity' of plants and colours 'must create confusion, and destroy all the masses upon which effect and grandeur depend'.[123] As Samuel Smith points out, contemporaries would undoubtedly have read these remarks as embodying a 'desire to increase the prerogative powers of the crown and to establish elite arbiters of taste'.[124] Peter Kitson observes that Chambers effectively reverses the political polarities of chinoiserie, converting it from a 'disruptive, hybrid, and proto-Jacobinical aesthetic' to a Tory trope of 'rightful obedience'.[125]

This coded political critique further intensifies in the *Dissertation*'s later reception history. Mason's satirical riposte, *An Heroic Epistle to William Chambers* (1773), attempts to expose its Tory politics by transferring the scene from China to England, presenting George III as a cossetted Chinese emperor, shielded from his subjects by the 'Barbaric glories' and 'August Pagodas' built by Chambers at Kew.[126] Chambers responds with an 'Explanatory Discourse by Tan Chet-qua', appended to the second edition, in which he effectively doubles down on the satire, allowing a fictional Chinese narrator to speculate how the whole island of Britain might be shaped into one vast imperial garden, 'with the imperial mansion towering on an eminence in the center, and the palaces of the nobles scattered like pleasure-pavilions among the plantations'.[127] By this point, it was unlikely that any readers took this seriously as objective discussion of China ('Chet-qua' is surely intended as a pseudo-oriental rendering of 'Chambers'). By the end of Chambers's career as a Sinologist, the 'Chinese garden' had thus attained a status it would hold in British imaginative and visual culture into the first half of the nineteenth century, as a self-consciously fictional and hyperbolic space for commentary upon domestic debates about class, politics and taste.

Chambers and Romantic Ecologies of China

This chapter has explored how the 'small cargo' of information Chambers brings back with him from China is repeatedly redeployed, over the course of three decades, in different domestic debates about taste and social class, producing on each occasion a different vision of the country. This perspective requires us to distinguish between 'China', the cultural and political reality encountered by a handful of eighteenth-century Britons who travelled to the Far East or were directly connected with the trade, and 'China' as it was understood and experienced by most Britons during this period: a largely aesthetic concept, essentially produced within domestic debates about class, taste and material consumption.

One benefit of this distinction is that it avoids overly reductive geopolitical connections between aesthetic ideas and external trade relations. An established critical narrative has sought to explain the shift from Enlightenment praise of Chinese hierarchy to Romantic ideas of Chinese inequality and despotism largely in terms of British imperialism and anxieties about the balance of trade.[128] However, there is a danger here of too readily elevating the self-interested complaints of merchants at Canton to the status of 'the British view of China'. In addition, as the example of Chambers demonstrates, merchants themselves could hold ambiguous or conflicting views towards the country. George Anson (1697–1762), for example, who famously attacks the Chinese as insolent and obstructive during his visit to Canton in 1743,[129] also uses his visit to acquire furniture, porcelain and lanterns, which are placed on his return in a newly constructed 'Chinese House' on his family estate at Shugborough.[130] Finally, the use of the failed Macartney Embassy of 1793 as a crucial 'turning point' in British attitudes is problematic given that the shift to more critical ideas of China is evident from some decades earlier, and (as I have explored elsewhere) the ramifications of the Embassy are politically contested for years after its return to England.[131]

Chambers's *Dissertation*, by contrast, allows us to understand how changes in the representation of China might be seen as driven primarily by domestic debates about class, taste, consumption and power relations. 'China' in this work is a space in which to represent and reconfigure the social relations between Britons, allowing Chambers to propose (while maintaining ironic distance from) a deliberately exaggerated vision of aristocratic control, in differentiation to emergent Whiggish and bourgeois styles of gardening. Importantly, this vision of Chinese landscape does not merely structure expressions of Chambers's own Tory aesthetics, but also appeals to later writers with divergent aesthetic and political views. Echoes of Chambers's *Dissertation* are found in Romantic poems as different as Coleridge's 'Kubla Khan' (1797/1816) and Wordsworth's *The Prelude* (1799), while the essay also (I have argued elsewhere) shapes the descriptions of actual Chinese gardens by Macartney Embassy diplomats, allowing them a way to figuratively present their own powerless encounters with the Chinese state.[132]

Ironically, Chambers, had he chosen, was one of the best-positioned Britons during this period to promote a more accurate understanding of Chinese gardens and garden buildings. Arguably, his achievements in this field have been under-credited: most notably, in the resemblance of his Great Pagoda to the Chigang Pagoda at Canton, and in his descriptions of mercantile gardens at Canton. Nevertheless, a broader view of his career as a Sinologist shows that, in his eagerness to distance 'China' from middle-class rococo tastes and produce a version of the country acceptable to an aristocratic audience, he creates an even more lurid and enduring orientalist vision. Kara Blakely has shown, focusing on the Royal Pavilion in Brighton, how by the early nineteenth century chinoiserie designs exhibit a 'clear ideological departure from mid eighteenth-century iterations',[133] rejecting any semblance of authenticity in favour of 'exaggerated, flamboyant, and repurposed manifestations of signs that were already known to British audiences'.[134] The arc of Chambers's career thus reinforces Peter Kitson's arguments about the 'ambivalent' position of the early 'Romantic Sinologists', caught between a desire for accurate knowledge and a growing British suspicion of Chinese culture.[135] It also suggests some broader conclusions about the ways in which Romantic environmentalism – often grounded in imaginative and rhetorical oppositions between British and 'Eastern' landscapes – tends to foreclose Enlightenment attempts at intellectual and aesthetic dialogue with Asian traditions.

Notes

1. This research was supported by a JSPS Grant-in-Aid for Scientific Research (18K12316).
2. Giovanni Paolo Marana, *Letters Writ by a Turkish Spy*, trans. William Bradshaw, 8 vols (London: Hindmarsh and Sare, [1684] 1687–94).
3. Oliver Goldsmith, *The Citizen of the World; or Letters from a Chinese Philosopher, Residing in London, to his Friends in the East*, 2 vols (London: Printed for the author, 1762), p. vi.
4. Elizabeth Chang, *Britain's Chinese Eye: Literature, Empire, and Aesthetics in Nineteenth-Century Britain* (Stanford: Stanford University Press, 2010), p. 29.
5. Maxine Berg, *Luxury and Pleasure in Eighteenth-Century Britain* (Oxford: Oxford University Press, 2007), p. 19.
6. Eugenia Zuroski Jenkins, *A Taste for China: English Subjectivity and the Prehistory of Orientalism* (Oxford: Oxford University Press, 2013), p. 3.
7. Nicholas Rowe, *The Biter. A Comedy* (London: Tonson, 1705), p. 25.
8. William Hogarth, *The Tête à Tête* (1743), from the *Marriage A-la-Mode* series (1743–5), <https://www.nationalgallery.org.uk/paintings/william-hogarth-marriage-a-la-mode-2-the-tete-a-tete> (accessed 16 March 2020). Hogarth's class satire is echoed (although reversed) in a letter in *The World* (20 September 1753) in which Samuel Simple, a wealthy tradesman, marries a lady from an upper-class but impoverished family who engages the Chinese craftsman Mr Kifang to remodel his home in hideous rococo style; see vol. 1, no. 38 (1753): 240–1.
9. John Brown, *An Estimate of the Manners and Principles of the Times*, 7th edn (Boston: Green and Russell, 1758), p. 28.
10. David Porter, *The Chinese Taste in Eighteenth-Century England* (Cambridge: Cambridge University Press, 2010), p. 24.
11. See Chi-ming Yang, *Performing China: Virtue, Commerce, and Orientalism in Eighteenth-Century England, 1660–1760* (Baltimore: Johns Hopkins University Press, 2011); Jenkins, *A Taste for China*.
12. Nicholas Hudson, 'Literature and Social Class in the Eighteenth Century', *Oxford Handbooks Online* (Oxford: Oxford University Press, 2015), <doi: 10.1093/oxfordhb/9780199935338.013.007> (accessed 19 March 2020).
13. Ibid.

14. Ann Laura Stoler, 'Cultivating Bourgeois Bodies and Racial Selves', in *Race and the Education of Desire: Foucault's History of Sexuality and the Colonial Order of Things* (Durham, NC: Duke University Press, 1995), pp. 95–136.
15. Saree Makdisi, *Making England Western: Occidentalism, Race, and Imperial Culture* (Chicago: University of Chicago, 2014).
16. Gerard Cohen-Vrignaud, *Radical Orientalism: Rights, Reform, and Romanticism* (Cambridge: Cambridge University Press, 2015).
17. Jeng-Guo S. Chen, 'The British View of Chinese Civilization and the Emergence of Class Consciousness', *The Eighteenth Century* 45, no. 2 (2004): 193.
18. John Harris speculates that Chambers's reputation as a Sinologist led to his introduction to the Swedish minister in Paris, Count Carl Fredrik Scheffer, who may have smoothed his recruitment into Blondel's École des Arts. See John Harris, 'Chambers, Sir William (1722–1796)', *Oxford Dictionary of National Biography Online* <https://www.oxforddnb.com/view/10.1093/ref:odnb/9780198614128.001.0001/odnb-9780198614128-e-5083> (accessed 15 December 2019).
19. Yu Liu, 'The Real vs the Imaginary: Sir William Chambers on the Chinese Garden', *The European Legacy* 23, no. 6 (2018): 687; Peter Kitson, *Forging Romantic China* (Cambridge: Cambridge University Press, 2013), pp. 184–8.
20. *The Gentleman's Magazine* 27 (1757): 216–19.
21. Goldsmith, *Citizen of the World*, 1: 126–30.
22. Chang, *Britain's Chinese Eye*, p. 28.
23. David Porter, 'Beyond the Bounds of Truth: Cultural Translation and William Chambers's Chinese Garden', *Mosaic* 37, no. 2 (2004): 51.
24. Chang, *Britain's Chinese Eye*, p. 29.
25. C. C. L. Hirschfeld, *Theory of Garden Art* (1779–85), quoted in Richard E. Strassberg, 'War and Peace: Four Intercultural Landscapes', in Marcia Reed and Paola Demattè (eds), *China on Paper: European and Chinese Works from the Late Sixteenth to the Early Nineteenth Century* (Los Angeles: Getty Research Institute, [2007] 2011), p. 127.
26. The Scottish physician John Bell also gives an account of two gardens and parks in Beijing, as well as the emperor's hunting lodge near the capital, during his time at a Russian embassy in 1719–22. This was published as *Travels to St Petersburg in Russia to Diverse Parts of Asia* (1763). See Bianca Maria Rinaldi (ed.), *Ideas of Chinese Gardens: Western Accounts, 1300–1860* (Pittsburgh: University of Pennsylvania Press, 2016), pp. 126–31.
27. Quoted in John Harris, *Sir William Chambers: Knight of the Polar Star* (University Park: Pennsylvania State University Press, 1970), p. 4.
28. Matthew Smith Anderson, *Europe in the Eighteenth Century, 1713–1783*, 4th edn (Oxford: Routledge, 2000), p. 300.
29. Charles Noble, *A Voyage to the East Indies in 1747 and 1748* (London: Becket and Dehondt, 1762), p. 215.
30. Leonard Blussé, *Visible Cities: Canton, Nagasaki, and Batavia and the Coming of the Americans* (Cambridge, MA: Harvard University Press, 2008), p. 52.

31. Peter Perdue, 'Boundaries and Trade in the Early Modern World: Negotiations at Nerchinsk and Beijing', *Eighteenth-Century Studies* 43, no. 3 (2010): 354.
32. Noble, *Voyage to the East Indies*, pp. 231–2.
33. Porter, 'Beyond the Bounds of Truth', p. 47.
34. William Chambers, *Designs of Chinese Buildings, Furniture, Dresses, Machines, and Utensils. Engraved by the best hands, from the originals drawn in China by Mr. Chambers, architect* (London: printed for the author, 1757), p. 12.
35. Ibid. p. 1.
36. Noble, *Voyage to the East Indies*, pp. 214–15.
37. Chambers, *Designs*, p. 14.
38. Ibid. p. 14.
39. Ibid. 'Preface'.
40. Fa-ti Fan, *British Naturalists in Qing China: Science, Empire, and Cultural Encounter* (Cambridge, MA: Harvard University Press, 2004), pp. 33–4.
41. On cross-cultural discourses of sociability between England and China, see Laurence Williams, 'Anglo-Chinese Caresses: Civility, Friendship and Trade in English Representations of China, 1760–1800', *Journal for Eighteenth-Century Studies* 38, no. 2 (2015): 277–9.
42. Noble, *Voyage to the East Indies*, p. 225.
43. Chambers, *Designs*, p. 9. The price is glossed in a footnote as 'Above 300 guineas'.
44. Porter, *The Chinese Taste*, p. 110.
45. Lisa Hellman, *This House is Not a Home: European Everyday Life in Canton and Macao, 1730–1830*, Studies in Global Social History 34 (Leiden and Boston: Brill, 2019), p. 101.
46. Ibid. p. 101.
47. Chambers, *Designs*, p. 8.
48. Ibid. p. 11. Plate IX (Canton merchant's house, towards the river) is mislabelled in the text as Plate XI.
49. Engraving of a Cantonese merchant's house by Edward Rooker, in William Chambers, *Designs of Chinese Buildings* (London: printed for the author, 1757), pl. ix.
50. Yu Liu, 'Transplanting a Different Gardening Style into England: Matteo Ripa and His Visit to London in 1724', *Diogenes* 55, no. 2 (2008): p. 90.
51. David Porter, 'Monstrous Beauty: Eighteenth-Century Fashion and the Aesthetics of the Chinese Taste', *Eighteenth-Century Studies* 35, no. 3 (2002): 396.
52. David Lambert, 'The Prospect of Trade: The Merchant Gardeners of Bristol in the Second Half of the Eighteenth Century', in Michael Conan (ed.), *Bourgeois and Aristocratic Cultural Encounters in Garden Art* (Washington, DC: Dumbarton Oaks Research Library, 2002), p. 123.
53. Horace Walpole, letter to John Chute, 4 August 1753, in Peter Cunningham (ed.), *The Letters of Horace Walpole, Fourth Earl of Orford*, 9 vols (London: Bentley, 1891), 2: 348. Walpole was speaking of the Chinese buildings at Wroxton, which he thought were 'of the very first' of this style.

54. William Halfpenny, *Rural Architecture in the Chinese Taste*, 3rd edn (London: Robert Sayer, [1752] 1755), 'Preface'.
55. Anthony, Earl of Shaftesbury, *Characteristics of Men, Manners, Opinions, Times, etc.*, 2 vols (Bristol: Thoemmes Press, 1995), 1: 219.
56. Halfpenny, *Rural Architecture*, pl. 45.
57. Miles David Samson, *Hut Pavilion Shrine: Architectural Archetypes in Mid-Century Modernism* (Farnham: Ashgate, 2015), p. 33.
58. William Chambers, *Desseins des édifices, meubles, habits, machines, et ustenciles des Chinois* (London: printed for the author, 1757).
59. J. Fleming, *Robert Adam and His Circle, in Edinburgh and Rome* (1962), quoted in Harris, 'Chambers, Sir William'.
60. Chambers, *Designs*, 'Preface'.
61. Ibid. 'Preface'.
62. Ibid. 'Preface'.
63. Ibid. p. 12.
64. Harris, *Sir William Chambers*, p. 146.
65. Harris, 'Chambers, Sir William'.
66. Chambers, *Designs*, 'Preface'.
67. David Hume, 'Of the Standard of Taste', in Stephen Copley and Andrew Edgar (eds), *Selected Essays* (Oxford: Oxford World's Classics, 1998), pp. 135–9 and 144.
68. It has been argued that this structure was in fact designed by Chambers; he himself denied this. See Porter, 'Beyond the Bounds of Truth', p. 46.
69. Chambers, *Plans, Elevations, Sections, and Perspective Views of the Gardens and Buildings at Kew in Surry* (London: Haberkorn, 1763), p. 4.
70. Ibid. p. 4.
71. Chambers, *Designs*, p. 6.
72. Ibid. p. 8.
73. Lee Prosser, 'The Great Pagoda at Kew: Colour and Technical Innovation in Chinoiserie Architecture', *Architectural History* 62 (2019): 72.
74. Ibid. p. 75. The dragons were returned to the pagoda in a 2018 restoration.
75. See entry for 'pagoda' in *OED*. The first use of the word to mean 'An ornamental building or structure in imitation' (1.b.) is 1789.
76. See entry for 'gazebo' in *OED*. The etymology is unclear: *OED* speculates that it 'may possibly be a corruption of some oriental word'.
77. Patrick Connor, 'Chinese Style in Nineteenth-Century Britain', in David Beevers (ed.), *Chinese Whispers: Chinoiserie in Britain, 1650–1930* (Brighton: Royal Pavilion Libraries, 2008), p. 62.
78. Chambers, *Designs*, p. 6.
79. Aldous Bertram, 'Cantonese Models for the Great Pagoda at Kew', *The Georgian Group Journal* 21 (2013): 47–57.
80. Chambers, *Designs*, p. 4.
81. Vanessa Alayrac-Fielding, 'From Jehol to Stowe: Ornamental Orientalism and the Aesthetics of the Anglo-Chinese Garden', in Claire Gallien and Ladan Niayesh (eds), *Eastern Resonances in Early Modern England: Receptions and Transformations from the Renaissance to the Romantic Period* (London: Palgrave, 2019), p. 141.
82. Zaheer Baber, 'The Plants of Empire: Botanic Gardens, Colonial Power

and Botanical Knowledge', *Journal of Contemporary Asia* 46, no. 4 (2016): 675–6.
83. On copies of the Great Pagoda, see Adolf Reichwein, *China and Europe: Intellectual and Artistic Concepts in the XVIIIth Century*, trans. J. C. Powell (Oxford: Routledge, [1925] 2000), p. 119.
84. William Marlow, 'View of the Wilderness at Kew' (1763); Metropolitan Museum of Art, 25.19.43 (Harris Brisbane Dick Fund, 1925).
85. Lambert, 'The Prospect of Trade', p. 137.
86. Ibid. p. 132.
87. Sarah Easterby-Smith, 'Botanical Collecting in Eighteenth-Century London', *Curtis's Botanical Magazine* 34, no. 4 (2018): 281–2.
88. Chambers, *Designs*, p. 17.
89. Liu, 'The Real vs the Imaginary', p. 687. On possible Japanese origins of the word, see Wybe Kuitert, 'Japanese Art, Aesthetics, and a European Discourse: Unraveling *Sharawadgi*', *Japan Review* 27 (2014): 77–101.
90. Chambers, *Designs*, p. 15.
91. Ibid. p. 15.
92. John Butt (ed.), *Twickenham Edition of the Poems of Alexander Pope*, p. 590.
93. Chambers, *Designs*, p. 16.
94. Ibid. 'Preface'.
95. Ibid. p. 15.
96. Ibid. p. 15.
97. Edmund Burke, *A Philosophical Enquiry into the Origin of Our Ideas of the Sublime and the Beautiful* (Oxford: Oxford World's Classics, [1757] 2015), pp. 60–1.
98. Chambers, *Designs*, p. 15.
99. Edward S. Harwood, 'Luxurious hermits: asceticism, luxury and retirement in the eighteenth-century English garden', *Studies in the History of Gardens & Designed Landscapes* 20, no. 4 (2000): 276–7.
100. William Hogarth, *The Analysis of Beauty* (London: Reeves, 1753).
101. Liu, 'The Real vs the Imaginary', p. 680.
102. Samson, *Hut Pavilion Shrine*, p. 33.
103. The posthumous essay 'The Life of Sir William Chambers' states that, at the time of publication of the *Dissertation*, 'it was invidiously suggested, that the intention of our author was to depreciate English gardeners, in order to divert his Royal Master from his plan of improving the gardens at Richmond'; see *Scots Magazine* 58 (1795), p. 225.
104. Chambers, *A Dissertation on Oriental Gardening*, 2nd edn (London: Griffin, 1772), p. 14.
105. Ibid. p. 13.
106. Ibid. pp. v and vii.
107. Ibid. p. vii.
108. Eric Hayot, *The Hypothetical Mandarin: Sympathy, Modernity, and Chinese Pain* (Oxford: Oxford University Press, 2009), p. 8.
109. Ibid. p. 15.
110. Jean-Denis Attiret, *A Particular Account of the Emperor of China's Gardens Near Pekin*, trans. Joseph Spence (London: Dodsley, 1752).
111. Chambers, *Dissertation*, p. 42–3.

112. Ibid. p. 107.
113. Ibid. p. 39.
114. Chambers, *Designs*, p. 15.
115. Chambers, *Dissertation*, p. 29.
116. Ibid. p. 43.
117. John Dixon Hunt and Peter Willis (eds), *The Genius of the Place: The English Landscape Garden 1620–1820* (Cambridge, MA: The MIT Press, [1988] 2000), p. 318.
118. Horace Walpole, 'On Modern Gardening', in *Anecdotes of Painting in England*, 2nd edn, 4 vols (London: Dodsley, 1782), 4: 289.
119. Ellen Rosenman, 'On Enclosure Acts and the Commons', in Dino Franco Felluga (ed.), *BRANCH: Britain, Representation and Nineteenth-Century History* (Extension of *Romanticism and Victorianism on the Net*, 2012), para. 5 <http://www.branchcollective.org/?ps_articles=ellen-rosenman-on-enclosure-acts-and-the-commons> (accessed 16 March 2020).
120. Ibid. para. 10.
121. Chambers, *Dissertation*, p. 105.
122. William Mason, *The English Garden: A Poem. Book the First*, 3rd edn (London: Dodsley, 1778), p. 5.
123. Chambers, *Dissertation*, p. 91.
124. From Samuel Peter Smith, *William Mason: Nature and The English Garden, 1750–1785*, PhD thesis (University of York, 2014), p. 130.
125. Kitson, *Forging Romantic China*, pp. 186–7.
126. Mason, *An Heroic Epistle*, p. 10.
127. Chambers, *Dissertation*, p. 134. A footnote explains 'the center' as 'Windsor'.
128. See David Porter, *Ideographia: The Chinese Cipher in Early Modern Europe* (Stanford: Stanford University Press, 2001), especially chapter 4. See also Robert Markley, *The Far East and the English Imagination, 1600–1730* (Cambridge: Cambridge University Press, 2006).
129. George Anson, *The History of Commodore Anson's Voyage Round the World* (London: Mason, 1764), pp. 198–212.
130. Stephen McDowall, 'Imperial Plots? Shugborough, Chinoiserie and Imperial Ideology in Eighteenth-Century British Gardens', *Culture and Social History* 14, no. 1 (2017): 18–22. Stacey Sloboda also explores how *chinoiserie* decorations at Shugborough intertwine 'imperial ideology' with expressions of 'upwardly mobile social status', in *Chinoiserie: Commerce and Critical Ornament in Eighteenth-Century Britain* (Manchester: Manchester University Press, 2014), p. 177.
131. Laurence Williams, 'British Government Under the Qianlong Emperor's Gaze: Satire, Imperialism, and the Macartney Embassy to China, 1792–1804', in *Lumen* 32 (2013): 104. See also McDowall, 'Imperial Plots?', p. 18.
132. Williams, 'Anglo-Chinese Caresses', 287–92.
133. Kara Blakely, 'Domesticating Orientalism: Chinoiserie and the Pagodas of the Royal Pavilion, Brighton', *Australian and New Zealand Journal of Art* 18, no. 2 (2018): 206.
134. Ibid. p. 216.
135. Kitson, *Forging Romantic China*, p. 14.

Chapter 3

Ecogothic Chinatown

Li-hsin Hsu

Reminiscing upon his stay in San Francisco in 1879, Robert Louis Stevenson described the Chinese quarter as 'the most romantic' among 'all the romantic places to loiter in'. Stevenson's gothic representations of Chinatown have more in common, however, with what Catherine Cook calls the spectacle of ethnic slumming,[1] than with the rural landscapes evoked by Wordsworth and other British Romantic poets. As 'an actual foreign land' just 'three doors from home', the Chinese quarter in Stevenson's imagination is a multi-layered urban space with 'cellars ... alive with mystery; opium dens, where the smokers lie one above another, shelf above shelf, close-packed and grovelling in deadly stupor; the seats of unknown vices and cruelties, the prisons of unacknowledged slaves and the secret lazarettos of disease'.[2] Such a mysterious vision of Chinatown ties in with what Stevenson claims to be the nature of romances in 'A Gossip on Romance' (1882): that they 'may be nourished with the realities of life, but their true mark is to satisfy the nameless longings of the reader, and to obey the ideal laws of the day-dream. The right kind of thing should fall out in the right kind of place; the right kind of thing should follow.'[3] Stevenson's 'romance' of the Chinese quarter as an underground world brimming with filth, disease and illegality is entirely in tandem with the default mode of nineteenth-century orientalism ('the nameless longings of the reader', 'the ideal law of the day-dream'), where the portrayal of the racial other, while 'nourished with the realities of life', exists in spatial and epistemological obscurity with its real-life consequence in threatening moral and physiological corruption as well as environmental contamination.

In the 1870s and the 1880s, Chinatowns in California were depicted as overpopulated, deprived and impure places. Nayan Shah has commented on the association of Chinatown in the late nineteenth century with a 'subterranean world' that was 'noxious and degraded'.[4] As Shah elaborates, 'the public-health knowledge of dens, density, and the labyrinth cast Chinatown as a deviant transplantation of the traditional East in the modern Western city[.] Chinatown was impervious to progress and was instead liable to rot and regress like the enervated Chinese empire across the Pacific.'[5] This was developed in stark contrast to the image many Americans had of the expanding American empire, who saw the US foray into the Pacific Ocean in the nineteenth century as the logical extension of the completion of transcontinental railroads.[6] Indeed, David Palumbo-Liu identifies as 'the defining mythos' of American manifest destiny the desire they shared to 'form a bridge westward from the Old World, not just to the western coast of the North American continent, but from there to the trans-Pacific regions of Asia'.[7] Traffic on a bridge runs both ways: even as the development of steam technology facilitated American expansionist ambitions, it was also bringing in from the other side of the ocean thousands of Chinese. Considering how the vast population of China had already haunted the European imagination for at least a century, this transpacific connection raised (and still raises in the Far Right quarter) the dystopia of reverse colonisation. Looking westwards wistfully and yet fearfully across the Pacific Ocean, Raphael Pumpelly's 1871 travelogue *Across America and Asia* opposes China as 'a giant spectre slowly defining its shadowy form against the western heavens' to 'the splendid sunrise of our national morning': its 'population of more than four hundred millions treads closely upon the capacity of the soil for supporting existence'.[8] The Malthusian language of overpopulation was deployed to visualise China as a menacing ecological threat: teetering on the edge of environmental collapse, the unmistakable warning was of an overwhelming 'influx' of millions of Chinese.[9]

The context for this was anti-Chinese feeling, which rose along with Chinese immigration. Having initially come to participate in the California Gold Rush, due to the productivity and efficiency of Chinese labour, the Chinese were by the late nineteenth century intimately interwoven into the fabric of American society: they had built its railroads; they were servicing its restaurants, laundries, helping with household chores, mining, fishing, canning, etc. As Pumpelly remarked, 'when a pressing necessity arose for labor on the public works of California and Nevada, the Chinaman was found to answer every need; and now, having become identified with our internal improvements, he has obtained recognition as a necessary element of population'.[10] If Chinese people were indispensable, they were also unwelcome. Congress debated the restriction of Chinese immigration; in the decade running up to the passing of the 1882 Chinese Exclusion Act, Chinese immigrants experienced an intensification of racial violence inflicted verbally and physically through numerous anti-coolie and anti-Chinese movements.[11] Californian Chinatowns were emblematic and symptomatic of the racial and political tensions of the time.[12] San Francisco Chinatown functioned for many visitors as a kind of 'eternal frontier', according to Daphne Pi-Wei Lei.[13] Occupying a twelve-block space in between the city and the seaport, Chinatown was presented as a perverted Romantic landscape that was profoundly unsettling of the social and environmental order, revealing the fragility and unpredictability of Sino-American relations from its inception.

This chapter considers the politics of Twain and Stevenson's use of haunting as a literary device not only to depict Chinatown artefacts and commodities, houses and cellars, but also the daily living and spatial practices of the Chinese immigrants. Being one of the most racialised and contested of landscapes in 1870s America, Californian Chinatowns magnify the intersectionality between literary representation and racial politics, between environmental materiality and orientalist imagination.[14] Chinatown as an urban space is both haunted and quotidian, its corporeal presence consistently shadowed by a history of racial violence.[15] In *Immigrant Acts*, Lisa Lowe suggests Asian immigrants were 'a screen', 'a phantasmatic site' onto which the US government 'projects a series of condensed, complicated anxieties regarding external and internal threats to the mutable coherence of the national body'.[16] Informed by the social and political practices of ethnographic tourism, the history of westward expansionism, industrial urbanisation and racial segregation in California, this chapter reveals the subtle processes of ecological othering that take place in the representations of Chinatown by these two middle-class writers, who publicly opposed racism.

The concept of 'ecogothic' is helpful to my reconceptualisation of Chinatown as a perverted Romantic landscape. While the representations it describes might appear to be pre-modern, agricultural and phantasmagoric, they are in fact urban and un-pastoral-like; in other words, cognitively disorientating and yet ecologically relevant. Allan Lloyd Smith points out the four major features of the gothic in nineteenth-century American literature: 'the frontier, the Puritan legacy, race, and political utopianism'.[17] Chinatown is a contested borderline space providing local materials for Western writers to project their orientalist landscapes, in which the boundary between the rural and the urban, the innocent and the deviant, the natural and the unnatural, the native and the foreign, is called into question. Dawn Keetley and Matthew Wynn Sivils observe that in American ecogothic literature 'relations of predation, edibility, and environmental exploitation have often been expressed specifically within the system of racial hierarchy and oppression'.[18] One category of the ecogothic that Keetley and Sivils provide is especially pertinent to my discussion of Twain and Stevenson's Chinatown: 'a terrain in which the contours of the body are mapped, contours that increasingly stray beyond the bounds of what might be considered properly "human"'.[19] I will also associate Twain and Stevenson's representations of Chinese working-class men with what Sarah Jaquette Ray calls 'the ecological other', who challenges the boundary between purity and pollution, both corporally and environmentally. Environmental discourse as 'a discourse of disgust', in Ray's words, 'enforces social hierarchies even as it seeks to dismantle other forms of hegemony'.[20] Finally, I consider the extent to which Twain and Stevenson's respective engagements with a discourse of disgust in their Chinatown accounts disrupt the naturalised divisions between health and filth, native and foreign.

Mark Twain's Necromantic Realism

Twain's 1872 *Roughing It*, a collection of essays about his sojourn in California in the 1860s, includes an ethnographic depiction of Chinatowns on the West Coast. Chinese people in California could produce 'surprising crops of vegetables on a sand pile', as well as 'marketable tin and solder' out of disposed waste and garbage like 'the old oyster and sardine cans' and 'old mining claims that white men have abandoned as exhausted and worthless'.[21] The essay continues: 'They waste nothing. What is rubbish to a Christian, a Chinaman carefully preserves and makes useful in one way or another. He gathers up old bones and turns them into manure.'[22] While othering these thrifty, economised practices as un-Christian and non-white, it reveals Twain's true political colours by proceeding to notice a signal injustice: the application of a '"foreign" mining tax ... inflicted on no foreigners but Chinamen' once or even twice in a month.[23] The us-and-them juxtaposition is thus ironic, highlighting the legalised racial oppression of these Chinatown residents: the 'Chinaman' gardened and recycled in this way because of the precarious circumstances in which 'Christian' white lawmakers had placed him through their 'exorbitant swindle'.

Nevertheless, Twain's portrait of Chinese economic frugality is problematically sensational. It sways uncomfortably close to the anti-coolie propaganda of the time, which emphasised the 'wasting nothing' ethic of Chinese labourers.[24] Moreover, it soon descends from a depiction of their ingenuity in 'gather[ing]' of 'old bones' and 'turn[ing] them into manure' to an account of lurid necrophilia. The Chinese reverence for their ancestors was such that 'in China, a man's front yard, back yard, or any other part of his premises, is made his family burying ground, in order that he may visit the graves at any and all times'. This familial longing to be closer to one's ancestors was supposedly so pervasive as to turn 'that huge empire' into 'one mighty cemetery', 'ridged and wrinkled from its centre to its circumference with graves'.[25] This projection of China as a massive graveyard is hardly dissimilar from Pumpelly's inflammatory image of China as 'a giant spectre'. But Twain pushes the envelope further still by elaborating how 'inasmuch as every foot of ground must be made to do its utmost, in China, lest the swarming population suffer for food, the very graves are cultivated and yield a harvest, custom holding this to be no dishonor to the dead'.[26] The corpses of the deceased are not only held in physical proximity, but they are recycled in a way that inevitably recalls the reusing of 'old bones' as 'manure' by the Chinatown residents. By this point, Twain's essay has not only imposed the Malthusian discourse of overpopulation on China like Pumpelly, but through the scandalous implication of cannibalism also stereotypes them as anti-technological and anti-modern. The passage ending on the Chinese bitterly opposing the building of railroads closely echoes the observation by Anson Burlingame, US diplomatic minister to China, that 'a road could not be built anywhere in the empire without disturbing the graves of their ancestors or friends'.[27]

Twain's queering of the practice of recycling and reusing limited resources borders on supernatural surrealism. The Chinese obsession with ancestral worship and deep attachment to their native land further mandates that 'their bodies shall be restored to China in case of death'.[28] The Chinese, coming to America in their thousands, literally leave feet first: 'Every ship that sails from San Francisco carries away a heavy freight of Chinese corpses.'[29] While Twain's take on the Chinese prioritisation of practicality and productivity is intended to be humorous, it was also predicated upon the receptiveness of his readers to the stereotypical notion of them as inhuman, or even anti-human. The Chinese body in the late nineteenth century, as scholars have noted, was closely associated with industrialisation and capitalism, and thus was considered to be more machine than human.[30] Twain's observation reverses the logic and points to an alternative discourse of disgust with the Chinese necrophiliac fear of modernisation, which inhibits their Americanisation. Their excessive attachment to their homeland and obsession with ancestral worship leads to their inability to become truly modern American citizens. As Twain comments, 'They [the Chinese] are penned into a "Chinese quarter" – a thing which they do not particularly object to, as they are fond of herding together.'[31] Twain's use of 'penned' and 'herding' implies the animalistic nature and subhuman existence of the

Chinese. It also ties in with the anti-Chinese sentiment of the time to see Chinese immigrants as essentially alien to American soil and unassimilable, unlike Native Americans, who were more receptive of Christianity and Westernisation generally.[32]

The practices and body of the 'Chinaman' in Twain's writing match what Ray discerns as 'the ecological other' in upsetting the boundary between what is wholesome and what is contaminated, both in a bodily and an environmental sense. 'Disgust shapes mainstream environmental discourses', she explains, 'by describing which kinds of bodies and bodily relations to the environment are ecologically "good," as well as which kinds of bodies are ecologically "other["].'[33] While the Chinese were able to subsist on fewer resources than their American counterparts, the practice of composting human biological components for food crops was scarcely palatable to Twain's readers, who would have considered it gruesome and uncivilised. The proximity to which the Chinese practice allows Twain to draw together petrification and consumption, death and vitality, waste disposal and food production, respect and disrespect, preservation and perversion demonstrates his recognition of an alternative social-ecological philosophy, even as it exposes through his discourse of disgust the deep divide between the sacred and sacrilegious, pure and corrupted in American culture.

Turning to the opium smokers in the Chinese quarter of Virginia, which according to Twain was like any other along the Pacific coast, he was again consciously eliciting disgust from the reader. In an opium den, 'cooped-up' and 'dingy', 'faint with the odor of burning Josh-lights' and lighted only by 'the sickly, guttering tallow candle, were two or three yellow, long-tailed vagabonds' seen 'coiled up on a sort of short truckle-bed, smoking opium, motionless and with their lustreless eyes turned inward from excess of satisfaction'.[34] Though 'the stewing and frying of the drug and the gurgling of the juices in the stem would well-nigh turn the stomach of a statue', as Twain observed, 'John likes it.'[35] The visceral feelings evoked here differentiate Twain from the working-class Chinese opium addict he conjures for other white, middle-class people: a 'motionless', 'soggy creature' with 'lustreless eyes'. Twain moves on to imagine how the filthy, cadaverous man might 'feast on succulent rats and birds'-nests in Paradise' in his opiate dream.[36]

Admittedly, the figure of the opium addict is an easy target, but Twain's ecogothic othering of the Chinese is a recurring device. In 'The Mysterious Chinaman', Twain's parody of Edgar Allan Poe's 'The Raven', whilst clearly expecting a female visitor, the poetic persona on opening his bedroom door instead sees 'Ah Chung', a 'Ghastly, grim and long-tailed scullion'.[37] Where Poe's raven visitor was an insidious intrusion from the (super)natural world, the unexpected Chinese laundryman in Twain conveys – to quote Hsuan L. Hsu – 'the troubling intimacy of racialized labor'.[38] To the persona's archly formal enquiry – 'Tell me what thy lordly will is, ere you leave my chamber door[?]' – Ah Chung casually answers: 'No shabby "door"'.[39] The human-animal encounter in Poe is revised through Twain's nonsensical exchange into one between the civilised and uncivilised: the illiterate Chinese domestic is an animalistic communicator, an 'ungainly brute'.[40] Hsu notes how 'Twain's poem highlights the unsettled boundaries of race, labor, gender, and nation that would characterize his later engagement with U.S.-Asia relations.'[41] In terms of the ecogothic, Twain's revision of Poe further illuminates the subtle role a perturbed ecology plays in Sino-American cultural (mis)understandings, when what might be considered properly human is complicated by racial and social class divisions.

Stevenson's Eco-Fantastic Romance

Across the Atlantic Ocean, Stevenson's writing confers on Chinatown yet another form of ecogothic obscurity.[42] Where Chinatown in Twain is a nightmarish place of physical decay and perverted consumption, in Stevenson it is translated into a romantic orientalist fantasy. In 1879, Stevenson travelled from Scotland to New York and then to California, where he stayed from the autumn of 1879 to the summer of 1880 in Monterey and San Francisco. *The New and Old Capitals*, which he published in 1882, contain such recollections as '[T]he very barber of the *Arabian Nights*' being 'at work before him in the Chinese quarter, shaving heads', as well as 'Aladdin playing on the streets'.[43] Stevenson draws on a familiar vein of representation in fictionalising and reinventing Chinatown's exoticism. His Chinatown has an ambient fuzziness, audible yet unknowable: 'who knows but among those nameless vegetables the fruit of the nose-tree itself may be exposed for sale? [. . .] Below, you hear, the cellars are alive with mystery[,] the prisons of unacknowledged slaves and the secret lazarettos of disease.'[44] The alien fruits and vegetables, the strange, unidentifiable sounds emanating from the filthy cellars below, imply a contagious environment that might well pose a public health hazard to visitors.

Stevenson's Chinatown is a collage of characters, commodities, plants and diseases transplanted from the *Arabian Nights*, which disrupts and disorients rather than consolidates and materialises one's sense of locality.[45] As Stevenson exults in writerly reverie – 'the interest is heightened with a chill of horror' – the empiricist impulse to catalogue and categorise is continually excited as it is thwarted, or threatened, by the cornucopia of sights, sounds and experiences.⁴⁶ The foreignness of Chinatown derives from its indescribability, its allusive and illusive generic vagueness, its transporting ability to invoke images and objects elsewhere and nowhere in particular. Despite its cosmopolitanism, it being intelligible and accessible to readers across the Atlantic world only because of the transglobal network of cultural transmission, knowledge transplantation and commodity circulation, Stevenson's account of Chinatown is predicated, like Twain's, on the gothicisation of a racial other. With the former, however, the thrill is generated through visual imperceptibility as well as epistemological indeterminacy.

The image Stevenson proffers of the Chinese immigrant can be strangely different from that of his habitat, however: Chinatown may be a place of disease and impurity, but the Chinese labourer himself is clean and hygienic. In 'Despised Races', Stevenson comments on the negative stereotype of the Chinese as being dirty to the point of vomit-inducing: '[my fellow Caucasians] declared them hideous vermin, and affected a kind of choking in the throat when they beheld them'. To combat this visceral racism, Stevenson proceeds to highlight the exceptional pains the Chinese took during the railway journey across the American continent: their 'washing' of 'their feet' and 'their whole bodies' constantly, 'as far as decency permitted', 'put the rest of us to shame'. As he notes, 'these very foul and malodorous Caucasians entertained the surprising illusion that it was the Chinese waggon, and that alone, which stank. I have said already that it was the exception, and notably the freshest of the three.'⁴⁷ Quite remarkably, Stevenson turns the discourse of disgust back on himself and his 'fellow Caucasians', exposing themselves as the 'ecological other'. Bodily odour and sanitation, as he makes clear, had become racialised as a result of labour market competition: 'They [the Chinese] could work better and cheaper in half a hundred industries, and hence there was no calumny too idle for the Caucasians to repeat, and even to believe.'⁴⁸

Stevenson further declares his admiration for Chinese antiquity in a manner that evokes a sense of deep time. In 'Across the Plains', he states that 'I could not look but with wonder and respect on the Chinese. Their forefathers watched the stars before mine had begun to keep pigs.'⁴⁹ And yet, for Stevenson, there is a temporal (as well as physical) discontinuity between China and the West: 'They walked the earth with us, but it seems they must be of different clay. They hear the clock strike the same hour, yet surely of a different epoch.'⁵⁰ Nevertheless, Stevenson manages to find common ground in their shared attachment as migrants to their respective homelands (Scotland and China):

Heaven knows if we had one common thought or fancy all that way, or whether our eyes, which yet were formed upon the same design, beheld the same world out of the railway windows. And when either of us turned his thoughts to home and childhood, what a strange dissimilarity must there not have been in these pictures of the mind – when I beheld that old, gray, castled city, high throned above the firth, with the flag of Britain flying, and the red-coat sentry pacing over all; and the man in the next car to me would conjure up some junks and a pagoda and a fort of porcelain, and call it, with the same affection, home.[51]

Stevenson juxtaposes the railway journey westward and the movement towards a new world of opportunities with their backward glance and longing for home. Images like 'that old, gray, castled city' and 'junks and a pagoda and a fort of porcelain' from their native environment fail to be entirely compensated by American modernity. What Stevenson perceives to be 'a strange dissimilarity' between himself and his fellow Chinese passenger turns out to be interlocking and co-present, rather than dissimilar and segregated. In effect, Stevenson conducts a geo-poetic mapping that reimagines the segregated space of the train carriage as a romanticised utopic space of dreams and sense of spatial-emotional intimacy.

For Stevenson, the relatively fluid social space of the transcontinental train connects the Atlantic and the Pacific – Edinburgh and Canton – with a potentially equalising force through the shared longing of the Scottish and Chinese migrant for home. Furthermore, in Stevenson, despite being an anachronism, Chinatown is very much in its place as part of a multicultural urban environment. Initially, Chinese agricultural produce is perceptually uncanny: 'The goods they offer for sale are as foreign as the lettering on the signboard of the shop: dried fish from the China seas; pale cakes and sweetmeats – the like, perhaps, once eaten by Badroubadour; nuts of unfriendly shape; ambiguous, outlandish vegetables, misshapen, lean, or bulbous.'[52] They convey to visitors like him 'a country where the trees are not as our trees, and the very back-garden is a cabinet of curiosities'.[53] But this segregation is mentally and physically broken down by the flow of trade and commodities, of 'mercantile Jack, the Italian fisher, the Dutch merchant, the Mexican vaguero, go[ing] hustling by'.[54] If the streets of Chinatown appear to be 'narrower', 'cool, sunless, a little mouldy', they are also filled with houses 'of Occidental build' and 'lines of a hundred telegraphs'.[55] Even though Chinatown is presented in such a way as to be clearly discordant with Stevenson's notion of modern architecture, he also conveys how intimately enmeshed it is with the Western character of the city: 'one European' and 'one Chinese' kite hang together, with 'the high, musical sing-song' of the Chinese language transposing by 'the sunny end of the street' into the roaring of 'European traffic'.[56] While the dark, narrow alleyways of Chinatown, its outlandish plants and the joss-house 'heavy with incense, packed with quaint carvings and the paraphernalia of a foreign ceremonial' are intended to be sensuously jarring, the passing through of telegraph lines and merchants of various national origins also materially contribute to the sense of San Francisco as an emerging transoceanic metropolis of international networks.[57]

While the Chinese immigrant might well have functioned as the ultimate other in the ecological imagination of the time, Stevenson was more vigorous than Twain in exposing the fragility and fluidity of us versus them distinctions. Critics like Edward Said, Homi K. Bhabha and Michel Foucault have shown how orientalism operates upon the fixity and fixability of the other, but because the boundaries between the self and the other are porous and shifting, these projections are radically open to disruption or subversion.[58] Twain, in *Roughing It*, pictures Chinatown as a farm and cemetery that embodies the economic ingenuity and necrophilia of its denizens. Stevenson's Chinatown is unsettling, spatially and psychologically, but its alterity is contained by its presentation as an eco-paradise: a spatially intimate and aurally porous, multilingual and egalitarian place.[59] Stevenson's Chinatown, however antediluvian, dystopic or even apocalyptic in appearance, is nonetheless central to the vitality of the city: energised by the forces of technology and commerce, it seems nonetheless safely quarantined. If it reminds Stevenson of 'a country where the trees are not as our trees', he also makes it amply clear that '[t]he Chinese', like the other immigrants from Europe, 'are settled as in China.'[60] The 'foreign' Chinese quarter is in fact an economically vibrant and ecologically co-present part of San Francisco.

The most ecogothic moment in Stevenson's travelogue takes place when the whole city of San Francisco is transformed into a double of Chinatown. 'I wonder what enchantment of the *Arabian Nights* can have equalled this evocation of a roaring city, in a few years of a man's life, from the marshes and the blowing sand.' San Francisco itself becomes an *Arabian Nights* theme park with its mirage-like development: here this moment, gone the next. 'Such swiftness of increase, as with an overgrown youth,' he writes, 'suggests a corresponding swiftness of destruction.' Indeed, the unstable geology of the land continually promises this example of human civilisation some catastrophe that will return the city to wilderness: 'The sandy peninsula of San Francisco, mirroring itself on one side in the bay, beaten on the other by the surge of the Pacific, and shaken to the heart by frequent earthquakes, seems in itself no very durable foundation.'⁶¹ Soon after this point, Stevenson steps a little out of the orientalist mode. Perhaps it can't quite capture the land's uncanny volatility. To him, the whole Californian landscape has an 'unfinished look'. The hills are not yet properly shaped by the weather, 'forests spring like mushrooms from the unexhausted soil; and they are mown down yearly by the forest fires'. The land is imaginary yet geological, magical yet primitive, and brimming with apocalyptic potential: 'We are in early geological epochs, changeful and insecure; and we feel, as with a sculptor's model, that the author may yet grow weary of and shatter the rough sketch.'⁶²

The aesthetic in Stevenson's travel account is a hybrid of orientalist sensationalism and environmental realism, where Chinatown is a mythical emblem for California's ecological rawness. The unsettling development of the city is a synecdoche for an environment that is radically volatile. Overtly an almost supernatural zone of shadowy characters, dislocated in time and place, Stevenson's embrace of the rhizomic co-existence of Chinatown with the rest of the city is also indicative of its potential as a utopian urban space. In *The Amateur Emigrant*, Stevenson suggested that the United States was 'a sort of promised land' holding out a potentiality 'beyond the ... imagination' of Europeans like himself, who were given to 'compromise, customs, forms of procedure, and sad, senseless self-denial'.⁶³ San Francisco 'is essentially not Anglo-Saxon; still more essentially not American. The Yankee and the Englishman find themselves alike in a strange country[.] Here, on the contrary, are airs of Marseilles and of Pekin[.] The passers-by vary in feature like the slides of a magic-lantern[.] For every man, for every race and nation, that city is a foreign city[,] yet each and all have made themselves at home.'⁶⁴ As more of an exoticised, disjunctive vision of interconnectedness than a wishful Whitmanian transcendental unity,⁶⁵ Stevenson's San Francisco is a magic lantern whose diversity, disorientating as it may be, also democratically promises every visitor a home.

As the American policy on Chinese immigration swung between the 1860s and the 1880s from an open door to downright exclusion, Stevenson offered a very different image of the Chinese migrant from Twain. Twain focused on the extreme ecological queerness of the Chinese labourer (his inhuman frugality, his macabre customs and habits) to emphasise his physical and mental intractability, despite his ingenuity and entrepreneurship, whereas Stevenson's Chinese figures, taken from elsewhere in Asia, have a more familiar and therefore understandable exoticism (being transplanted from the *Arabian Nights*). The Chinese in Stevenson are obviously an anachronism, not unlike Twain's Chinatown residents and laundryman Ah Chung, and yet they clearly demonstrate greater individual mobility and the potential for integration. Admittedly, Stevenson's Chinatown account is mostly a tableau of orientalist fantasy rather than an empirical reality,[66] but it is also a fluid social space connecting people across Asia, Europe and America. If, in Twain, Chinatown represents a human-nature, race-class relationship distorted by 'predation, edibility, and environmental exploitation', Stevenson's republican utopia goes the other way around, communicating a sense of belonging through Romantic re-enchantment and ecological co-presence.

Conclusion

California Chinatown, with its palimpsest-like co-existence of the quotidian and the mythical, the edenic and the fallen, the utopic and the apocalyptic, manifests itself as an ecogothic fantasy world for writers like Twain and Stevenson to inscribe their understanding of transpacific racial-environmental encounters. Both Twain and Stevenson demonstrate the potency of haunting as an aesthetic strategy to expose the fragile and unstable boundary between the human and the non-human, subhuman and inhuman, by subverting seemingly fixed categories about the self and the other, as well as preconceived notions about race and environment. However, the process of gothicisation also risks concealing a racially motivated objectification of the other, equating the racial other with the ecological other by naturalising normative divisions between the pure and the impure, the civilised and the uncivilised. Drawing on Rob Nixon's notion of 'slow violence', Leilani Nishime and Kim D. Hester Williams comment on the devastating effects of the 'continued endangerment' of poor persons of colour that the 'dominant, racialized views of these groups as docile, unsophisticated, uncivilized, and unappreciative of the natural world serve to justify . . . by validating the idea that [they] have created, or at least are complicit in, the degradation of their environment'.[67] Indeed, apart from the physical brutality suffered by Chinese immigrants, Chinatowns in the nineteenth century further illustrate the 'slow violence' of racial ghettoisation. As Guenter B. Risse notes, while the Chinese (along with a number of other ethnic groups) were excluded from citizenship and as non-citizens did not have the right to own property in California, their white landlords, mostly 'prominent citizens' of the city who charged them exorbitant rents, allowed the buildings in Chinatown to grow dilapidated and grimy; 'in their view, the "barbaric Mongolians" deserved to live in such condition'.[68] In other words, environmental degradation is a by-product of systematic racism. By examining the 1870s Chinatown accounts by Twain and Stevenson, this chapter foregrounds the symbiotic connection between notions of race, corruption and pollution.

Keetley and Sivils note that 'The American ecogothic ... grows in a soil too often fed by the blood of violent oppression.'[69] Ecogothic Chinatown in Twain and Stevenson shows diverging attitudes towards a 'romantic' landscape imprinted by these traces of violence. Twain's Chinatown episode in *Roughing It* concludes with the assertion: 'No Californian *gentleman or lady* ever abuses or oppresses a Chinaman[.] Only the scum of the population ... and, naturally and consistently, the policemen and politicians', 'for these are the dust-licking pimps and slaves of the scum, there as well as elsewhere in America'.[70] This vindication of gentlemen and ladies essentially suggests that racism is a problem of the lower classes ('the scum of the population'), policemen (stereotypically illiberal) and populist politicians ('the dust-licking pimps and slaves of the scum'). Nevertheless, writing to his mother in 1853 from New York, a younger Twain did comment on the crowds of people of colour and labourers as capable of 'rais[ing] the ire of the most patient person that ever lived'.[71] His Chinatown accounts show a shift of focus from race to class. Twain's evocation of visceral feelings with respect to China exposes the volatility and reversibility of human-non-human, East-West, class-race boundaries, as well as the relationship between racial hierarchy and environmental injustice in the late nineteenth century. Stevenson's Chinatown, from a transatlantic point of view, forms a compelling contrast to Twain's: a cognitive paradigm segueing from a writerly preoccupation with a romantic orientalist fantasy to empathy with Chinese people as a fellow migrant.

Through the discourse of disgust, both Stevenson and Twain unveiled the direct relationship between class and racial oppression and environmental degradation. Lance Newman's argument seems pertinent here: 'achieving race, gender, and class liberation will require transforming human relations with nature'.[72] My analysis of Twain and Stevenson's Chinatown accounts showcases how environmental discourse and romantic orientalism in late nineteenth-century America operated in multiple modes to shape the cultural perceptions of their time of the racial as well as ecological other. The transatlantic context of the 1870s magnified the arbitrary nature of human-non-human interactions in Twain and Stevenson's perverted Romantic-Oriental-American Chinatown, but it also offered the potential of intimate ecological coexistence, in which – as Stevenson stated – 'The Chinese are settled as in China.'[73]

Notes

1. Catherine Cocks, *Doing the Town: The Rise of Urban Tourism in the United States, 1850–1915* (Berkeley: University of California Press, 2001), p. 174.
2. Robert Louis Stevenson, 'The New and Old Pacific Capitals', in *The Works of Robert Louis Stevenson*, 20 vols (London: Chatto and Windus, 1911), 2: 164–5.
3. Glenda Norquay (ed.), *R. L. Stevenson on Fiction* (Edinburgh: Edinburgh University Press, 1999), p. 56.
4. Nayan Shah, *Contagious Divides: Epidemics and Race in San Francisco's Chinatown* (Berkeley: University of California Press, 2001), pp. 43–5. See also Guenter B. Risse, *Plague, Fear, and Politics in San Francisco's Chinatown* (Baltimore: The Johns Hopkins University Press, 2012).
5. Ibid. p. 43. Recent scholarship on nineteenth-century American orientalism includes John Kuo Wei Chen, *New York before Chinatown: Orientalism and the Shaping of American Culture, 1776–1882* (Baltimore: The John Hopkins University Press, 1992); Malini Johar Schueller, *U.S. Orientalisms: Race, Nation, and Gender in Literature, 1790–1890* (Ann Arbor: The University of Michigan Press, 1998); Robert G. Lee, *Orientals: Asian Americans in Popular Culture* (Philadelphia: Temple University Press, 1999); Anthony W. Lee, *Picturing Chinatown: Art and Orientalism in San Francisco* (Berkeley: University of California Press, 2001); Mari Yoshihara, *Embracing the East: White Women and American Orientalism* (Oxford: Oxford University Press, 2003); Colleen Lye, *America's Asia: Racial Form and American Literature, 1893–1945* (Princeton: Princeton University Press, 2005); Christopher Benfey, *The Great Wave: Gilded Age Misfits, Japanese Eccentrics, and the Opening of Old Japan* (New York: Random House, 2007); John Rogers Haddad, *The Romance of China: Excursions to China in U.S. Culture: 1776–1876* (New York: Columbia University Press, 2008); Josephine Nock-Hee Park, *Apparitions of Asia: Modernist Form and Asian American Poetics* (Oxford: Oxford University Press, 2008); Jim Egan, *Oriental Shadows: The Presence of the East in Early American Literature* (Columbus: Ohio State University Press, 2011); Wenxian Zhang, *China through American Eyes: Early Depictions of the Chinese People and Culture in the U.S. Print Media* (Singapore: World Scientific Publishing, 2017).
6. For transpacific connections from the late nineteenth century onwards, see Akira Iriye, *Across the Pacific: An Inner History of American-East Asian Relations* (New York: Harcourt, Brace & World, 1967); Ronald Takaki, *Strangers from a Different Shore: A History of Asian Americans* (Boston: Little, Brown and Company, 1989); David Palumbo-Liu, *Asian/American: Historical Crossings of a Racial Frontier* (Stanford: Stanford University Press, 1999); Rob Wilson, *Reimagining the American Pacific: From South Pacific to Bamboo Ridge and Beyond* (Durham, NC: Duke University Press, 2000); Christina Klein, *Cold War Orientalism: Asia in the Middlebrow Imagination, 1945–1961* (Berkeley: University of California Press, 2003); Colleen Lye, *America's Asia: Racial Form and American*

Literature, 1893–1945 (Princeton: Princeton University Press, 2005); and Josephine Park, *Apparitions of Asia: Modernist Form and Asian American Poetics* (New York: Oxford University Press, 2008).
7. Palumbo-Liu, *Asian/American*, p. 7.
8. Raphael Pumpelly, 'The Chinese as Emigrants and Colonizers', in *Across America and Asia* (New York: Leypoldt & Holt, 1870), p. 274.
9. Ibid. p. 251.
10. Ibid. p. 249.
11. The anti-Chinese movements in California in the 1860s and 1870s have attracted considerable scholarly attention. For example, Gunther Barth, *Bitter Strength: A History of the Chinese in the United States, 1850–1870* (Cambridge, MA: Harvard University Press, 1964); Stuart Creighton Miller, *The Unwelcome Immigrant: The American Image of the Chinese, 1785–1882* (Berkeley: University of California Press, 1969); Alexander Saxton, *The Indispensable Enemy: Labor and the Anti-Chinese Movement in California* (Berkeley: University of California Press, 1971); Roger Daniels, *Asian America: Chinese and Japanese in the United States Since 1850* (Seattle: University of Washington Press, 1995); Charles J. McClain, *In Search of Equality: The Chinese Struggle against Discrimination in Nineteenth-Century America* (Berkeley: University of California Press, 1994); Lisa Lowe, *Immigrant Acts* (Durham, NC: Duke University Press, 1996); Yong Chen, *Chinese San Francisco, 1850–1943: A Trans-Pacific Community* (Stanford: Stanford University Press, 2000); Moon-Ho Jung, *Coolies and Cane: Race, Labor, and Sugar in the Age of Emancipation* (Baltimore: The John Hopkins University Press, 2004) and 'Outlawing "Coolies": Race, Nation, and Empire in the Age of Emancipation', *American Quarterly* 57, no. 3 (2005); Jean Pfaelzer, *Driven Out: The Forgotten War against Chinese Americans* (New York: Random House, 2007); Joshua Paddison, *American Heathens: Religion, Race, and Reconstruction in California* (Berkeley: University of California Press, 2012); Gary Y. Okihiro, *Margins and Mainstreams: Asians in American History and Culture* (Seattle: University of Washington Press, [1994] 2014); Beth Lew-Williams, *The Chinese Must Go: Violence, Exclusion, and the Making of the Alien in America* (Cambridge, MA: Harvard University Press, 2018); Gordon H. Chang and Shelley Fisher Fishkin (eds), *The Chinese and the Iron Road: Building the Transcontinental Railroad* (Stanford: Stanford University Press, 2019).
12. While the 1844 treaty of Wanghai and the Burlingame Treaty of 1868 encouraged open trade and the free movement of people between China and the United States, rising anti-Chinese sentiment culminated in the passing of the 1877 Page Act forbidding the immigration of Asian women, and the Chinese Exclusion Act in 1882 that ended Chinese immigration.
13. Daphne Pi-Wei Lei, 'The Production and Consumption of Chinese Theater in Nineteenth-Century California', *Theater Research International* 28 (2003): 298.
14. For more on the conflicting images of Chinatown, refer to Anderson, 'The Idea of Chinatown: The Power of Place and Institutional Practice in the Making of a Racial Category', *Annals of the Association of American Geographers* 77, no. 4 (1987): 580–98; K. Scott Wong, 'Chinatown:

Conflicting Images, Contested Terrain', *Melus* 20 (1995): 3–15; Li-hsin Hsu, 'The "phantasmatic" Chinatown in Helen Hunt Jackson's "The Chinese Empire" and Mark Twain's *Roughing It*', in *Spatial Imageries in Historical Perspective* (Amsterdam: Amsterdam University Press, 2021), pp. 191–217.
15. For more on racial conflict in a broader context, refer to Jung's *Coolies and Cane*; Paddison's *American Heathens*; Natalia Molina, *How Race Is Made in America: Immigration, Citizenship, and the Historical Power of Racial Scripts* (Berkeley: University of California Press, 2014); Lisa Lowe, *The Intimacies of Four Continents* (Durham, NC: Duke University Press, 2015); Hsuan L. Hsu, *Sitting in Darkness: Mark Twain's Asia and Comparative Racialization* (New York: New York University Press, 2015); Quynh Nhu Le, *Unsettled Solidarities: Asian and Indigenous Cross-Representations in the Américas* (Philadelphia: Temple University Press, 2019).
16. Lowe, *Immigrant Acts*, p. 18.
17. Allan Lloyd Smith, 'Nineteenth-Century American Gothic', *A New Companion to the Gothic* (London: Blackwell, 2012), p. 163.
18. Dawn Keetley and Matthew Wynn Sivils (eds), *Ecogothic in Nineteenth-Century American Literature* (New York: Routledge, 2018), p. 8.
19. Ibid. p. 4.
20. Sarah Jaquette Ray, *The Ecological Other: Environmental Exclusion in American Culture* (Tucson: University of Arizona Press, 2013), p. 1.
21. Mark Twain, *Roughing It* (Berkeley: University of California Press, [1872] 2011), p. 370.
22. Ibid. p. 370.
23. Ibid. p. 370.
24. The poem 'Plain Language from Truthful James', published in September 1870 in *The Overland Monthly Magazine*, which made Bret Harte an overnight sensation, shows how prevalent the idea 'We Are Ruined by Chinese Cheap Labor' was among white working-class people.
25. Twain, *Roughing It*, pp. 370–1.
26. Ibid. p. 371.
27. Ibid. p. 371. For more details about the impact of Twain's friendship with Burlingame on his view of the Chinese, see Hsin-yun Ou, 'Mark Twain, Anson Burlingame, Joseph Hopkins Twichell, and the Chinese', *Ariel* 42, no. 2 (2012): 43–74.
28. Twain, *Roughing It*, p. 372.
29. Ibid. p. 372.
30. For more on the association of the Chinese body with machines, refer to Lye, *America's Asia*; Eric Hayot, *The Hypothetical Mandarin: Sympathy, Modernity, and Chinese Pain* (Oxford: Oxford University Press, 2009); David S. Roh, Betsy Huang and Greta A. Niu (eds), *Techno-Orientalism: Imagining Asia in Speculative Fiction, History, and Media* (New Brunswick, NJ: Rutgers University Press, 2015).
31. Twain, *Roughing It*, p. 369.
32. Paddison, *American Heathens*, p. 4.
33. Ray, *The Ecological Other*, p. 1.
34. Twain, *Roughing It*, pp. 372–3.
35. Ibid. p. 373.

36. Ibid. p. 373.
37. Mark Twain, *Early Tales & Sketches, Vol. 2: 1864–1865* (Berkeley: University of California Press, 1981), pp. 64–5.
38. Hsu, *Sitting in Darkness*, pp. 14–5.
39. Twain, *Early Tales*, p. 65.
40. Ibid. p. 65.
41. Hsu, *Sitting in Darkness*, pp. 14–5.
42. Twain and Stevenson met in April 1888, when the Stevensons visited New York, which Twain recorded in his personal notebook and autobiography. For more details, see Leland Krauth, *Mark Twain & Company: Six Literary Relations* (Athens: University of Georgia Press, 2003), pp. 166–8.
43. Stevenson, 'The New and Old Pacific Capitals', 2: 164.
44. Ibid. 2: 165.
45. In 'A Gossip on Romance', Stevenson considers the *Arabian Nights* 'more generally loved than Shakespeare' (Norquay, *Stevenson on Fiction*, pp. 58–9). On the cultural influences of the Arabian Nights on nineteenth-century American culture, refer to Egan, *Oriental Shadows* and Susan Nance, *How the Arabian Nights Inspired the American Dream, 1790–1935* (Chapel Hill: University of North Carolina Press, 2009).
46. Stevenson, 'The New and Old Pacific Capitals', 2: 165.
47. Stevenson, 'Across the Plains', 2: 130–1.
48. Ibid. 2: 130.
49. Ibid. 2: 131.
50. Ibid. 2: 131.
51. Ibid. 2: 131.
52. Stevenson, 'The New and Old Pacific Capitals', 2: 163.
53. Ibid. 2: 163.
54. Ibid. 2: 163.
55. Ibid. 2: 163.
56. Ibid. 2: 163.
57. Ibid. 2: 163.
58. Refer to Michel Foucault, *The Order of Things: An Archaeology of the Human Sciences*, trans. unknown (London: Routledge, [1966] 2005); Edward Said, *Orientalism* (London: Routledge, 1978); Homi K. Bhabha, 'The Other Question', *Screen* 24, no. 6 (1983): 18–36. Recent scholarship focuses more on the elasticity of orientalist imagination. See, for example, Michael Haldrup and Jonas Larsen, *Tourism, Performance and the Everyday: Consuming the Orient* (London: Routledge, 2010); Chi-ming Yang, *Performing China: Virtue, Commerce, and Orientalism in Eighteenth-Century England, 1660–1760* (Baltimore: The John Hopkins University Press, 2011).
59. In the chapter 'Monterey' in 'The New and Old Capital', Stevenson criticises Dennis Kearney's 'dictatorship' and the inflammatory rhetoric against the Chinese, 2: 158. In the chapter 'Despised Races' in *Across the Plains* (1892), he further laments that 'we may regret the free tradition of the republic, which loved to depict herself with open arms, welcoming all unfortunates'.
60. Stevenson, 'The New and Old Pacific Capitals', 2: 163.
61. Ibid. 2: 161.

62. Ibid. 2: 161.
63. Stevenson, 'The Amateur Emigrant', 2: 80–1.
64. Stevenson, 'The New and Old Pacific Capitals', 2: 162.
65. Stevenson's admiration for Walt Whitman's *Leaves of Grass* is plain in *Familiar Studies of Men and Books* (1882).
66. This is all the more puzzling considering Stevenson's cultural knowledge. The year before his trip to California, Stevenson met Japanese scholar Taizo Masaki at a dinner party. From Masaki, Stevenson learned of Yoshida Shoin, the revolutionary and scholar of classical Chinese, about whom he published a biographical sketch. For more information, refer to Michael Gardiner, 'Robert Louis Stevenson and the Meiji Enlightenment', *The Yearbook of English Studies* 41, no. 2 (2011): 58–72.
67. Leilani Nishime and Kim D. Hester Williams (eds), *Racial Ecologies* (Seattle: University of Washington Press, 2018), p. 6.
68. Risse, *Plague, Fear, and Politics in San Francisco's Chinatown*, pp. 22, 25 and 26; see also Charlotte Brooks, *Alien Neighbors, Foreign Friends: Asian Americans, Housing, and the Transformation of Urban America* (Chicago: University of Chicago Press, 2009).
69. Keetley and Sivils, *Ecogothic*, p. 8.
70. Twain, *Roughing It*, pp. 374–5.
71. Edgar Marquess Branch (ed.), *Mark Twain's Letters, Volume 1: 1853–1866* (Berkeley: University of California Press, 1988), p. 10.
72. Lance Newman, *The Literary Heritage of the Environmental Justice Movement* (New York: Palgrave Macmillan, 2019), p. 23.
73. Stevenson, 'The New and Old Pacific Capitals', 2: 163.

Chapter 4

Climate Change, Inequality and Romantic Catastrophe

David Higgins

The idea of the Anthropocene has been enormously generative and largely beneficial for academic discourse on human interactions with the environment. But, as is increasingly well understood, it also has significant problems. Perhaps the trickiest one is its implication of a species-wide agency. In his influential article 'The Climate of History' (2009), Dipesh Chakrabarty argues that traditional forms of cultural critique do not provide a sufficient framework for addressing climate change, which, after all, is a problem for humanity as a whole.[1] He has since been taken to task, perhaps unfairly, by scholars who argue that the emphasis on 'species being', implied by the idea of the Anthropocene, effectively ignores the considerable economic, social and political inequalities that have created climate change and that are further fed by it.[2] Like the casual invocation of 'we' in climate discourse, a key danger of the term 'Anthropocene' is that it distracts from understanding the history of anthropogenic environmental change as a history of carbon capitalism, for which a relatively small number of nations and multinationals have the bulk of responsibility.[3] Crises such as global heating and biodiversity loss are inevitably intertwined with inequalities between individuals, classes and nations, and with imperialism, colonialism and their legacies.[4] As noted in a 2015 Oxfam report on 'Extreme Carbon Inequality', the richest 10 per cent of the global population are responsible for 50 per cent of global emissions.[5] Richer countries engage in a kind of neocolonialism by driving ecological destruction in the Global South, largely for their own benefit. The wealthier and more educated are disproportionately over-represented with respect to the discourse on climate change, despite being the most sheltered from its effects. This may explain the kind of binary thinking that produces apocalypticism, techno-utopianism and pure denialism: all the products of privilege that are less likely to attract people who are already having to make deep adaptations to climate change.[6]

The climate emergency is of course unprecedented, but it is also the product of a long history of global inequality and therefore should be understood genealogically. I attempted to do this in my recent book on British Romanticism and the Anthropocene, which analyses how texts produced around the 'Year without a Summer' of 1816 addressed topics such as the relationship between human and non-human agency, the precarity of human life on an increasingly volatile planet, and the interplay of individual consciousness, political structures and earth systems.[7] When Paul Crutzen and Eugene F. Stoermer outlined their newly coined term 'Anthropocene' two decades ago, they proposed a start date for the new geological epoch of 'the latter part of the 18th century', in part because it 'coincides with James Watt's invention of the steam engine in 1784'.[8] Since then, other start dates have been suggested, but if we accept that the Anthropocene is intertwined with the rise of what Andreas Malm calls 'fossil capital', then the late eighteenth century seems as plausible as any.[9] Romantic literature can be understood as Anthropocene literature, not just because of the historical coincidence, but in its concern with human-non-human entanglements and with what it means to be alive at a catastrophic turning point in planetary history.[10] As well as being characterised by increasing numbers of environmental catastrophes, such as extreme weather events and species extinctions, the Anthropocene is itself a catastrophe in the etymological sense, from the Greek *katastrophē* meaning an 'overturning' or 'sudden turn'. Its beginning, whenever that might have been, is a turn from the Holocene to a new geological epoch. This shift is also an epistemological catastrophe, a turning point in individual and cultural self-consciousness: the catastrophe of perceiving the catastrophe.[11]

This chapter will focus on four Romantic texts that understand catastrophe in environmental, political and epistemological terms: Byron's 'Darkness' (1816), Percy Bysshe Shelley's *Prometheus Unbound* (1820), and Mary Shelley's *Frankenstein* (1818) and *The Last Man* (1826). On the face of it, they can be read in the light of Chakrabarty's claim that climate change offers 'no lifeboats for the rich and the privileged'.[12] In 'Darkness', the dimming of the sun eventually leaves earth a lifeless rock; in *Prometheus Unbound*, the entire universe initially suffers the deadening effects of Jupiter's oppression and Prometheus's curse; in *Frankenstein*, a new species is created that threatens to supplant humanity; and in *The Last Man*, the whole human race is seemingly wiped out by a plague that leaves non-human nature untouched. All four texts are influenced by the stormy summer of 1816, during which Byron and the Shelleys were living by the shores of Lake Geneva.[13] They did not know that the bad weather was one of the after-effects of the Tambora eruption the previous year, but it nonetheless had a powerful impact on their creativity, in combination with their interest in contemporary natural philosophy and their experience of the sublime Alpine landscapes around them. Their writings reflect on the vulnerability of human communities living with uncontrollable geophysical and climatic forces, the entanglement of humans and non-human nature, and the possibility of human extinction. However, they are also the result of a privileged perspective available to these expatriate authors, who were largely sheltered from the post-Tambora subsistence crisis that afflicted most Europeans.[14] This chapter will investigate how these texts understand the relationship between politics, inequality and environmental catastrophe. My genealogical claim is that there is a parallel between their elite perspectives on apocalypse and utopia, and present-day responses to climate change. That is, ecological pessimism and optimism have a long lineage, and, then as now, are most attractive to those least affected by climate disruption.

'Darkness', *The Last Man* and the Politics of Human Extinction

Although Mary Shelley's novel *The Last Man* was written ten years after the 'Year without a Summer', it is very much shaped by the same concerns and images shared by the Diodati Circle in that period and particularly by Byron's 'Darkness'.[15] It also offers an extended and bleak reflection on the politics of catastrophe, presenting a counterpoint to the utopian politics of Percy Shelley, as most obviously reflected in *Prometheus Unbound*. 'Darkness' and *The Last Man* are very different texts, but both imagine human extinction in the context of rapid environmental change. They show that this process has a politically equalising effect, in so far as it dissolves distinctions of rank and wealth, but the catastrophic context means that such equality can only be viewed with grim irony.

'Darkness' has a broad range of influences, from the climate of 1816, to various apocalyptic passages in the Bible, to natural philosophy, to the European sun-spot panic of the same year.[16] But the poem's imagining of the heat-death of the universe, and particularly of human extinction, without any form of eschatological recompense moves far beyond its intertexts to produce a vision of nihilistic horror that is akin to recent philosophical work in the field of speculative realism. For example, Raymond Brassier considers the philosophical implications of the future death of the sun: 'The extinction of the sun is a catastrophe, a mis-turning or over-turning (*kata-strophe*), because it blots out the terrestrial horizon of future possibility relative to which human existence, and hence philosophical questioning, have hitherto oriented themselves.'[17] There is a sense, therefore, in which imagining the death of the sun means that human extinction has already happened – not in the sense of 'the termination of a biological species', but in that it destroys any idea of human transcendence by revealing our contingency and superfluousness: 'if the extinction of the sun is catastrophic, this is because it disarticulates the correlation' (that is, the idea that reality can only be understood in terms of the human relationship to it).[18] Furthermore, because the 'time of extinction' entails '*the extinction of space-time* [...]' it is not so much that extinction *will* terminate the correlation, but that it *has already* retroactively terminated it'.[19] The paradoxical temporality of extinction is reflected in Byron's poem. The speaker has a prophetic 'dream, which was not all a dream' (4: 40, l. 1), and as a result is able to describe the destruction of all life on earth and the universal triumph of Darkness in the past tense, as if it has already happened. The poem simultaneously affirms human exceptionality – our unique power to imagine our own absence – while presenting our destruction alongside that of all other lifeforms and forces in the universe.

From its opening, Byron's poem describes a planet no longer able to sustain human life, for 'the bright sun was extinguish'd' (4: 40, l. 2). The stars wander 'rayless' and 'pathless', and the earth is 'moonless' (4: 40, ll. 4–5): the poem is defined by absence, loss and confusion. The image of the earth swinging 'blind and blackening' (4: 40, l. 5) suggests a movement that deviates from its normal orbital trajectory. The usual order of the universe has collapsed; the darkening of the sun is mirrored by the other stars, which now wander without a clear path. Ultimately leaving the planet 'lifeless', the dwindling of the sun leads initially to a population so desperate for light and warmth that they set fire to everything they can:

And the thrones,
The palaces of crowned kings – the huts,
The habitations of all things which dwell
Were burnt for beacons; cities were consumed (4: 41, ll. 10–13)

'Darkness' is remarkable for its compressions. The single line referring to 'palaces' and 'huts' suggests how environmental catastrophe on this scale sweeps away social distinctions. Similarly, the meeting of the last two people on earth in a ruined church or temple, 'Where had been heap'd a mass of holy things / For an unholy usage', suggests the complete collapse of cultural norms.

What remains is a brutally Hobbesian world. With the planet deprived of the sun's energy and unable to grow more food, bloody conflicts arise around increasingly scarce resources. 'War [. . .] / Did glut himself again', and

> All earth was but one thought – and that was death,
> Immediate and inglorious; and the pang
> Of famine fed upon all entrails – men
> Died, and their bones were tombless as their flesh;
> The meagre by the meagre were devoured (4: 41–2, ll. 38 and 42–6)

Citing this passage, Wood argues that 'with a remarkable, prescient sympathy, Byron's "Darkness" anticipates the full-blown humanitarian disaster as it was to unfold in Switzerland and around the world over the subsequent three-year global climate emergency'.[20] The bad weather of 1816 certainly led to a subsistence crisis in Europe. Switzerland, which already had many inhabitants who were barely surviving, was particularly affected; in 1817, the price of grain almost tripled. As a result, many labouring-class people in agricultural areas and industrial towns could not afford even a subsistence diet, leading to social instability, widespread begging and vagrancy, and excess mortality.[21] I'm not sure, however, that 'sympathy' is the right word to describe the perspective adopted by the speaker in 'Darkness'. Byron's poem treats human suffering with a kind of horrified irony. Its distanced perspective is made possible by political and cultural capital accrued as a result of Byron's birth and his education at Harrow and Cambridge. It can be understood as an extreme version of the 'prospect view' supposedly available only to the gentleman-poet, although Byron's prospect is not a landscape apprehended from an eminence but the earth observed from a position of cosmic removal. In the above passage, famine paradoxically feeds, men are reduced to 'tombless' flesh and bones, and the starving consume the starving, presumably with little success. The mode of the poem is sceptical rather than sympathetic. Perhaps its most terrifying aspect is the way in which it condenses a period of global cooling that the natural philosopher Buffon had imagined taking place over millennia, so that civilised rules and ethics, and whole ecosystems, are shown to collapse in the speed it takes to read a few lines of text. Beginning with the blindly wandering planet and stars of the poem's opening lines, much of the poem gives a feeling of chaotic and futile energy that dissipates as we arrive at the final few lines. They continue the emphasis on loss and absence from the beginning of the text – 'Seasonless, herbless, treeless, manless, lifeless' (4: 43, l. 71) – but also present a new sense of stillness after the death throes of all human, creaturely and even elemental agencies (4: 43, ll. 78–81). Given our increasing understanding of the speed with which climate change can take place – and the extent to which natural variation can be escalated by human action – the poem's powerful compressions are far more resonant today than any sympathy.²²

The journal that Byron kept of his Alpine tour in September 1816 reveals that he was generally impressed by the poor Swiss whom he encountered ('free & happy and *rich*').²³ This contrasts with the damning description by Percy Shelley in the Shelleys' *History of a Six Weeks' Tour* (1817), which reflects on 'the degradation of the human species – who in these [Alpine] regions are half deformed or idiotic, and most of whom are deprived of any thing that can excite interest or admiration'.²⁴ Mary Shelley's position is more nuanced, describing 'exceedingly disgusting' individuals of 'the meanest class' on a boat trip, but also noting that 'there is more equality of classes here than in England. This occasions a greater freedom and refinement of manners among the lower orders than we meet with in our own country.'²⁵ Her willingness to offer different perspectives is in keeping with critical understanding of her work as challenging the elite masculine hyperbole of Byron and Percy Shelley. The critique of the sublime genius and Enlightenment utopianism in *Frankenstein* has been much discussed. And *The Last Man* is well known for its not uncritical portrayals of Percy and Byron in the characters of Adrian and Raymond. There have been excellent attempts to find a recuperative posthuman ethics in Shelley's novel. For example, Kate Rigby argues that it subverts 'patriarchal and anthroparchal assumptions': 'the demise of Man (as defined in accordance with the logic of colonization), it is hinted, might just open the way for the emergence of a new kind of human-non-human collectivity'.²⁶ Chris Washington suggests that it shows us 'the philosophical outline of a workable posthuman contract'.²⁷ Both critics offer more extensive and nuanced accounts of *The Last Man* than I can manage in this essay. However, I remain unconvinced by their overall arguments. For me, the novel is profoundly pessimistic. The detailed account provided of its characters' romantic and political schemes only serves to emphasise their fruitlessness. Dreams of political equality can only be realised ironically:

> As the rules of order and pressure of laws were lost, some began with hesitation and wonder to transgress the accustomed uses of society. Palaces were deserted, and the poor man dared at length, unreproved, [to] intrude into the splendid apartments, whose very furniture and decorations were an unknown world to him. [. . .] We were all equal now; magnificent dwellings, luxurious carpets, and beds of down, were afforded to all. Carriages and horses, gardens, pictures, statues, and princely libraries, there were enough of these

even to superfluity; and there was nothing to prevent each from assuming possession of his share. We were all equal now; but near at hand was an equality still more levelling, a state where beauty and strength, and wisdom, would be as vain as riches and birth. (p. 317)

As in Byron's poem, the fate of 'palaces' is metonymic for a general breakdown in hierarchy. But in Shelley's novel, everyone now gets their 'share'. The plague breaks down barriers between rich and poor, rather than cementing inequalities, and the passage's lists suggest that those who remain alive experience luxurious abundance, very different from the brutal resource wars in 'Darkness'. While the parallel with the present climate emergency is inexact, the fact that wealthy nations and individuals are able to afford greater resilience to a hostile environment is at least observable in Shelley, where the privileged characters have places to take refuge away from large groups of people. (I began this essay in the early stages of the Covid-19 pandemic, at a point when celebrities, royals and politicians could seemingly easily access the test for the virus that was not yet available to most front-line medical professionals.)

Initially the main characters are able to shelter at Windsor Castle, due to their wealth and status. When even that place proves not to be 'a spot sacred from the plague', they resolve to go abroad: 'perhaps, in some secluded nook, amidst eternal spring, and waving trees, and purling streams, we may find Life' (p. 326). But to what extent does 'Life' require humanity? As the novel's narrator, Lionel Verney, contemplates the landscape around Windsor, he reflects that

> for the last time we looked on the wide extent of country visible from the terrace, and saw the last rays of sun tinge the dark masses of wood variegated by autumnal tints; the uncultivated fields and smokeless cottages lay in shadow below; the Thames wound through the wide plain, and the venerable pile of Eton college, stood in dark relief, a prominent object; the cawing of the myriad rooks which inhabited the trees of the little park, as in column or thick wedge they speeded to their nests, disturbed the silence of evening. Nature was the same, as when she was the kind mother of the human race; now, childless and forlorn, her fertility was a mockery; her loveliness a mask for deformity. Why should the breeze gently stir the trees, man felt not its refreshment? Why did dark night adorn herself with stars – man saw them not? Why are there fruits, or flowers, or streams, man is not here to enjoy them? (p. 329)[28]

Unlike Byron's 'Darkness', which imagines the end of everything, here the end of the world is conflated with the end of humanity. The crux of reading this passage is the degree to which the novel encourages Verney to be viewed ironically. Is his anthropocentrism suspect? After all, his questions might be compared to the famous one at the end of 'Mont

Blanc' (1816) – 'And what were thou, and earth, and stars, and sea, / If to the human mind's imaginings / Silence and solitude were vacancy?' – and might similarly seem to imply that the world has no meaning without human perception.[29] To suggest that Shelley is ironising Verney's position would neatly fit her in with an anti-anthropocentric ethic with which many of us might agree. But I'm sceptical. As Timothy Clark has pointed out, too many ecocritical readings expend a great deal of labour in an attempt to show that their texts reflect the ethical-environmental truisms that the critic and their readers probably already hold.[30] There is no evidence that Verney's elegiac portrayal of a depopulated landscape is not to be taken seriously. The plague has achieved a kind of extreme picturesque by occluding all rural labour and transforming elite social institutions such as Eton into empty ruins. For Verney, and I think for Shelley, the flourishing of other forms of life do not make up for this loss.

Admittedly, there are moments in which the narrator's anthropocentrism seems comically overwrought, not to mention erroneous, in the context of the imminent destruction not just of human civilisation but of the human species: 'look at this thought-endued countenance, his graceful limbs, his majestic brow, his wondrous mechanism – the type and model of this best work of God is not to be cast aside as a broken vessel – he shall be preserved, and his children and his children's children carry down the name and form of man to latest time' (p. 261). Verney's model for the Anthropos is, of course, an exclusionary one: the reference to the 'majestic brow' is the giveaway in the context of early nineteenth-century ideas about racial physiognomy. That he sees some humans as more human than others is made apparent when he encounters a Black man, half-dead from the plague, on the city street:

> O a pernicious scent assailed my senses [. . .] while I felt my leg clasped, and a groan repeated by the person who held me. I lowered my lamp, and saw a negro half clad, writhing under the agony of disease, while he held me with a convulsive grasp. With mixed horror and impatience I strove to disengage myself, and fell on the sufferer; he wound his naked festering arms on me, his face was close to mine, and his breath, death-laden, entered my vitals. For a moment, I was overcome, my head bowed by aching nausea; till, reflection returning, I sprung up, threw the wretch from me, and darting up the staircase, entered the chamber usually inhabited by my family. A dim light shewed me Alfred on a couch; Clara trembling, and paler than whitest snow, had raised him on her arm, holding a cup of water to his lips. I saw full well that no spark of life existed in that ruined form, his features were rigid, his eyes glazed, his head had fallen back. I took him from her, I laid him softly down, kissed his cold little mouth, and turned to speak in a vain whisper. (p. 337)

The contrast between the stranger's disgusting, infectious embrace and the purity of Verney's wife ('paler than whitest snow') and dead son could hardly be clearer. In Shelley's plague, as so often in discourse around current catastrophes, there is a kind of hierarchy of victimhood, with members of the white elite sympathised with as individuals and imagined very differently from the great mass of generic Black and Brown sufferers who are not worth naming. (This hierarchy is inflected by class as well as race, of course, with poor white sufferers sometimes imagined as similarly anonymous and amorphous.) The problem here is not anthropocentrism per se, nor is that the key factor in anthropogenic climate change. The problem is grotesquely unequal racial, social, political, imperial and economic structures, and their impact on how the Anthropos is defined.

Frankenstein, Prometheus Unbound and Eco-Optimism

Both *Frankenstein* and *Prometheus Unbound* associate climate change with the fate of the human species as a whole. *Frankenstein* is a novel about schemes for human progress that go horribly wrong, and lead to the creation of a type of being that may supplant humanity due to its superior cold resilience in a world undergoing global cooling. *Prometheus Unbound* imagines love transforming the earth into a paradise of eternal summer. Broadly speaking, Percy Shelley's poem can be compared to the more utopian side of climate discourse, while Mary Shelley's novel can be usefully understood as offering a critique of it. Over the years, *Frankenstein* has been the victim of various moralistic interpretations, usually along the lines of humans not transgressing natural or divine boundaries. Bruno Latour has recently drawn a more interesting conclusion. Victor Frankenstein's crime 'was not that he invented a creature through some combination of hubris and high technology, but rather that he abandoned the creature to itself'. The lesson, therefore, is that, rather than trying to limit our effects on the environment, we should take responsibility for those effects; we should continue 'innovating, inventing, creating, and intervening' and show 'the same type of patience and commitment to our creations as God the Creator, Himself'.[31] This interpretation was published in the online journal of the ecomodernist Breakthrough Institute, a think tank based in California. Ecomodernism, in effect, wants us to double down on the Anthropocene by embracing our power as a species to shape the world. It sees technologies such as 'urbanization, agricultural intensification, nuclear power, aquaculture, and desalination' as interventions that will reduce environmental degradation and improve human life.³² Victor Frankenstein can be understood as a prototypical ecomodernist, optimistic about the potential of technology to improve the world and ascribing to it a kind of magical power. Given that, by pursuing their dreams of a better world, both he and the polar explorer Walton end up destroying the people around them, it seems reasonable to suggest that Mary Shelley is wary of the Enlightenment utopianism apparent in the writings of her father William Godwin and husband Percy Bysshe Shelley, which shows a deep faith in the perfectibility of humanity even while it rejects the traditional apparatus of religion. Ecomodernism can be understood as the latest iteration of this utopianism, with even apparently secular groups such as the Breakthrough Institute having a quasi-religious belief in the eventual triumph of 'Progress'.

Frankenstein endorses neither an anti-technological agenda nor humanity's supposed elevation to the role of 'God species'. Rather, it challenges utopian ideas about scientific progress while also suggesting that returning to a more 'primitive' state is itself a fantasy. It therefore speaks to some of the tensions that trouble Anthropocene thinking. Key to its complexity is the Creature's narrative, which lies at the centre of the novel and offers a kind of counterpoint to Walton's and Victor's projects by presenting the viewpoint of a marginalised Other. Rather than imposing his will onto the world, he seeks only the sympathy of others and, when this proves impossible, to find somewhere free of human influence:

> I will go to the vast wilds of South America. My food is not that of man; I do not destroy the lamb and the kid, to glut my appetite; acorns and berries afford me sufficient nourishment. My companion will be of the same nature as myself, and will be content with the same fare. We shall make our bed on dried leaves; the sun will shine on us as on man, and will ripen our food. The picture I present to you is peaceful and human.³³

This is exactly the sort of primitivism that ecomodernists lambast. It presents an ideal of 'wild', untouched nature that offers a refuge from the problems of modernity and, in the Creature's case, the cruel treatment that he receives from humanity. It also offers an ecocentric view of mutual co-existence with non-human creatures based on a vegan diet. The Creature implies that his vision is more authentically 'human' than the modern world; resembling the 'state of nature' celebrated by Jean-Jacques Rousseau, whose works have a major influence on *Frankenstein*.³⁴ However, by the time that he presents this vision to Victor, the Creature has already discovered fire. He therefore has access to a source of energy that – unlike the sun's rays – he can manipulate and control, and he has experienced the benefits of this technology. The return to a pre-technological state is a confidence trick, and the novel never makes it to the 'wilds of South America'. It offers instead a kind of parody of that utopian vision of the state of nature when Victor travels to 'one of the remotest of the Orkneys'. In this 'desolate and appalling landscape', he is able to find the solitude that he requires in order to make the Creature a companion (3: chap. 2, para. 20). As he comes close to completing his task, he reflects on the risks involved and particularly the idea that a new species might be propagated that would threaten the existence of humanity.

The Creature desperately wants to be part of the Anthropos, but he soon learns that even that would not guarantee him full personhood. As he listens to Felix De Lacey teach French to Safie, 'the strange system of human society was explained to me. I heard of the division of property, of immense wealth and squalid poverty, of rank, descent, and noble blood' (2: chap. 5, para. 16). This leads him to reflect on his own predicament:

> I learned that the possessions most esteemed by your fellow creatures were, high and unsullied descent united with riches. A man might be respected with only one of these acquisitions; but without either he was considered, except in very rare instances, as a vagabond and a slave, doomed to waste his powers for the profit of the chosen few. And what was I? Of my creation and creator I was absolutely ignorant; but I knew that I possessed no money, no friends, no kind of property. I was, besides, endowed with a figure hideously deformed and loathsome; I was not even of the same nature as man. I was more agile than they, and could subsist upon coarser diet; I bore the extremes of heat and cold with less injury to my frame; my stature far exceeded theirs. When I looked around, I saw and heard of none like me. Was I then a monster, a blot upon the earth, from which all men fled, and whom all men disowned? (2: chap. 5, para. 17)

In this passage, the Creature's appearance is only a secondary factor in his marginalisation from society. The primary factor is his uncertain genealogy and lack of wealth and influence. It therefore supports readings of the novel that have emphasised the Creature as standing for oppressed groups. Latour's argument that we should embrace catastrophic technologies is a powerful one, but it may also distract from the dangers of a technocracy run by and for the benefit of elites, and the socio-political overturnings required at a time of climate catastrophe.[35] *Frankenstein* offers a more nuanced approach than he suggests. In its complex portrayal of the Creature as a marginalised other, it asks us to be wary of invocations of humanity as a unified agent, given the inequalities that drive, and are driven by, catastrophic change. It also shows how difficult it can be to control our technologies, even if we wish to do so. For when one reads the myriad of statistics and reports reflecting our Anthropocene catastrophe, it is hard to share the ecomodernists' optimism about our capacity to make well-managed interventions to the earth's systems. We live on a volatile planet and the idea that we can shape it to our whims is a fantasy.[36] Of course, technological interventions to address environmental problems are sometimes necessary, and are likely to be increasingly so in a rapidly warming world. But to be safe and effective, they need to be made with due humility, with attention to environmental justice and with an understanding that they are not a substitute for systemic change.

In *Prometheus Unbound*, the planet seems volatile, but is in fact entirely shaped by the protagonist's imagination. Its wintry climate is a result of his brutal cursing of Jupiter; once the curse is revoked, love spreads, Jupiter is defeated, and an eternal summer begins. Unlike the other three texts discussed, a genuine socio-political equality (systemic change) emerges in life rather than in death: 'thrones were kingless, and men walked / One with the other, even as spirits do, / None fawned, none trampled'.[37] As in 'Darkness' and *The Last Man*, buildings act as metonyms for inequality and their fate reveals its demise:

> Thrones, altars, judgement-seats and prisons; wherein
> And beside which, by wretched men were borne
> Sceptres, tiaras, swords, and chains, and tomes
> Of reasoned wrong glozed on by ignorance,
> Were like those monstrous and barbaric shapes,
> The ghosts of a no more remembered fame,
> Which from their unworn obelisks look forth
> In triumph o'er the palaces and tombs
> Of those who were their conquerors, mouldering round.[38]

The apparatus of modern oppression here is compared to the ruins of Egyptian despotism, and particularly the unreadable hieroglyphs on 'unworn obelisks'. Not only is inequality ended, it is no longer comprehensible. All that is left is 'man: / Equal, unclassed, tribeless and nationless'.[39] It's a powerful and alluring vision of what ecomodernists call the 'good Anthropocene'. The value of that vision is that it emphasises human power and responsibility to shape the world for the better, both politically and ecologically. But one of its weaknesses is that, paradoxically, it offers a highly elite view of the end of inequality that depends on decisions made by a small number of the rich and powerful. Modern-day paeans to 'homo deus' tend to obscure political complexities and the dangers of top-down solutions. As Dale Jamieson puts it, given the reality of the environmental crisis, 'we will have to abandon the Promethean dream of a certain, decisive solution and instead engage with the messy world of temporary victories and local solutions while a new world comes into focus'.[40] *Frankenstein*, of course, is subtitled 'The Modern Prometheus'; fantasies of the lone tech genius saving the world still have surprising traction. Such fantasies are unlikely to end well; real solutions require close attention to local conditions and needs. Byron and the Shelleys can hardly be blamed for paying little attention to environmental justice, given their education and historical circumstances. Present-day elites do not have that excuse.

Notes

1. 'The Climate of History: Four Theses', *Critical Inquiry* 35 (2009): 220. Chakrabarty has nuanced his position in several subsequent articles: for example, 'Postcolonial Studies and the Challenge of Climate Change', *New Literary History* 43 (2012): 1–18. For a useful collection of essays, including a response from Chakrabarty, see Robert Emmett and Thomas Lekan (eds), 'Whose Anthropocene? Revisiting Dipesh Chakrabarty's "Four Theses"', *RCC Perspectives: Transformations in Environment and Society* 2 (2016), <http://www.environmentandsociety.org/perspectives/2016/2/whose-anthropocene-revisiting-dipesh-chakrabartys-four-theses> (accessed 30 March 2020).
2. See, for example, Andreas Malm and Alf Hornborg, 'The geology of mankind? A critique of the Anthropocene narrative', *The Anthropocene Review* 1 (2014): 62–9.
3. Genevieve Guenther, 'Who is the we in "We are causing climate change"?', *Grist*, 13 October 2018, <https://grist.org/article/who-is-the-we-in-we-are-causing-climate-change/> (accessed 22 May 2020).
4. Amitav Ghosh, *The Great Derangement* (Chicago: University of Chicago Press, 2016); Kyle Whyte, 'Indigenous Climate Change Studies: Indigenizing Futures, Decolonizing the Anthropocene', *ELN* 55 (2017): 153–62.
5. Oxfam International, 'Extreme Carbon Inequality', 2 December 2015, <https://www.oxfam.org/en/research/extreme-carbon-inequality> (accessed 30 March 2020). See also Yannick Oswald, Anne Owen and Julia K. Steinberger, 'Large inequality in international and intranational energy footprints between income groups and across consumption categories', *Nature Energy* 5 (2020): 231–9.
6. For deep adaptation and its implications for researchers, see Jem Bendell, 'Deep Adaptation: A Map for Navigating Climate Tragedy', *IFLAS Occasional Paper* (2018), <http://lifeworth.com/deepadaptation.pdf> (accessed 30 March 2020). For a critique, see Thomas Nicholas, Galen Hall and Colleen Schmidt, 'Is Deep Adaptation flawed science?', *The Ecologist*, 15 July 2020 <https://theecologist.org/2020/jul/15/deep-adaptation-flawed-science> (accessed 18 August 2020).
7. David Higgins, *British Romanticism, Climate Change, and the Anthropocene: Writing Tambora* (London: Palgrave, 2017).

8. Paul Crutzen and Eugene F. Stoermer, 'The Anthropocene', *IGBP Newsletter* 41 (2000): 17.
9. Andreas Malm, *Fossil Capital: The Rise of Steam Power and the Roots of Global Warming* (London: Verso, 2016).
10. For a discussion of further ways in which Romantic literature can usefully be read as Anthropocene literature, see Thomas H. Ford, 'Punctuating History Circa 1800: The Air of Jane Eyre', in Tobias Menely and Jesse Oak Taylor (eds), *Anthropocene Reading: Literary History in Geologic Times* (University Park, PA: The Pennsylvania State University Press, 2017), pp. 78–95; David Higgins and Tess Somervell, 'Catastrophe', forthcoming in John Parham (ed.), *The Cambridge Companion to Literature and the Anthropocene*.
11. This self-consciousness is not necessarily enlightening. While Kate Rigby suggests that 'true catastrophes' are 'opportunities for deeper understanding and, potentially, new directions', Timothy Clark argues that a catastrophe like the Anthropocene may preclude deeper understanding due to the 'derangement of given norms' that it produces. See Kate Rigby, *Dancing With Disaster: Environmental Histories, Narratives, and Ethics for Perilous Times* (Charlottesville: University of Virginia Press, 2015), p. 18; Timothy Clark, *Ecocriticism on the Edge: The Anthropocene as a Threshold Concept* (London: Bloomsbury, 2015), p. 195.
12. Chakrabarty, 'The Climate of History', p. 221.
13. The best study of this phenomenon is Gillen D'Arcy Wood, *Tambora: The Eruption that Changed the World* (Princeton: Princeton University Press, 2014).
14. John D. Post, *The Last Great Subsistence Crisis in the Western World* (Baltimore: The Johns Hopkins University Press, 1977).
15. See, for example, the appearance of the 'black sun': Mary Shelley, *The Last Man*, ed. Morton D. Paley (Oxford: Oxford University Press, 1994), p. 222. Quotations from this novel are hereafter all from this edition with the page number in parentheses.
16. For the poem's sources, see the relevant endnote in Lord Byron, *The Complete Poetical Works*, ed. Jerome McGann, 7 vols (Oxford: Clarendon Press, 1980–93); see also R. J. Dingley, '"I had a Dream . . .": Byron's "Darkness"', *Byron Journal* 9 (1981): 20–33; Catherine Redford, '"No love was left": The Failure of Christianity in Byron's "Darkness"', *Byron Journal* 43 (2015): 131–40; Jeffrey Vail, '"The Bright Sun Was Extinguish'd": The Bologna Prophecy and Byron's "Darkness"', *Wordsworth Circle* 28 (1997): 183–92. Quotations from Byron's poetry are hereafter from McGann's edition with volume, page and line numbers in parentheses.
17. Raymond Brassier, *Nihil Unbound: Enlightenment and Extinction* (Basingstoke: Palgrave, 2007), p. 223.
18. Ibid. p. 224.
19. Ibid. p. 230.
20. Wood, *Tambora*, p. 69.
21. Ibid. pp. 60–4.
22. See Nigel Clark, 'Volatile Worlds, Vulnerable Bodies: Confronting Abrupt Climate Change', *Theory, Culture & Society* 27, nos 2–3 (2010): 31–53.
23. Peter Cochran (ed.), 'Byron's Alpine Journal', p. 9 <https://petercochran

.files.wordpress.com/2009/03/alpine_journal.pdf> (accessed 18 August 2020).
24. [Mary Shelley and Percy Bysshe Shelley,] *History of a Six Weeks Tour* (London: Hookham and C. & J. Ollier, 1817), p. 163.
25. Ibid. pp. 56 and 103–4.
26. Kate Rigby, *Dancing*, pp. 77–9. See also Olivia Murphy, 'Apocalypse Not Quite: Romanticism and the Post-human World', in Ben P. Robertson (ed.), *Romanticism and Sustainability: Endurance and the Natural World, 1780–1830* (Lanham: Lexington Books, 2015), pp. 245–59.
27. Chris Washington, *Romantic Revelations: Visions of Post-Apocalyptic Life and Hope in the Anthropocene* (Toronto: University of Toronto Press, 2019), p. 75.
28. I have corrected a minor typographical error in the final sentence of the quotation.
29. [Shelley and Shelley,] *History*, p. 183.
30. Clark, *Ecocriticism*, p. 78.
31. Bruno Latour, 'Love Your Monsters', *Breakthrough Journal* 2 (2011) <https://thebreakthrough.org/journal/issue-2/love-your-monsters> (accessed 5 April 2019).
32. John Asafu-Adjaye, Linus Blomqvist, Stewart Brand, Barry Brook, Ruth Defries, Erle Ellis, Christopher Foreman, David Keith, Martin Lewis, Mark Lynas et al., *An Ecomodernist Manifesto* (2015), p. 18, <https://ecomodernistmanifesto.squarespace.com/> (accessed 5 April 2019).
33. Mary Wollstonecraft Shelley, *Frankenstein*, ed. Stuart Curran, 3 vols (College Park, MD: Romantic Circles, [1818] 2009), <https://romantic-circles.org/editions/frankenstein/1818_contents> (accessed 29 March 2020), 2: chap. 9, para. 9. Quotations from the novel are hereafter cited from this edition with volume, chapter and paragraph numbers in parentheses.
34. For a useful early ecocritical discussion of *Frankenstein* and Rousseau, see Jonathan Bate, *The Song of the Earth* (London: Picador, 2000), chap. 2.
35. Andreas Malm, *The Progress of this Storm* (London: Verso, 2018), pp. 153–6.
36. Nigel Clark, *Inhuman Nature: Sociable Life on a Dynamic Planet* (London: Sage, 2011).
37. Percy Bysshe Shelley, *Prometheus Unbound*, in Donald H. Reiman (ed.), *Shelley's Poetry and Prose*, 2nd edn (New York: Norton, 2002), p. 267.
38. Ibid. p. 268.
39. Ibid. p. 269.
40. Dale Jamieson, *Reason in a Dark Time* (Oxford: Oxford University Press, 2014), p. 10.

Chapter 5

Governing from the Country House: Landscape and the Aesthetics of Colonial Rule in India, 1780–1830

Rosie Dias[1]

Arrived in England, the destroyers of the nobility and gentry of a whole kingdom will find the best company in this nation[.] ... Here the manufacturer and husbandman will bless the just and punctual hand, that in India has torn the cloth from the loom, or wrested the scanty portion of rice and salt from the peasant of Bengal, or wrung from him the very opium in which he forgot his oppressions and his oppressor. They marry into your families; they enter into your senate; they ease your estates by loans; they raise their value by demand; they cherish and protect your relations which lie heavy on your patronage; and there is scarcely an house in the kingdom that does not feel some concern and interest that makes all reform of our eastern government appear officious and disgusting[.][2]

In his speech of 1 December 1783 to Parliament on the introduction of Fox's India Bill, Edmund Burke presented his colleagues with the troubling spectre of a socially disruptive class of men easing their way into British society on the basis of their destruction of another society thousands of miles away. Assuming positions that were not theirs by birthright, these returnees from India were exerting a contaminating presence in the metropole, marrying the daughters of the aristocracy and gentry, buying country estates, taking up seats in Parliament and positioning themselves as the financial sponsors of their social superiors. The elevating mechanisms of their wealth, for Burke, could not – and should not – conceal its iniquitous origins, the basis of which was the destruction of another longstanding social order which had been affected in its entirety by the East India Company's (EIC) mercantile imperialism, from the peasant in the field and the weaver at the loom, to the Indian 'nobility and gentry' that these so-called 'nabobs' had usurped.[3] Burke thus articulated the destabilising social consequences of East Indian wealth for both India and Britain, connecting the Company's practices in the subcontinent and its employees' return to Britain to the erosion of two traditional social orders. In Britain itself, he envisaged these

Indian returnees as firmly embedded within an elite social, political and economic class (enjoying advantageous marriages, country houses, parliamentary seats and financial status), but he configured them, through the repetition of 'they', as irrevocably other.

Burke's perception of this process of social advancement enjoyed by EIC returnees to Britain, while undoubtedly pitched for rhetorical effect, offers a useful starting point for thinking through some of the issues with which this chapter will engage. Burke's fears coalesced within a very specific social domain – that of the British landowning and governing elite – and this essay will take up that thread which he identified as connecting India and Britain, in order to examine how this path to social distinction was carved out imaginatively by high-ranking EIC administrators before they returned to Britain. Focusing on the imagery of the colonial country house in India, the chapter explores some of the questions which Burke's oratory prompts: what was the relationship between elite practices in India and in Britain, and how did those whose lives and careers straddled the two countries navigate and connect them through their relationship with land? More precisely, how was this new group of merchant imperialists able to navigate its own social elevation, not economically (for that story is well known) but in cultural terms? Here I examine a selection of visual works which represent the very basis of that social distinction, the country house, considering how its representation in colonial India offers a way of imagining a relationship to land and governance not only in terms of an emerging colonial practice, but with an eye on a return to the metropole. I differentiate my focus from two preceding kinds of analysis, both of which have offered immensely useful insights into the representation and architecture of the colonial country house and estate in India. The first of these is the investigation of the development of the outdoor conversation piece in India, a genre which pictures European sitters, sometimes with their servants, within the estate in what is essentially a form of portraiture adapted from its European origins to a colonial context.[4] The second is the consideration of the garden house (the term by which colonial country houses occupied by colonial and local elites in India were known, a derivation from the Bengali *bagan bari*) in terms of its status as a site of conspicuous consumption consistent with the emergence of – and resistance to – a colonial-capitalist economy, as well as the experiences and desires which its spaces fulfilled.[5] Here, I am primarily concerned with how the garden house (rather than its inhabitants) is situated pictorially within and in relation to its twofold rural setting, in which a cultivated European-style garden setting adjoins (and sometimes pictorially accommodates) a wider landscape, a process which might usefully be described as negotiating a transition from comfort zone to 'contact zone'.[6] The works I analyse depict not their owners or inhabitants, but Indian figures, indicating a concern with the relationship of the colonial country house to the Indigenous environment and peoples, and to the control of that wider landscape.

That these two zones are imagined and connected visually is indicative of an emerging colonial regime which saw the EIC make the transition from a company of traders to a quasi-imperial power, for which economic benefit was now to be derived no longer from trade but through the administration of land. But it is also an imaginative process which is connected to the metropole and – as we shall see – to aesthetic frameworks for the representation of landscape which are profoundly class-based. Most Company men were not settlers but aimed to return to Britain, where the most successful were able to achieve the kind of social distinction which Burke described. But while Burke drew upon the stereotype established within satirical prints and critical writings during the third quarter of the eighteenth century of these returnees as problematic nabobs, this trope has recently been called into question by scholarship which emphasises the carefully crafted respectability of these Company men (and, occasionally, women) as they established themselves back in Britain.[7] What is in fact clear from surviving imagery of country houses inhabited by them is that this self-fashioning took place even before they disembarked on British shores, with Palladian villas featuring prominently in drawings and watercolours by amateur artists who depicted Anglo-Indian life or colonial landscapes. In much the same way that Swati Chattopadhyay has described the effect of European travellers' recognition of familiarity within the white neoclassical Calcutta cityscape in terms of a 'colonial uncanny', we might also note the extent to which imagery of the colonial garden house both replicated and prefigured its British equivalent, drawing on established representations and constructions of the English country house, and anticipating the kind of homecoming that returnees might enjoy.[8] Such imagery inevitably raises issues around social status or class, and the ways in which social structures were configured in the colony, beyond the obvious one of colonised-coloniser. Here it is worth noting how little attention the question of class has received in relation to colonial activity. If – as this volume proposes – class has been obscured from environmental histories, this problem pertains doubly in relation to the representation of colonial landscapes. During the 1980s and early 90s, several scholars working on British landscape painting developed and deployed the methodologies of a social history of art, emphasising issues of class, society and nation in order to illuminate the ideological underpinnings of eighteenth- and nineteenth-century British landscape painting.[9] A decade or so later, history's – and indeed, art history's – global turn saw the critical lens shift from issues of class and society to those of colonialism, race and transnationalism. In the process, class-based analysis remained tied to the nation, not enjoying the mobility of, say, feminist scholarship, which has spanned both national and global histories. Christof Dejung, for example, writing in the recently published *Routledge Handbook of Transregional Studies*, notes that global historians and scholars, 'primarily interested in imperial expansions, global regimes of racism, and transnational networks ... barely connect these topics explicitly to the examination of a particular social order or the examination of class'.[10]

And yet class seems like an important lens through which to analyse imagery of the colonial country house, a location implicated within practices of elite display and self-fashioning which parallel those in the metropole. Burke's speech can help us further in establishing a few of the issues here, for at its core is a tension not just between types of people, but between two different ways of visualising social distinctions. Burke's own conception of society is one based on an organisation of what was commonly, in the eighteenth century, referred to as 'rank': that is to say, those 'fixed, invariable external rules of distinction ... which create no jealousy, as they are allowed to be accidental' (that is to say, derived from the accident of birth).[11] In contrast to the fixed classification of rank, a more mobile system developed in the emerging capitalist culture of eighteenth-century Britain, one with which the term 'class' increasingly became associated. Penelope Corfield notes how 'class' 'glided into the language, and for some time ... was deployed alongside older terms, sometimes almost interchangeably with them'.[12] This is well exemplified in Burke's thinking (if not in his actual vocabulary), which recognises the emergence of this newly mobile and imprecisely defined social order, and its intersection and tension with an established, codified one.[13] Forming a key part of Britain's vigorous trading and financial landscape, the EIC offered unprecedented opportunities for economic advancement including, in some cases, for the recovery of depleted family fortunes: it acted as a lever, in effect, for class mobility.[14] But, uniquely within Britain's commercial terrain, its transition from a mercantile to a merchant-imperialist entity allowed men employed by the EIC to govern peoples and territories. The colonial country house is emblematic of this dual activity, acting not only as a repository and signifier of capital – one which obscured some of those iniquitous origins pointed to by Burke – but also as a space from which colonised land can be managed and conceptualised through landscape organisation and representation. In pictorial form, it offered an imaginative space through which to articulate a relationship to land and to people, one which leveraged aesthetic frameworks developed within the European art tradition and which were tied to concepts of landscape that were almost invariably elite. Such representations worked against Burke's narrative of moral failure, stolen resources and social disruption by visually articulating the social and political accomplishments of elite men in empire in ways which were both natural and affirmative, and inflected with more than a touch of imperial propaganda.

* * * * *

In 1781, the landscape painter William Hodges – who had arrived in India the previous year to work under the patronage of the EIC's Governor General, Warren Hastings – embarked on a painting of his patron's garden house at Alipur, a recently built villa a few miles downstream from the centre of the colonial city of Calcutta. A preliminary drawing of the subject frames Hastings's house centrally, with a tree acting as a *repoussoir* to draw attention to the building's Palladian features while its tenant stands in the foreground, sheltered beneath a parasol held by an Indian servant (Fig. 5). To the left of the building is Belvedere, an older Palladian house on Hastings's estate, and between the two buildings a small thatched hut.[15] In spite of its exotic markers, the composition adheres closely to the conventions of estate portraiture that had been established in paint and print by topographical artists in Britain over the course of the eighteenth century, with a centrally positioned house providing the focus of the image, and the landowner (sometimes with his family) often featuring in the foreground.[16] The work ultimately painted for Hastings (Fig. 6), however, departs significantly from the drawing. Hastings and his servant no longer appear in the composition, and the garden house features less centrally, placed further back and additionally made less prominent through the use of aerial perspective. A new foreground arrangement with the addition of native figures shifts the emphasis of the painting. The barely noticeable pool of water from the drawing has been elongated to connect the foreground with the middle ground of the painting, and it is now the focus of human activity: one person washing their hair, and another two collecting water from it. The unassuming sapling has morphed into a much larger tree, now placed centrally in the composition and extending sheltering branches over the Bengali figures. The tiny hut, which barely registers in the drawing, is moved further to the left of the composition, but a much more prominent one now appears in the space that Hastings and his servant had originally occupied.

A few years after the painting was executed, the Calcutta banker Benjamin Mee wrote from India to his brother-in-law, Viscount Palmerston, that: 'Mr Hodges's pictures of India make it look like gentleman's seats.'[17] Mee's disparaging assessment of Hodges's Indian oeuvre economically points to underpinning practices and notions around aesthetics, class and possession which inhere in Hodges's work, drawing as it did upon the idealising aesthetic modes that shaped the estates – and the pictorial views made of them – belonging to aristocratic families and landed gentry in Britain. In other words, Hodges's Indian landscapes weren't merely reminiscent of the works of Claude Lorrain or of Canaletto (just two examples of the august Continental influences detected by contemporary critics viewing Hodges's Indian scenes), but they were seen by Mee to draw upon a specific sifting and repurposing of those artists' compositions for the requirements of picturesque landscaping on British estates such as Stourhead (a garden which viewers such as Mee might well have called to mind on seeing Hodges's pendant view to Figure 6, *A View of Marmalong Bridge with a Sepoy and Natives in the Foreground*).[18] Visually processed by means of such elite aesthetics, the Indian landscape came to resemble, to Mee's eyes, not only Claude's compositions, but also the country estates of those English gentlemen who, in the eighteenth century, collected his paintings and modelled their landscapes on them. Hodges's own writings on India confirm this tendency to view the landscape as though it were an English estate. In the course of his travels upcountry from Calcutta, he assessed the countryside around Colgong as the 'most beautiful' he had seen in India, explaining that the 'waving appearance of the land, its fine turf and detached woods, backed by the extensive forests on the hills, brought to my mind many of the fine parks in England'.[19] For *Natives Drawing Water from a Pond*, Hodges was drawing upon another kind of estate view, of the kind sometimes painted by his former teacher, the landscape painter Richard Wilson. In *Dinas Bran from Llangollen* (Fig. 7), Wilson had carefully obscured the landowner Sir Watkin William-Wynn's dominance of the landscape through a conception which was 'organic and paternal'.[20] Sir Watkin's house does not appear in the painting (his presence is instead alluded to through the distant ruins of Castell Dinas Bran) and the estate view, prefiguring Hodges's, is structured around a pool-like section of the River Dee, with local inhabitants using the landscape for collecting wood and washing clothes, while sheep graze in the background.

If Burke detected individualistic, profit-motivated and rapaciously commercial tendencies underpinning the EIC's regime in Bengal, Hodges's vision of his patron's management of the region offered instead a rural idyll based on a benevolent and paternalistic moral economy. These contrasting visions correspond to distinct conceptions of eighteenth-century landscape, which Nigel Everett has characterised respectively as Whig and Tory.[21] While Everett acknowledges that these two categories do not always equate with political positions (Burke, who frequently contrasted the 'chearful face of paternal government and protected labour' with the destructive way in which the EIC managed land, was, after all, a Whig), they are nonetheless useful for comprehending the different social and aesthetic conceptions underpinning estate management, controversies around the 'improvement' of land, and the relationship of the mansion to the wider landscape.[22] Increasingly criticised in the final decades of the eighteenth century, the 'Whig' idea of landscape linked taste with obvious possession and with the tight control of the estate's wider landscape: with 'little . . . left to nature, accident, or discretion; the end of improvement is the clear distinction of personal property from the common, the rustic, the public'.[23] Conversely, the older, paternalistic mode of landscape associated with Toryism emphasised traditional social relations over new liberal ideologies, elevating moral and spiritual values over those of commercial self-interest. Hodges's pastoral idyll falls clearly on the latter side of this binary and was evidently intended to do so. Not only does his painting represent a considerable conceptual shift from the preliminary drawing, but it also engenders a synthesis of two kinds of imagery, that of the country house and the village. A contemporary drawing by Hodges of an Indian village suggests a template for the foreground composition of the painting, featuring a tree placed centrally between a native hut and a village pond utilised by local figures and livestock (Fig. 8).[24] One modification to the Indian village drawing is to make the hut in the painting more recognisably Bengali (the hut in the drawing could be mistaken for an English cottage); another is to extend the branches of the central tree to span most of the width of the canvas and to offer shade to the native figures. Finally, the tiny seated figure to the left of the tree in the drawing is given a more prominent position in the painting and is connected visually with the tree. His pose is suggestive of the kind of meditative or spiritual activity which often took place under a peepal tree, a possible candidate for the species depicted here.

    This carefully managed vision of sheltering yet unobtrusive paternalism (suggested by the spreading branches of the tree, in conjunction with the distancing of the garden house) did not, in fact, correspond with the actual features of Hastings's land, which a contemporary survey map shows was rather more regimented in its arrangement of trees and water sources than the painting would imply.[25] We also know that, far from being left to nature's will, Hastings's Alipur estate was purposed for pleasure and use, consisting of 'partly lawn but chiefly garden ground in high cultivation and well stocked with a great variety of fruit trees', in a configuration which aligned more closely with Whig ideas of landscape than with the traditional social ideal of Hodges's pictorial conception.[26] However, there was more at stake in this representation than a nod to estate management in the metropolis. Hastings had been appointed Governor of Calcutta in 1771 amidst the ongoing effects of the catastrophic Bengal famine of 1770, which had wiped out an estimated third of the region's native population, or ten million people in total. In the subsequent years, interpretations of the famine shifted between ascribing its causes to nature (drought) or to culture (land management), and in assessing the EIC's role in relation to both.[27] Criticism of the Company was widespread; it was blamed for monopolising grain during the crisis, as well as for its rapacious insistence in pursuing, and even increasing, land taxation during the famine period. Moreover, it was recognised that the land policies which the EIC had pursued prior to the famine – which served the needs of the Company's revenue extraction rather than food provision for the local population – had eradicated traditional land use by restricting longstanding local practices such as nomadism and investment in irrigation systems in favour of demarcating easily calculable plots of land for the purposes of taxation.[28] For famine to have occurred in such a location as Bengal was, to many Europeans, unthinkable. Bengal was considered to be the most fertile region in India, even in Asia, the place which the Mughal emperor, Aurengzeb, had pronounced to be the 'Paradise of Nations'. In the European imagination, parts of India, and the Gangetic Plain in particular, had long existed as candidates for the location of the Garden of Eden.[29] Abbé Raynal had described India as a kind of earthly Eden, in which nature's bounty provided abundantly for man and beast, with species which would be incompatible elsewhere co-existing in perfect harmony, while the Indian, 'exempt from necessity, has nothing to pursue but pleasure'. Famine, for him, was not a lapse of nature, but had been brought about by the EIC's greed, which had 'ravaged and oppressed the finest country on the globe'.[30] In alluding to this fabled region, Burke emphasised the role of 'man' in prudently managing God's generous provision:

> the moisture, the bounty of Heaven, is given but at a certain season. Before the aera of our influence, the industry of man carefully husbanded that gift of God. The *Gentûs* [Hindus] preserved, with a provident and religious care, the precious deposit of the periodical rain in reservoirs ... and from these, as occasion demanded, they fructified the whole country. To maintain these reservoirs, and to keep up an annual advance to the cultivators, for seed and cattle, formed a principal object of the piety and polity of the priests and rulers of the *Gentû* religion.[31]

This pre-colonial idyll Burke contrasted with the system the Company had introduced, which ensured that 'reservoirs of water went to decay ... and sterility, indigence, and depopulation, overspread the face of these once flourishing provinces'.

Underpinning both Raynal and Burke's critiques of the Company's management of its territories is an understanding that nature provides abundantly for the sustenance and benefit of humankind, but that its stewards have to manage it prudently, storing its gifts and neither wasting nor restraining them. This model of stewardship can be traced back to an environmental consciousness which had emerged in Britain over the previous century and which was underpinned by the concept of 'usufruct'. Derived from Roman civil law, the model of usufruct which established itself in eighteenth-century theological, moral and literary writings envisaged humans as the custodians rather than the true owners of the non-human environment, bearing a responsibility to preserve the land they owned for posterity or for God, and not simply exercise mastery over it.[32] In Burke's rhetoric, the bounty of heaven, its 'precious deposit', is respected and managed more successfully through a rural economy structured by Hindu beliefs and practices than it is by the mercenary and destructive methods of emergent European capitalism. This is a view consistent with early modern conservationist thinking, which Richard Grove has argued 'emerged as a corollary of, and in some sense as a contradiction to ... the mental and material colonisation of the world by Europeans' and which paid increasing attention to indigenous practices of land management.[33] For many, the famine was not so much the result of environmental factors, but the consequence of gross human mismanagement. Its effects were encountered and visualised not simply in terms of its colossal human fatalities, but as a nightmarish reversal of nature's harmonic order. Overturning Raynal's vision of a paradisiacal settlement in which Indian fauna co-existed in exceptional harmony, contemporary famine accounts observed dogs, jackals, hogs and vultures feasting on the remains of the human dead. As David Arnold has shown, for later writers who sought to evaluate the longer-term effects of the famine, the severe depopulation and desolation of the Bengal countryside had opened the way for the 'nihilism of unrestrained nature' where 'tigers (symbolising nature at its most predatory and opportunistic) prowled and elephants plundered in places where villages had once thrived', and where dense impenetrable jungle sprung up in previously cultivated areas.[34] The Edenic environment of Bengal was fundamentally and deleteriously transformed, with the famine being as much an environmental catastrophe as a human tragedy, affecting the land for decades after the event.

Sustained criticisms of the EIC in the metropole, of which its role in the famine was only one, led to the Regulating Act of 1773, and to increasing state intervention in the Company's business thereafter. In light of these events, Hodges's painting offers a pictorial sense of the restoration of Bengal's Eden under Hastings's apparently benign and unobtrusive regime. Hodges's *Travels in India*, published in 1793 at the height of Hastings's impeachment trial, took care to note the probity of the Company in managing its territory in Bengal: 'the care that was taken in the government, and the minute attention to the happiness of this people, rendered this district, at this time (1781) a perfect paradise'.[35] As Kate Teltscher has noted, the emphasis in Hodges's text on the flourishing populations of the Bengali villages he passes through implies an environment which has recovered from the deathly effects of the famine;[36] one might infer a similar message from *Natives Drawing Water from a Pond*, which depicts Indians resting in contentment rather than busily working to replace the significant loss of labour that the famine had caused.

Although Hodges's painting suggests a lack of interference in Bengal's rural life, the famine actually resulted in increased European involvement in the management of Indian land. The EIC's policies, it was claimed, had exacerbated the famine, but critiques were also levelled at Indians themselves, who were deemed too inert and fatalistic to overcome its threats. Thus, rather paradoxically, more European management of the landscape was deemed necessary to prevent future recurrences, a belief which we might observe as underpinning a later work by the artist James Baillie Fraser (Fig. 9).[37] Presenting a carefully framed view on the bend of Garden Reach, another suburb south of Calcutta, Fraser's aquatint captures the extremity of the Botanic Garden, specifically the superintendent's house at the edge of the River Hooghly, which faces a series of Palladian garden houses on the opposite bank. In the English topographical imagination, a proliferation of country villas in areas such as Surrey was indexical of the nation's accumulation of wealth, and this was no less so in the colony, with Eliza Fay observing along Garden Reach 'a constant succession of whatever can delight the eye or bespeak wealth and elegance in the owners'.[38] In his other published views of Calcutta, Fraser habitually structured the pictorial space to emphasise divisions, mostly between the so-called 'black' and 'white' towns and populations of Calcutta.[39] Here, space is articulated differently, not only delineating but also balancing two distinct colonial processes: the accumulation of capital, and the management of land through scientific and political means. While the country villas on the right-hand bank 'bespeak wealth', the left-hand bank is carefully cropped to single out the dwelling and administrative building occupied by the Botanic Garden's superintendent. The Calcutta Botanic Garden had been established in 1787 with famine prevention as its primary concern. Its founding superintendent, Thomas Kyd, had advocated for the development and dissemination of stocks of drought-resistant crops as a means of averting future disasters (though the EIC's Board of Directors was ultimately only swayed when Kyd stressed the commercial advantages which the garden might secure).[40] Kyd's successor, William Roxborough, integrated his predecessor's interests in crop experimentation and medicinal botany within broader scientific concerns, namely his pioneering study of meteorological data, undertaken in order to understand the relationship between climate change, the occurrence of famine and colonial land use.[41]

In Fraser's image, the house built by Roxborough contrasts with the houses on the opposite bank. While they 'bespeak wealth', the curved façade of the superintendent's house implies surveillance and control, its windows and deep verandas opening out on all sides to the Calcutta landscape. The tableau in the composition's foreground reinforces this idea. Here, a couple of native river boats approach the riverbank, where a flock of vultures stands innocuously among the vegetation. Back in 1770, vultures had infamously feasted on human remains. Now, in the same year Fraser's print was published, James Atkinson – a Deputy Assay Master in the Calcutta Mint and an amateur poet and artist – described the Hooghly's gruesome spectacle: bodies of dead Hindus 'the revolting prey / Of Vultures, festering fast and rolling to the Bay'.[42] In Atkinson's poem, this grisly sight formed part of a wider picture of Calcutta's ambiguous landscape, both the seat of a dazzling, opulent empire, and the destroyer of human morals and health. If human mortality represented a significant theme in Atkinson's poem (as, indeed, it did in countless colonial narratives centred upon Calcutta), Fraser offers a reassuringly stable and balanced landscape. Native figures and vultures co-exist in an equilibrium which is carefully managed by the Company botanists' scientific activity. The commercial gains of empire – signified by the succession of villas along the Hooghly's banks – are offset by responsible management of the land. And the squally sky, a climatic threat, fails to extend its storm clouds to the Garden House, whose denizens (both human and vegetable) work to alleviate its hazards. Visiting the Garden in 1824, Bishop Heber noted it to be simultaneously 'very beautiful and well-managed', offering a scene that 'more perfectly answers Milton's idea of Paradise ... than any thing which I ever saw'.[43] This 'paradise' garden restored and conserved the abundance of Bengal's natural resources, further enriching it with an encyclopaedic profusion of plants and trees collected from all over the world.

Fraser and Hodges's views, then, visualised the EIC's conscientious management of Bengal's landscape and reinforced the centrality of the human in the Garden of Eden as a beneficiary of its bounty and a conserver of its resources. They structured pictorial space carefully, using the relationship between the garden house and the surrounding landscape to couch associations with the historical and environmental catastrophe of famine within an affirmative expression of the EIC's subsequent political and scientific regimes. But it is worth, at this point, returning with more precision to the issue of class in the imagery of the garden house, beyond the neoclassical building's generalised association with government and empire. Class comes more clearly to the fore in an 1811 watercolour depicting the Madras garden house of Sir Thomas Strange, the Chief Justice of the Supreme Court of Madras (Fig. 10). The image draws upon an explicitly patrician concept of the Palladian villa, emphasising its relationship with nature, and reinforcing the building's stark classicism through the inclusion of three figures in the foreground: two holy men conversing with a woman, the latter attired in dress which looks almost Roman. The composition – so far as I can tell – is more or less unique in colonial imagery, but its iconography bears notable similarities with an early eighteenth-century portrait by John Closterman depicting the Earl of Shaftesbury and his brother in classical robes and conversing in a wooded grove, with an Ionic temple in the background (Fig. 11). Closterman's painting has been understood by art historians to embody the Horatian topos of virtuous rural retirement, as well as Shaftesbury's own political thought, which centred upon a commitment to the principles of civic humanism – that is to say upon the understanding that the possession of property was the fundamental basis of good government, securing public or 'civic' virtue by ensuring that the landowner's concerns 'would coincide with the public interest at large'.[44] The colonial garden house was a particularly resonant space with regard to the concept of virtuous retirement. Located neither in the city nor in such remote rural locations as Residents' bungalows or hill houses, it became established in the colonial imagination as a space of suburban retreat, not simply for leisure but as a necessary corrective to the frenzied and corrupting experience of the colonial city, one which could restore the colonial administrator's mind and virtue. The parallel with the Roman *villa urbana* was not lost on those who inhabited this landscape. A playful letter written in 1779 by an unidentified lawyer to Warren Hastings's neighbour in Alipur, Philip Francis, deploys the topography of Calcutta and its suburbs as an imaginative terrain through which the writer plays out an elaborate classical fantasy that envisions the city as a modern Rome:

> I was in pursuit of you last night near two hours without success. I went first to your '*villa inter paludes*' where I found not the smallest vestige of society. I then returned to town, and, quitting my chariot, I took to my litter and proceeded in it to your house near the Capitol, where, to my utter astonishment, I found the same appearance of desertion and desolation. It struck me that you might have repassed the Rubicon, and with your slaves have gone again upon some private plan of pleasures into Cis-alpine Gaul [Chandernagore, the French trading settlement on the Hooghly]. While I was ruminating upon these things, a Ligurian tax-gatherer, whom I remember to have seen among your followers, informed me that, having been forced by certain putrid exhalations from the marshes in which your villa stands to discontinue your weekly symposium there, and having at a late meeting at Nasidienus drank too deeply of Falerian, you had retired with two females (Contemplation and Temperance), with whom you had been very lately made acquainted, to the gardens of Rufillus near the fourth stone on the Falerian Way to enjoy with him and his freedman, Petronius Macer, the feast of reason and the flow of soul, or to prepare yourself for the more momentous matter that may be debated in the Senate this day.[45]

The letter is clearly humorous in its intent, but its author's affectation of the role of a modern-day Pliny was consistent with several contemporary writings (Atkinson's *City of Palaces* among them) which framed Calcutta in explicitly classical terms and stressed the parallels between the British and Roman empires. The rural counterpart to the neoclassical city, the colonial *villa urbana* in Porter's watercolour is emphasised as a place of virtuous retreat by the inclusion of the three figures, whose otherness is recast within the framework of the classical, not only in the dress of the woman but in the activity which takes place. Engaged in dialogue outdoors, the figures imply a visual equivalent to the Virgilian eclogue, a poetic form which was often reworked in the eighteenth century to extend the genre's original pastoral concerns to the experience of new, exotic locations.

While Porter's image evokes the paradigm of classical Rome and its political and literary modes, it is also structured in a way which emphasises the distinctive natural environment of the subcontinent. The watercolour's foreground creates an aperture onto the classical tableau and includes recognisably exotic flora such as banana trees to the right of the composition. Once again, we might consider how the space of the garden house connects with this indigenous landscape, and here it is worth noting that the figures in front of the house depict not the landowner – as was the case with Closterman's portrait – but Indians. Occupying the space between the house and the wider landscape, they suggest the ways in which EIC officials gained knowledge of the colony by drawing on the expertise of pandits, brahmins and other informants in areas such as natural history, law and religion. When Strange was later to publish a tome on Hindu law, he acknowledged the assistance he had received from local pandits; similarly, colonial botany was informed not only by European methodologies but by indigenous knowledge.[46] If Strange occupied a patrician role within the social order of colonial India, it was one which – Porter's image suggests – he undertook with respect for, and knowledge of, the local environment and its inhabitants. Like Hodges and Fraser's views, Porter's watercolour carefully mediates between colonial knowledge and power, and the moral and social concerns posed by the natural world and the resources it offered in this new Garden of Eden.

Conclusion

In *Green Imperialism*, Grove highlighted the importance of examining 'the metaphors and images used by Europeans to characterise, identify and organise their perceptions of nature at the expanding colonial periphery', a task which he notes illuminates the prevalence of the garden and the island in the colonial imagination.[47] This essay has taken up that invitation, focusing on a particular manifestation of the garden: the colonial suburban estate and the ways in which its garden house is put in dialogue with the surrounding landscape, the 'Paradise' of rural India. I am not attempting to argue here that the visual works which have been examined in this essay are at all representative of colonial garden house imagery. Indeed, a more extensive appraisal of the genre would recognise that my three examples are far more ideologically laden than are the majority of depictions of this subject, which tended to offer rather straightforward portraits of such houses. The difference between the two kinds of imagery – which could crudely be characterised as falling into the categories of the idealised and the topographical – hinges not only on the aesthetic frameworks which they draw upon, but also upon a claim to authority, one which is based not on the mere possession of wealth but on the moral, social and intellectual virtues necessary to colonial governance. Produced in the context of the growing visibility, awareness and criticism of what Rob Nixon would call the 'slow violence' of the multinational corporation, they served not merely as propaganda in support of the Company, but as a means of articulating a moral claim to the kind of social elevation to which Burke so fiercely objected, one which hinged upon the understanding and care of the wider landscape and the people it accommodated.[48]

In arguing for further regulation of EIC activity in 1783, Burke had dwelt on its abuse of nature's resources and the extraction of those resources from the hands of their rightful possessors: cotton torn from the weaver's loom, rice and salt from the peasant's bowl, and opium from the weary labourer's pipe. His troubled Georgic vision connected with criticisms made by other Europeans such as Abbé Raynal, who invoked Eden rather than the Georgic as the natural paradigm for empire: a divinely provided bounty proffered to humankind but in need of careful conservation, not mere extraction. If the responses to such concerns included further regulation of the corporation on the part of the State, accompanied by the articulation by colonialists of their relationship to the landscape they occupied in terms of legitimacy, responsible management and moral care, then what we appear to be seeing is the emergence of modern environmental anxieties, and of the specific corporate behaviours which developed in order to address them. Paul Warde has powerfully demonstrated that sustainability began to be articulated as a problem and to emerge in political discourse only towards the end of the early modern period, appearing 'in its full-blown form in the latter part of the eighteenth century'.[49] Key to Warde's analysis is the question of who gets to shape this discursive field: not, crucially, those who work the land and are most dependent upon it, but 'rich men', occasionally state officials, but more often men working 'in what we might call a "personal" capacity that embraced both their own interests *and* the discharge of public office, which was in any case often being done from their own splendid residences'.[50] While Warde does not address the specific manifestations of these practices in colonial South Asia, the imagery this essay has examined demonstrates all too clearly this broad picture of elite men straddling official and private interests to shape, and respond to, environmental discourse and anxieties, as well as the clear demarcation of this elite strata of individuals from the 'dumb and mute mass' which constituted the 'population' they governed.[51] Such social orderings are evident in the three main works considered here, which feature the estate or headquarters occupied by a specified colonial official, while the Indian figures on the property's peripheries remain undifferentiated. Indeed, in considering the images of colonial estates produced by British artists, the corporate-colonial practices that they addressed and the criticisms of metropolitan figures such as Burke and Raynal that they deflected, we can see how Warde's discursive field of sustainability works in practice and who its participants were. To answer Gayatri Chakravorty Spivak's rhetorical question, the subaltern evidently cannot speak; rather they are muted or spoken for – a problem which, in environmentalism, is far from resolved today.[52] Moreover if, as indicated earlier in this essay, one of the aims of images such as Hodges's was to provide reassurance about the recovery of the native population after the famine (or in the case of Fraser to point to the delicate equilibrium through which the EIC's environmental management staved off further disaster) we must ask why it was imperative to do so. Was this motivated purely by a humanitarian concern for the population of Bengal, or (given the concerns expressed about the shortage of labour the famine had caused) by a recognition that sustainability of the Company's activities and profits was dependent not only upon the environment it managed but on the population that generated the land's profits? Just as in those Dutch still life paintings of the seventeenth century (another crucial imagery through which a powerful trading empire articulated its understanding of the territories it spanned) in which Black slaves appear within a panoply of consumer goods on display, here we might recognise that the native population was itself conceived of as a resource, whose 'extraction' from the landscape threatens the Company's very sustainability.[53]

If, as Warde argues, we can witness the unmistakable arrival of sustainability as a concept in public discourse in the late eighteenth century, we can additionally perceive how swiftly the anxieties that this discourse embodied were countered by a specific corporate response. While, over time, the British State's reaction to criticisms of the multinational corporation's misdeeds was to impose incremental regulation, the EIC itself was able to leverage visual culture with varying degrees of deliberation to effect what we might recognise today as an embryonic form of greenwashing. As landscape imagery produced in colonial India made its way back to the metropole and was exhibited at the Royal Academy, circulated through print culture, or was shown in albums to friends, it anticipated some of the key deflective functions of twentieth-century greenwashing, promoting 'ethical leadership ... [and the] image of a committed corporate culture' while countering 'threats to [the] organisation's legitimacy' and attempting to thwart 'increased regulatory requirements'.[54] It is worth noting that British artists were only able to travel to India under the auspices of the EIC – whether subject to direct patronage (such as Hodges) or with the permission of Company officials (Fraser, who arrived in Calcutta as a trader). Many more who produced imagery of the Indian landscape (including Porter) were officers in the Company's armies, trained in draughtsmanship as cadets in the Royal Military Academy at Woolwich or, after 1809, at the Company's dedicated Military Seminary at Addiscombe. All these artists, therefore, participated in an imbrication of professional, ethno-cultural and social networks generated by the EIC's activities, and were cognisant of and responsive to the Company's practices, ambitions and controversies. The lack of objectivity of such works was widely understood, not least by the artists Thomas and William Daniell, who set out to remedy Hodges's idealised vision of India by using a camera obscura to enforce detachment and distance. The observation that colonial artists may have produced landscape works which anticipate twentieth-century greenwashing is not intended to be reductive or to hazard a claim that these works can be comprehended as mere exercises (and cynical ones at that) in corporate reputation salvaging. Clearly, they can be understood within many other frameworks. Rather, it is to suggest how an analysis of visual culture can usefully extend work such as Warde's, revealing the swiftness with which corporate, image-based responses to charges of environmental mismanagement emerged. It also allows us to consider that corporate strategies such as greenwashing, commonly understood to be a uniquely twentieth-century phenomenon, perhaps have a longer history than has been fully recognised.[55]

Notes

1. An early version of this research was delivered at a 2014 symposium on British Environmental Aesthetics at Nanzan University. I am grateful to Ve-Yin Tee for the invitation to this event and for his generous feedback on the first draft of this essay. I also gratefully acknowledge the financial support of the Grant-in-Aid for Scientific Research (C) in funding my visit to the symposium.
2. Edmund Burke, 'Speech on Fox's India Bill, 1 December 1783', in P. J. Marshall (ed.), *The Writings and Speeches of Edmund Burke. Vol V. India: Madras and Bengal, 1774–1785* (Oxford: Oxford University Press, 1981), p. 403.
3. 'Nabob' was the pejorative term which was applied to conspicuously wealthy returnees from India in the second half of the eighteenth century, in particular those who were able to exert political influence in the metropole through their purchase of land. See Tillman W. Nechtman, *Nabobs: Empire and Identity in Eighteenth-Century Britain* (Cambridge: Cambridge University Press, 2010).
4. Beth Fowkes Tobin, *Colonizing Nature: The Tropics in British Arts and Letters, 1760–1820* (Philadelphia: University of Pennsylvania Press, 2005), pp. 81–116.
5. Swati Chattopadhyay, 'The Other Face of Primitive Accumulation: The Garden House in British Colonial Bengal', in Peter Scriver and Vikramaditya Prakash (eds), *Colonial Modernities: Building, Dwelling and Architecture in British India and Ceylon* (New York: Routledge, 2007), pp. 169–97.

6. In deploying the term 'contact zone', I am of course referring to the work of Mary Louise Pratt, who uses it to describe spaces where 'cultures meet, clash, and grapple with each other, often in contexts of highly asymmetrical relations of power, such as colonialism, slavery, or their aftermaths'; see 'Arts of the Contact Zone', *Profession* (1991), p. 34.
7. For example, the various case studies in Margot Finn and Kate Smith (eds), *The East India Company at Home* (London: UCL Press, 2018), suggest 'Company men and women often worked sedulously to erase or obscure the provenance of their wealth' (p. 8).
8. Swati Chattopadhyay, *Representing Calcutta: Modernity, Nationalism and the Colonial Uncanny* (London and New York: Routledge, 2005).
9. See, for example, David Solkin, *Richard Wilson: The Landscape of Reaction* (London: Tate, 1982); Michael Rosenthal, *Constable: The Painter and His Landscape* (London and New Haven, CT: Yale University Press, 1983); John Barrell, *The Dark Side of the Landscape: The Rural Poor in English Painting, 1730–1840* (Cambridge: Cambridge University Press, 1980); Ann Bermingham, *Landscape and Ideology: The English Rustic Tradition, 1740–1860* (Berkeley: University of California Press, 1986); and Stephen Daniels, *Fields of Vision: Landscape Painting and National Identity in England and the United States* (Cambridge: Polity Press, 1993).
10. Christof Dejung, 'Transregional Study of Class, Social Groups and Milieus', in Matthias Middell (ed.), *The Routledge Handbook of Transregional Studies* (London: Routledge, 2019), p. 74.
11. Frederick A. Pottle (ed.), *Boswell's London Journal, 1762–63* (New Haven, CT: Yale University Press, 1950), p. 320.
12. P. J. Corfield, 'Class by Name and Number in Eighteenth-Century Britain', *History* 72, no. 234 (1987): 39.
13. On the difficulties and competing models of defining class in this period, see Corfield, 'Class by Name and Number'; David Cannadine, *The Rise and Fall of Class in Britain* (New York: Columbia University Press, 1999); and William M. Reddy, 'The Concept of Class', in M. L. Bush (ed.), *Social Orders and Social Classes in Early Modern Europe since 1500* (Harlow: Longman, 1992), pp. 13–25.
14. The standard work on the pursuit and mechanisms of East Indian wealth is P. J. Marshall, *East Indian Fortunes: The British in Bengal in the Eighteenth Century* (Oxford: Clarendon Press, 1976).
15. On the development of Hastings's Alipur estate, see Lord Curzon, *British Government in India: The Story of the Viceroys and Government Houses*, 2 vols (London, New York, Toronto and Melbourne: Cassell and Company Ltd, 1928), 1: 138–44.
16. An example of this genre published close to the time of Hodges's Indian travels is William Watts's *The Seats of the Nobility and Gentry in a Collection of Most Interesting and Picturesque Views* (Chelsea: W. Watts, 1779). Within that publication, several works, among them Watts's engraving after Paul Sandby's *West Combe in Kent, the Seat of the Marchioness of Lothian*, offer a useful point of comparison for Hodges's drawing.
17. University of Southampton, Harley Library Special Collections, Broadlands Papers, BR 11/11/4. Benjamin Mee to Viscount Palmerston, 9 January 1786. Quoted in John McAleer, *Picturing India: People, Places and*

the World of the East India Company (London: British Library, 2017), p. 83.
18. The painting, in the collection of the Yale Center for British Art, is catalogued in Geoff Quilley and John Bonehill (eds), *William Hodges, 1744–1797: The Art of Exploration* (London: National Maritime Museum, 2004), pp. 140–1. On Stourhead's relationship to seventeenth-century landscape painting, see Kenneth Woodbridge, 'The Sacred Landscape: Painters and the Lake Garden of Stourhead', *Apollo* 88 (1968): 210–14.
19. William Hodges, *Travels in India in the Years 1780, 1781, 1782 & 1783* (London, 1793), p. 25.
20. Solkin, *Richard Wilson*, p. 130.
21. Nigel Everett, *The Tory View of Landscape* (New Haven, CT: Yale University Press, 1994).
22. Edmund Burke, 'Speech on Fox's India Bill', p. 393.
23. Everett, *Tory View of Landscape*, p. 39.
24. Steube suggests that this drawing represents a hill village in Bhagalpur on the basis of similarities with an aquatint Hodges published of this subject in his 1787 *Select Views in India* (plate 25). I find these alleged similarities unconvincing, and the drawing crucially lacks the hilly background of the print. See Isabel Combs Stuebe, *The Life and Works of William Hodges* (New York and London: Garland Publishing, 1979), p. 215.
25. The estate can be seen in Mark Wood's 1785 *Survey of the Country on the Eastern Bank of the Hughly, from Calcutta to the Fortifications at Budgebudge* in the British Library (BL Maps K.Top.115.38).
26. Curzon, *British Government in India*, 1: 142.
27. David Arnold, 'Hunger in the Garden of Plenty: The Bengal Famine of 1770', in Alessa Johns (ed.), *Dreadful Visitations: Confronting Natural Catastrophe in the Age of Enlightenment* (New York and London: Routledge, 1999), pp. 81–111.
28. Vinita Damodaran, 'The East India Company, Famine and Ecological Conditions in Eighteenth-Century Bengal', in Vinita Damodaran, Anna Winterbottom and Alan Lester (eds), *The East India Company and the Natural World* (Basingstoke: Palgrave Macmillan, 2015), pp. 81–101.
29. Richard H. Grove, *Green Imperialism: Colonial Expansion, Tropical Island Edens and the Origins of Environmentalism* (Cambridge: Cambridge University Press, 1995), p. 4.
30. Abbé Raynal, *A Philosophical and Political History of the Settlements and Trade of the Europeans in the East and West Indies*, trans. J. Justamond, 2nd edn, 5 vols (London: T. Cadell, 1776), 1: 38.
31. Burke, 'Fox's India Bill', p. 422.
32. Erin Drew, '"'Tis Prudence to Prevent th'Entire Decay": Usufruct and Environmental Thought', *Eighteenth-Century Studies* 49, no. 2 (2016): 195–210.
33. Grove, *Green Imperialism*, p. 2.
34. Arnold, 'Hunger in the Garden of Plenty', p. 93.
35. Hodges, *Travels in India*, p. 27.
36. Kate Teltscher, *India Inscribed: European and British Writing on India, 1600–1800* (Oxford: Oxford University Press, 1995), p. 127.
37. Arnold, 'Hunger in the Garden of Plenty', pp. 94–100.

38. Eliza Fay, *Original Letters from India*, annotated by E. M. Forster, introduced by Simon Winchester (New York: New York Review of Books, 2010), pp. 171–2 [original letter dated 22 May 1780]. On the proliferation of country villas in England, see Daniel Defoe, *A Tour thro' the Whole Island of Great Britain*, 5th edn, 4 vols (London: Birt, 1753), 1: 250–1.
39. Amanda Sciampacone, 'Urban Ruin: James Baillie Fraser's Representation of the Black Hole Memorial of Calcutta', *Third Text* 25, no. 6 (2011): 751–62.
40. Grove, *Green Imperialism*, pp. 332–5.
41. Ibid. pp. 400–1.
42. James Atkinson, *The City of Palaces: A Fragment* (Calcutta: Government Gazette Press, 1824), p. 7.
43. Reginald Heber, *A Narrative of a Journey through the Upper Provinces of India, from Calcutta to Bombay, 1824–1825*, 2 vols (Philadelphia: Carey, Lea & Carey, 1829), 1: 70.
44. David Solkin, 'Re-Wrighting Shaftesbury: The Air-Pump and the Limits of Commercial Humanism', in John Brewer and Susan Staves (eds), *Early Modern Conceptions of* Property (London: Routledge, 1995), p. 239.
45. H. E. Busteed, *Echoes from Old Calcutta, being Reminiscences of the Days of Warren Hastings, Frances and Impey* (London: Thacker, 1908), pp. 119–20.
46. Thomas Strange, *Elements of Hindu Law, referable to British Judicature in India*, 2 vols (London: Payne and Foss, 1825). On the use of Indigenous knowledge in colonial botany, see Grove, *Green Imperialism*.
47. Grove, *Green Imperialism*, p. 13.
48. Rob Nixon, *Slow Violence and the Environmentalism of the Poor* (Cambridge, MA: Harvard University Press, 2011).
49. Paul Warde, *The Invention of Sustainability: Nature and Destiny, c. 1500–1870* (Cambridge: Cambridge University Press, 2018), p. 4.
50. Ibid. p. 8.
51. Ibid. p. 9.
52. Gayatri Chakravorty Spivak, 'Can the Subaltern Speak?', in Lawrence Grossberg and Cary Nelson (eds), *Marxism and the Interpretation of Culture* (Urbana: University of Illinois Press and Basingstoke: Macmillan, 1988), pp. 271–313.
53. On these Dutch paintings and the commodities which appear within them, see Julie Hochstrasser, *Still Life and Trade in the Dutch Golden Age* (New Haven, CT: Yale University Press, 2007).
54. William S. Laufer, 'Accountability and Corporate Greenwashing', *Journal of Business Ethics* 43, no. 3 (2003): 256.
55. The origins of greenwashing (not just as a term, but also as a practice) are conventionally pinpointed to as late as the 1980s. See, for example, Frances Bowen, *After Greenwashing: Symbolic Corporate Environmentalism and Society* (Cambridge: Cambridge University Press, 2014) and Toby Miller, *Greenwashing Culture* (London and New York: Routledge, 2018).

Chapter 6

On the Prowl: Tigers and the Tea Planter in British India

Romita Ray

A tiger's head hangs over a stack of rifles in a tea planter's bungalow in Assam (Fig. 12). In the distance, beyond the bungalow garden, tea pluckers are hard at work. A tangible reminder of the dense jungle out of which plantations were carved in Assam in the nineteenth century, the tiger trophy is indicative of the extent to which plantations remained entangled with the forest in 1945, when this illustration was published.[1] In such terrain, wild animals frequently wandered to the forest edge in search of food and shelter, or into plantations themselves. Perceived as intruders, they were either chased away or killed, and if they happened to be big cats, their skins and heads might be preserved as prized trophies. Growing tea meant coping with the extreme challenges of living in close proximity to the jungle. But as countless colonial photographs and planters' memoirs reveal, these human-animal encounters also had their advantages. Wildlife trophies made colonial heroes out of tea planters, repositioning them as brave *burra sahibs* (great masters)[2] in tea country, where they had successfully conquered the *jungli* – the wild, or the savage.[3] For what could be more impressive than bagging a tiger, that most ferocious of *jungli* predators?

Dead or alive, the tiger drew the *jungli* into the social, cultural and material realities of plantation life. It reiterated hierarchies of race, gender and class that were essential to running a plantation. It earned the planter the respect of his colonial brethren and constituted a point of entry into their orbit of camaraderie. It also gave the planter his personal and very conspicuous badge of honour: an animal trophy that promoted key ideas about masculine identity, while spatialising, visualising and memorialising the performance of his colonial authority. In other words, the tiger trophy enabled the planter to write himself into the topos of tea country by producing new mythologies of the wild that linked him back to the perceived 'wilderness' origins of the 'province of Assam', that place once described as 'covered with jungle and swamp, the abode of the tiger and wild animals of all kinds', which had 'now . . . become the home of an industrious peasantry'.[4] If the tea industry had brought a civilising touch to the jungle, then it had done so by transforming forest into landscape, natives into disciplined workers and tigers into personal memorabilia. After all, the very origins of Assam tea were rooted in the forested expanse of Upper Assam, where an indigenous *jungli* species of tea was found growing wild in the 1820s and 30s. Consumed by the Singhpo and Khamti tribes, the plant only gained complete acceptance after being cultivated under British supervision and fetching a high price at a London auction in 1839.[5] Despite the successful commodification of the plant, however, the animal was less easily tamed.

By the opening decades of the twentieth century, tales of violent confrontations between planters and tigers were the stuff of local legend, the ferocity of human-animal conflict made all the more conspicuous by the desire to photograph, preserve and display the tiger's remains long after the animal had been killed. Even in death, however, the tiger continued to instil some of the sense of fear and wonder it had inspired in life, that famously reclusive predator described by various planters as a 'brute', a 'man-eater' and a creature of 'extraordinary vitality'.[6] How, then, did such a dangerous creature become embedded in the physical and imagined realities of plantation life? How did it position the planter within the landscapes of tea cultivation? Equally importantly, how did its visual representations cement the planter's imaging as a *burra sahib*? While answering these questions, we need to keep in mind the slow yet steady transformation of 'jungly country' into 'tea-gardens' – changes which had been shaped by imperial agendas and capitalist networks that were shot through with Romantic ideas about science, nature and improvement.[7] For it was during the Romantic era that the commercial potential of the indigenous tea plant in Assam came to light, fuelling the need to authenticate the *jungli* plant as a genuine Camellia species (like the Chinese tea plant), and pulling the plant and its organic matter into the discourses and practices of botany. In effect, the Assam tea plant represented the very 'disciplinary and cultural array of practices and commentaries' that now constituted the field of imperial botany in which, as Theresa Kelley notes, 'botanical ideas operated across romantic culture, from taxonomic efforts to identify thousands of plants' to 'philosophical questions about life and agency and poetic and aesthetic notice of plants'.[8]

Key to these 'botanical ideas' in Assam was the jungle, a forbidding yet wondrous terrain filled with natural resources, whose ecologies would be radically rearranged by the tea industry and whose spatial and aesthetic imaginings could be traced back to conceptions of land

and nature in the Romantic era, when the English forest was perceived as a 'profane, eccentric space',[9] 'the lair of thieves' and 'fugitives' – a space where, as Kate Rigby points out, the notion of 'sylvan dwelling ... remained in some sense "savage"'.[10] The very idea of the forest as a place of 'savage' dwellers would intensify in India, where the discourses of empire frequently harnessed the paradigm of the 'savage' to construct the otherness of people and places. In the landscapes of Assam, this would also be applied to the *jungli* plants and animals that were displaced, replaced or simply erased. The Assam jungle mirrored the anxieties, fears and suspicions that revolved around the alien other, its 'savagery' signalled by powerful animals like the tiger whose ferocity rendered it an irrefutable site of mortal danger,[11] in sharp contrast to the English forest where 'the only dangers that one was likely to encounter ... would probably have stemmed from other humans'.[12] Yet, it was this very aspect of the *jungli* that appealed to the Romantic imagination as well as to the desire to harness its commercial potential. As David Arnold observes, Romanticism when combined with 'the doctrines and imagery of capitalism and Christianity ... helped forge a program for change' that 'emphasiz[ed] the need to transform the ruined and debased Indian landscape to create a peaceful and prosperous civilization modeled after an "improved" and industrious Britain'.[13] In order to become a civilised space the jungle had to be tamed, and integral to this was the cultivation of tea, the plant that would change this 'wild, jungle-laden frontier', a place of 'danger, disorder, and vegetative excess',[14] into a zone of 'economic prosperity' for the British empire.[15]

By the 1830s, the fate of the Assam jungle and that of the tiger would be entangled with the quest to authenticate the *jungli* Assam plant as a genuine species of tea. Clearing swathes of forest to create tea plantations also appealed to the desire to improve and manage wasteland, and bring discipline and order to Indigenous communities and animals.[16] Complicating this was the Romantic preoccupation with the thresholds of life and death that were rendered fragile in India by an unfamiliar climate and tropical diseases (including the virulent strain of malaria known as jungle fever) to which many a Briton succumbed throughout the eighteenth and nineteenth centuries.[17] In remote Assam, where it was impossible to avoid the jungle, death ushered in by the *jungli* created numerous opportunities to commemorate the living as well as to reify the distinction between life and death through artefacts like the tiger trophy, which reflected ongoing anxieties about the fragility of the European body in the Indian landscape.

Tigers had long been enmeshed in the fear of an untimely death.[18] This is perhaps best exemplified by the legacy of Hugh Munro, a young lieutenant who was mauled to death by a tiger during a hunting excursion in Bengal in 1792. Widely reported in India and Britain, his gory ending inspired a line of Staffordshire ceramics and the spectacular automaton of a tiger attacking an English soldier once owned by Tipu Sultan.[19] It may even have inspired William Blake's 'The Tyger' (1794), where the animal subject's 'fearful symmetry' and fiery eyes recall contemporary eyewitness accounts of Munro's killer with 'eyes darting fire'.[20] Imagined and reimagined as an agent of death, the tiger disrupted time, place and memory, accentuating, in Chase Pielak's words, 'what it means to be human, what happens at death, what it means to survive death, and what it means to be remembered'.[21] If poets and novelists in the Romantic period harnessed the tiger's capacity to rearrange spatial, temporal and ontological boundaries, then painters, sculptors and printmakers from Britain and Europe – Blake, George Stubbs, James Ward, Antoine-Louis Barye and Eugène Delacroix – frequently deployed the tiger to visualise the spectacle of death, their emphasis on the dissolution of the body and the intensity of dying fuelling the taste of the time for 'tragedy, torment, and violence'.[22]

Strikingly, their images were bound up with colonial bodies brought back to Europe, either as living specimens or as visual records created by other artists who had visited India and Africa. Recalibrated through these corporeal traces, the primeval was mobilised in such a way as to tantalise viewers with the anticipation of a bloody and spectacular death: tigers attacking gavials, horses, lions and women; tigers twisting and turning in space, sinking their teeth into their victims. Natural history authors also played a part in firing up the Romantic imagination by sensationalising the tiger as 'the most rapacious and destructive of all carnivorous animals',[23] while artists like Edward Armitage had Britannia lunging with sword in hand at a writhing Bengal tiger in her grip in his painting titled *Retribution* (1858). A response to the Indian Rebellion of 1857, Armitage's picture emphasised the ferocious beast as a symbol of India, thus adding one more arresting image to many others of the 'savageness and butchery' of the Indian 'native'[24] that proliferated following the massacre of British women and children at Kanpur by Indian soldiers. By then, killing a tiger was considered tantamount to conquering all that was considered primitive about the Indian subcontinent.[25]

But while paintings like Armitage's were fictitious representations of a distant India, a tiger trophy embodied the raw violence of a first-hand encounter with the Indian landscape. As such, it brought home the complex sensory registers of human experience even as it drew attention to what W. J. T. Mitchell calls a 'heightened perception of thingness – of materiality, physicality, objecthood'.[26] It was in the Romantic period that the understanding of the world on both local and global levels came to be defined by imports of plants and animals, their ontologies articulating new expectations of what it meant to be British at home and abroad. These exotica would generate intellectual inquiry and aesthetic imaginings, their bodies and body parts endorsing biology as the new 'frontier of science' alongside 'new forms of archaic and modern animism' that added layers of meaning and purpose to human life.[27] Against this backdrop, the tiger trophy coaxes us to contemplate the finality of the kill and the meaning of death in colonial places. At the very least it gives us pause to admire the handiwork of a skilful taxidermist, its remnants of fur and skin a far cry perhaps from the Romantic fantasies that European artists had created in their works, but no less brutal in the imaginaries they presented to viewers.

Here was something hard-won from the jungle, from an entity long mythologised as a cunning beast, a supernatural creature and a divine animal.[28] In the tiger's material transformation and visual imaging, therefore, we can trace something far more compelling and mystifying than a strictly rational engagement with the wild. For in its physical remains lies the conquest of the very primeval essence of the Assam jungle, one that invested the tiger with what Jonas Frykman and Maja Povrzanović Frykman have described as the 'affective charge of history, politics, and place',[29] which underscored in turn a profound longing for the *jungli*. And so, this essay returns first to the Assam jungle, that natural habitat of the tiger as well as daunting frontier where – according to the tea planter, hunter and ardent conservationist Edward Pritchard Gee – '[i]f one loses one's way ... there is little chance of returning'.[30] It was here that the tiger's mystique was cemented by the fear of the unknown that the jungle elicited. Next, I will turn to the tiger inside the plantation, where it posed a direct threat to the planter, labourer and domestic animal, its presence unsettling the quotidian rhythms of plantation life, its death infusing the planter with an aura of invincibility. Finally, I will analyse how the tiger trophy embedded the *jungli* in the domestic spaces of the plantation, its materiality inscribing the ways in which the Assam jungle tested the physical and psychological limits of the colonial body. Running through my discussion are the Romantic ideas about life, death and the 'savage' that became inseparable from readings of the tiger and jungle as they were reiterated by different generations of planters well into the twentieth century.

The Jungle

The mystique of Assam tea was first planted in the British imagination when a wild species of the tea plant was reported growing in the dense, forested expanse of Upper Assam. By 1835, Governor General Lord William Bentinck had dispatched a scientific expedition to explore the area with the explicit goal of authenticating the indigenous tea plant.[31] If found to be genuine, recommendations might be made for its cultivation. But first, there was the jungle, a thick, 'vast and fever-infested' frontier that was difficult to navigate, parts of it so bewilderingly dense that the young botanist William Griffith was compelled to note that it was unlike any other forest he had ever encountered.[32] The forest grew larger than life during the expedition, proving also to be a veritable treasure trove of exotic flora and fauna. Here, after remarking earlier in his journal that tigers were 'frequent' where 'large and small game abound[ed]' near Tezpur, Griffith would eventually stumble upon 'the tracks of a Tiger'.[33] Overlapping with tiger terrain, the physical and sensory geographies of the wild tea plant constituted an unstable threshold where the savage was interwoven with the benign: one signalled extreme danger whereas the other promised immense commercial profit. No two worlds could have been further apart, yet here they were together in the Assam jungle, each defining the *jungli* in different ways in the British imagination.

As K. Sivaramakrishnan reminds us, the 'work of the imagination' in colonial knowledge and place-making was labourious and time-consuming, its contours shaped through the 'forms it took in epistolary, scientific, and bureaucratic writing'.[34] Add to this artistic inscriptions and material objects whose workings were rooted in the body's ability to navigate space, time and memory both past and present. Imagination brought science to life and in this respect, it was charged with a characteristically Romantic emphasis on feeling, intuition and voice. Such an ontological approach could of course be deeply unsettling, especially considering the radically different environment of the Assam jungle that might well 'dislodge the certainty of self'.[35] In their quest to find *Thea assamica*, the members of the tea expedition unearthed far more about the jungle than they had anticipated. Immersed in a seemingly unending expanse of *jungli* flora and fauna, they had effectively entered the realm of the primordial, in which the tiger's muddy paw print was a stark reminder of the dangers that lay ahead.

How could tea be grown in such a formidable landscape? As William Prinsep, the Calcutta-based director of the Assam Company,[36] observed of Assam in 1841, the jungle 'prevailed everywhere', its density and scale posing serious challenges to the fledgling tea industry, which had to contend with the onslaught of 'abundant' 'wild beasts' that made the area dangerous to navigate, let alone to cultivate.[37] As the jungle was cleared to create the earliest plantations in the 1840s, wild animals were hunted far and wide, their decimation reaching an unprecedented scale in the 1860s and 70s when cash incentives were handed out for exterminating dangerous beasts.[38] In 1870 the Assam administration was offering five rupees to kill a tiger, with one army officer going as far as recommending spring guns be placed strategically along tiger trails in the forest.[39] The newly instituted Forest Department (1868) and the Indian Forest Act of 1878, which were meant to protect the forest, did little to deter the indiscriminate slaughter of wild animals even as the tea industry expanded in this north-eastern corner of India.[40] The Assam Forest Regulation Act of 1931 extended the government's hold to all of Assam's forests, and large tracts of land were given over to agricultural development, leading to a fresh wave of depleting wildlife.[41]

At the end of the nineteenth century, Assam was widely recognized as 'the best country in the world for affording every kind of big game shooting'[42] and the Brahmaputra valley had emerged as a favourite hunting ground for tea planters.[43] As the jungle was reduced, it became more accessible, rendering wild animals more visible and vulnerable than they had ever been before. The Romantic-era interest in the tropical wilderness as a space for imagining and inscribing human courage and curiosity was now a reality, making its way into the Indian jungle through colonial policies that formalised relations between land and nature, directly impacting the fate of the non-human occupants of the Assam jungle. Big game hunting aside, conflicts with tigers also took place in villages and labour lines situated near the jungle. Emerging from the forest in search of prey, tigers killed domestic animals and humans in these communities, the multi-spatial and multi-temporal dimensions of the confrontations confirming the uncertainties of life in such liminal territory.[44] At best, human-animal encounters resulted in the thrill of killing and bagging the beast, but more often than not a tiger's appearance resulted in fatalities and financial headaches. As Frank Nicholls observed, a 'planter's life can be very harassing when he is called upon to protect his labour from the attacks of leopards, tigers and elephants. The rhythm of work on his garden can be badly disrupted, and serious financial losses sustained thereby if the labourers are disturbed or even refuse to work, as has often been the case.'[45]

A planter's life was not for the faint-hearted. As Lieutenant Colonel Pollok, who tried his hand at tea-planting for a few years, advised, 'no man' should 'go in for a tea-garden unless he can look after it himself'.

This included 'spend[ing] three to four hours prowling about his garden' in the early hours of the morning with 'his gun, as he is almost sure to see jungle-fowl, pheasants, perhaps deer, and occasionally bears, pig, and more rarely perhaps a tiger, leopard, elephant, bison, or buffaloes'.[46] No other animal was as feared inside the plantation as the tiger. Mysterious and unpredictable like its natural habitat, the dreaded predator might well constitute a point of no return. Its very entry caused chaos, the disarray it left behind challenging the authority of the planter-in-charge, as the Victorian planter George Barker discovered when he was awakened 'in the middle of the night' by the cry of 'Barg, barg (tiger)':

> There is not a moment to be lost if the horses are to be saved. A light is secured, rifles, together with all the odd firearms that can be speedily collected together, are distributed, and the procession starts for the stables in the following order. First the sahib, behind him the light-bearer, succeeded a few yards off by the chowkeydar with a gun; then, some considerable distance in the rear, the establishment armed with anything handy, slowly come after.[47]

In the inky darkness of the night, the plantation throbs with tension. Unable to see the tiger yet acutely aware of its proximity, Barker's hunting instincts intensify as he tries to control the situation. The tiger's presence signals the anticipation of violence and the disruption of a well-managed landscape. Modern technology comes to the rescue: if the wilderness posed a threat, it could be systematically erased with the necessary guns and ammunition.[48] The affective power of the tiger, in this instance, relies not just upon its fearful symmetry (to borrow from Blake), but equally so upon the guns that Barker and his staff deploy to launch their assault on the predator.

An agent of death, the gun brings into sharp relief its capacity to bring the human body to a state of high alert when faced with grave danger. For Barker and his staff, the weapons of the planter and his staff also unite them as they prepare to kill the tiger. As the band of men draw closer to their target, the gun makes palpable their collective anxiety and the impending reality of the tiger's death. Here, I want to turn to Charles Fruehling Springwood's observation that firearms are fundamentally 'killing machines'. When 'grasped by a person, these killing machines insinuate themselves into the desiring and *gendered* body of the would-be shooter, and a new machine emerges'.[49] Merged with the human body, the gun draws out the atavistic tendencies of its holder, the act of aiming a gun and releasing the fatal bullets that sink into the tiger's flesh taming the fear and fascination inspired by the beast. Soon after the tiger was killed, it was measured, skinned and turned into an animal trophy, its affective power transferred from the living being to the inanimate artefact. To borrow from Pielak, the trophy embodies 'the trajectory from life to memory'.[50] Thus, the *jungli* becomes inseparable from the gun.

Inside the Plantation

With rifle in hand and one foot atop a dead tiger, Frank Nicholls stands in front of the camera (Fig. 13), his picture invoking countless other images of maharajas, viceroys and the occasional British royal posed with animal spoils at their feet.[51] The photograph also harks back to Stuart, Georgian and Romantic-era portraits of aristocratic hunters whose animal spoils were irrefutable signs of their landed wealth.[52] Like the Indian and British elite who were depicted as the natural custodians of the flora and fauna of the land they owned, Nicholls's conveys similar messages about power and masculine authority. While planters were neither royals nor members of the landed elite, in the eyes of their staff and labourers, their stewardship of acres of land and their superior position in the plantation hierarchy made them all-powerful figures.[53] It was a perception reinforced by them hunting and posing with their tiger trophies, their choreographed displays of masculinity appropriating the visual strategies deployed by the ruling classes to accentuate their mystique.

The ferocious feline stretched at his feet along with the rifle in his hand also reified Nicholls's aura of invincibility.[54] Weighing nearly six hundred pounds, the full-grown tiger was a daunting predator that challenged the skills and stamina of the most experienced of hunters.[55] Its ferocity was legendary and its image, so rooted in the iconography of Hindu gods and Indian royals, bestowed upon it a regal – if not divine – air.[56] Vanquishing a tiger was therefore enough to seal a person's reputation as a fearless *shikari* (hunter), the tiger's death itself a means of repudiating the fear of one's own mortality in a remote corner of the Indian empire. Why draw the *jungli* then (albeit as a lifeless form) into the confines of the plantation? As Michael Taussig reminds us, the 'savagery of the forest is contagious[.] Like a sponge the succulent jungle absorbs and magnifies human passion.'[57] Deposited in the plantation, the dead tiger continues to signal the 'human passion' for *shikar* (the hunt) and for acquiring something as spectacular from the jungle as an adult tiger. This also meant that the *jungli* had to be recalibrated on human terms and on a human scale. With its roar silenced and its ferocity terminated, the tiger's limp body transformed into a cultural artefact reveals the urge to convert the wild into something more controllable.

Death becomes a figment of the imagination as the dead tiger at Nicholls's feet invites the viewer to imagine both the tiger's brutal ending and the planter's courage while facing the possibility of his own death. Such mediations of death in life cycle back to the Romantic preoccupation with death and renewal, which is now repackaged to acknowledge the loss of the *jungli* and to reinstate the wild through a carefully curated display of masculinity before the camera. Coaxing us to take in the planter's unscathed body, the most credible sign of Nicholls's impressive victory, the photograph emphasises his unharmed, physical state that promotes his dexterity as a *shikari* who had triumphed over the *jungli*, the gun at his side drawing attention to his ability to take on such a deadly beast. What then do we make of the camera, the instrument trained on the tiger's body to 'shoot' a picture? It is worth mentioning here that by this time, big-game photography had evolved into a visual sport, with the colonial forester Frederick Champion promoting it as a viable alternative to killing wild animals. 'It provides all the excitement of the stalk', assured Champion, 'and the pitting of one's wits against those of the ever-alert inhabitants of the jungle.'[58] In effect, the camera was increasingly implicated in the complex dynamics of preserving the visual experience of wildlife, be it inside the jungle where it replaced the gun, or inside the plantation where it commemorated the violence inflicted upon the animal by the gun.

This brings me to the bungalow garden where the tiger's body was put on display for the camera. An ornamental space attached to the planter's bungalow, the garden instantly draws attention to the animal as a dislocated thing away from its *jungli* habitat. A retinue of servants ensured that Nicholls was photographed without any hindrance. Although they are left out of the picture, glimpses of their labour are everywhere: from the animal's corpse positioned in a well-chosen spot on the manicured lawn to the pruned flowerbeds and bush behind Nicholls. It was in the garden too that identifiably British leisurely activities like croquet, badminton, tea parties and gardening took place within the white colonial planting community, and where strict racial and cultural divisions were maintained between the planter, his family and the Indian servants. Only the Indian staff who worked in the planter's bungalow could access the garden, which remained off limits to other plantation labourers. As such, the garden drew a crucial boundary between the commercial life of the plantation and the social life of the plantocracy. In so stridently British a colonial domain, the indigene was undeniably the outsider. Not surprisingly, therefore, the tiger – the most indigenous of indigenes – was isolated as a foreign object.[59]

While the garden might stage the tiger as an alien thing, the camera facilitates the visual memorialisation of the tiger's otherness and embeds its alterity within the material and social realities of the plantation. After all, it is the camera that accentuates the tiger's value as a wildlife acquisition (something that belongs to Nicholls) even as it draws our attention to its dislocated wildness (something that belongs in the jungle). Thus, the very act of photographing situates the tiger as the locus of death, desire and belonging, while the photograph itself makes visible a famously elusive animal. As Matthew Brower explains, 'photographs show us animals we could not normally see'.[60] Photographs also show us how wild animals might be remembered by invoking the very traces of their lived existence. Every animal trophy photographed was personal memorabilia that evoked an incident which had taken place at a specific time and a specific site. 'A tigress shot in 1936. It had sprung upon a woman with her two small children washing clothes at the side of the Borgang River.'[61] The caption accompanying Nicholls's photograph in the planter's memoir takes us straight to the place where the animal had been found, some twenty kilometres away from the plantations that Nicholls managed for the Borgang Tea Company.[62] In as much as photography enshrined the tiger, it also memorialised the very spaces of confrontation and death.

If photographs translated human-animal encounters into accessible glimpses, stuffed animal heads and skins transformed bungalow interiors into galleries of conquest. Draped on walls, spread on floors and displayed on pedestals, these traces of once living wild animals complemented the wood, mud, rattan cane and jungle grass that were culled from the forest to construct the planter's traditional *chang* bungalow.[63] No matter where one looked, the *jungli* held sway in the planter's residence. Wild skins therefore produced a visual circuit of power that maintained the planter at the top of plantation society. The trophy memorialised the planter's contribution to the industry to which he belonged. It connected him to the planters who had come before him and forged a legacy for those who would follow in his footsteps. Every stuffed head, every wild skin up on the wall was a constellation of time, memory and space that asserted the white, predominantly male plantocracy's ability to survive and prosper in the *jungli* frontiers of the empire. Thus, animal trophies adorned as well the walls of the clubhouses frequented by planters: the billiards room, bar and dining and smoking rooms where the planter community converged and bonded in tea country.

If, as Harriet Ritvo asserts, 'ferocious wild animals' represent 'what seems most threatening about the natural world', then it follows that wildlife trophies might be destabilising objects that disconcert the viewer.[64] For white manhood to be asserted in remote tea country, it was essential that the fear of the wilderness be kept alive. Part sculpture and part still life, their skins stretched over manikins, trophies did precisely that. For it was in their material makeover that the fear of the *jungli* was writ large. The tiger head was almost always presented jaws agape, to suggest the fierce roar unleashed during its confrontation with the hunter. In death, as in life, the tiger had to be brutal. And it is in this macabre visual echo of its former self that the tiger trophy preserved the deep-seated fear and awe of the jungle in which tea plantations continue to be nestled in the twenty-first century.

To conclude, the tiger trophy was a concrete fragment of the complex biodiversity of the jungle. In the tea country of Assam, it challenged the boundary between forest and plantation by drawing the jungle into the man-made landscapes of tea estates where it shaped the scopic regimes that validated the planter's authority. The tiger trophy may have functioned as a badge of honour, but its silent roar also indexed the very real human fear of being subsumed by the wild. As human and non-human worlds collided, the planter was forced to reconcile the jungle with the plantation and the *jungli* with the human. Such mediations were rooted in the Romantic period when the tea industry was first developed in the forested expanse of Assam, and when the longing for the primordial was cemented by colonial flows of knowledge about Indigenous peoples, spaces, and flora and fauna. Settling into images and literary musings inspired by colonial bodies and spaces, the primordial became sedimented in the Romantic imagination, where it created a profound preoccupation with life and death even as its lived realities in tea country were played out in human-animal encounters like the tiger hunt. In the mixed terrain of plantation and jungle, the primordial invested the tiger's corpse with an affective power that when drawn into the planter's orbit, framed the planter's body as a triumphant sign of survival. Simply put, the image of the tiger was deployed to enhance the masculine authority of the *burra sahib* over the plantation labourer while earning him the respect and camaraderie of his colonial brethren. For its part, the tiger trophy drew out the primordial in the planter-hunter, bringing into sharp focus the very foreignness of being British in colonial-era Assam.

Notes

1. Jacket cover illustration, A. R. Ramsden, *Assam Planter: Tea Planting and Hunting in the Assam Jungle* (London: John Gifford, 1945).

2. Henry Yule and A. C. Burnell, *Hobson-Jobson: The Anglo-Indian Dictionary* (Hertfordshire: Wordsworth Editions, [1886] 1996), p. 132.
3. I use the term *jungli* throughout this essay because it was a vernacular term appropriated by colonial botanists, writers and administrators to characterise the wild and the savage, be it with regard to the jungle or the Indigenous body. As Jayeeta Sharma notes, the term 'blended indigenous notions of primitiveness and civilization with western typologies borrowed from race science', in *Empire's Garden: Assam and the Making of India* (Durham, NC and London: Duke University Press, 2011), p. 31.
4. Captain J. Shakespear, 'The Lushais and the Land They Live In', *Journal of the Society of Arts* 43, no. 2,201 (1895): 204.
5. Andrew Charlton, *Correspondence Regarding the Discovery of the Tea Plant of Assam* (Calcutta: Printed by E. P. de Beaufort, 1841), p. 3; George Watt, *A Dictionary of Economic Products of India*, vol. 6, part 3 (Calcutta: Office of the Superintendent of Government Printing, 1893), pp. 429–34; Sharma, *Empire's Garden*, pp. 30–2.
6. J. R. S. C., 'Killing an Assam Tiger', in *Chatterbox*, ed. J. Erskine Clarke (Boston: Dana Estes and Company, 1902), p. 276; Frank Sheffield, *How I Killed the Tiger: Being an Account of my Encounter with a Royal Bengal Tiger. With an Appendix Containing Some General Information about India* (London: Frank Sheffield, 1902), p. 13; Reginald George Burton, *A Book of Man-Eaters* (Delhi: Mittal Publications, [1936] 1984), p. 146.
7. John Lindley, 'On Substances Used as Food, Illustrated by the Great Exhibition', in William Whewell et al., *Lectures on the Progress of Arts and Science, Resulting from the Great Exhibition in London, Delivered Before the Society of Arts, Manufactures, and Commerce* (New York: A. S. Barnes, 1856), p. 174; A. C. Newcombe, *Village, Town, and Jungle Life in India* (Edinburgh: William Blackwood, 1905), p. 281.
8. Theresa M. Kelley, *Clandestine Marriage: Botany and Romantic Culture* (Baltimore: Johns Hopkins University Press, 2012), p. 7.
9. Robert Pogue Harrison, *Forests: The Shadow of Civilization* (Chicago: University of Chicago Press, 1992), p. 165.
10. Kate Rigby, *Topographies of the Sacred: The Poetics of Place in European Romanticism* (Charlottesville: University of Virginia Press, 2004), p. 234.
11. On the subject of the tiger defining the jungle as a formidable frontier, see Ranjan Chakrabarti, 'Reading the Government Reports and the European Memoirs: Glimpses of Hunting or *Shikar* in Colonial India', in Ranjan Chakrabarti (ed.), *Does Environmental History Matter? Shikar, Subsistence, Sustenance, and the Sciences* (Kolkata: Readers Service, 2006), pp. 185–221.
12. Rigby, *Topographies of the Sacred*, p. 231.
13. David Arnold, *The Tropics and the Traveling Gaze: India, Landscape, and Science, 1800–1856* (Seattle: University of Washington Press, 2006), p. 75.
14. Ibid. p. 81.
15. Sharma, *Empire's Garden*, p. 3.
16. Rajib Handique, *British Forest Policy in Assam* (New Delhi: Concept Publishing Company, 2004), p. 39; Sarah Hilaly, 'Imagining Colonial Assam: The Figuring of "Wastelands" in its Making', *Economic and Political Weekly* 51, no. 3 (2016): 55–62. As Handique explains, the

term 'wasteland' was used for 'uncultivated' and 'unsettled' land that did not produce any 'revenue' for the imperial government. It comprised 'forests and highland' with 'extensive high reed and grass' as well as 'grasslands'.
17. Arnold, *Tropics and the Traveling Gaze*, p. 54; Sujata Mukherjee, 'Environmental Thoughts and Malaria in Colonial Bengal: A Study in Social Response', *Economic and Political Weekly* 43, nos 12–13 (2008): 54–61.
18. Dane Kennedy, 'T is for Tiger', in Antoinette Burton and Renisa Mawani (eds), *Animalia: An Anti-Imperial Bestiary for Our Times* (Durham, NC: Duke University Press, 2020), pp. 171–7.
19. Examples of the Staffordshire porcelain pieces can be found in the collections of the Metropolitan Museum of Art (New York City), the Victoria and Albert Museum (London) and the National Army Museum (London). Popularly known as 'Tipu's Tiger', the automaton can be seen today in the Victoria and Albert Museum. For more about the Staffordshire pieces, see John M. MacKenzie, *The Empire of Nature: Hunting, Conservation, and British Imperialism* (Manchester: Manchester University Press, 1988), p. 179. For 'Tipu's Tiger', see Mildred Archer, *Tippoo's Tiger* (London: H. M. Stationary Office, 1959).
20. Colin Pedley, 'Blake's Tiger and the Discourse of Natural History', *Blake/ An Illustrated Quarterly* 24, no. 1 (1990): 238–46. The eyewitness account of Munro's death was widely disseminated in the newspapers of the time.
21. Chase Pielak, *Memorializing Animals During the Romantic Period* (New York: Routledge, 2016), p. 6.
22. Colta Ives, 'Eugène Delacroix', in Colta Ives and Elizabeth E. Barker, *Romanticism and the School of Nature: Nineteenth-Century Drawings and Paintings from the Karen B. Cohen Collection* (New York: The Metropolitan Museum of Art, 2000), pp. 76–8.
23. Thomas Bewick, *General History of Quadrupeds* (London: Robinson, [1790] 1800), p. 206. For a discussion of tigers in the latter half of the nineteenth century, see Ralph Crane and Lisa Fletcher, 'Picturing the Indian Tiger: Imperial Iconography in the Nineteenth Century', *Victorian Literature and Culture* 42 (2014): 369–86.
24. Ann C. Colley, *Wild Animal Skins in Victorian Britain* (Surrey: Ashgate, 2014), p. 95. Armitage's *Retribution* (1858) is now in the collection of the Leeds Art Gallery. The preliminary drawing for the picture is at the Yale Center for British Art.
25. Joseph Sramek, '"Face Him Like a Briton": Tiger Hunting, Imperialism, and British Masculinity in Colonial India, 1800–1875', *Victorian Studies* 48, no. 4 (2006): 660; MacKenzie, *Empire of Nature*, pp. 17–23 and 80.
26. W. J. T. Mitchell, 'Romanticism and the Life of Things: Fossils, Totems, and Images', *Critical Inquiry* 28, no. 1 (2001): 173.
27. Ibid. p. 173.
28. Patrick Newman, *Tracking the Weretiger: Supernatural Man-Eaters of India, China, and Southeast Asia* (Jefferson, NC: McFarland, 2012), pp. 3–8 and 135–66.
29. Jonas Frykman and Maja Povrzanović Frykman, 'Affect and Material Culture: Perspectives and Strategies', in Jonas Frykman and Maja

Povrzanović Frykman (eds), *Sensitive Objects: Affect and Material Culture* (Lund: Nordic Academic Press, 2016), p. 18.
30. E. P. Gee, *The Wild Life of India* (New York: Dutton, 1964), p. 12.
31. Lord Bentinck created an official Tea Committee in 1834 to examine the possibility of cultivating tea in India. The tea expedition to Assam was a direct outcome of that Committee. Sharma, *Empire's Garden*, 29–32; 'Cultivation of the Tea-Plant in Assam-II', *The Penny Magazine of the Society for the Diffusion of Useful Knowledge* 506 (1840): 71.
32. H. A. Antrobus, *A History of the Assam Company, 1839–1953* (Edinburgh: Constable, 1957), p. 2; William Griffith, *Posthumous Papers Bequeathed to the Honorable The East India Company, and Printed by Order of the Government of Bengal. Journals of Travels in Assam, Burma, Bootan, Affghanistan and the Neighbouring Countries* (Calcutta: Bishop's College Press, 1847), p. 14.
33. Griffith, *Posthumous Papers*, pp. 13 and 79.
34. K. Sivaramakrishnan, 'Science, Environment and Empire History: Comparative Perspectives from Forests in Colonial India', *Environment and History* 14 (2008): 47.
35. Felix Driver and Luciana Martins, 'Views and Visions of the Tropical World', in Felix Driver and Luciana Martins (eds), *Tropical Visions in an Age of Empire* (Chicago: University of Chicago Press, 2005), p. 7.
36. Established in 1839, the Assam Company was one of the earliest colonial tea companies. It was formed by merging the Calcutta-based Bengal Tea Association with the London-based Assam Company. The former was created by a group of merchants including Prinsep (who hailed from a prominent Anglo-Indian family) and Dwarkanath Tagore, scion of a prominent Bengali merchant family; the latter was a joint-stock company formed by a group of merchants in London. Sharma, *Empire's Garden*, p. 32.
37. William Prinsep, *Autobiographical Memoir*, vol. 3 (1838–1842), British Library, Mss Eur D1160/3, p. 153.
38. Handique, *British Forest Policy in Assam*, pp. 37–8.
39. Arupjyoti Saikia, *Forests and Ecological History of Assam, 1826–2000* (New Delhi: Oxford University Press, 2011), pp. 256–7.
40. Ibid. pp. 114–21.
41. Ibid. p. 257.
42. George M. Barker, *A Tea Planter's Life in Assam* (Calcutta: Thacker and Spink, 1884), p. 90.
43. Saikia, *Forests and Ecological History of Assam*, p. 260.
44. For one such account, see J. R. S. C., 'Killing an Assam Tiger', pp. 276–8.
45. Frank Nicholls, *Assam Shikari: A Tea Planter's Story of Hunting and High Adventure in the Jungles of North East India* (Auckland: Tonson Publishing House, 1970), p. 33.
46. Lieutenant Colonel Pollok, *Sport in British Burmah, Assam, and the Cassyah and Jyntiah Hills: With Notes of Sport in the Hilly Districts of the Northern Division, Madras Presidency, Indicating the Best Localities in those Countries for Sport, With Natural History Notes, Illustrations of the People, Scenery, and Game, Together with Maps to Guide the Traveller or Sportsman, and Hints on Weapons, Fishing-Tackle, etc., Best Suited for*

Killing Game Met With in Those Provinces, 2 vols (London: Chapman and Hall, 1879), 2: 69–70.
47. Barker, *Planter's Life*, p. 211.
48. Guns designed to shoot specific animals like tigers and elephants were manufactured by Manton and Company of 13 Old Court House Street in Calcutta; specific examples were displayed at the Calcutta International Exhibition of 1883–4. Also on display was a gold 'arm-gun, formerly used for tiger hunting', valued at 'Rs. 10', from Tanjore. *Official Report of the Calcutta International Exhibition, 1883-84: Compiled Under the Orders of the Executive Committee*, 2 vols (Calcutta: Bengal Secretariat Press, 1885), 2: 493 and 701.
49. Charles Fruehling Springwood, 'Gun Concealment, Display, and Other Magical Habits of the Body', *Critique of Anthropology* 34, no. 4 (2014): 459. Italics are Springwood's.
50. Pielak, *Memorializing Animals*, 4.
51. It is worth noting here that Indian history abounds with fables of kings and emperors who were famous huntsmen. The Mughal emperor Akbar, for instance, was lauded by his vizier Abu'l Fazl as a benevolent hunter. Anand S. Pandian, 'Predatory Care: The Imperial Hunt in Mughal and British India', *Journal of Historical Sociology* 14, no. 1 (2001): 89–91. An elaborate and expensive affair, the royal tiger hunt involved a retinue of trained elephants, Indian *shikaris* (hunters), gun-bearers, beaters, cooks, bheesties (water-bearers), dhobis (washermen), blacksmiths, porters, and mahouts, and a host of other servants who were tasked with setting up tents, washing dishes and taking care of supplies. Simply put, it was a tradition that only the elite could afford, its complex social hierarchies and rituals shoring up the spectacle of authority that it was meant to promote. James Moray Brown, *Shikar Sketches: With Notes on Indian Field-Sports* (London: Hurst and Blackett, Publishers, 1887), 156; William K. Storey, 'Big Cats and Imperialism: Lion and Tiger Hunting in Kenya and Northern India, 1898–1930', *Journal of World History* 2, no. 2 (1991): 135–73.
52. Robert Peake the Elder (1551–1619), Sir Anthony Van Dyck (1599–1641), Sir Peter Lely (1618–80), John Wootton (1686–1765), Thomas Gainsborough (1727–88), Sir Joseph Wright of Derby (1734–97), Sir Nathanial Dance-Holland (1735–1811) and Edwin Landseer (1802–73), among many other acclaimed artists, depicted British royals and the landed elite at their hunting best.
53. According to George Watt, 'most gardens average 500 acres, the larger concerns owning 2,000, 3,000, and even 10,000 acres'. Watt, *Pests and Blight of the Tea Plant*, p. 9.
54. Nicholls managed the Borgang, Kettela and Rangaghur tea estates for the Borgang Tea Company.
55. Frank Nicholls, *Assam Shikari*, p. 28.
56. The god Shiva meditates while seated on a tiger skin; the triumphant goddess Durga or Jagaddhatri rides atop a snarling tiger; and tiger stripes were emblazoned across the banners, seals and insignia of Tipu Sultan and several Hindu Rajput kings.
57. Michael Taussig, *Shamanism, Colonialism, and the Wild Man: A Study in Terror and Healing* (Chicago: University of Chicago Press, 1987), pp. 76–7.

58. Frederick Walter Champion, *With a Camera in Tiger-Land* (London: Chatto and Windus, 1928), p. xi.
59. Even the grass upon which the tigress is displayed was planted from seeds imported from nurseries in Calcutta to create the verdant lawn, that quintessential British garden feature. Judith Roberts, 'English Gardens in India', *Garden History* 26, no. 2 (1998): 122–3.
60. Matthew Brower, '"Take Only Photographs": Animal Photograph's Construction of Nature Love', *Invisible Culture: An Electronic Journal for Visual Culture* 9 (2005): <http://www.itc.rochester.edu/in_visible_culture/Issue_9/issue9_brower.pdf>.
61. Nicholls, *Assam Shikari*, n.p., figure 16.
62. Nicholls also shot a leopard, which had attacked 'eight labourer's goats' near the same river. Nicholls, *Assam Shikari*, n.p., figure 15.
63. Barker, *Planter's Life*, pp. 94–7.
64. Harriet Ritvo, 'Beasts in the Jungle', *Daedalus* 137, no. 2 (2008): pp. 22–3.

Figure 1   Mei Leng, *Bishu Shanzhuang* [Mountain Resort to Escape the Heat], 1713. © The Palace Museum, Beijing. See p. 23.

Figure 2   Giuseppe Castiglione (aka Shining Lang), *Xieqiqu Nanmian* [South Façade of the Palace of Delightful Harmony], 1785. Copper Engraving. © The National Information Study Institute Digital Archive, Toyo Bunko, Tokyo. See p. 29.

Figure 3 Cantonese merchant's house from William Chambers, *Designs of Chinese Buildings* (London: printed for the author, 1757), plate ix. Engraving by Edward Rooker. Public domain. See p. 41.

Figure 4 William Marlow, *View of the Wilderness at Kew*, 1763. Watercolour. © Metropolitan Museum of Art, 25.19.43. See p. 46.

Figure 5   William Hodges, *View of Warren Hastings' House at Alipur and Two Figures in the Foreground*, c. 1781–3. Drawing and watercolour. Yale Center for British Art, Paul Mellon Collection. See p. 97.

Figure 6   William Hodges, *Natives drawing Water from a Pond with Warren Hastings' House at Alipur in the Distance*, c. 1781. Oil on canvas. Private collection. See p. 97.

Figure 7   Richard Wilson, *Dinas Bran from Llangollen*, 1770–1. Oil on canvas. Yale Center for British Art, Paul Mellon Collection. See p. 98.

Figure 8   William Hodges, *View of an Indian Village with a Man Seated in the Foreground*, c. 1781–3. Gray wash, pen and black ink and graphite on laid paper. Yale Center for British Art, Paul Mellon Collection. See p. 99.

Figure 9   James Baillie Fraser, 'A View of the Botanic Garden House and Reach' from *Views of Calcutta and its Environs* (London: Smith, Elder & Co., 1826). Coloured aquatint. © The British Library Board, X644(4). See p. 102.

Figure 10   John Young Porter, *Palladian Garden House in a Wooded Park*, 1811. Watercolour on paper. © The British Library Board, WD4417. See p. 104.

Figure 11 John Closterman, *Maurice Ashley-Cooper and Antony Ashley-Cooper, 3rd Earl of Shaftesbury*, c. 1700–1. Oil on canvas. © National Portrait Gallery, London. See p. 104.

Figure 12 Jacket cover illustration, A. R. Ramsden, *Assam Planter: Tea Planting and Hunting in the Assam Jungle* (London: John Gifford, 1945). Author's private collection. See p. 113.

Figure 13 Frank Nicholls with Tigress shot at Borgang River, Assam, 1936. Reproduced in Frank Nicholls, *Assam Shikari: A Tea Planter's Story of Hunting and High Adventure in the Jungles of North East India* (Auckland: Tonson, 1970), figure 16. Author's private collection. See p. 121.

Figure 14 Map of The Leasowes from Robert Dodsley's 'A Description of the Leasowes', *The Works in Verse and Prose of William Shenstone*, 3 vols (London: Dodsley, 1764–9), II: facing page 333. Engraving. Author's private collection. See p. 160.

Figure 15 'Wolverhampton from the Penn Road', from William West, *Picturesque Views in Staffordshire* (Birmingham: Emans, 1834), plate v. Engraving by T. Radclyffe after Frederick Calvert's drawing. © The Bodleian Library. See p. 179.

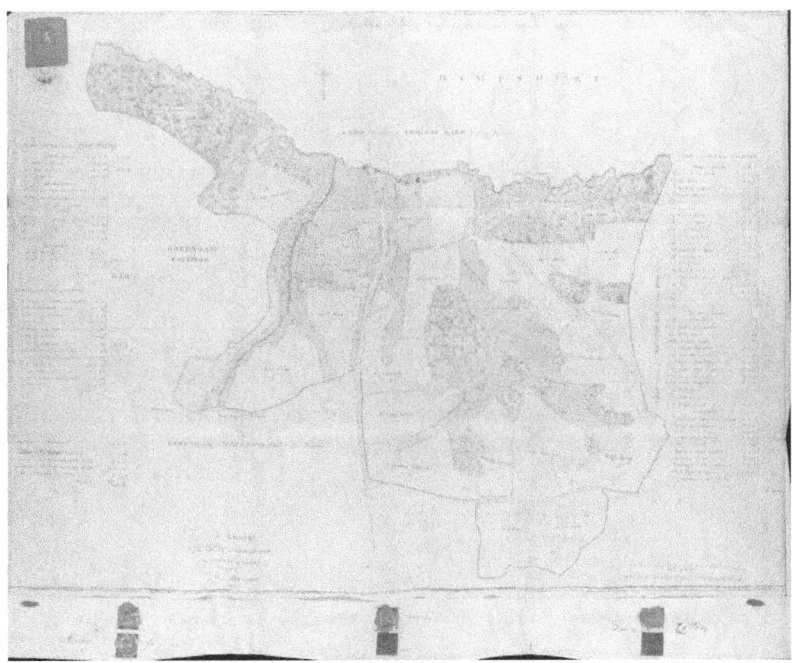

Figure 16 *A Survey of the Estate of Sandleford in the County of Berkshire belonging to Mrs Montagu*, 1781. © Berkshire Record Office, BRO:D/ELM/T19/2/13. See p. 184.

Part II
Land and Creature Ethics

'Recreational development is a job not of building roads into the lovely country, but of building receptivity into the still unlovely human mind.'

Aldo Leopold, *A Sand County Almanac* (1949), pp. 176–7

Chapter 7

William Cowper and Suburban Environmental Aesthetics

Kaz Oishi

Robert Lloyd's 'The Cit's Country Box' (1754) is one of the earliest satires on the middle-class penchant for suburban living. In the poem, a rich merchant is persuaded by his wife to leave behind their London townhouse for a home in the suburbs after learning from her that a business rival has already done so. The wife's remarks also contain the primary reason motivating such a migration: to gain a healthier environment in which one might enjoy the 'country air' (26).[1]

> What signify the loads of wealth,
> Without that richest jewel, health?
> Excuse the fondness of a wife,
> Who doats upon your precious life!
> Such ceaseless toil, such constant care,
> Is more than human strength can bear. (ll. 17–22)

For Lloyd, suburban taste represented bourgeois snobbism and vulgarity: merchants, traders and bankers were keen to distance themselves from the world of dirt and toil in the city, but could not quite afford to fully retire to the countryside like the gentry or the aristocracy. The merchant and his wife move to a villa, mocked as 'a country box', whose lawn they furbish with modish chinoiserie and show off as a 'paradise' (l. 62).

Lloyd's caricature is interesting principally for what it reveals about the hygienic, social and aesthetic values of middle-class aspirational culture. Taking two poems by William Cowper, *The Task* (1785) and 'Retirement' (1782), this chapter situates their increasing awareness of the relationship between human well-being and the living environment in the context of eighteenth- and nineteenth-century suburbanisation. Especially following his traumatic liaison with the Calvinist Evangelical John Newton, Cowper became painfully perceptive to the beneficent influence of natural surroundings upon the suffering human mind and body. He thought the suburbs could provide bodily as well as spiritual relief, despite them being less green and blissful than the countryside. Fundamentally, suburbs were secular human habitations, and yet still they contained a trace of Edenic felicity. Clapham in south London epitomised such a bourgeois suburb. It was a hub for Evangelicals, who, while prioritising a pious and peaceful life away from what they saw as a morally corrupt metropolitan centre, yet remained deeply committed to it politically and commercially. I will argue that this position of theirs and their environmental sensibility were shared by and large by urban middle-class people during the Romantic period.

Cowper's Environmental Sensibility

'God made the country, and man made the town' is perhaps William Cowper's best-known dictum from *The Task* (1: 749).[2] For him, rural living was a religious topos. On the completion of his treatment at Dr Cotton's hospital for a nervous breakdown, Cowper continued to reside reclusively in the countryside of south-east and east England. His picturesque descriptions of rural scenery are suffused with sensitivity to the workings of the divine will. 'The Lord of all, himself through all diffus'd', he exclaims, 'Sustains, and is the life of all that lives' (6: 221–2). In contrast to the city as the nursery of vices, such as 'sloth and lust', and replete with 'wantonness and gluttonous excess' (1: 686–8), the beauty of the rural environment delights the eye and refreshes all. Those formerly cloistered in dark unsanitary rooms recover their 'healthful hue', their eyes spark with fire again: 'He walks, he leaps, he runs – is wing'd with joy, / And riots in the sweets of ev'ry breeze' (1: 441–4). The passage anticipates Wordsworth's 'Glad Preamble' in *The Prelude*, which records his joy of returning to the Lake District: liberated 'from yon City's walls . . . where he hath been long immured', he felt 'free, enfranchis'd and at large' (1: 6–9).[3] The sweet breeze Cowper feels in the countryside reveals the Christian roots of Wordsworth's 'corresponding mild creative breeze' (1: 43).[4]

> From dearth to plenty, and from death to life,
> Is Nature's progress when she lectures man
> In heav'nly truth; evincing, as she makes
> The grand transition, that there lives and works
> A soul in all things, and that soul is God. (*The Task*, 6. 181–5)

The last line also fairly resonates with Wordsworth's 'something far more deeply interfused' in nature, 'A motion and a spirit, that impels / All thinking things, all objects of all thought, / And rolls through all things' in 'Tintern Abbey' (ll. 97–103), and more strongly with 'God / Diffus'd thro' all, that doth make all one whole' in Coleridge's 'Religious Musings' (ll. 130–1).[5] Cowper's depiction of the operation of the divine will in nature's seasonal rhythms, however, is more specifically Arminian, both in the sense that the country is a gift from God, and in the lurid language that it is 'the liberty of heart' procured by the 'blood' of Jesus Christ and given to all mankind (*The Task* 5: 545–6).

What Cowper appreciated most, moreover, was not merely an effect of God's divine power in nature. The famous dictum is followed by the assertion that rural surroundings enhance our 'health and virtue', which soften our bitter experiences of life.

> God made the country, and man made the town.
> What wonder then that health and virtue, gifts
> That can alone make sweet the bitter draught
> That life holds out to all, should most abound
> And least be threaten'd in the fields and groves? (*The Task*, 1: 749–52)

Cowper's emphasis on the effect of the country air upon human 'health and virtue' has not been paid sufficient attention. Clearly, according to him, our living environment not only impacts upon our physical well-being but also exerts a moral influence.

Cowper repeatedly emphasised the remedial effects of nature on people in *The Task*. Blooming flowers banish the 'lower'ing eye, the petulance, the frown, / And sullen sadness' and restore 'Sweet smiles' (*The Task*, 1: 456–61). Both the patient who has 'long endur'd / A fever's agonies, and fed on drugs', and the mariner whose health is damaged by 'acrid salts' through a long voyage, yearn after 'Nature in her green array' (1: 445–9). Cowper considers the human mind as a sensitive organ and calls this tendency to the curative influence of nature 'sympathy' (6: 323). Thus, it is a sympathy that is different from the misanthropy of Rousseau's solitary walker, or from the stoic impartial sympathy Adam Smith upheld as the basic principle of social intercourse in *The Theory of Moral Sentiments* (1759). It is a biological as well as spiritual connection with the natural world, corresponding with the rhythm of seasons, resonating with the vital impulses of animals and plants, and imbibing the energy of all sentient beings. It is taken to be essential not only for 'human fellowship', but for the fellowship of all living creatures: the sympathetic person delights at 'sight of animals enjoying life' and 'feels their happiness augment of his own' (6: 321–6). The interest in animal welfare, so prominent in Cowper's poetry and life, is based on this sense of the emotional and physical exchange we have with our surroundings.

J. Baird Callicott's concept of bioempathy in the field of environmental ethics also extends the concept of human sympathy to other members of the biotic community.[6] Cowper's environmental sensibility, however, has a biological implication as well as an ethical one. I would suggest it anticipates the scientific research of the 1980s that reveals the beneficial effects green environments have on physical and mental welfare. Most famously, after tracing the medical records of post-cholecystectomy patients for ten years, Roger S. Ulrich discovered that convalescents in rooms with a view of a more natural landscape were in a more stable condition, less in need of painkillers, and recovered more quickly than those in rooms without a view.[7] This so-called 'asphalt complex' is ultimately an aesthetic response to environment, which Ulrich himself admits elsewhere.[8] Damaged minds and bodies then have a better chance at healing when surrounded by greenery than by asphalt streets and concrete walls. Other researchers have shown that environmental degradation brought about by urban development, pollution or the ongoing climate crisis gravely affect the behaviour, immune system, even the genes of all creatures, human, animal or plant.[9] Indeed, Robert J. Lefkowitz and Brian K. Kobilka's study of the response of G-protein-coupled receptors (GPCRs) has shown that the environment around the cell determines most physiological processes, including the working of genes.[10] In this sense, an environmental sensibility delicately interrelated with homeostasis, health and welfare might be held in common between all living things down to the cellular and DNA level.[11]

Given the secularism of mainstream academic discourse, the fact that Cowper's environmental sensibility operates in a markedly religious framework cannot be overstated. Due to a constant fear of damnation under the influence of John Newton, Cowper was particularly sensitive to the way in which the afflicted mind could be soothed, consoled or restored by God in nature.[12] God's grace, he insisted, is available to all in the wholesome sunshine and sweet breeze:

> 'Tis free to all – 'tis ev'ry day renew'd;
> Who scorns it starves deservedly at home.
> He does not scorn it, who, imprison'd long
> In some unwholesome dungeon, and a prey
> To sallow sickness, which the vapours, dank
> And clammy, of his dark abode have bred,
> Escapes at last to liberty and light:
> His cheek recovers soon its healthful hue;
> His eye relumines its extinguish'd fires;
> He walks, he leaps, he runs – is wing'd with joy,
> And riots in the sweets of ev'ry breeze. (1: 433–44)

Throughout *The Task*, he discerns the working of God's infallible hand in nature's blessings. For him, the enjoyment of health, liberty and light are the basic fundamentals of human happiness.

Ethically, Cowper's sensibility is not exactly identical with what Jonathan Bate sees as operating in Wordsworth's 'green' language. In both, the fulfilment of humanity lies outside itself, but unlike Cowper, who rests it in the hands of God, the environmental tradition Bate builds on Wordsworth involves a surrender to nature's 'œconomy': an adoption of a simple way of life in 'harmony with the environment'.[13] Cowper's bioempathy should also be distinguished from 'Deep Ecology', which posits 'organisms as knots in the biospherical net or field of intrinsic values' to advocate an 'ecological egalitarianism'.[14] Instead, it is the hierarchical concept of the Great Chain of Being that *The Task* endorses, which places humankind at the very apex of earthly creation:

> Distinguish'd much by reason, and still more
> By our capacity of grace divine,
> From creatures that exist but for our sake,
> Which, having serv'd us, perish, we are held
> Accountable; and God, some future day,
> Will reckon with us roundly for th'abuse
> Of what he deems no mean or trivial trust.
> Superior as we are, they yet depend
> Not more on human help than we on their's. (6: 601–9)

As Cowper put it, human interests override that of all other creatures and plants: '[i]f man's convenience, health, / or safety, interfere, his rights and claims / Are paramount' (6: 581–3). Finally, in place of rights, Cowper extends an ethics of care: it is our duty to treat fairly and well the other-than-human beings whom God has placed on earth to serve and feed us.[15] In other words, Cowper's environmental sensibility would not be valued by biocentrists, who oppose the anthropocentric stewardship Christian environmentalists currently advocate.[16]

Cowper on the Suburb

Cowper did not restrict himself to idyllic rural scenery. He also wrote on that increasingly significant locale of human habitation in his time: the suburb. Though close to the busy, densely populated urban centre, suburbs are comparatively greener and therefore still capable of refreshing their dwellers physically and spiritually. 'A breath of unadult'rate air, / The glimpse of a green pasture', Cowper exclaims, 'how they cheer

/ The citizen, and brace his languid frame!' (*The Task*, 4: 750–2). The divine gifts of 'health and virtue' can be enjoyed in the suburbs, because the residential environment is reminiscent of the countryside and therefore touched by the divine. This is clear enough in Cowper's delineation of the suburbs in 'Retirement':

> To regions where, in spite of sin and woe,
> Traces of Eden are still seen below,
> Where mountain, river, forest, field, and grove,
> Remind him of his Maker's power and love. (ll. 27–30)

There is a hint of sarcasm in the heroic couplets. As a residential area, suburbs are a little too artificial and therefore not entirely free from 'sin and woe'. To Cowper, they are not quite Edenic enough when compared to the rural landscape.

Cowper's ambivalence spills over in his description of suburban villas – in Robert Lloyd's satirical voice – as confined and box-like, whose inhabitants aspiring to enjoy fresh country air in reality breathe city dust.

> Suburban villas, highway-side retreats,
> That dread th'encroachment of our growing streets,
> Tight boxes, neatly sash'd, and in a blaze
> With all a July sun's collected rays,
> Delight the citizen, who, gasping there,
> Breathes clouds of dust, and calls it country air. (ll. 481–6)

Suburban development, by reinforcing the expansion of city roads, eventually reduces the green spaces suburbanites so value. Hot July sunshine reflecting on the windows of long lines of suburban housing glares in the dust. Nature in the suburbs is tainted by human design and art. Instead of enjoying more solitary country sports, like riding, hunting or fishing, suburbanites are engaged in rounds of social intercourse with friends: 'prison'd in a parlour snug and small / Like bottled wasps upon a southern wall' (ll. 493–4). In Cowper's words, they are not country gentlemen, but the 'man of bus'ness and his friends', who commute to the urban centre 'safe' in their stage coach (ll. 492–5).

Engaged in business, economic as well as social, middle-class suburbanites never truly withdraw from the metropolitan centre. Yet – as Cowper interjects –

> But still 'tis rural – trees are to be seen
> From ev'ry window, and the fields are green;
> Ducks paddle in the pond before the door,
> And what could a remoter scene show more? (497–500)

Trees and green fields stretch blissfully before the house. The pond on which ducks swim is just in front of the door. 'Nature' is readily accessible in the suburbs, but it is one that is arranged and created for its urban residents. As Cowper notes in *The Task*, people have 'burning instinct' for nature (4: 773). Even at the heart of the town, they console themselves growing plants or flowers in a pot in order to remind themselves 'That nature lives' (4: 759). For Cowper, nature and art are not necessarily at odds with each other. As the poem outlines, 'art ... acts in nature's office' to secure the crop that brings joy to farmers and agricultural labourers (3: 541). When he compares a human being to 'a flow'r / Blown in its native bed', he means 'Man in society', not a person living in wild nature (4: 659–60). In his view, the suburb offers a sociable and ecological milieu nurtured by nature, cultivated by art. It offers nature-loving city people a more sustainable alternative to the holy grail of countryside living.

Clapham as Bourgeois Ecotopia

Suburbanisation has been a socio-geographical phenomenon at least since Roman times, but the suburbs truly became the topoi of wealth and health for the bourgeoisie only in the eighteenth century. Robert Fishman delineates the process of the emergence of the suburb as an idealised locale for middle-class people in Britain and the United States. In the case of eighteenth-century Londoners, with their wealth increasing to levels comparable to the rural squirearchy and even the aristocracy, prosperous merchants, bankers and tradesmen began to form a close-knit elite society and adopt a new mode of living, gradually distancing their seat of domesticity from their business at the core of the metropolis, first for weekend villas and then for permanent residence in the suburbs. For them, city living had been essential, given the access it offered to information, markets and customers. Merchants resided above the shop, with goods stored in the cellar below and apprentices and servants above in the attic, while bankers and tradesmen commuted to banks and markets conscious of their superiority to the labourers and the destitute thronging the vicinity. Their domestic lives were restricted to a walking distance from this mixed and congested public space.[17] By the middle of the eighteenth century, however, they began to pull away from the bonds of commerce and industry towards the city fringes.

> The merchant elite leaped over the belt of poverty that had constrained the metropolis and used their wealth to establish a new kind of rapidly expanding urban periphery, which we now call suburbia. They realized that, with their

private carriages and ample funds, they were no longer limited to the area traditionally considered the city. On the relatively inexpensive land still a surprisingly short commute to the core, they could build a world of privilege, leisure, and family life that reflected their values.[18]

According to Fishman, modern suburbanisation was not the result of an innovative architect, but 'a collective creation of the city's bourgeois elite, a gradual adoption of a new way of living by a class that had the wealth and confidence to remake the world to suit its values'.[19]

As for the driving forces of suburbanisation, however, Fishman does not offer an explanation beyond their growing desire to decamp from a congested living environment, and the developments in transport that facilitated it. I would suggest the influence here of Evangelicalism, which reified domesticity as a peaceful sphere separated from the immorality and corruption it associated with the metropolis. Clapham is an archetype of such a bourgeois suburb, springing into existence in 1735 when John Thornton, with wealth amassed through the Russian and Baltic trades, purchased land overlooking picturesque Clapham Common and parcelled it out to fellow Evangelicals. He was a prominent philanthropist funding a number of charities and supporting the likes of Newton and Cowper. The suburban residence portrayed in Cowper's 'Retirement' is based in part upon this Evangelical suburb. Thornton invited Henry Venn to serve as curate, and from the 1780s Evangelicals gathered in sufficient numbers to form a distinct community. The Clapham Sect thus formed included the abolitionist William Wilberforce and the statistician and philanthropist Zachary Macaulay. Henry Thornton, John Thornton's son, MP and banker, also moved into the area. The younger Thornton followed in the footsteps of his father sponsoring diverse charitable activities.[20] It was imperative for them to keep their domestic life aloof from what they saw as sins in the city, their campaign for the reformation of manners being in essence a critique of degenerate urban life.[21]

Their ideal of a pious domestic life was materialised in the layout of the village.[22] The whole had a picturesque arrangement, elegant villas distributed around the pastoral common and the streets drawing gracefully curved lines. We have an idea of what the area might have looked like through the paintings of J. M. W. Turner. Thornton's daughter Marianne, who was also E. M. Forster's great aunt, had fond memories of her home on the west side: 'to the day of my death I shall think nothing so lovely as the trees and the lawn at Battersea Rise'.[23] Woodland Cottage at Clapham, though not actually owned by a member of the community, was represented by John Hassell as an exemplary picture of tranquil, rural picturesqueness. It was a 'homely, yet elegant little cottage', 'a perfect model of rustic beauty' for a businessperson looking for a welcoming community to relax away 'from the fatigues of a professional employment'.[24] The area was 'now converted into the rural and picturesque',[25] where houses fronted by green pastures and shady trees leading to walled gardens and orchards behind fulfilled 'Evangelical ideals of family life and contact with nature'.[26] A pious domestic life in picturesque surroundings is also clearly the ideal pattern of 'the closed domesticated nuclear family', which Lawrence Stone describes as the fashionable mode of living for the eighteenth-century bourgeoisie.[27]

This sanitary, virtuous and picturesque landscape would have appealed to William Gilpin. He had hoped while admitting its difficulty that 'every admirer of *picturesque beauty*, is an admirer also of the *beauty of virtue*'; he had also written to the effect that 'every lover of nature reflects, that "Nature is but a name for an *effect*, / Whose *cause* is God"'. His idea of the picturesque is full of ambiguities and paradoxes, as the case in fact is with the idea of the suburb. It includes sublime scenes which inspire 'religious awe', as well as pretty landscapes that provide 'a rational and agreeable amusement'.[28] The picturesque also occupies a middle ground between nature and art. John Whale summarises Gilpin's dilemma: 'The further he travels towards nature, the more he must admit artifice'; 'the more he defines his idea of beauty, the further he flies from nature'.[29] Indeed, the Evangelicals had aimed to create a place that aroused 'religious awe' and virtue through a mixture of art and nature.

Despite the religious connotations, the suburb was very much like the picturesque landscape – as Fishman himself admits – artificially organised for consumption.[30] The appreciation and aestheticisation of 'nature', brought about by urbanisation and agricultural improvement, led to a conspicuous increase in upper-class investment in landscape designing and an even greater expansion of the middle-class market in tourism. Guide books like Gilpin's to picturesque places in Britain not only increased tourism in the countryside, but also resulted in a massive proliferation of landscape paintings and prints. Enchanted with the view of Derwentwater, Thomas Gray speculated that were he a painter he would fix the scene 'in all the softness of its living colours [to] sell for a thousand pounds'.[31] As John Brewer has indicated, the cultural impetus behind this monetisation of the landscape was upper-class estate development. It was the gentry and aristocrats who, greatly expanding their holdings through the enclosure of common and forest lands, landscaped their properties in the aesthetic patterns that inspired the picturesque.[32] It was 'nature' designed by 'art' and created by 'wealth'. As the landscape designer Humphry Repton put it, the country manor should occupy an elevated location in order to command a prospect since landscape is about '*appropriation*[, a] charm which only belongs to ownership, the *exclusive right* of enjoyment'.[33] To upper-class people, a beautiful landscape not only testified to the owner's taste and refinement, but also symbolised his political and financial power.[34]

Suburbanisation can be understood as a middle-class response to the taste for the picturesque. A walking guide published in 1801, for instance, admired as 'picturesque' the suburbs south of the Thames and Hampstead in north London.[35] Picturesqueness was also a regularly touted feature of suburban properties, whose sales surged in the last decades of the eighteenth century. As a point of advertisement, the term was commonly used to characterise a home with gardens or orchards (or both) arranged over several acres, and easy access to central London. These advertisements also frequently highlighted the drainage and sanitariness of the property, as well as the availability of clean water, which was of course indicative of the premium the bourgeoisie placed on a healthy living environment. In other words, cleanliness, fresh air and a good supply of water were part of the rhetoric used to distinguish the suburban house from its counterpart in the metropolis.[36]

The following advertisement for a villa at Clapham is a typical example:

> The Lease of a very chearful [sic], well-fitted, comfortable FAMILY DWELLING, with Garden, Coach-house, Stabling, small Paddock and Fish-pond, situate near the Church, on that healthy and delightful spot Clapham Common, comprising a substantial Brick Dwelling, in excellent state of repair, containing 5 good bed-chambers, powdering-room, and store-closets; a drawing-room, dressing-room, and dining-parlour; good entrance hall and stair case, kitchen, wash-house, and other domestic offices; cellaring, coach-house, and stabling for 4 horses. The pleasure-ground is laid out with taste; a garden, profitably cropped and planted with choice fruit trees, a small paddock, drying-ground, and fish-pond well stored, and fore-court. The Premises are well supplied with water, and are held for a term, of which 9 years were unexpired at Mid-summer last, at the low rent of 47*l*. per ann.[37]

The advertisement clearly had in mind a wealthy middle-class family, who expected to commute to the city by carriage and be waited upon by servants. Though close to the urban core, they also expected some of the advantages of country living, including access to fresh fruit and fish, a paddock to keep horses and other animals, a drying area for crops or hay and a cellar to lay down drink and provisions for the winter. As this advertisement shows, suburban villas were presumably like country manors, with similar appointments but smaller in scale. The advertisement is also peppered with the kind of jargon attractive to a middle-class elite preoccupied with comfort, gentility and luxury, such as 'delightful spot' and 'laid out with taste'.[38]

What was healthy was also picturesque to these urbanites, who were concerned about the unsanitary living conditions of London long before John Snow traced cholera to sewage-contaminated water in London slums in 1854. The environmental sensibility of suburban Evangelicals is indicative of a social position elevated from the seamy urban underbelly and hard field labour, shielded in other words from what John Barrell has called 'the dark side of the landscape'.[39] The elision of labour and poverty is consistent across middle-class depictions of the suburb, from adverts and guidebooks to the complete absence of agricultural labourers in *The Task*. As Peter Stallybrass and Allon White show, an increasing regulation of labouring-class behaviour, including the suppression of local seasonal festivities, accompanied the rise of middle-class power and presence in society.[40] The process is conspicuous in the Evangelical activism against local festivities and conduct they perceived to be paganistic, disorderly, immoral or indecent, particularly in London.[41] For the Evangelicals, then, the ideal environment connected human and non-human in relationships that were both religious and worldly.

The Legacy

The picturesque suburb was firmly established as an aesthetic by the nineteenth century. John Nash was not an Evangelical, but he was inspired by Clapham, applying a similar style to Park Village near Regent's Park, which was completed in 1820. Georgian houses in London were traditionally organised around town squares, but Park Village was *rus in urbe*, a village in the middle of the city. This was facilitated, of course, by the development being next to a huge park, and Nash completed the illusion by installing trees, curving streets and meandering canals. Nash thus brought the Clapham model to middle-class people in general, which could essentially be reproduced wherever suitable land became available. According to Nicholas Pevsner, Nash transformed suburbia into a marketable product in London, contributing materially to the rise in land prices and the development of similar residential areas in St John's Wood, Hampstead and Chelsea.[42]

Hampstead was described in an 1851 London guide as being 'extremely picturesque', with 'the salubrity of its air, the loveliness of its scenery, and its magnificent heath ... render[ing] it a favourite abode with invalids and with persons of rank and fortune'.[43] Another London handbook also recorded in 1850–1 how 'the picturesque hills of Surrey, near Dulwich and Norwood' were 'studded with the villas' of those who wished to retreat from the clamour of city life.[44] The suburbs of Dulwich and Camberwell were portrayed in Dickens's *Sketches of Boz* as an ideal residential area for genteel families, with green fields and leafy streets.[45] With the expansion of the city, places like Camberwell became less suburban, with more people from the lower classes moving in.[46] Nevertheless, even as late as 1894, George Gissing could say of Camberwell: 'The houses vary considerably in size and aspect, also in date, – with the result of a certain picturesqueness, enhanced by the growth of fine trees on either side.'[47] The suburbs continued to embody health and respectability, if not exactly Evangelical virtue, against the insanitary living conditions that supposedly prevailed at the heart of the city.

It would be misleading, however, to deny religious implications entirely with respect to the picturesque suburb. The church was an indispensable feature of the suburb. Furthermore, when Octavia Hill emphasised the importance of fresh air, green landscape and picturesque scenery to street children, she was extrapolating not from a medical tenet but from an Evangelical standpoint:

> The gay spring fields, the village green, the bright brooks should have surrounded the young beings at that age when most subtle, enduring impressions are sealed on the soul. Oh, for power to cast away from them the misery around, to remove them from air poisoned and close, to give them God's free light, for here from side to side, from window to window at every height were lines hung with clothes till the court was darkened.[48]

As a matter of fact, the idea that communion with nature was morally edifying was one of the assumptions underlying the foundation of the National Trust.

Health and moral virtue were the qualities that Cowper found in the countryside and extended to the suburb. As a bourgeois ecotopia, suburbs such as Clapham were conditioned by their ambivalent position, ideologically and physically, towards the city and the countryside. As a landscape, it was circumscribed by the middle-class standards of politeness and respectability. It had to be clean as a place, both physically and morally, whilst retaining its connections to the dirty heart of the town. Cowper's representation of Clapham encapsulates this paradoxical ethos imbibed by a middle-class people who increasingly chose to reside in the suburbs.

Notes

1. Robert Lloyd, 'The Cit's Country Box', in David Fairer and Christine Gerrard (eds), *Eighteenth-Century Poetry: An Annotated Anthology* (Oxford: Blackwell, 2004), p. 408. Quotations from the poem are hereafter from this edition with line numbers in parentheses. I would like to thank David Fairer for drawing my attention to this poem.
2. H. S. Milford (ed.), *The Poetical Works of William Cowper*, 4th edn (Oxford: Oxford University Press, [1934] 1971), p. 145. Quotations from Cowper's poems are hereafter all from this edition with book and line numbers in parentheses.
3. Mark L. Reed (ed.), *The Thirteen-Book Prelude . . . by William Wordsworth* (Ithaca, NY: Cornell University Press, 1991), p. 107. Quotations from the poems are hereafter all from this edition with book and line numbers in parentheses.
4. Martin Priestman points out that Wordsworth's 'Glad Preamble' is an echo of Cowper's in *Cowper's Task: Structure and Influence* (Cambridge: Cambridge University Press, 1983), pp. 167–8.
5. James Butler and Karen Green (eds), *Lyrical Ballads, and Other Poems, 1797–1800* (Ithaca, NY: Cornell University Press, 1992), p. 119; J. C. C. Mays (ed.), *Poetical Works*, 3 vols in 6 parts (Princeton: Princeton University Press, 2001), 1, part 1 (Reading Text): 180.
6. See 'On the Intrinsic Value of Nonhuman Species', in J. Baird Callicott (ed.), *In Defence of the Land Ethic: Essays in Environmental Philosophy* (Albany: State University of New York Press, 1989), pp. 129–55.
7. Roger S. Ulrich, 'View through a Window may Influence Recovery from Surgery', *Science* 224, no. 4647 (1984): 420–1.
8. Roger S. Ulrich, 'Aesthetic and Affective Response to Natural Environment', in Irwin Altman and Joachim F. Wohlwill (eds), *Behavior and the Natural Environment* (New York: Plenum, 1983), pp. 85–125.
9. On this issue, see Peter Calow and R. J. Berry (eds), *Evolution, Ecology and Environmental Stress* (London: Academic Press, 1989); Ary A. Hoffmann and Peter A. Parsons, *Evolutionary Genetics and Environmental Stress* (Oxford: Oxford University Press, 1991); Sheldon Cohen, Gary W. Evans, Daniel Stokols and David S. Krantz, *Behavior, Health, and Environmental Stress* (New York: Plenum, 1986), pp. 103–42.
10. See Lizzie Buchen, 'Cell Signalling Caught in the Act: Receptor Imaged in Embrace with its G protein', *Nature* 475 (2011): 273–4; Ruth Williams, 'Robert Lefkowitz: Godfather of G Protein-Coupled Receptors', *Circulation Research* 106 (2010): 812–4.
11. G. R. Elliot and Carl Eisdorfer, *Stress and Human Health: Analysis and Implications of Research* (New York: Springer, 1982); Hoffmann and Parsons, *Evolutionary Genetics*, pp. 5–39.
12. Gilbert Oliver Thomas pointed out the contradiction between Cowper's anxiety about his own salvation and his assertion of free Grace, in *William Cowper and the Eighteenth Century* (London: Allen and Unwin, [1935] 1948), pp. 186–9. The eighteenth-century critic John Knox perceived that it was Cowper's own inner suffering that gave his poetry its soothing

power. It made him 'a benefactor of human kind', who provided 'harmless satisfaction' for all distressed souls restoring them to their 'safe and natural habits' with 'sweet strains of the poetic lyre'. See 'Cowper III', in Scott Elledge (ed.), *Eighteenth-Century Critical Essays*, 2 vols (Ithaca, NY: Cornell University Press, 1961), 2: 1113. A Methodist inclination, however, is evident in Cowper. Cowper 'admired' Walter Churchey's elegy for John Wesley, whose name he was delighted to find among the subscribers to his 1791 translation of Homer; James King and Charles Ryskamp (ed.), *The Letters and Prose Writings of William Cowper*, 5 vols (Oxford: Clarendon Press, 1979–86), 3: 591.

13. Jonathan Bate, *Romantic Ecology: Wordsworth and the Environmental Tradition* (London: Routledge, 1991), p. 40.
14. Arne Naess, 'The Shallow and the Deep: Long-Range Ecology Movements', *Inquiry* 16 (1973): 95–6. 'Deep Ecology' is in principle committed to the well-being of all living beings, but it calls for 'fundamental changes' in understanding human welfare and the goals of politics and economy, which should be based not on 'vast material consumption', but on 'friendships, the development of talents, and ties to a local environment'; see Jason Kawall, 'A History of Environmental Ethics', in Stephen M. Gardiner and Allen Thompson (eds), *The Oxford Handbook of Environmental Ethics* (Oxford: Oxford University Press, 2017), p. 19. For the idea of animal rights based on the 'principle of equal considerations of interests and the indefensibility of limiting this principle to members of our own species', see Peter Singer, 'Not Humans Only: The Place of Nonhumans in Environmental Issues', in Andrew Light and Holmes Rolston III (eds), *Environmental Ethics: An Anthology* (Oxford: Blackwell, 2003), p. 58.
15. Cowper's ethics of care can be seen as a prototype for the feminist care tradition, which, as Carol J. Adams and Lori Gruen explain, 'focuses on affective connections, including compassion and empathy, and shows how these connections have a cognitive or rational component'; see *Ecofeminism: Feminist Intersections with Other Animals and the Earth* (London: Bloomsbury, 2014), p. 3.
16. See for example Roger S. Gottlieb, *A Greener Faith: Religious Environmentalism and Our Planet's Future* (Oxford: Oxford University Press, 2006).
17. Robert Fishman, *Bourgeois Utopias: The Rise and Fall of Suburbia* (New York: Basic Books, 1987), pp. 21–5.
18. Ibid. p. 26.
19. Ibid. p. 26.
20. For the formation of Thornton's Evangelical community and their communal engagement with politics, commerce and philanthropy, see Stephen Tomkins, *The Clapham Sect: How Wilberforce's Circle Transformed Britain* (Oxford: Lion, 2010), pp. 112–24 and 145–66.
21. Wilberforce emphasises the virtue of child education and family life in *A Practical View of the Prevailing Religious System of Professed Christians, in the Higher and Middle Classes with Real Christianity* (London: Cadell and Davies, 1797), p. 117.
22. Raymond Williams observes these qualities in the enclosed landscape of the period: 'The clearing of parks as 'Arcadian' prospects depended on

the completed system of exploitation of the agricultural and genuinely pastoral lands beyond the park boundaries. There, too, an order was being imposed: social and economic but also physical. The mathematical grids of the enclosure awards, with their straight hedges and straight roads, are contemporary with the natural curves and scatterings of the park scenery'; see *The Country and the City* (London: Hogarth, 1985), p. 124.
23. E. M. Forster, *Marianne Thornton 1797–1887: A Domestic Biography* (London: Edward Arnold, 1956), p. 18.
24. John Hassell, *Picturesque Rides and Walks, with Excursions by Water, Thirty Miles Round the British Metropolis: Illustrated in a Series of Engravings, Coloured after Nature: with an Historical and Topographical Description of the Country within the Compass of that Circle* (London: Hassell, 1817), pp. 13–14.
25. Ibid. p. 14.
26. Fishman, *Bourgeois Utopia*, p. 55.
27. Lawrence Stone, *The Family, Sex and Marriage in England, 1500–1800* (New York: Harper and Row, 1977), p. 7.
28. William Gilpin, *Three Essays on Picturesque Beauty, on Picturesque Travel; and on Sketching Landscape: to which is added a Poem, on Landscape Painting* (London: Blamire, 1792), p. 47.
29. John Whale, 'Romantics, Explorers and Picturesque Travellers', in Stephen Copley and Peter Garside (ed.), *The Politics of the Picturesque: Literature, Landscape and Aesthetics Since 1770* (Cambridge: Cambridge University Press, 1994), p. 178. See also Ann Bermingham, *Landscape and Ideology: The English Rustic Tradition 1740–1860* (London: Thames and Hudson, 1986), p. 65: 'Gilpin's notion that "nature is the archetype" had some interesting consequences. If nature prefigures the picturesque, then there must exist in nature a purely picturesque landscape, one that is all roughness, irregularity, and variousness. Yet if there were such a landscape, the hand of art, unable to improve it, would become secondary and even superfluous.' Walter J. Hippie also argues: 'There is a paradox here: a system which isolates a certain property of nature for admiration [picturesque beauty], a property defined by its excellence as a subject for art, comes at last to reject the art for the nature which was at first only its subject.' See *The Beautiful, the Sublime and the Picturesque in Eighteenth-Century British Aesthetic Theory* (Carbondale: Southern Illinois Press, 1957), pp. 198–9.
30. Fishman, *Bourgeois Utopia*, p. 49.
31. William Mason, *The Works of Thomas Gray, Esq,: Collated from the Various Editions: with Memoirs of His Life and Writings* (London: Dove, 1827), p. 294.
32. John Brewer, *The Pleasures of the Imagination: English Culture in the Eighteenth Century* (London: Routledge, 1997), pp. 495–502.
33. Humphry Repton, *Fragments on the Theory and Practice of Landscape Gardening* (New York: Garland, [1816] 1982), p. 233. See Brewer, *The Pleasures of the Imagination*, p. 496. On the sense of ownership driving enclosure, landscape design and the construction of the country manor in the eighteenth century, see Thomas Oles, *Walls: Enclosure and Ethics in the Modern Landscape* (Chicago: The University of Chicago Press, 2015), pp. 66–113.

34. Brewer, *The Pleasures of the Imagination*, p. 497.
35. James Edwards, *A Companion from London to Brighthelmston, in Sussex; Consisting of a Set of Topographical Maps from Actual Surveys, on a Scale of Two Inches to a Mile* (London: Bensley, 1801), pp. 12–13.
36. For more examples of advertisements for properties in the newly developed suburbs, including Clapham, refer to *The Times*, 6 August 1799 and 29 May 1799.
37. *The Times*, 29 July 1799.
38. For 'comfort' as an indicator of a bourgeois value system, see Franco Moretti, *The Bourgeois: Between History and Literature* (London: Verso, 2013), pp. 44–51.
39. John Barrell, *The Dark Side of the Landscape: The Rural Poor in English Painting 1730–1840* (Cambridge: Cambridge University Press, 1980).
40. Peter Stallybrass and Allon White, *The Politics and Poetics of Transgression* (London: Methuen, 1986). The ideological mechanism underlying the picturesque suburb has affinities with the aestheticisation of labouring-class people and itinerants like gypsies to appeal to the taste of their social superiors, as John Barrell explores in the work aforementioned.
41. Sunday schools, promoted by Hannah More and sponsored by the Thorntons, were one of the avenues by which the Evangelicals disseminated their ideals of practical piety and orderly conduct among working-class people. For the connections between consumerism, sensibility and the reformation of manners, see George J. Barker-Benfield, *The Culture of Sensibility: Sex and Society in Eighteenth-Century Britain* (Chicago: The University of Chicago Press, 1992), pp. 37–103 and 224–31.
42. John Summerson, *The Life and Work of John Nash, Architect* (London: Allen and Unwin, 1980), pp. 114–29; Dana Arnold, *Rural Urbanism: London Landscapes in the Early Nineteenth Century* (Manchester: Manchester University Press, 2005), pp. 54–8 and 61–71.
43. William Gaspey, *Tallis's Illustrated London in Commemoration of the Great Exhibition of All Nations in 1851. Forming a Complete Guide to the British Metropolis and its Environs*, 2 vols (London: Tallis, 1851–2), 1: 319.
44. J. R. McCulloch, *London in 1850–51* (London: Longman, 1851), p. 108.
45. Charles Dickens, *The Posthumous Papers of the Pickwick Club*, ed. Robert L. Pattern (Harmondsworth: Penguin, 1972), p. 895; Charles Dickens, *Sketches by Boz*, ed. Dennis Walder (London: Penguin, [1833–6] 1995), p. 416.
46. The social history of suburbanisation in London suburbs in the nineteenth century is mapped out by Olsen, *Victorian London*, pp. 118–264; Fishman, *Bourgeois Utopia*, pp. 3–102; F. M. L. Thompson (ed.), *The Rise of Suburbia* (Leicester: Leicester University Press, 1982). H. J. Dyos explores the development and degeneration of Camberwell in *Victorian Suburb: A Study of the Growth of Camberwell* (Leicester: Leicester University Press, 1961).
47. George Gissing, *In the Year of Jubilee*, ed. Paul Delany (London: J. M. Dent, 1994), p. 15.
48. Octavia Hill, *Octavia Hill: Early Ideals*, ed. Emily S. Maurice (London: Allen and Unwin, 1928), p. 48.

Chapter 8

Exclusionary Landscapes: Shenstone and the Development of a Romantic Aesthetics of Enclosure

Ve-Yin Tee[1]

It did not occur to me until the green, undulating slopes of the Yorkshire Dales came to the train windows that I had taken the scenic route out of Glasgow Central. It was 10 August 2015, a typical English summer's day of cloud and dappled sunshine. Looking upon the land of sheep, cows, horses, dogs and their walkers, hurtling past at sixty miles an hour, I asked myself: what makes a landscape beautiful? On recalling the places I'd been to, or experienced second-hand through the mass media, I was at once struck by how few of the scenes in my mind's eye had people in them and how many had none at all.

Assuming that 'notions of what makes a beautiful landscape are' – to quote Swiss sociologist and economist Lucius Burckhardt – 'historically determined',[2] what then is the provenance of this misanthropy underlying my sense of the beautiful, which seems to me remarkably widespread and durable? The French geographer Augustin Berque voices the sense that people today have lost the ability to produce beautiful landscapes,[3] and across the developed world the restriction of human activity, if not of the human presence itself, is accepted as the necessary corollary to the maintenance of 'places of great natural beauty'. Indeed, the activists of Earth Liberation Front and the Sea Shepherd Society believe that the best thing we can do for our rapidly degrading world is to leave it alone. To restore our planet's biodiversity, they argue that we have to commit ourselves as a species to depopulation and economic recession. This misanthropic sentiment is recapitulated in sources as diverse as the anarchistic graphic novels of Alan Moore, James Lovelock's proposal of sustainable retreat in *The Revenge of Gaia* (2006), and the videos uploaded to YouTube on the return of nature to retreated environments, most notably to the irradiated landscapes of Chernobyl and Fukushima.

Returning to the Yorkshire Dales and other green spaces in and about the cities, towns and villages of England, is it going too far to assert that the etiquette of picking up after a dog, or conceiving whatever a human being might leave behind these places as 'litter', is yet another manifestation of the same misanthropic feeling? I am not arguing here for anarchism, nor am I simply chafing at the heavy-handedness of the various land management agencies which have stopped the kicking of a ball or the throwing of a Frisbee across many a green. Rather, I am taking aim at the cultural forces that enforce our detachment from the land. Consider this: on Hampstead Heath, which includes over 300 acres of common land, not only are the games that people normally think of playing in such a place strictly regulated, but also any effect they might have on the spaces they pass through. I cannot plant a rosemary bush to mark the favourite spot of a loved one there, for example, without contravening the local byelaw that 'No person shall . . . cut . . . any turf, sod, gravel, sand, clay or other substance in any open space.'[4] Thus, a public place paradoxically denotes a space we cannot live on, and about which there is furthermore the understanding that we are to erase all traces of ourselves when we leave.

I think the aesthetics I have outlined at the outset – the underlying misanthropy, not to mention the anti-human detachment we have towards wide swathes of land – have been inherited from the eighteenth century; specifically, from the strand of the enclosure movement that imposed upon England that ideological rearrangement of physical and biological material known as the landscape garden. If it was among (mostly) upper-class people that landscape thinking arose, it was (mostly) middle-class people with the leisure time and the access to these estates who imbibed this ethic and took it to the lands without. I will demonstrate this transference of an upper-class aesthetics of enclosure to the middle class by comparing the responses William Shenstone consciously cultivated towards the Leasowes Park, with Coleridge's towards the green places he did not own. Shenstone is, of course, known as one of the pioneering creators of the English garden. Less well known, however, was his unusual liberality in allowing for almost two decades visits to his estate by anyone, free of charge. One frequent visitor was James Woodhouse, the 'Poetical Shoemaker', a descendant of freeholders who had worked on land that the family had farmed for over three hundred years.[5] Landscape thinking was instrumental in the dispossession of people who lived off the land, like the Woodhouse family, and his representations of landscape gardens like The Leasowes help us to understand the tragic consequences of landscape thinking for his time and ours.

It is probably helpful to point out that the places referred to in this chapter are considered from two perspectives: as 'land', to denote a physical and material location, and as 'landscape', to connote immaterial and invisible relations. Two hundred and twelve years before me, seated by his cottage window sixty miles away in the Lake District, Coleridge wrote down in his notebook:

> Oct 19, 1803. The general Fast Day – and all hearts anxious concerning the Invasion. – A grey Day, windy – the vale, like a place in Faery, with the autumnal Colours, the orange, the red-brown, the crimson[,] the light yellow, the yet lingering Green, Beeches ~~all~~ & Birches, as they were blossoming Fire & Gold! – & the Sun in slanting pillars, or illuminated small parcels of mist, or single spots of softest grayish Light, now racing, now slowly gliding, now stationary / – the mountains cloudy – the Lake has been a mirror so very clear, that the water became almost invisible – & now it rolls in white Breakers, like a Sea; the wind snatches up the water, & drifts it like Snow . . . why have I not an unencumbered Heart! [T]hese beloved Books still before me, this noble Room, the very centre to which a whole world of beauty converges, the deep reservoir into which all these streams & currents of lovely Forms flow – my own mind so populous, so active, so full of noble schemes, so capable of realizing them / this heart so loving, so filled with noble affections – O Ἀσρα! wherefore am I not happy? [W]hy for years have I not enjoyed one pure & sincere pleasure! – one full Joy! – one genuine Delight, that rings sharp to the Beat of the Finger! – all cracked, & dull with base Alloy![6]

Preparations across the country against invasion had moved up a gear following the declaration of war on France in May, effectively ending the fourteen-month-long Peace Treaty of Amiens.[7] A rebellion against British rule had also taken place in Ireland over the summer. Though it was quickly suppressed, the fact that Robert Emmet, the young man who led it, was of Coleridge's class and temperament might have deepened his sense of crisis.[8] Back home at Greta Hall, it was becoming painfully clear as well that he could not live under the same roof as Mrs Coleridge. Fulfilling his domestic obligations only made him dream more fervently of Sara Hutchinson and of escape, as the mystical pseudonym ('Ἀσρα', i.e. Asra, which he inked over) and the longing numinous depiction of the view outside attest. The latter, ostensibly of Keswick, is at one level so generic in detail that it could be almost anywhere in the Lake District, perhaps even in rural France or Germany. On another level, it does not really exist, since no window at Greta Hall actually has the elevation to offer such an expanse of 'vale', 'Lake' and 'mountains cloudy'. Coleridge was not aiming for topographical accuracy, of course. The purpose rather was to generate pathos through the slideshow of autumn colours, desolate places and an approaching rainstorm. It is this creation of a landscape to draw the mind away from a troubled public situation towards private, melancholic feelings that is the characteristic oeuvre of an aesthetics of enclosure.

The literati of China had a long tradition of manifesting their disagreement with the ruling government by retiring to their lands and imagining themselves anchorites. Considering how exalted Chinese landscape gardens were in Georgian England, and how many estates had a hermitage without actually having a hermit,[9] the upper-class aesthetics of enclosure was probably a development from this fantasy eremitical tradition. Indeed, the Whig statesman George Lyttelton, who had retreated to the country in the face of a government he opposed like the Chinese scholars of old, developed Hagley into one of 'the three gardens that a late eighteenth century visitor to the West Midlands had to see'.[10] The other two were Enville, the estate of Harry Grey, fourth earl of Stamford, and The Leasowes. From the northern part of Shenstone's grounds (Fig. 14, number 34) facing south,[11] his residence – to quote Robert Dodsley's 'Description of the Leasowes' (1764) – 'appears in the center [sic] of a large swelling lawn, bushed with trees and thicket. The pleasing variety of easy swells and hollows, bounded by scenes less smooth and cultivated, affords the most delightful picture of domestic retirement and tranquility.'[12] Though The Leasowes was a fraction of the size of Enville or Hagley – and Shenstone considerably lower in social rank than Grey or Lyttelton, who were members of the aristocracy – the three gardens combined formed a sectorial cluster whose programmatic influence on landscape thinking must have been huge. Not only do the properties all lie within ten miles of each other, they also had the same terrain and 'a similar gardenist repertory (cascades, pools, seats, urns and gothic belvederes)'.[13] What Coleridge's notebook entry further reveals, which Dodsley's use of 'pleasing' and 'delightful' might obscure for readers today, was the principal sentiment land reified as landscape was supposed to evoke in the gentrified onlooker: melancholia. In the 1760s, polite visitors – that is, 'company ... with ... horses or equipage' – generally began their tour of The Leasowes at the 'root-house'.[14] A house made of tree roots was stereotypically the dwelling of a hermit, who has – according to Shenstone – become who he is because of a setback in life.[15] This developed into a kind of self-referential promotion; Shenstone never married, and the plaintive poetical voice he cultivated, notably in works such as 'A Pastoral Ballad, in Four Parts', suggested that he had suffered disappointment in love: 'How she smil'd, and I could not but love; / Was faithless, and I am undone!'[16] Placed in the 'beautiful gloomy' wooded parts of The Leasowes Park was a commemorative urn to a beloved niece who died young from smallpox,[17] wooden benches or stone seats dedicated to poets or friends who had passed on, and sentimental verses stuck to trees, all to elicit that paroxysm of 'delicious melancholy' – which was a popular collocation in the Romantic period.

According to Shenstone, 'GARDEN-SCENES may be divided into the sublime, the beautifull [sic], and the melancholy or pensive; to which ...

we may assign a middle place betwixt the former two, as being in some sort composed of both'.[18] But what makes a landscape beautiful? In the mid-eighteenth century the answer would unquestionably be 'variety'. The Leasowes had a circuit of interconnected streams, waterfalls, reservoirs and fish ponds. It had mature woods, tree clumps, shady groves and a functioning coppice ground (Fig. 14, number 21). In addition to the melancholic garden features mentioned at the end of the previous paragraph, there was a ruined priory (Fig. 14, number 9), a gothic-style alcove (Fig. 14, number 20) and a visually arresting gothic building (Fig. 14, number 34). Shenstone installed a range of classically themed follies and statues as well; for example, a Greek temple (Fig. 14, number 31) and piping fauns placed among the shrubbery like garden gnomes (Fig. 14, number 11). There was a life-sized sculpture of Faunus (Fig. 14, number 14) and one of Venus presiding over a basin of goldfish (Fig. 14, number 38). The circuitous path that Shenstone laid round the property not only ensured the individual decorations could be seen from multiple angles, it also offered commanding views over the surrounding country. At his house, there was a menagerie for doves and stables for horses. He planted native wildflowers, shrubs and trees, as well as foreign exotics.[19] There could be such a thing as too much variety, however, given Shenstone's clear statement of what constitutes a 'pensive' garden (that is, as being 'betwixt' the sublime and the beautiful). In fact, he took pains to ensure there was not such a cornucopia of flowers as to turn The Leasowes into a flower garden. He wrote, 'A sufficient quantity of undecorated space is necessary to exhibit such decorations to advantage,'[20] and the greater part of the property was in fact plain grassland for sheep and dairy. In other words, as contrary to the beautiful, the sublime can be understood as an industrial aesthetic associated with uniformity and utility. (The frightening productivity of machine culture later conjured by the Romantics, for example, by Blake in 'The Tyger' (1794), or by Wordsworth in the final two books of *The Excursion* (1814), is simply an accentuation of this variant of the sublime to accompany the advancement of industrialisation.) That The Leasowes occupied a 'middle place', somewhere between the meretricious and the utilitarian, is perhaps best conveyed by Shenstone himself, who declared to a correspondent in 1748: 'I give my place the title of *ferme ornée*.'[21]

Shenstone would have chosen a different design had he a larger canvas to work with than The Leasowes, which he privately deprecated as a 'pitiful parterre-garden'.[22] Quite apart from its limited extent, the 'decorations' themselves were decidedly economical: the ruined priory accommodated a single, paying tenant, the Greek temple was really a fancifully named rustic cottage, and the eye-catching gothic edifice actually a painting on a few pieces of board. That 'the sensibilities of Georgian polite society could perceive ... the pleasures of his *ferme ornée* ... akin to ... Hagley and ... Enville'[23] was because of the time and energy he put in to promote the place. The Leasowes was consciously the constant and concrete example behind Shenstone's pronouncements on gardening, as well as behind the Virgilian landscapes of love and loss evoked in his elegiac and mock-pastoral poetry. The liberal admissions policy of The Leasowes was almost certainly strategic as well. As he had neither the social standing nor the personality to cultivate as wide a circle of polite friends and associates as his aristocratic neighbours, opening his doors to all would enable him to make up for the lack of quality with quantity. Up until 1747, he was still begging friends to come: 'My wood grows excessively pleasant, and its pleasantness vexes me; because nobody will come that can taste it.'[24] Shenstone did not just rely on penmanship to pull people in; he rolled out the red carpet to those who came, taking the time to talk to everyone, and personally conducted tours even when visitor numbers rose considerably two years later. As he wrote to regular correspondent Richard Jago, 'I have been exhibiting myself in my walks to no less than a hundred and fifty people, and that with no less state and vanity than a Turk in his seraglio.'[25] Finally, the fact that a property as modest as Shenstone's could hold its own against an Enville or a Hagley would have made him that much more impressive in the eyes of his middle-class visitors, for whom an expenditure on the scale of The Leasowes was not completely out of reach.

Even if the number of people who were tempted by Shenstone's example into gardening projects of their own was very small, these parkland visits would have educated them to read green spaces in general with a gardenist eye. The association of 'nature' with melancholy, which was the organising principle of The Leasowes, became a common enough trope in the poetry of the urban middle class for Coleridge to lambast it in 'The Nightingale' (1798) as a cultural imposition:

> And hark! the Nightingale begins its song,
> 'Most musical, most melancholy'* Bird!
> A melancholy Bird? O idle thought!
> In nature there is nothing melancholy.
> – But some night-wandering Man, whose heart was pierced
> With the remembrance of a grievous wrong,
> Or slow distemper or neglected love,
> (And so, poor Wretch! fill'd all things with himself
> And made all gentle sounds tell back the tale
> Of his own sorrows) he and such as he

First nam'd these notes a melancholy strain;
* 'Most musical, most melancholy.' This passage in Milton possesses an excellence far superior to that of mere description; it is spoken in the character of the Melancholy Man, and has therefore a dramatic propriety. The author makes this remark, to rescue himself from the charge of having alluded with levity to a line in Milton; a charge than which none could be more painful to him, except perhaps that of having ridiculed his Bible.[26]

The poem, like The Leasowes, has both gothic and classical elements, and who could possibly be a better fit for the 'Melancholy Man' here than Shenstone? Not only was he the acknowledged master of pathetic verse,[27] but he would also peg Latin inscriptions and his own verses to trees, or seats by streams, ponds and waterfalls so that the sounds of rustling leaves and flowing water literally told 'back the tale / Of his own sorrows'. Though there are no hermits in 'The Nightingale', they do appear in the poems that Coleridge wrote at about the same time: in 'The Rime of the Ancyent Marinere'[28] and in 'Christabel', where the eponymous heroine is portrayed as a 'hermitess'.[29] Finally, understanding the melancholy of nature as a gardenist gesture helps shed light on the subversive decision Coleridge took in the poem to situate a whole flock of happily singing nightingales in a landscape garden.[30]

I wonder whether the place at which Coleridge's poetical persona of 'The Nightingale' insists he has never seen 'So many Nightingales' is fact or fiction.

> Of large extent, hard by a castle huge
> Which the great lord inhabits not . . .
> This grove is wild with tangling underwood,
> And the trim walks are broken up, and grass,
> Thin grass and king-cups grow within the paths.[31]

The same question clearly occurred to J. C. C. Mays, who has suggested a number of locations in Somerset,[32] of which Enmore Castle seems to me to be the most likely. However, as with the view from Greta Hall, Coleridge's depiction is such that it could be almost anywhere in the West Country, or nowhere in particular. After all, Enmore Castle was in good repair, with its lord and his family in residence. Furthermore, considering that the south of England is currently just within the northern limit of the range of the nightingale, and that the weather back then was colder,[33] it might be doubted whether there were any nightingales in Somerset. In short, even if Coleridge had been inspired by a specific place, his evocation of it is almost certainly a case of what Peter De Bolla has labelled 'imaginative doodling'.[34] While Coleridge's poetical depictions of green spaces have clear affinities with Shenstone's, it is important to note with Coleridge the gulf between the land he experienced and his projection of it. Indeed, as De Bolla observes in his fine elucidation of landscape aesthetics, there was greater willingness among middle-class exponents of the picturesque like William Gilpin to dispense with the protocols of vraisemblance.[35] Why this might be so is connected with their very different relationships to the land. Shenstone's landscape projections were inspired by a land on which he invested considerable resources and lived the greatest part of his life. The landscape projections of urban middle-class people like Coleridge, on the other hand, were invariably inspired by land they did not own. That middle-class people did not deploy the aesthetics of enclosure over their own land meant they could deploy it virtually everywhere. As the case was with Coleridge, land merely to be crossed, merely experienced as an obstacle, such as the forest of 'The Picture; or, the Lover's Resolution' (1802), could be made to recall the melancholic features of a landscape garden: 'No myrtle-walks are here! These are no groves / For love to dwell in'.[36]

Treating land as landscape has serious consequences, however, on people-to-people relations and their relationship to the broader biotic community, at least in the mode inspired by the process of emparkment in the eighteenth century. Landscape implies an aesthetic standard that requires cultural and physical resources to maintain. Furthermore, success begets the desire for more success, which unfortunately was also the case with Shenstone. He arranged the visits of friends to coincide with the seasons when The Leasowes could be seen in its best possible light. Since there was not enough water to supply all the water features simultaneously, a servant had to be stationed to direct it from one part of the estate to another to follow the flow of visitors.[37] The improvements to the property increased in frequency and scale, gradually taking over his life. The lake below the priory (Fig. 14, number 8) was his final, most ambitious project. Begun in 1758, it '*employed* . . . servants, and *enslav'd* . . . Horses all year' to excavate,[38] it made his streams and ponds run dry filling it, and yet 'the grand water in the valley' did not appear until several months after his death in 1762.[39] 'I think the landskip [sic] painter is the gardiner's [sic] best designer,'[40] Shenstone wrote, but treating The Leasowes as if it were a painting in an exhibition resulted in rules and conventions that were exclusionary. In the hermitage at the start of the walk was a tablet with the following lines:

> . . . tread with awe these favour'd bowers;
> Nor wound the shrubs, nor bruise the flowers;
> So may your path with sweets abound!
> [. . .]

But harm betide the wayward swain,
Who dares our hallow'd haunts profane!⁴¹

Nature was reduced to a look-but-don't-touch spectacle, and in this respect The Leasowes is truly the ancestor of parks and gardens today. As Shenstone explained to Jago in June 1749, he wrote these verses for 'the admonition of my good friends the vulgar'.⁴² The 'multitudes [who came] every Sunday evening' only grew, and the day eventually came in 1759 when James Woodhouse and his friends suddenly found the gates of The Leasowes firmly barred against them.

In June that same year, Woodhouse sent 'An Elegy to William Shenstone', giving birth to the legend of the 'Poetical Shoemaker'. According to the 'Advertisement' for Woodhouse's *Poems on Sundry Occasions* (1764), Shenstone was so impressed that he 'not only gave him the liberty of passing many leisure hours' in The Leasowes, but also became his patron and teacher.⁴³ The poem itself is an interesting revelation of the cultural capital one had to amass in order to access a landscape. Its introduction of him as a 'village swain' echoes the rustic register of the verses Shenstone used for 'the admonition'. The landscape it describes is in Shenstone's neoclassical style, for example, a pond with 'crystal waves' where 'bounding fish the dimpling surface spurn' to 'hail the Naiad as she stoops her urn'.⁴⁴ More crucially, it signals his understanding of the proper code of conduct: 'My joyful feet explor'd the mazy road; / Whence not a sacrilegious footstep strays, / Nor, lawless, seeks to tread forbidden ways'.⁴⁵ The regime of the picture that Shenstone imposed was so strict it reportedly angered him when people strayed from the circuit walk, or started from the wrong point, or took it anticlockwise instead of clockwise. No surprise then that 'The Lessowes' (1764), the longest poem in Woodhouse's first publication, takes the reader through the park in the same order prescribed by Dodsley's official guide. Nevertheless, there are significant differences in the experience Woodhouse conveys of the Leasowes. He did not have the education to appreciate the park's many classical motifs and allusions. Instead, as he touchingly confessed later in 'The Lessowes, after Shenstone's Death' (1766), 'These mazey rills, these fringed glades, / I love because he' – that is, Shenstone – 'lov'd'.⁴⁶ Woodhouse correctly understood The Leasowes as a landscape of feeling, but as he could 'feel no GRECIAN, ... no ROMAN fire',⁴⁷ and could not borrow the aestheticised pathos of the Classics, he instead drew upon the visceral experiences of his own hard life. 'Spring' (1764), another poem in the first collection, is about how the beauty of nature failed to divert him from a life of unrelenting labour and worry. In it, the poetical persona pines for the past, when much of the day might be spent writing poetry, wandering about the land looking for medicinal herbs to treat people, or simply daydreaming.

Unlike Shenstone, Woodhouse did not always stay within the pastoral range of emblematic detail. In his version of 'The Lessowes', the 'blushing milkmaid', 'saunt'ring plough-boys' and other labouring figures appear.[48] Woodhouse also demonstrated a very different herbalist eye by naming the thirty or so species of plants around the statue of Venus (Fig. 14, number 38).

> By these prickly-leaved oak you see,
> And, with frontated leaves, the tulip-tree;
> Here, yellow blows the thorny barberry-bush;
> And velvet roses spread their bright'ning blush;
> And here the damask, there the provence rose,
> And cerasus's, double blooms disclose;
> With rip'ning fruit domestic raspberries glow,
> And sweets americans their scents bestow;
> White lilacs and syringas shed perfumes,
> And gelder-roses hang their bunchy blooms;
> And tow'ring planes erect their heads sublime,
> And, by the sweet-briar flow'ring willows climb;
> Here flimsy-leav'd acacia drooping weeps,
> And lowly laurustinus humbly creeps;
> The foreign dogwood shoots its sanguine sprays,
> And sable yews combine with cheerful bays;
> While, by the double-blossom'd hawthorn, stands
> Curl'd laurel, brought from Portugalian strands;
> And arbor-vitae's rear their fetid heads,
> And stinking tithymal effluvia spreads;
> Here Scotch and silver firs, the shrubs among,
> And lovely larch with hairy verdure hung,
> And sycamores their lofty summits rear,
> And silver-border'd foliage hollies wear;
> While these above, with various others, twine,
> Beneath, the piony and catch-fly shine;
> Narcissus fair, and early daffodil,
> Between their stems and vacant spaces fill.[49]

The vraisemblance of Woodhouse's poem is such that Mark Laird, a modern expert on landscape garden design, turns to it in order to understand the actual situation of The Leasowes, rather than Shenstone's poem, or Dodsley's prose guide. In his words, 'the horticultural content of the poem rings true'.[50] These lines of Woodhouse are not simply an empirical catalogue aiming for objectivity, however, but 'a composite picture of the shrubbery's flowering throughout the seasons' in the style of the illustrations in books on gardens and the natural world.[51] It is a landscape, in other words, but one with a greater fidelity to locality than Coleridge's. Reading these lines, can it not be said that from Shenstone to Woodhouse, we move from the emblematic to the environmental?[52]

Perhaps Woodhouse could not deploy the pastoral as consistently as Shenstone because his socioeconomic background did not allow it. Certainly, Bloomfield and Clare, male poets of a similar social status, found the georgic a more conducive vehicle than the pastoral to communicate their experiences. Woodhouse's dissatisfaction with the pastoral can be detected in 'The Lessowes' itself where it refers to him as 'a poor plebian [sic] swain'.[53] With the closure of the park to the general public, wandering around in 'russet garb, whose ragged rent-holes grin',[54] Woodhouse would have been painfully conscious of the gulf between himself and the rarefied company which Shenstone kept. In fact, this dissatisfaction breaks out most spectacularly over the next two pages, which throw the entire melancholic premise of the pastoral into question:

To range among my lawns, my streams, my trees,
[. . .]
Or, in deep meditation stretch'd along,
I'd court the muses with a sylvan song;
[. . .]
To scan with judgment the works of taste and wit.
Would bounteous heav'n my whole petition give,
Like thee, O SHENSTONE! would I wish to live.[55]

With this 100-acre rural retreat, with this life of ease, with good food and good friends, what possible reason could there be for anyone to feel miserable? Looking upon the green grass of England almost a century later, Karl Marx penned one of his most resonant lines on the land enclosure movement embroiling Woodhouse and Shenstone: 'The labourers are first driven from the land, and then come the sheep.'[56] While the struggling young poet was lent books, had his verses proof-read and was promoted to wealthy people, he was never given any direct financial support.[57] Shenstone was often short of money, but the picture-perfectness of having a lone ragged figure on his estate might not have been entirely lost on him too. Woodhouse had also asked for access for 'friends select' in 'An Elegy to William Shenstone',[58] yet he was the only one granted this privilege. One ragged figure a hermit might make,[59] but to allow him like company was to raise the spectre of banditti or worse, a hungry mob.

Despite the cultural prominence of hermits and hermitages, the eighteenth century was far from convinced of the value of an eremitical life.[60] Shenstone's *The Judgment of Hercules* (1741), ostensibly a celebration of Lyttelton's political retirement, is haunted by a fear of indolence and the desire for public distinction.[61] While the upper-class originators of the aesthetics of enclosure turned to their estates to quiet these uneasy sensations, the answer of young middle-class people – as Coleridge communicated in 'Reflections on Having Left a Place of Retirement' (1797) – was activism:

> Ah quiet Dell! dear Cot! and Mount Sublime!
> I was constrain'd to quit you. Was it right,
> While my unnumber'd Bethren toil'd and bled,
> That I should dream away the trusted Hours
> On rose-leaf Buds, pamp'ring the coward Heart
> With feelings all too delicate for use?[62]

That activism and the aesthetics of enclosure might be bedfellows in our middle-class psyche makes sense to me when I see vast tracts of land made useless in the name of conservation, like the Yorkshire Dales and the Lake District. Environmentalists are generally unable to reconcile the land with work that utilises the land productively. They equate such work with destruction, and the few who appreciate the process of knowing the land through work accommodate only archaic work like traditional farming, which would not yield a living for most people. Richard White has a succinct comment on the subject:

> Environmentalists have come to associate work – particularly heavy bodily labour, blue-collar work – with environmental degradation. This is true whether the work is in the woods, on the sea, in a refinery, in a chemical plant, in a pulp mill, or in a farmer's field ... Environmentalists usually imagine that when people who make things finish their day's work, nature is the poorer for it. Nature seems safest when shielded from human labor.[63]

The use of land for modern blue-collar work, including environmentally friendly wind and solar farms, is opposed as an ugly blemish on the landscape. If any relationship is accepted at all between people and the land it is of recreation, of which the Yorkshire Dales and the Lake District are the most spectacular consequences. I accept that the rapid population growth we have experienced globally over the last two centuries has generally been deleterious to the land, and virtually every plant and every other animal that lives on the land. I would question the credentials of any environmentalist who is not suspicious of the continuing thirst for economic development, or concerned about how not a single government – no matter how wealthy or developed the country – is even aiming for something as moderate as economic equilibrium. While I generally support the argument for sustainable retreat, I am persuaded that the leave-nature-alone ethos underlying it is misguided.

By seeking to exclude human beings, I fear it is simply another mutation of the aesthetics of enclosure that has already dispossessed millions from the land.

Notes

1. I am grateful for the funding extended to me through the Grant-in-Aid for Scientific Research (C) for the 2014 academic year and the Nanzan University Pache Research Subsidy I-A-2 for the 2015 academic year. This essay has benefited from discussions I've had with Jim and Marianne Mays at the Kyoto conference on Coleridge and Contemplation. I also wish to thank Simon J. White for giving me the opportunity to participate in the English and Modern Languages Seminar series at Oxford Brookes University, where I received pressing questions, in particular from Simon Kövesi and Adam Bridgen. Last but not least, I would like to acknowledge David Vallins's helpful comments on an early version of this essay, and if there are any omissions and oversights they are all my own.
2. Lucius Burckhardt, *Why is Landscape Beautiful? The Science of Strollology*, trans. Jill Denton (Berlin: Birkhäuser, 2015), p. 280.
3. Augustin Berque, *Thinking Through Landscape*, trans. Anne-Marie Feenberg-Dibon (London: Routledge, 2013), p. 5.
4. City of London, 'Damage or Injury', *Hampstead Heath Byelaws* No. 2, <http://www.cityoflondon.gov.uk/things-to-do/green-spaces/hampstead-heath/visitor-information/Pages/byelaws.aspx> (accessed 28 September 2019).
5. R. I. Woodhouse (ed.), *The Life and Poetical Works of James Woodhouse*, 2 vols (London: Leadenhall Press, 1896), 1: 1.
6. Kathleen Coburn (ed.), *The Notebooks of Samuel Taylor Coleridge* (London: Routledge & Kegan Paul, 1957), 1 (Text): 1577.
7. Jeffrey N. Cox, *Romanticism in the Shadow of War* (Cambridge: Cambridge University Press, 2014), p. 25.
8. Timothy Webb, 'Coleridge and Robert Emmet', *Irish Studies Review* 8 (2000): 304–24.
9. There is no firm evidence that any of these hermitages ever hosted a real live hermit, despite recent attempts by Gordon Campbell to prove otherwise in *The Hermit in the Garden: From Imperial Rome to Ornamental Gnome* (Oxford: Oxford University Press, 2013).
10. Sandy Haynes, 'William Shenstone and the Enville Landscape', *Arcadian Greens Rural* 53 (2002): 74.
11. The numbering here of the landscape features of The Leasowes basically follows Robert Dodsley's 'Description of the Leasowes', in William Shenstone, *The Works in Verse and Prose of William Shenstone*, 3 vols (London: Dodsley, 1764–9), 2: 331–72. Figure 14 is basically of the map he provided (facing p. 333), with a few additions of my own. Specifically, I have added the directional arrow, indicated the location of 'Virgil's Grove' and penned in numbers 20 and 38.
12. Ibid. p. 362.

13. Patrick Eyres, 'Introduction: Shenstone, The Leasowes and the Heritage Lottery Fund', *Arcadian Greens Rural* 53 (2002): 7.
14. Dodsley, 'Description of the Leasowes', in Shenstone, *The Works*, 2: 334–5.
15. Shenstone, *The Works*, 2: 30–5.
16. Ibid. 1: 198.
17. Dodsley, 'Description of the Leasowes', in Shenstone, *The Works*, 2: 363.
18. Shenstone, *The Works*, 2: 125.
19. As John Andrew Hemingway makes clear in his PhD thesis, *The Origins, Development and Influence of William Shenstone's Landscape Garden Design at The Leasowes, Halesowen* (University of Birmingham, 2017), pp. 290–301. My thanks to Adam Bridgen for drawing my attention to this work.
20. Shenstone, *The Works*, 2: 127.
21. Ibid. 3: 162.
22. Ibid. 3: 161.
23. Eyres, 'Introduction', p. 6.
24. Shenstone, *The Works*, 3: 141.
25. Ibid. 3: 183.
26. [Samuel Taylor Coleridge and William Wordsworth,] *Lyrical Ballads, With a Few Other Poems* (London: Arch, 1798), p. 64.
27. According to William Mason, *The English Garden: A Poem. Book the First*, 3rd edn (London: Dodsley, 1778), p. 33.
28. [Coleridge and Wordsworth,] *Lyrical Ballads*, pp. 44–8.
29. Samuel Taylor Coleridge, *Christabel: Kubla Khan, a Vision; The Pains of Sleep* (London: Murray), p. 22. I would have missed this if not for Peter Cheyne.
30. Coleridge and Wordsworth, *Lyrical Ballads*, p. 66.
31. Ibid. p. 66.
32. Samuel Taylor Coleridge, *Poetical Works*, J. C. C. Mays (ed.), 3 vols in 6 parts (Princeton: Princeton University Press, 2001), 1, part 1 (Reading Text): 518.
33. The Thames freezing over in winter was a regular occurrence from 1776 onwards until well into Victorian times. For more information on the climatic conditions refer to Mark Laird, *A Natural History of English Gardening 1650–1800* (New Haven, CT: Yale University Press, 2015), pp. 19–20.
34. Peter De Bolla, *The Education of the Eye: Painting, Landscape, and Architecture in Eighteenth-Century Britain* (Stanford: Stanford University Press, 2003), p. 121.
35. Ibid. p. 120.
36. Coleridge, *Poetical Works*, 2, part 2 (Variorum Text): 913–4.
37. Hemingway, *William Shenstone's Landscape Garden Design at The Leasowes*, p. 200.
38. Quoted by Christopher Gallagher, 'The Leasowes: A History of Landscape', *The Garden History Society* 24 (1996): 211.
39. Shenstone, *The Works*, 3: 373.
40. Ibid. 2: 129.
41. Dodsley, 'Description of the Leasowes', in Shenstone, *The Works*, 2: 336.
42. Shenstone, *The Works*, 3: 180.

43. James Woodhouse, *Poems on Sundry Occasions* (London: Dodsley, 1764), p. iv.
44. Ibid. p. 4.
45. Ibid. p. 3.
46. James Woodhouse, *Poems on Several Occasions*, 2nd edn (London: Dodsley, 1766), p. 124.
47. Woodhouse, *Poems on Sundry Occasions*, p. 6.
48. Ibid. p. 48.
49. Ibid. pp. 97–8.
50. Mark Laird, *The Flowering of the Landscape Garden: English Pleasure Grounds 1720–1800* (Philadelphia, PA: University of Pennsylvania Press, 1999), p. 114.
51. Ibid. p. 114.
52. Woodhouse's work is not an 'environmental poem', as defined by Ann Fisher-Wirth and Laura-Gray Street in *The Ecopoetry Anthology* as 'poetry propelled by and directly engaged with active and politicized environmentalism' (San Antonio, TX: Trinity University Press, 2013), p. xxiv; nor does it seem to me even able to fully satisfy Lawrence Buell's more capacious idea of an 'environmental text' in *The Environmental Imagination* (Cambridge, MA: Harvard University Press, 1995), pp. 7–8. Rather, it is environmental in the sense of its ecological detail, exceptional for a landscape poem of the time, and of featuring an engagement with the non-human world that could interest people like Buell, Fisher-Wirth and Street, who are directly engaged with environmentalism today.
53. Woodhouse, *Poems on Sundry Occasions*, p. 53.
54. Ibid. p. 63.
55. Ibid. pp. 63–4.
56. Karl Marx, *Capital Volume One: A Critique of Political Economy*, trans. Samuel Moore and Edward Aveling (New York: Dover Publications, [1906] 2011), p. 470.
57. This is not to belittle in any way the considerable assistance that Shenstone rendered to Woodhouse, which Sandro Jung has highlighted on several occasions; for example, in 'Shenstone, Woodhouse, and Mid-Eighteenth-Century Poetics', *Philological Quarterly* 88, nos 1–2 (2009): 129–30.
58. Woodhouse, *Poems on Sundry Occasions*, p. 8.
59. The possibility that Woodhouse might have served as an ornamental hermit for Shenstone was suggested to me by Simon J. White.
60. Stephen Bending, 'Uneasy Sensations: Shenstone, Retirement and Fame', *Arcadian Greens Rural* 53 (2002): 32–3.
61. William Shenstone, *The Judgment of Hercules, a Poem* (London: Dodsley, 1741), pp. 25–7.
62. Samuel Taylor Coleridge, *Poems, by S. T. Coleridge*, 2nd edn (London: Robinsons, 1797), pp. 102–3.
63. Richard White, 'Are You an Environmentalist or Do You Work for a Living?', in William Cronon (ed.), *Uncommon Ground: Rethinking the Human Place in Nature* (New York: Norton, 1996), p. 172.

Chapter 9

A World of Fire and Drought: Ecosocialism, Improvement and Apocalypse in James Woodhouse's *Crispinus Scriblerus*

Adam Bridgen

Labouring-class writing is emerging as one of the new frontiers of ecocriticism in British Romantic studies. Previously, owing to Jonathan Bate's influential *Romantic Ecology* (1991), it was maintained that the Romantic poets, led by William Wordsworth, offered a powerful vision of human harmonisation with nature that we would do well to emulate in the present.[1] Scholars have since questioned this paradigm, however, exploring how Romantic naturalism may in fact be a problematic model of environmental writing. Timothy Morton's *Ecology Without Nature* (2007) argues that Romanticism's transcendental vision of 'Nature', as something existing outside of human culture, accommodated rather than resisted the destructive processes of enclosure, industrialisation and imperialism.[2] As Morton contends, this vision was a kind of psychological compensation to assuage concerns about the rapacious drives of capitalism, a case of applying 'aesthetic[s] as an anaesthetic'.[3] Many of the literary works Romantic ecocritics have drawn attention to in fact perpetuate a mode of environmentalism that 'impedes a proper relationship with the earth and its life-forms'.[4] As a consequence, critics now stress the need to reorient Romantic ecocriticism. In his 2018 review article, Jeremy Davies calls for a shift away from Whiggish claims about 'the origins of contemporary environmental sensibilities, [. . .] towards a critical history of regimes of environmental exploitation'.[5] The school of ecocritics Davies hails – Timothy Morton, Timothy Clark, Katey Castellano, Alan Bewell and Simon Kövesi – 'resituate Romanticism within the real process of historical change'.[6] With this new aim in mind, Davies stresses that 'one of the more promising ways forward for Romantic ecocriticism' is 'a closer entwinement with the study of labouring-class writing'.[7] The poetry of John Clare features prominently in Romantic ecocriticism, but Davies draws attention to the revisionary potential of a far broader corpus, first highlighted by Bridget Keegan's *British Labouring-Class Nature Poetry, 1730–1837* (2008). Rejecting the primitivist platitude that labouring-class poets were somehow 'closer to nature', Keegan demonstrates how these authors adapted existing poetical genres to their own views, as well as to deftly critique elite ideology.[8] For instance, Keegan considers Robert Bloomfield's inventive experimentation with the neoclassical georgic mode, resulting in an affective poetics of environmental stewardship that 'model[s] a responsible relationship to the non-human'.[9] By attending to labouring-class writing, we can better appreciate how social class mediates literary representation. In ecocritical terms, moreover, by diversifying the sources we draw upon, we stand to gain a richer and more layered understanding of environmental writing and of the various responses that the social, economic and political transformations of this period elicited.

Central to any such project is the Staffordshire-born shoemaker-poet James Woodhouse (1735–1820), whose discussion of landscape parks and troubled career as steward of Sandleford Priory – the estate of the Bluestocking socialite and businesswoman Elizabeth Montagu (1718–1800) – make him an invaluable point of reference for exploring the politics of late eighteenth-century nature writing. Eighteenth-century society was prevailingly hierarchical,[10] but thanks to his astute social skills Woodhouse gained the support of patrons.[11] While this was no longer the only route into print, patronage remained a crucial stepping stone for labouring-class poets in this period.[12] In 1759, Woodhouse addressed a poem to the English poet and designer of The Leasowes, William Shenstone (1714–63), petitioning him for access to the famous garden. The Leasowes was an archetype of the less formalised, naturalistic landscape aesthetic which came to dominate in Georgian Britain, but had recently been closed to the public due to acts of vandalism. Shenstone was impressed by Woodhouse's efforts, and over the next four years supported his development as a poet.[13] Through Shenstone, he was introduced to wealthier patrons – including John Ward, 1st Viscount Dudley and Ward, and Lord George Lyttelton – and consequently many of his early poems pay tribute to even grander gardens. Woodhouse's depiction of Sandleford Priory came later, however, and under very different circumstances. Elizabeth Montagu also played a critical role in Woodhouse's success, using her extensive social network to gather subscriptions for a second edition of his *Poems* in 1766. Following their publication, she offered Woodhouse the position of land steward at her estate in Berkshire. In addition to collecting rents and keeping accounts, maintaining buildings and intercepting intruders, he oversaw the agricultural development of the 500-acre property. Indeed, evidence suggests he had little opportunity to write in this period. As time went on, he fell out of Montagu's favour, and was dismissed in 1778. Though Montagu rehired Woodhouse as her house steward in 1781, she dismissed him again in 1788. He subsequently went into business as a London bookseller and it was in the 1790s that he started composing his magnum opus, *The Life and Lucubrations of Crispinus Scriblerus*. This extraordinary seventeen-chapter, 28,013-line poetic autobiography lays bare his anger at Montagu, but also gives voice to a radical Christian egalitarianism only seen darkly in his earlier works.[14] Due to its incendiary nature, only the first and most unobjectionable chapter saw publication during Woodhouse's lifetime (in 1814).[15] It was not until 1896 that the work was published in full, in the two-volume *Life and Poetical Works of James Woodhouse* brought out by his grandson. Recognised now as 'one of the most important literary records of plebeian social and ideological critique of the late eighteenth century', critics since William Christmas have found much of interest in *Crispinus Scriblerus*, including its extensive passages on emparkment and enclosure.[16] Woodhouse's time in Montagu's employ was evidently a signal influence upon his thinking, especially when she hired Lancelot 'Capability' Brown to redesign Sandleford in the 1780s. This experience resulted in a significant revision of Woodhouse's position on landscape gardens, as Keegan and Peter Denney have pointed out: gone was the equanimity of his earlier poetry, which was replaced by a politicised exposure of the exclusionary and exploitative violence that underlay the Brownian aesthetic of untouched nature, free from any signs of use or industry.[17] Both critics also note Woodhouse's georgic ethos, and his preference for land that was productive rather than purely ornamental. Keegan further argues that Woodhouse advocated an 'environmental ethic of Christian stewardship', which emphasised the preservation of nature as a religious duty; moreover, considering his account of the ruinous effects of Montagu's drive for profits at Sandleford, Keegan explores how he developed a conception of nature's limits.[18]

The complex social and environmental argument Woodhouse developed in his vast autobiography – or 'Novel, in Verse', as he also styled it – however extends beyond simply expressing care or respect for nature. As Steve Van-Hagen writes, *Crispinus Scriblerus* 'remain[s] to a large extent critically unexplored',[19] a fact made all the more unfortunate when we consider its curious parallels with Wordsworth's *Prelude*.[20] Developing on Denney and Keegan's insights, this chapter examines the georgic ethos Woodhouse articulates in *Crispinus Scriblerus*, but also his apprehension of the devastating directions of eighteenth-century 'improvement'. Where Woodhouse's land politics and his environmental expressions have previously been considered separately, therefore, I treat the two as intertwined. As I argue, just as *Crispinus Scriblerus* traces 'the poet's life of servitude and his evolving social and moral consciousness',[21] so too does it chart the emergence of a labouring-class ecosocial sensibility, as Woodhouse begins to perceive the ways in which the ascendance of capitalist ideology not only led to the exclusion and impoverishment of working people, but also severely degraded the environments they relied upon.[22] In Woodhouse, a utilitarian georgic emphasis on agricultural production is tempered by a critical awareness of the social and ecological cost of profit-driven maximisation.[23] Undoubtedly, Woodhouse's experience at Sandleford was central to this recognition. He realised that the pastoral idyll Montagu sought to create at her country estate was in fact funded by aggressive agricultural improvements, as well as the lucrative coal-mining operations she oversaw in the north of England. Consequently, he sought to expose the Brownian aesthetic as a lie, a pleasing fantasy which cloaked the colonialist extraction of wealth from places and peoples elsewhere. To measure *Crispinus Scriblerus* by the conventional yardstick of 'green' expressions of care for nature, therefore, does not comprehend the social and political thrust of the work's environmental argument. Substantiating this, I conclude with a novel account of how Woodhouse conceptualised the apocalyptic ramifications of elite consumption through metaphors of fire and drought. Evidently, Woodhouse apprehended the large-scale effects which human activity might have upon the world. Quite different from either the agrarian utopianism of this period or, by contrast, the fatalistic Malthusian theory of overpopulation, Woodhouse imagined that it was capitalist wealth extraction which threatened social and ecological collapse, by depleting the land until it could no longer support life. By thus combining a georgic understanding of nature with resistance to the socio-economic drives slowly degrading it, I argue, Woodhouse's ecosocial imagination was both pragmatic and prophetic.

Extravagant Wastes: Woodhouse's Alternative Landscape Aesthetic

While one aim of Woodhouse's in writing *Crispinus Scriblerus* was to process the trauma he had endured as Elizabeth Montagu's steward (a 'Tyrant's Tool', as he bitterly put it), the work also grounds a powerful claim, on behalf of himself and his class, to be able to 'judge of right and wrong – of woe *and* weal / Awake, to reason; and alive, to feel!' (my emphasis).[24] As a matter of fact, the work engages both with subjective emotional experiences and with national and political matters. Alongside issues such as corruption and the integration of church and state, the politics of land was of signal importance to Woodhouse. It is a subject he engaged with repeatedly from the outset of *Crispinus Scriblerus*, and one to which he clearly distinguishes his approach on the basis of his working background. In an intriguing anticipation of Wordsworth's poetic reclamation of the 'plainer and more emphatic language' of '[l]ow and rustic life' in the *Lyrical Ballads* (1800),[25] Woodhouse claimed that a 'language like his own' might be salutary, in addition, on public matters, because

> Tho' neither classic lore, nor lofty lays,
> Nor genuine genius, plead[s] just claims for praise;
> Some simple hint may, haply, have its use,
> In strengthening Truth, or baffling foul abuse, –
> Expose base Villainy to public view –
> Distinguish spurious Patronage from true –
> Prove happiness, on Earth, may Penury wed,
> When Piety prepares the board and bed;
> Or urge more generous, energetic, Mind,
> To sketch some nobler scheme to bless Mankind! (p. 11)

This is a practically minded Romantic manifesto, in which Woodhouse proposed to use his writing to condemn contemporary abuses of power while also recommending a different model of terrestrial behaviour – a 'nobler scheme' – to better serve humankind. Not apologising for poverty but its importance as a source of insight, Woodhouse argued that poetry like his could offer a valuable perspective on nature and humankind's place within it.[26] Asking '[w]hy may not poor Crispinus' native Hill' be the subject of verse, he explained that in contrast to the 'swelling strains' of highbrow poets, who applauded the 'vain ornaments, and vile attire' of aristocratic estates, he was 'unperverted' by the desire for wealth or fame (p. 12). By his account, he was an 'unaspiring' poet whose aim was not to 'exalt' nature, nor 'to preclude contentions thro' the Earth', but rather to describe the world around him according to what 'integrity and truth require' (p. 12).

Woodhouse's critique of the obsequiousness and fake harmony of eighteenth-century topographical poetry, such as Alexander Pope's *Windsor-Forest*,[27] finds further purchase in his opening descriptions of the aristocratic parks situated around his 'native Hill' of Rowley Regis in Staffordshire, including Himley, Hagley and The Leasowes. On Himley, in particular, Woodhouse offers a nuanced appraisal of the discourse of improvement that clearly illustrates the social basis of his environmental thinking. It is important to note that 'improvement' has today acquired a peculiarly negative valency which might not be entirely merited. Marxist critics tend to think of it as a deceptive 'code word' for capitalist farming, enclosure and landscape gardening, which was deleterious to rural populations and destructive of a whole way of life.[28] However, the effects of enclosure were uneven, and historians distinguish two stages of agricultural change, the first taking place in the seventeenth century, which increased productivity among yeoman farmers, and the second in the eighteenth century, which infamously increased the possessions and profits of large landowners, to the detriment of peasant farmers and labourers.[29] Undoubtedly, Woodhouse was a supporter of this earlier model of improvement and the enclosure enabling it. This is evident in the account of Viscount Dudley's enclosure of the 'wild wastes' adjourning Himley (p. 15), a rapturous description of how he 'Call'd out the mattock, axe, and probing spade' to cultivate the land, so that

> Soon o'er the smiling wilderness were seen
> Rich clover grass, and turnips' vivid green;
> While bordering Peasantry, with hopes, behold,
> Fields gladly float in waves of wheaten gold! (p. 16)

As Keegan has noted, this georgic ethos 'praise[s] land that is fertile and productive rather than ornamental but fallow'.[30] Woodhouse was keen to stress this practical aesthetic, stating that 'None touch'd with sympathy, or blest with taste, / Loves barren wild, or drear deformed waste' (p. 16). Lest we think him an unqualified supporter of enclosure, however, this instance of agricultural intrepidity is swiftly inverted by the attention he drew to its unequal distribution:

> But, ah! how seldom Scenes, like these, supply
> One gleam of hope to Penury's eager eye!
> How rare one real privilege impart,
> To meagre Misery's hapless, pining, heart! (p. 16)

Rather than improving the lives of the 'bordering Peasantry', the use of enclosure '[t]o make exclusive claims o'er all the plain' (p. 17) forced people off the land and into a desperate dependence on wage-labour to gain the shelter and food that they formerly had free access to. While it is the case that Woodhouse held 'improvement [as] a Christian duty', as Keegan suggests, this sense of duty was also partnered by communitarian values, which required that improvement not override the rights of the poor to access land: 'The Earth [was] meant for all Mankind' (p. 17).[31]

Recalling Woodhouse's egalitarian convictions helps to explain the ecosocial nature of his critique of late eighteenth-century improvement, and his emerging conception of its destructive social and environmental effects. For Woodhouse the greatest so-called 'wastes' were not tracts of unproductive land, such as the former 'wild wastes' of Himley, but land which was enclosed in order to create private parks, and hence egregiously 'wasted' (p. 12) to gratify elites.[32] Instead of contributing to the betterment of society as a whole, such improvements achieved the very opposite: 'Nature reduc'd to savage state agen, / Excluding culture, and expunging Men!' (p. 20). The fashionable Brownian aesthetic, which erased sites of labour with 'unproductive Shades', and 'Streams, that useless glide' (p. 21), was actually destructive of human growth and cultivation:

> Thus countless acres lie, in worthless waste,
> To banish all that frets fastidious Taste –
> All squeamish Pomp, or Arrogance, disgusts,
> That low'rs Life's pride, or Eyes' deluding lusts –
> Ev'n Population's springs, and Culture's course,
> Must stop their currents, and dry up their source,
> The Country's riches, and the Kingdom's dow'r,
> To Ostentation, sacrificed by Pow'r! (pp. 21–2)

The political economist Adam Smith had praised expensive estate improvements in terms of their trickle-down effect, by which an 'invisible hand' would provide for the needs of local people, advance society and 'afford means to the multiplications of the species'.[33] Woodhouse argued otherwise, casting this as an improvident hubris reaping catastrophic drought: enclosing land for this purpose 'dr[ied] up' the 'source' of 'Population's springs, and Culture's course' (that is, agriculture) and by doing so undermined the actual basis of national prosperity: its people.

Woodhouse would probably have questioned the environmental activism that created the national parks of the nineteenth and twentieth centuries, in which designated 'natural' areas were preserved from human activity. For him, nature was land rather than landscape, a site of continual and even redemptive struggle by which the necessities of life might be won by human invention and labour. He dismissed the fine works of landscape art that obscured this as 'Expensive Caricatures! belying Life; / Where Art and Nature wage continual strife!' (p. 50). Given the economic dependency he faced for most of his life, it is understandable that he looked to agricultural improvement as a means of bettering the lives of working people. One cannot overlook the fact that Woodhouse was writing during a period of acute poverty and famine in Britain.[34] Accordingly, he hailed the 'new volcanoes' (p. 25) of coal-driven industry sprouting across Birmingham and Wolverhampton – one of the most industrialised areas of Britain at the time – because of the 'benefits Mankind' might gain from them.[35] Of course, his subsequent imagery of 'clanking engines vomit[ing] scalding streams' (p. 25) strays into a more bleak and threatening portrayal than the more distant, harmonious scene-setting of the picturesque (see Fig. 15), suggesting that Woodhouse was not completely unsuspicious of these industrial technologies. In any case, he was concerned less with production per se than with broader patterns of elite consumption driving it, which he astutely perceived to be the greater threat to both society and the land. At the end of Chapter 2, following an account of Shenstone's straitened circumstances (owing to the cost of The Leasowes' improvement), *Crispinus Scriblerus* proceeds to satirise 'Taste's pregnant pow'rs, / Still more voracious while he more devours' (p. 49). While depicting the exorbitant cost of fashionable improvements, where 'glitt'ring guineas fuse in waterfalls' and 'And youthful woods, ag'd houses renovate', the passage culminates with a vision of the damage done to both land and workers in the process, as 'Earth's womb, incarnate, fate ordains to feel / Hard labour's pangs, with instruments of steel' (p. 49). Unlike more leisured critics of industrial change who held workers culpable for the destruction of nature, Woodhouse thus took aim at the wealthy elites and their consumptive demands.[36] In fact, the fiery imagery that Woodhouse had earlier used to describe industry is redeployed here as a metaphor for the insatiable desires of large landowners. They are described as 'Volcanoes!' who

> Would scorch, with cruel heat, each prostrate plain,
> Did not the hand of Heav'n their wrath restrain;
> Turn their fierce fires – reverse their vengeful aims,
> And broil themselves, while belching furious flames! (p. 56)

While some solace is found in the fact that the 'voracious' appetites of landlords often proved personally ruinous for them, the implication remains that, if left unchecked, their destructiveness could potentially be apocalyptic – burning through everything in their path.[37] With this subtle shift from new industries to landowners as 'Volcanoes!', Woodhouse seems here to literalise aspects of J. M. W. Turner's threatening industrial landscapes. As John Gold and George Revill suggest, specifically in relation to his 1835 painting of Dudley, Turner saw industrialisation, 'aristocratic wealth, and traditional authority' as 'driving forces for environmental change'.[38]

Natural and National Limits: Ecology as a Response to Globalisation

Undoubtedly, it was Woodhouse's time as land steward at Sandleford which most clearly revealed to him the threat that commercial improvement posed, both to labouring people and to the land itself. In 1767, Woodhouse was hired by Elizabeth Montagu to take over as land steward at Sandleford. Their relationship was mutually 'rapturous' at first.[39] Montagu was keen to develop the estate's agricultural potential, and saw him as the man to do it. As she noted to her husband, Edward, Woodhouse not only possessed 'modesty & humility' but also a 'surprising disposition to sciences'.[40] Moreover, Woodhouse was no stranger to agricultural work, having often helped at his father's small freehold farm. Montagu romanticised the Woodhouses' settlement at Sandleford, writing to Lord Lyttelton on 24 July 1767: 'My Poet Laureate, his wife & babes are all here. I reckon I have made the finest plantation at Sandleford that could be. I have brought these roots of virtue, ingenuity, & innocence, & I hope they will flourish here.'[41] Despite these pastoral fantasies, Montagu was in her later years increasingly concerned 'with utility, industry, and improvement'.[42] Given the scale of the task of making Sandleford agriculturally productive, Woodhouse was left with little time to write. Indeed, Montagu celebrated the fact that she had 'taken him from [A]pollo to give him to Ceres'.[43] In 1768, she wrote: '[Woodhouse] exceeds even my hopes & wishes', adding, 'Integrity, diligence, & sagacity, are by him employ'd for me with unremitting zeal from the rising to the setting sun.'[44] By Woodhouse's estimate, he increased agricultural revenue '[f]rom nearly nothing to ten hundred pounds!' (p. 79). On her part, Montagu had noted in 1771 that '[t]he Farm is in very good order & will now be very profitable.'[45] But Montagu expected ever greater rewards, pithily stating in 1774: 'I exhort Mr Woodhouse to make [Sandleford] every year carry out & bring in more money.'[46] After Edward's death in 1776, Montagu took over the management of the family estates, including the coal mines in the North. She became, as Betty Rizzo has described, 'a notable captain of industry and something of a domestic tyrant'.[47] Indeed, this shift seems to have intensified her expectations of the farm. She had long deemed Woodhouse 'rather too mild' as an overseer, and was also vexed by his management of livestock (judging from his sensibilities, it appears he may have been 'too mild' on this front also).[48] In 1777 Montagu thus recruited someone 'capable of improving [the livestock] which [Woodhouse] does not understand, or will not attend to'.[49] Unbeknown to him, Woodhouse ended up training his replacement: he was subsequently fired in 1778. Although Montagu, in a letter to her sister, professed never to have doubted Woodhouse's abilities, his 'pride & impertinence' was more than she could tolerate.[50]

While Montagu's demands ultimately proved calamitous for Woodhouse, the experience offered him an important first-hand insight into the darker side of eighteenth-century agricultural improvement. In turn, this experience contributed to his remarkable conception of ecological sustainability in *Crispinus Scriblerus*. As Woodhouse had made clear in Chapter 1, he was a supporter of economic development insofar as it benefited local populations. In a similar vein, Chapter 4 recounts Woodhouse's first decade at Sandleford, detailing his eager engagement in the science of agriculture to cultivate the 'wilderness' of Sandleford, including drainage, fencing and the planting of crops such as turnips to feed animals over winter, as well as his battles against weather, weeds and wanton human activity (pp. 76–9). While exulting in the farm's newfound productivity, Woodhouse however stresses nature's limits:[51]

> Predestin'd limits bound all earthly things,
> Terrestrial Kingdoms, and terrestrial Kings!
> A providential point still strongly stands
> Like polar ice, or Ocean's rocks and sands!
> Some *ne plus ultra* runs all Nature through,
> No art can counteract, or strength subdue! (pp. 79–80)

Drawing upon the 'curving courses' of sun and moon as an analogy, Woodhouse presents the physical universe as a carefully balanced, self-limiting, cyclical system, which it is inadvisable to push beyond. The phrase '*ne plus ultra*', from Latin, originally meant 'not further beyond', and is fabled to have been inscribed onto the Pillars of Hercules to warn sailors against travelling beyond the Mediterranean into the Atlantic Ocean. As this allusion suggests, Woodhouse's stress on 'limits' was likely reinforced by a sense of the risks that accompanied European colonisation, and the unprecedented transmission of different natures that it had led to.[52] In fact, Woodhouse's farming theories indicate a complex understanding of the symbiosis of plants and soil, and by connection his advocacy of native plants over foreign. In contrast to the 'experimental' (p. 80) capitalist practices of his time, which often supplanted native biomes with more profitable cash crops (the most infamous example being, of course, sugar in the Caribbean), Woodhouse sided with the view that 'Each plant, and tree, thrives best on parent-ground' (p. 81). He concluded that while transplanting 'pleads best for speculative pride', a surer policy, favoured by 'Nature's Lovers', was a native one. Many labouring-class poets before him had favoured domestic agriculture and plant varieties over nouveau colonial projects and imports,[53] but Woodhouse goes further to frame this nativist position in ecological terms. He arraigned the speculative improvements Montagu demanded of him by describing the resulting crop failures. For example, her 'Siberian Barley' required the use of vast quantities of 'Exsiccant soot' which damaged the topsoil: not only was the resulting crop a failure, therefore, but the process was also laborious and 'at heavy cost / While better soils from native surface [were] lost' (p. 83–4). Montagu was disappointed by the results and lamented 'the meager condition of the soil' at Sandleford in general, which prevented her from living in the dignified 'state of a Shepherdess Queen'.[54] While Woodhouse was ultimately blamed for the failure of these experiments, his account suggests they were performed against his better judgement, and in spite of his preference for 'crops of [more] durable delights' (p. 86).

Extraction to Extremes: Anticipating the Anthropocene

Woodhouse's time at Sandleford exposed him to some of the dire consequences of capitalism's inexorable triumph over slower, more traditional modes of land management. Importantly, it also revealed to him the pernicious, naturalistic landscape aesthetic which attended and accommodated this transition. As alluded to above, Montagu was an exemplar of this shift from an 'ancient, public, and (implicitly) masculine' ideal of estate management, which stressed the subordination of private desires to the preservation of social harmony, to a more individualistic, commercial outlook, in which 'social relations were reduced to purely economic relations between consumers and producers'.[55] This change in Montagu's attitudes was likely precipitated by her involvement in coal mining at Denton Hall, an estate her husband inherited in 1758. As Montagu wrote to Lord Lyttelton on her first visit there, 'we are possess'd with the Northumberland Demon covetousness, I find there is no resisting the contagion. I thought myself secured from it by many fine sentiments but I am now as deeply infected as the natives themselves.'[56] Although Montagu was often reluctant to admit her inculcation in this commercial mindset, it grew more difficult to deny. With Edward's death in 1776, she became one of the wealthiest independent women in eighteenth-century Britain, with control over land and estates in London and Berkshire as well as a lucrative coal-mining operation in Tyneside.[57] Juggling the roles of 'A Critick, a Coal Owner, a Land Steward, a Sociable Creature' was no doubt challenging, and Montagu's proclivity for business was inevitably at odds with her rather more genteel reputation as a leading Bluestocking.[58] The tension between the commercial and aristocratic aspects of her character is exhibited quite clearly in her letters on the management of Sandleford. Insisting on the one hand on profit, yet on the other desiring to appear as a bountiful 'Shepherdess Queen', Montagu demonstrates a characteristically modern and contradictory view of nature which, in Donna Landry's words, 'is unthinkingly instrumental and unthinkingly pastoral at the same time'.[59] This contradictory view is further manifest in Montagu's hiring of Capability Brown, whom she praised as 'the first man in the innocent & lovely art of adorning the Pastoral scene'.[60] Brown's designs aimed to create rural idylls; so where Sandleford had previously been 'fully integrated with the working countryside', with outbuildings, barns and a kitchen garden around the Priory, soon these blemishes were moved to the peripheries as informal clumps of trees, sprawling lawns, ornamental walks and artificial lakes took their place.[61]

Sandleford's landscaping during the early 1780s was a decisive stimulus for Woodhouse's ecosocial perspective, particularly in terms of his sense of the damaging effect that commercial forces were having on human relations with nature, as well as towards each other. Requiring his skills once again, in 1781 Montagu rehired Woodhouse as her house steward. Promised 'full command of town, and country, domes' (p. 130), he was to oversee domestic arrangements at Sandleford Priory as well as Montagu's newly built London house on Portman Square. The improvements Montagu commissioned were of considerable expense, but she justified them – in accordance with liberal economic thinking – on the grounds of the employment that they might provide for local people.[62] Also, as Stephen Bending argues, this rural paradise at Sandleford functioned as a 'necessary foil to the self-display of a fine lady in the metropolis', a means to naturalise her wealth and distinguish her use of it 'from the false aspirations of the vulgar rich'.[63] Not surprisingly, Woodhouse exposed the falsity of such representations in *Crispinus Scriblerus*. Clearly signposting the extractive industries that were the basis of her wealth, he insisted she 'Racks every tenant, ransacks all her Mines, / To build her Temple, and adorn her Shrines!' (p. 145).[64] In Chapter 9, which offers a behind-the-scenes view of Woodhouse's part in the estate renovations, he revealed Montagu's 'innocent [. . .] Pastoral scene' as a project in fact underpinned by vanity and violence. It was just one of many of her 'vast schemes' to 'exhibit more Wealth, Wit, and Taste' (p. 165), such that after a winter closeted away in fashionable London society, she might

[. . .] in gothic Mansion, on the Plain,
Through leafy, flowery, fruitful, Seasons, reign;
That there, her sylvan Votaries, all, might view
Her grand achievements, and give glory due! (p. 166)

Crispinus Scriblerus also destroys any notion of the charitableness of Montagu's improvements. Although Woodhouse's new role was 'different from the former burdens borne', he stressed the significant continuities it had with the kind of maximising, profit-driven behaviour that Montagu had previously demanded of him as a farmer: 'Self-interest [was] *primum mobile* in both – ', he wrote, 'Here – cool Economy – there – greatest growth' (p. 166). As house steward, Woodhouse's responsibilities would traditionally have been limited to domestic economy and staff, but Montagu also charged him with overseeing the 'servile Band' of 'Builders – Labourers – Gardeners' (p. 167) assembled for the renovations at Sandleford. Woodhouse was tasked with provisioning the workers as 'cheaply' as possible, 'Providing needfuls, and preventing spoil', while also 'urg[ing] full effort, and preclud[ing] neglect' (p. 167). Far from a 'Christian Scheme', *Crispinus Scriblerus* drives home the point that Montagu's extravagance belied her extreme miserliness – 'A System', as Woodhouse sagely put it, which 'Wealth must form in Self-defence' (p. 166). While *Crispinus Scriblerus* makes clear the oppressive nature of Woodhouse's new role, it also draws attention to the underlying exploitation of other people and places which Montagu's sentimental fantasy obscured.[65]

In Woodhouse's eyes, Montagu's money motives left her ill-equipped to fulfil the traditional responsibilities of a landowner. While in Chapter 4 he had detailed how Montagu's drive for profit eventually overturned Sandleford's agricultural productivity, in Chapter 9 he proceeded to explain how this desire also corrupted his employer's aesthetic vision. Woodhouse presented 'One cruel Anecdote' to instantiate this: Montagu's picking and selling the flowers he had lovingly planted in a 'small sequester'd space' of the estate. Intended for her pleasure, as well as his own, the site he cultivated was 'Contiguous to each common Office' (p. 168) – a detail that suggests the location was likely the wooded area between the Priory and the farmhouse known as 'The Wilderness Walk' (see Fig. 16). Woodhouse's description of the place suggests his flower gardening was, not unlike his farming, informed by a more restrained ethos that supplemented rather than supplanted existing natures. As Keegan notes, Woodhouse worked on a small scale, and chose to cultivate 'indigenous plants'.[66] In selecting a 'squalid, weedy, wild, and waste' area to plant 'rare flowers and fruits' (pp. 168–9) he was performing 'wilderness planting' (such as Shenstone had popularised at The Leasowes).⁶⁷ This was a pleasant, beautifying activity, as well as a social one: the various flowers he had planted – 'alpine strawberries', 'Pinks', 'Carnations', 'Convolvuluses', 'evening Primrose', 'Stocks' and 'Roses' – were the 'gifts of Friends, benevolent, and kind' (p. 169). Woodhouse was horrified, therefore, when Montagu decided to cut these flowers to sell. To add insult to injury, she also forbade him from inviting others to enjoy the garden. Woodhouse did not so much charge Montagu for her lack of consideration of his 'care and toil', however, as for her inability to apprehend the difference that these flowers made to the place, by imprinting 'beauty on that barren Site' (pp. 169–70).⁶⁸ As such Woodhouse expresses just how debased Montagu's aesthetics were: how, for all her talk of the pastoral, she was woefully 'unable to appreciate nature's beauty, seeing it only as an instrument for her profit'.⁶⁹ Moreover, as Denney notes, this 'cruel Anecdote' also illuminates how Montagu had effectively denied people like Woodhouse the capacity for aesthetic appreciation, enforcing an even more rigid distinction between the propertied rich and the landless labourer.⁷⁰

By bringing into focus the joint social and environmental damages of landscape improvement, Woodhouse's account of Sandleford's emparkment is central to the ecosocial thrust of *Crispinus Scriblerus*. This personal recollection, moreover, anticipates a significant development in the overarching argument of the work. Emboldened by his experiences, Woodhouse developed a more far-reaching condemnation of the capitalistic ethos which Montagu had come to exemplify:

> [. . .] Cunning's distillation drains
> From reeking vallies, and from weeping plains;
> From reservoirs, in mines, which skill can draw
> With forcing-pumps, and engines, fram'd by Law –
> Or what State-chemistry extracts, in drops,
> From furnaces and forges; sheds and shops –
> From sweat of toiling Man, or labouring Beast,
> The mighty mass grows, constantly increas'd;
> From every melting eye, and moisten'd hand,
> Till every source seems dry, thro' all the Land –
> But scarce a single particle returns,
> To feed those Fountains, or to fill those Urns –
> To make more fresh and fair each rude retreat,
> Each Plain more pleasant, each Recess more sweet;
> All only pouring from its plenteous stores,
> A showery deluge on dependent shores;
> Or arrogantly swells Ambition's tides,
> Flooding rank pastures, on proud river-sides –
> Replenishing each pouch before too rich,
> And mounting Pride to more mischievous pitch. (p. 209)

Portraying the degrading effects of extractive, profit-driven industries on both labouring people and the British nation, this concluding vision of capitalist political economy is quintessentially ecosocial. As it traces the 'distillation' of wealth, first as 'drops' drawn from the earth and then from the 'sweat of toiling Man, or labouring Beast', it develops a picture of the nefarious shackling of productive potential by powerful elites and legislators, who do not diffuse wealth but extract 'Till every source seems dry, thro' all the Land'. Developing upon Chapter 1's critique of the wastefulness of landscape improvement (for inhibiting the agricultural potential of the land), Chapter 11 envisages a far more unjust and injurious system of wealth extraction upon which elite lifestyles were based. Likewise, while landowners had earlier been imagined as 'Volcanoes!' whose desires might overwhelm the land about them, here Woodhouse further explicated his sense of the destructive potential of such urges: specifically, by imagining landscape parks not as 'wastes' but as 'dependent shores' (language no doubt informed by an awareness of European colonisation), he conceptualised not just the national but the global dimensions of elite extravagance, which depended upon, if not demanded, the despoliation of places and people elsewhere. As Woodhouse suggests in this striking anti-capitalist sublime, which contrasts the 'romanticized capitalism' of coal-owners like Montagu,[71] such extraction came at an unforeseeable cost, as the wealth it rendered became an end in itself and a means of ever further mischief.

Conclusion

The social and environmental argument *Crispinus Scriblerus* makes is, like the poem itself, tirelessly sustained. It might well be concluded that Woodhouse, like many labouring-class poets of his time, promoted a georgic view which 'struggles with nature, recognises diversity, tries to understand how an interdependent system can be sustained and properly exploited'.[72] Certainly, Woodhouse's work as a land steward and farmer led him not only to recognise nature's limits, but also to sharpen his sense of plant-soil relationships, which seems to anticipate modern conservationist thinking and sustainable agricultural practices. However, as this chapter argues, Woodhouse's stewardship ethos was just one part of a much wider response to the increasing ascendance of capitalist socio-economic relations and their erosion of more traditional, and arguably more equitable, modes of living upon the land. In particular, through his experience at Sandleford under the Bluestocking businesswoman Elizabeth Montagu, he came to understand that the urge to 'improve' the land economically, but also visually, were but two sides of the increasing instrumentalisation of land locally, nationally and internationally, for private gain. In exposing this, Woodhouse not only critiqued the back-to-nature fantasies of wealthy landowners but offered also a proleptic vision of where these appropriative and colonialist tendencies might lead in future: a world of fire and drought, as the rich eventually render the land unfit for life.

While the ponderous form of *Crispinus Scriblerus* may test the patience of modern readers, it nevertheless reveals a distinctive, 'redder' type of environmental writing to which ecocritics are increasingly (re)turning their attention.[73] In particular, based on his bottom-up view of social inequality and contemporary land improvement, Woodhouse arrived at a highly original imagining of environmental collapse. In 1798 Thomas Malthus offered his infamous theory of overpopulation, arguing that the multiplication of the labouring classes would, if unchecked, lead to a depletion of resources and hence population collapse – a position which rebutted the utopian thinking of agricultural reformers like Arthur Young, for whom technological innovation would provide abundantly for all.[74] Both positions were undoubtedly extreme: the former was fatalistic and stigmatised the poor, while the latter was utopian and 'underestimated the biophysical limits of the earth'.[75] Woodhouse, however, presented a very different futurity: while he was certainly receptive to the principles of agricultural improvement, he soon doubted it in view of the intensifying social inequalities that resulted from its application.[76] Asking 'Will Nature's Wealth, with all the Works of skill, / E'er satisfy the faithless human Will?' (p. 177), Woodhouse points to future ecological collapse resulting not from overpopulation but from the excessive and unsustainable exploitation needed to meet conspicuous consumption. Through his apocalyptic metaphors of fire and drought, Woodhouse imaginatively connected environmental extremes with the 'extravagant extremes' (p. 209) of social inequality. If this coincidence seems rather too neat, it is sadly also accurate. In envisioning the capitalistic accumulation of wealth as a kind of 'distillation' that would ultimately lead to the draining of the land of all life, Woodhouse offered a notably early articulation of the concept of the Anthropocene and what has since been termed 'slow violence': the unintended consequences, and unseen, attritional damage, of capitalism, falling particularly on the poor.[77] Likewise, he anticipates the slowly dawning realisation of modern ecological theory: namely, 'that major ecological problems have their roots in social problems'.[78]

In Woodhouse, as this essay shows, the combination of a georgic understanding of the natural world with radical social politics contributes to a distinctive conception of social and environmental destruction. This complicates how we might think of environmental writing in this period. Certainly, it further indicates 'the existence of a radically different concept of "Nature" to the one which the canonical Romantic poets were helping to define and establish'.[79] No doubt, Woodhouse's devotion to nature, not to mention his references to 'mystic Memory' and 'nature's treasured forms' (p. 13), can be situated within what we might term the Romantic reification of nature. However, Woodhouse's social background pulls his poetry in a different direction, away from the meditative and into an understanding of 'nature' as a locus of social and political contestation.[80] To use his own terms: rather than 'exalt[ing]', Woodhouse's position as a member of the labouring class drew him to consider the natural world not as a constant, but as something which could be appropriated and destroyed by humans. As such, *Crispinus Scriblerus* contributes ample evidence for 'an altogether new kind of environmental writing', based on 'georgic ecology' but also 'social responsibility', which Richard Pickard first observed of Mary Leapor's 'Crumble Hall' (1751).[81] As well as other 'agent[s] and victim[s] of improvement' like Robert Bloomfield, John Clare and also Robert Burns,[82] we might turn to more radical writers like Thomas Holcroft, whose Jacobin novel *Anna St Ives* (1792) critiques the mania of aristocratic landscape improvement and envisions a more egalitarian and enlightened alternative.[83] Many other writers, now discoverable in the extensive catalogue edited by John Goodridge, may offer further insights, not least given the various gardeners listed there (such as John Learmont, whom Keegan discusses).[84] While thanks to these critics we now can better appreciate the various distinctive ways in which labouring-class poets wrote about the natural world, much work remains to be done – particularly in regard to how these writers conceived of, and found expression for, the emerging social, economic and technological forces threatening it. The opportunities this archive offers for uncovering a more critical history of environmental exploitation are considerable.

Notes

1. Jonathan Bate, *Romantic Ecology: Wordsworth and the Environmental Tradition* (London: Routledge, 1991).
2. Timothy Morton, *Ecology Without Nature: Rethinking Environmental Aesthetics* (Cambridge, MA: Harvard University Press, 2007), pp. 5 and 92.
3. Ibid. p. 10.
4. Ibid. pp. 2 and 144.

5. Jeremy Davies, 'Romantic Ecocriticism: History and Prospects', *Literature Compass* 15, no. 9 (2018): 1.
6. Davies, 'Romantic Ecocriticism', p. 6. See also Timothy Clark, *The Cambridge Introduction to Literature and the Environment* (Cambridge: Cambridge University Press, 2011) and *Ecocriticism on the Edge: The Anthropocene as a Threshold Concept* (London: Bloomsbury, 2015); Katey Castellano, *The Ecology of British Romantic Conservatism, 1790–1837* (Basingstoke: Palgrave Macmillan, 2013); Simon Kövesi, *John Clare: Nature, Criticism and History* (Basingstoke: Palgrave Macmillan, 2017); Alan Bewell, *Natures in Translation: Romanticism and Colonial Natural History* (Baltimore: Johns Hopkins University Press, 2017).
7. Davies, 'Romantic Ecocriticism', p. 8. For an explanation of the term 'labouring-class' and its distinction from later, more proletarian 'working-class' writing, see William J. Christmas, *The Lab'ring Muses: Work, Writing, and the Social Order in English Plebeian Poetry, 1730–1830* (London: Associated University Press, 2001), pp. 41–3.
8. Bridget Keegan, *British Labouring-Class Nature Poetry, 1730–1837* (Basingstoke: Palgrave Macmillan, 2008), pp. 5–7.
9. Ibid. p. 15.
10. J. O. Lindsay (ed.), *The New Cambridge Modern History: Volume 7, The Old Regime, 1713–1763* (Cambridge: Cambridge University Press, [1957] 1988), p. 2.
11. Steve Van-Hagen, 'Patrons, Influences, and Poetic Communities in James Woodhouse's *The Life and Lucubrations of Crispinus Scriblerus*', in Ileana Baird (ed.), *Social Networks in the Long Eighteenth Century: Clubs, Literary Salons, Textual Coteries* (Newcastle upon Tyne: Cambridge Scholars, 2014), pp. 309–33. I wish to acknowledge here as well Van-Hagen's helpful comments on the penultimate draft of this essay.
12. On the importance of patronage for success as a labouring-class poet, see Dustin Griffin, *Literary Patronage in England, 1650–1800* (Cambridge: Cambridge University Press, 1996), pp. 189–95.
13. Sadly Shenstone died before Woodhouse's *Poems on Sundry Occasions* (London: R. & J. Dodsley, 1764) was published. For specific details of the assistance he gave to Woodhouse, see Christmas, *The Lab'ring Muses*, p. 192.
14. For discussion of the covert egalitarianism of Woodhouse's early poetry and his Methodist influences, see Adam J. Bridgen, 'Patronage, Punch-Ups, and Polite Correspondence: The Radical Background of James Woodhouse's Early Poetry', *Huntington Library Quarterly* 80, no. 1 (2017): 99–134. For a biographical overview, see Steve Van-Hagen, 'The Life, Works and Reception of an Evangelical Radical: James Woodhouse (1735–1820), the "Poetical Shoemaker"', *Literature Compass* 6, no. 2 (2009): 384–406.
15. The first chapter, which recounts Woodhouse's early development, was published pseudonymously in 1814, notice of which appeared in *The New Monthly Magazine* 3 (1815): 152 and *The Monthly Review* 80 (1816): 216–17.
16. Christmas, *The Lab'ring Muses*, p. 198.
17. Peter Denney, '"Unpleasant, tho' Arcadian Spots": Plebeian Poetry, Polite Culture, and the Sentimental Economy of the Landscape Park', *Criticism*

47, no. 4 (2005): 496–7 and 509–10; Keegan, *Labouring-Class Nature Poetry*, pp. 52–3. Steve Hindle contextualises Woodhouse's response to Sandleford's redesign in 'Representing Rural Society: Labor, Leisure, and the Landscape in an Eighteenth-Century Conversation Piece', *Critical Inquiry* 41, no. 3 (2015): 647.
18. Keegan, *Labouring-Class Nature Poetry*, pp. 51 and 57.
19. Van-Hagen, 'Patrons, Influences, and Poetic Communities', p. 333.
20. Wordsworth began *The Prelude* in 1798 and completed it in 1805, although he would continue 'retouching and revising' it for the rest of his life. William Wordsworth, *The Prelude*, ed. Ernest De Selincourt (London: Oxford University Press, 1950), p. xlii. Like *Crispinus Scriblerus*, Wordsworth's poetic autobiography was only published in full after the author's death; in both cases, when early parts were published to test public opinion (both in 1814), they were poorly received by critics at the time. See Jasper Cragwell, 'Wordsworth and the Ragged Legion; Or, The Lows of the High Argument', in Eugene Stelzig (ed.), *Romantic Autobiography in England* (Farnham: Ashgate, 2009), p. 187.
21. Christmas, *The Lab'ring Muses*, p. 200.
22. While Michael Löwy and Joel Kovel are the modern pioneers of this concept, ecosocialism has demonstrable historical roots. See, for instance, Kohei Saito's *Karl Marx's Ecosocialism: Capital, Nature, and the Unfinished Critique of Political Economy* (New York: Monthly Review Press, 2017).
23. For a recent definition of georgic ecology, see David Fairer, '"Where fuming trees refresh the thirsty air": The World of Eco-Georgic', *Studies in Eighteenth Century Culture* 40 (2011): 201–18.
24. *The Life and Poetical Works of James Woodhouse*, ed. R. I. Woodhouse, 2 vols (London: Leadenhall Press, 1896), 1: 12. Further references to *Crispinus Scriblerus* will be sourced from the first volume of this edition (which contains chapters 1 to 13) and cited parenthetically in the text by page number.
25. William Wordsworth and Samuel Taylor Coleridge, *Lyrical Ballads, and Other Poems, 1797–1800*, ed. James Butler and Karen Green (Ithaca, NY: Cornell University Press, 1992), p. 743.
26. Notably, the famous Bristolian poet and forger Thomas Chatterton (1752–1770) is referenced in the opening lines of *Crispinus Scriblerus*, further indicating Woodhouse's sense of belonging to a labouring-class tradition.
27. The line immediately following Woodhouse's promise not to erase 'contentions thro' the Earth' refers to a 'second Homer', that is, Pope, who first became famous for his translation of Homer's *Odyssey*. Describing the strategic erasure of 'contentions' as a technique 'To fix the sight of second Homer's birth' (i.e. Britain), it seems Woodhouse may have had in mind the various idealisations Pope deployed in *Windsor-Forest* (1713). This influential poem offered a glorifying (but necessarily oblique) view of British empire and commerce, as Suvir Kaul discusses in *Poems of Nation, Anthems of Empire: English Verse in the Long Eighteenth Century* (Charlottesville: University Press of Virginia, 2000), p. 26.
28. Roy Porter, *The Enlightenment*, 2nd edn (Basingstoke: Palgrave Macmillan, [1990] 2001), p. 306.
29. This argument is persuasively set out in Robert C. Allen's *Enclosure and the*

Yeoman: The Agricultural Development of the South Midlands, 1450–1850 (Oxford: Clarendon Press, 1992).
30. Keegan, *Labouring-Class Nature Poetry*, p. 53.
31. Ibid. p. 51.
32. For a historical discussion of the use of the concept of wasteland in discussions of land reform, and particularly its customary use as a means of justifying enclosure, see Sophie Gee, *Making Waste: Leftovers and the Eighteenth Century Imagination* (Princeton: Princeton University Press, 2010), pp. 47–50.
33. Adam Smith, *The Theory of Moral Sentiments*, ed. Knud Haakonssen (Cambridge: Cambridge University Press, 2002), pp. 215–16. Woodhouse had critiqued this providentialist economic sophistry in his poem 'On Benevolence', as I discuss in 'Patronage, Punch-Ups, and Polite Correspondence', pp. 129–31.
34. Roger A. E. Wells, *Wretched Faces: Famine in Wartime England, 1793–1801* (Gloucester: Alan Sutton, 1988).
35. This area was later renamed the 'Black Country' due to the discolouring effects of heavy industry and coal-mining. See Peter M. Jones, *Industrial Enlightenment: Science, Technology and Culture in Birmingham and the West Midlands, 1760–1820* (Manchester: Manchester University Press, 2009), pp. 22–3 and 38–9.
36. For a discussion of the colonialist tendency of middle- and upper-class environmental perspectives, in which 'the desire to preserve or recover the virginal purity of one realm seems to justify the exploitation of dark others', see Sharon Setzer, '"Pond'rous Engines" in "Outraged Groves": The Environmental Argument of Anna Seward's "Colebrook Dale"', *European Romantic Review* 18, no. 1 (2007): 77.
37. Woodhouse offers an interesting gloss on subsequent Romantic responses to volcanic activity, which were troubled by humankind's 'vulnerability to elemental forces apparently beyond our control', as David Higgins writes in *British Romanticism, Climate Change, and the Anthropocene: Writing Tambora* (Basingstoke: Palgrave Macmillan, 2017), p. 3.
38. John Gold and George Revill, *Representing the Environment* (London: Routledge, 2004), p. 48. I thank Seth T. Leno's *Early Anthropocene Literature in Britain, 1750–1884* (Cham: Palgrave Macmillan, 2020), p. 95, for this connection. Leno however misses the distinctiveness of Woodhouse's volcanoes metaphor (p. 76), largely due to the error in thinking *Crispinus Scriblerus* was written in 1820 (the year of Woodhouse's death). However, the book offers a welcome overview of early Anthropocene thinking, much of which emerges from the Black Country region.
39. Katherine G. Hornbeak, 'New Light on Mrs. Montagu', in *The Age of Johnson: Essays Presented to Chauncey Brewster Tinker* (New Haven, CT: Yale University Press, 1949), p. 350.
40. Elizabeth Montagu to Edward Montagu, 8 January 1765, National Library of Wales, MS.5433C.
41. Elizabeth Montagu to George Lyttelton, 24 July 1767, Huntington Library, MO 1455.
42. As Nicolle Jordan argues in 'From Pastoral to Georgic: Modes of Negotiating Social Mobility in Elizabeth Montagu's Correspondence', in

Linda Troost (ed.), *Eighteenth-Century Women: Studies in Their Lives, Work, and Culture*, vol. 6 (New York: AMS Press, 2011), p. 107.
43. Elizabeth Montagu to George Lyttelton, 3 November [1767], Huntington Library, MO 1457.
44. Elizabeth Montagu to George Lyttelton, 8 [May 1768], Huntington Library, MO 1458.
45. Elizabeth Montagu to Elizabeth Carter, [6 October 1771], Huntington Library, MO 3292.
46. Elizabeth Montagu to Elizabeth Carter, 5 September 1774, Huntington Library, MO 3341.
47. Betty Rizzo, *Companions without Vows: Relationships among Eighteenth-Century British Women* (Athens: University of Georgia Press, 1994), p. 112.
48. Elizabeth Montagu to Sarah Scott, September 1768, Huntington Library, MO 5902. Keegan discusses Woodhouse's attentiveness to animals, and reluctance to cause them harm, in *Labouring-Class Nature Poetry*, pp. 54–5.
49. Elizabeth Montagu to Edward Bridgen, 16 June 1777, Huntington Library, MO 689. Woodhouse however appears to have been keenly interested in husbandry: in 1781, he wrote a detailed letter to the *Monthly Review* on the subject of sheep rot, which he had (correctly) ascertained was due to parasitical infection, a theory he had arrived at by earlier observing 'by the microscope' the bodies of small 'insects' in the blood of deceased sheep. A longtime herbalist, he also cites a Birmingham physician's recommendation of elder bark as a remedy. *Monthly Review* 66 (January 1782): 79–80.
50. Elizabeth Montagu to Sarah Scott, [4 October 1778], Huntington Library, MO 6042.
51. As Keegan argues; see *Labouring-Class Nature Poetry*, p. 57.
52. Evidence of a more global and translocal understanding of the natural world in Romantic period writing is the subject of Bewell's recent *Natures in Translation*.
53. Keegan, *Labouring-Class Nature Poetry*, pp. 29, 43–4 and 107.
54. Quoted in Hindle, 'Representing Rural Society', pp. 640–1.
55. Denney, 'Sentimental Economy of the Landscape Park', p. 494.
56. Elizabeth Montagu to George Lyttelton, 20 October 1758, Huntington Library, MO 1499.
57. See J. V. Beckett, 'Elizabeth Montagu: Bluestocking Turned Landlady', *Huntington Library Quarterly* 49 (1986): 149–64; Elizabeth Child, 'Elizabeth Montagu, Bluestocking Businesswoman', *Huntington Library Quarterly* 65 (2002): 153–73.
58. Elizabeth Montagu to Sarah Scott, 26 December 1767, quoted in Les Turnbull, 'Elizabeth Montagu: "A Critick, a Coal Owner, a Land Steward, a Sociable Creature"', *Huntington Library Quarterly* 81, no. 4 (2018): 657.
59. Donna Landry, 'Georgic Ecology', in Simon J. White, John Goodridge and Bridget Keegan (eds), *Robert Bloomfield: Lyric, Class and the Romantic Canon* (Lewisburg, PA: Bucknell University Press, 2006), p. 255.
60. Elizabeth Montagu to Elizabeth Carter, 16 September 1781, Huntington Library MO 3516, quoted in Denney, 'Sentimental Economy of the Landscape Park', p. 506.
61. Ibid. pp. 505–6.

62. See Hindle, 'Representing Rural Society', p. 648.
63. Stephen Bending, *Green Retreats: Women, Gardens and Eighteenth-Century Culture* (Cambridge: Cambridge University Press, 2013), pp. 160 and 168.
64. That Montagu's coal-mining business financed her improvements at Sandleford is a point Turnbull makes in '"A Critick, a Coal Owner, a Land Steward, a Sociable Creature"', p. 669.
65. Denney, 'Sentimental Economy of the Landscape Park', p. 509.
66. Keegan, *Labouring-Class Nature Poetry*, p. 59.
67. John Phibbs, 'Mingle, Mass and Muddle: The Use of Plants in Eighteenth-Century Gardens', *Garden History* 38 (2010): 35.
68. To add insult to injury, following Brown's redesigns 'The Wilderness Walk' was planted with rhododendrons, a species introduced to England at the end of the eighteenth century which has been responsible since for the destruction of many native habitats throughout the British Isles. See Historic England, 'Sandleford Priory', <https://historicengland.org.uk/listing/the-list/list-entry/1000333> (accessed 31 August 2020).
69. Keegan, *Labouring-Class Nature Poetry*, p. 60.
70. Denney, 'Sentimental Economy of the Landscape Park', p. 510.
71. For Montagu's contrasting description of coal-mining, see Jordan, 'From Pastoral to Georgic', p. 25.
72. Fairer, 'The World of Eco-Georgic', p. 212.
73. For discussion of this more apocalyptic and activist form of ecology, see Tobias Menely and Margaret Ronda, 'Red', in Jeffrey Cohen (ed.), *Prismatic Ecology: Ecotheory Beyond Green* (Minneapolis: University of Minnesota Press, 2013), 22–41.
74. Gary Harrison, 'Ecological Apocalypse: Privation, Alterity, and Catastrophe in the Work of Arthur Young and Thomas Robert Malthus', in Tim Fulford (ed.), *Romanticism and Millenarianism* (New York: Palgrave Macmillan, 2002), 103–19.
75. Ibid. p. 115.
76. Shockingly, Malthus defended poverty as a necessary means of limiting population increase. As Greg Garrard notes in *Ecocriticism*, 2nd edn (London: Routledge, [2004] 2012), p. 103, 'Malthus's *Essay* is basically anti-apocalyptic in that population and food are supposed to remain in permanent competition, rather than building to a dramatic crisis'.
77. Rob Nixon, *Slow Violence and the Environmentalism of the Poor* (Cambridge, MA: Harvard University Press, 2011).
78. Murray Bookchin, *Remaking Society: Pathways to a Green Future* (Montreal: Black Rose Books, 1990), p. 154.
79. David Worrall, 'Agrarians against the Picturesque: Ultra Radicalism and the Revolutionary Politics of Land', in Stephen Copley and Peter Garside (eds), *The Politics of the Picturesque: Literature, Landscape and Aesthetics since 1770* (Cambridge: Cambridge University Press, 1994), p. 245.
80. For a more detailed discussion of the differences of working-class autobiography from the political detachment of more leisured writers, see Martin A. Danahay, *A Community of One: Masculine Autobiography and Autonomy in Nineteenth-Century Britain* (Albany: State University of New York Press, 1993), p. 4.

81. Richard Pickard, 'Environmentalism and "Best Husbandry": Cutting Down Trees in Augustan Poetry', *Lumen* 17 (1998): 117. Not unlike Woodhouse, Leapor's satirical take on fashionable improvement in 'Crumble Hall' was based upon her experiences as a servant in a country house.
82. Nigel Leask, 'Was Burns a Labouring-Class Poet?', in Kirstie Blair and Mina Gorji (eds), *Class and the Canon: Constructing Labouring-Class Poetry and Poetics, 1750–1900* (Basingstoke: Palgrave Macmillan, 2013), p. 26.
83. Sandro Jung, 'The Politics of Improvement in Thomas Holcroft's *Anna St Ives*', *Orbis Litterarum* 66, no. 1 (February 2011): 21–43.
84. Keegan, *Labouring-Class Nature Poetry*, pp. 62–4. John Goodridge (ed.), 'A Catalogue of British & Irish Labouring-Class & Self-Taught Poets & Poetry *c.* 1700–1900' is regularly updated and freely available on Academia.edu.

Chapter 10

Clifton Walks:
Milkmaids Real and Imaginary[1]

Yuko Otagaki

Since Maria Rollinger declaring in 2007, 'There is no historical book about milk history in Europe or the near East in any language of this region,'[2] several books have appeared on the subject, including Deborah Valenze's *Milk: A Local and Global History* (2011), which reveals the profound culturalisation of something as overtly natural as milk.[3] Beginning with the figure of the milkmaid in Ann Yearsley's 'Clifton Hill' (1785) and Henry Kirke White's 'Clifton Grove' (1803), this essay proceeds on to more recent representations of Japanese and French farm labourers – in Tōson Shimazaki's *Chikuma River Sketches* (1911) and John Berger's *Pig Earth* (1979) respectively – to offer a meditation not only on the relationship between cows and people, but also between people, domestic animals and wildlife generally. In his prime, when he served as viceroy of India from 1899–1905, Lord Curzon was once lauded for having 'the complexion of a milkmaid and the stature of Apollo'.[4] In 1918, Elmer McCollum claimed 'milk-using peoples' were taller, longer-lived and also 'more aggressive'.[5] Sadly, such fascistic sentiments are now resurgent. Using archaeological and genetic research connecting milk with European civilisation, such as Andrew Curry's for the scientific journal *Nature* (2013),[6] white supremacists have adopted milk as their symbol.[7] Partly to explore alternative human and non-human relationships, and partly from a desire to counter the triumphalist narrative of milk as a catalyst of Western civilisation, I will communicate how economic exploitation and animal suffering have gone hand in hand with the modernisation of British dairy farming.

'Clifton Hill' concludes *Poems, on Several Occasions* (1785), the book in which Hannah More first brought Yearsley to public attention as 'a milk-woman' and 'Poetess'.[8] Taking advantage of the eighteenth-century fad for natural genius, she managed to secure almost a thousand subscribers to support her discovery, ensuring an enthusiastic reception of the volume. The first edition made £350,[9] or more than £50,000 in today's terms.[10] The lifelong altercation that resulted between the two women as a consequence of More's decision to allocate to her only the interest drawn from the earnings – an annual allowance of £18 – was understandable, as Yearsley doubtless wanted to liberate herself from dairying,[11] perhaps the most arduous form of women's agricultural work in the eighteenth century.[12] It is revealing to me the way More policed class boundaries by separating Yearsley from herself and other middle- and upper-class readers on the grounds of literacy,[13] and how Yearsley stridently repudiated this in subsequent publications.[14] Explaining 'her defiance . . . as resentment against a middle-class woman she considered more her equal than her superior',[15] as Feldman has argued after Waldron,[16] somewhat misses the point, however. What I think Yearsley was resentful of was not her social rank, but that the choice of writing professionally might be denied to her because of that background.[17] Yearsley was proud of being a milkmaid. She venerated her mother, who was a milkmaid too; after all, milkmaids were the elite of the labouring class. The position of milkmaids in Clifton, who sold milk door-to-door directly to customers, was far removed from that of the wage-dependent farm labourer, at the mercy of bad weather and bad times.[18] Moreover, milkmaids had special skills that were passed down from mother to daughter over many generations. Yearsley's mother would have taught her how to sing while milking, to keep the cow calm and the milk flowing.[19] Indeed, animal history studies suggest there were cows who refused to be milked unless they were sung to.[20] Besides milking, seemingly a lost art by the time of William Cobbett's *Cottage Economy* (1821),[21] Yearsley would have learnt how to make the 'white meats' (that is, the products of milk, such as butter and cheese) that were a principal source of nutrition for labouring people. Understanding this history gives a whole new meaning to Yearsley's commemoration of her mother 'ever living [in her] mind', '[whose] firm precepts vibrate in [her children's] ear'.[22]

In 'Clifton Hill', various thoughts come to the speaker's mind, sparked by scenes of Clifton Church, St Vincent's Rocks, the Hotwells, the Avon River and Leigh Woods. As a loco-descriptive poem it differs from Alexander Pope's *Windsor Forest* (1713), the outstanding example of the genre in the eighteenth century, in at least two respects: in the mode of travel, where Yearsley's persona walks, Pope's rides; and in the views on offer, where Yearsley describes her own locale, Pope touches upon India to the east, Mexico to the west, the North Pole and the tropics. Certainly the locomotion and the narrower prospects are indicative of Yearsley's more humble situation, but with the publication of Jean-Jacques Rousseau's *Les Rêveries du Promeneur Solitaire*

(1782) and the rise of democratic sentiments, writers of Pope's social class were adopting the walking perspective as a political act.[23] Also, if Yearsley's work loses out intellectually to Pope's in terms of range, she gains on him ecologically in terms of situatedness. I say ecologically because, despite the authority that might be accorded to 'Clifton Hill' as a poem written by a real milkmaid, the descriptions of dairying life and traditions are generalised rather than documentary. By the 1780s, there were more plebeian writers, and they were less likely to provide the kind of visceral representations of labour that predecessors such as Stephen Duck and Mary Collier had offered in their antipastorals.[24] Nevertheless, when Yearsley invokes the pastoral-georgic, as she does at the beginning of 'Clifton Hill', it is shot through with a knowing irony:

> The Swain neglects his Nymph, yet knows not why;
> The Nymph, indifferent, mourns the freezing sky;
> Alike insensible to soft desire,
> She asks no warmth – but from the kitchen fire;
> Love seeks a milder zone; half sunk in snow,
> Lactilla, shivering, tends her fav'rite cow;
> The bleating flocks now ask the bounteous hand,
> And crystal streams in frozen fetters stand. (ll. 15–22)[25]

Opening the poem in winter instead of spring, hers is far from the pastoral in which the swain sings love songs to the nymph in a land at its greenest and most beautiful. There is labour and suffering, if half-hidden: she takes care of cow and sheep, 'shivering'. With the string of labouring poets behind her, men as well as women role models, it is as if she is saying to the gentlemen and gentlewomen readers of the day, enamoured with gentrified representations of country life: you know we don't live like that.

In fact, I would argue that the exposure of a false worldview in Yearsley goes deeper than Duck's or Collier's, as her poem subverts the class and gender inflections of the pastoral-georgic. The romantic love between a man and a woman (which no one truly believed in anyway) is replaced by the sense of duty shown by a woman towards animals that are utterly dependent on her. Cows had a special place on the early modern farm, not only because of the incredibly important nutrition they provided, but also because woman and cow were 'physically close[:] someone leaned up against a cow's flank twice a day, day-in, day-out'.[26] Yes, treating cows gently led to higher milk production, and, as Yearsley makes clear in the vignette that shortly follows, Lactilla and her sisters also exercise love's stratagems out of affection as much as practicality: 'The ruddy swain'

> By screaming milk-maids, not unheeded, seen;
> The downcast look ne'er fixes on the swain,
> They dread his eye, retire, and gaze again.
> 'Tis mighty Love – Ye blooming maids, beware,
> Nor the lone thicket with a lover dare.
> No high romantic rules of honour bind
> The timid virgin of the rural kind;
> No conquest of the passions e'er was taught,
> No meed e'er given them for the vanquish'd thought.
> To sacrifice, to govern, to restrain,
> Or to extinguish, or to hug the pain,
> Was never theirs; instead, the fear of shame
> Proves a strong bulwark, and secures their fame;
> Shielded by this, they flout, reject, deny,
> With mock disdain put the fond lover by;
> Unreal scorn, stern looks, affected pride,
> Awe the poor swain, and save the trembling bride. (ll. 50–66)

Although she likes what she sees and knows he is in earnest, she is not sure he will always be true. For the sake of her reputation, a milkmaid does not usually admit her desire until marriage, as no labouring woman could afford to be a single mother. Due to their social and economic circumstances, the milkmaids work together and completely frustrate 'the poor swain'. Yearsley's position is firmly with the milkmaid she represents, who refuses marriage and reveals in no uncertain terms that although she may lack the formal education of her social superiors, she is far from a hapless ingenue.[27]

Though largely forgotten now, Henry Kirke White was remembered for much of the nineteenth century as a poet of precocious genius who died young. Under the encouragement of Capel Lofft, the patron of the labouring-class poet Robert Bloomfield, White published *Clifton Grove, a Sketch in Verse, with other Poems* (1803) when he was only seventeen. A milkmaid features in the title poem, which also narrates a walk through the scenic spots of a local wooded area. But from here all resemblance between White's 'Clifton Grove' and Yearsley's 'Clifton Hill' ends. Yearsley detailed specific landmarks and landscape features, but of his favourite retreat about four miles from Nottingham where he resided, White provides only the most generalised depictions drawn from the conventions of picturesque description. The gaze White settles upon the working people of town and country is not the empathetic one of a fellow labourer, but the distancing anthropological one of a social superior:

Now, when the Rustic wears the social smile,
Releas'd from day and its attendant toil,
And draws his Household round their evening fire,
And tells the oft-told tales that never tire:
Or, where the Town's blue turrets dimly rise,
And Manufacture taints the ambient skies,
The pale Mechanic leaves the lab'ring loom,
The air-pent hold, the pestilential room,
And rushes out, impatient to begin
The stated course of customary sin:
Now, now, my solitary way I bend
Where solemn Groves in awful state impend,
And cliffs, that boldly rise above the plain,
Bespeak, blest Clifton! thy sublime domain.[28]

In the eyes of this persona, freedom from toil only gives bumpkins and menials the opportunity to feed their baser instincts. A butcher's son, first placed at a stocking loom but then later apprenticed to a law office, White's persona needs no company for gossip, to drink with or to have sex with, for he is a self-possessed gentleman who prefers to keep to himself. Unlike Yearsley's persona, for whom the countryside is a workplace, White's is comparable to the middle-class city-dweller of today, for whom it is a playground.

It is White's milkmaid, 'beauteous MARGARET', 'the peerless fair',[29] whose life the latter half of the poem recounts, who is perpetuated in poetry and in painting, which Donna Landry observes conflates the rustic and the polite in such a way 'that effaces female labor as productive work and reestablishes the country woman solely as an object of the spectator's desire'.[30] In 'Clifton Grove', she vows to be faithful to her fiancé Bateman, who has been drafted into war. Ominously, the moment she stops speaking, 'The death-bird gave a dismal cry, / The river moan'd, the wild gale whistled by'.[31] Indeed, Margaret proves faithless: Bateman returns three years later to find her married to a man of wealth. Where Yearsley's allegiance was to the milkmaid, White's was clearly to the proverbial swain. Inconsolable, Bateman drowns himself in the River Trent. In the 'Fair Maid of Clifton' from which he took his milkmaid, a story passed down for generations through song and poetry,[32] she had been forced to marry another man because her family was in financial difficulty. It is also worth noting that the milkmaid's cow does not appear in White's version at all, nor does White's milkmaid demonstrate anything like the sense of shared precarity Lactilla has with the sheep on St Vincent's Rocks, the highest point of elevation in the entire region.

Here nibbling flocks of scanty herbage gain
A meal penurious from the barren plain;

> Crop the low niggard bush; and, patient, try
> The distant walk, and every hillock nigh: (ll. 100–3)

As Yearsley shortly interjects, 'My woe-struck soul in all your troubles shares' (l. 107).

Indeed, Yearsley's poem makes readers aware of the thoughts and feelings of beings other than humans, in whom she reads her own anxieties and helplessness in a world of violence, class hatred and female exploitation. This extends beyond domestic animals to encompass wild nature. Together with Pope, James Thomson was one of the seminal figures of the eighteenth-century poetical landscape, except that Thomson was regarded as the master of the pastoral mode. This is largely on the strength of *The Seasons* (1726–30), and in the part on winter there is an episode about a person sharing his home with a robin, who 'pays to trusted Man / His annual Visit'. As Catherine Keohan has pointed out, the first thirty-four lines of 'Clifton Hill' are a striking revision of Thomson, in which Yearsley changes the story from a demonstration of man's bounty into an illustration of his cruelty:[33]

> The beauteous red-breast, tender in her frame,
> Whose murder marks the fool with treble shame,
> Near the low cottage door, in pensive mood,
> Complains, and mourns her brothers of the wood.
> Her song oft wak'd the soul to gentle joys,
> All but his ruthless soul whose gun destroys. (ll. 23–8)

Even if she were describing 'the reality of the countryman's relationship with wild things', as Waldron suggests,[34] it is more importantly a situation she has clearly singled out for criticism.[35] Given the diminutiveness of the species, it is highly unlikely that the cottager killed the birds for food. The nature of her criticism rather suggests he did it for sport. Scolding him 'rough clown' (l. 29) and suggesting equivalences between herself and the robin as female, as sister and as fellow singer, Yearsley arraigns him essentially for a lack of fellow feeling. The curse she calls down upon his head is instructive: 'For these fell murders may'st thou change thy kind, / [. . .] / Go, be a bear of Pythagorean name' (ll. 31–3). Bears were stereotypically savage, but the Greek philosopher she references here also propagated the belief in the transmigration of souls. This is significant because reincarnation implies a more expansive kinship by extending the existence of the soul to all living things, unlike Christianity.

As Jeremy Bentham, the utilitarian philosopher and one of the earliest proponents of animal rights, famously observed in *An Introduction to the Principles of Morals and Legislation* (1789):

The French have already discovered that the blackness of the skin is no reason why a human being should be abandoned without redress to the caprice of a tormentor. It may come one day to be recognized, that the number of legs, the villosity of the skin, or the termination of the *os sacrum*, are reasons equally insufficient for abandoning a sensitive being to the same fate. [. . .] But a full-grown horse, or dog, is beyond comparison a more rational, as well as a more conversable animal, than an infant of a day, or a week, or even a month, old. But suppose the case were otherwise, what would it avail? the question is not, Can they *reason*? nor, Can they *talk*? but, Can they *suffer*?[36]

Because animals feel pain as we do, they are deserving of moral consideration. The cult of sensibility was at its apogee, and the connection between the abolition movement, concern for animal welfare, and the concept that we are feeling beings in a sensitive universe is clear and obvious. We can see these same intersections in Charlotte Smith's *Conversations Introducing Poetry* (1804), a children's book that aims to raise awareness among them of animal suffering and the plight of Black people. For example, in 'The Hedge-Hog Seen in a Frequented Path', Smith asks: 'Should man, to whom his God has given / Reason, the brightest ray of heaven, / Delight to hurt, in senseless mirth, / Inferior animals?' To young readers who might be tempted to molest the creature for their amusement, she reminds them that the 'spiny ball' has a 'simple negro face'.[37] While there are certainly affinities between Yearsley's criticism of the 'fell murders' of the 'rough clown' and Smith and Bentham's idea of animal cruelty, from which the modern opposition to hunting or fishing as a sport originates, there are also crucial differences. Sensibility was a key aspect of bourgeois femininity during the late eighteenth century and the similarity of register in Yearsley is an example of a 'canny deployment of the discourse',[38] but the sense of equality between human and animal as fellow suffering beings does not exist in Smith. Smith's father was a member of the landed gentry, and socially elevated women like her tended to regard the small animals (as well as the Black and poorer peoples) for whom they were advocating as objects of charity.

For anything like the equivalence between human and non-human in Yearsley's 'Clifton Hill', it is to the poetry of the people of her class that we have to turn: for instance, the working animals seen as fellow labourers in Robert Bloomfield's *The Farmer's Boy* (1800), or the wildlife John Clare identifies with as fellow loafers or allies against land enclosure in the poems he wrote during the middle period of his life (1822–37). As Katey Castellano notes, land enclosure subjects 'commoners, animals, and plants all . . . to biopolitical discipline', but the molehills surfacing in forty-five of these poems 'mark a topography of animal territory that undermines private property'.³⁹ In 'The Mole', a creature hated by farmers and landscape gardeners is appreciated for giving rest to 'the cow boy' and receiving the poet as a 'guest'.⁴⁰ Typically covered with furze and other wildflowers, molehills are soft, fluffy and fragrant places of repose. Clare takes the position of moles and other so-called vermin, his poetry marking the improved landscape with 'evidence of the silent work of non-human life' such as birds' nests and rabbit tracks.⁴¹ He is regarded with justification as 'the most important British poet of natural history';⁴² but, as the following depiction of Leigh Woods suggests, Yearsley is not far behind in terms of her interest in the local flora and fauna:

> Its lovely verdure scorns the hand of Toil.
> Here the deep green, and here the lively plays,
> The russet birch, and ever-blooming bays;
> [. . .]
> The barren elm, the useful feeding oak,
> Whose hamadryad ne'er should feel the stroke
> Of axe relentless, 'till twice fifty years
> Have crown'd her woodland joys and fruitful cares.
> The pois'nous reptiles here their mischiefs bring,
> And thro' the helpless sleeper dart the sting;
> The toad envenom'd, hating human eyes,
> Here springs to light, lives long, and aged dies.
> The harmless snail, slow journeying, creeps away,
> Sucks the young dew, but shuns the bolder day.
> (Alas! if transmigration should prevail,
> I fear LACTILLA's soul must house in snail.)
> The long-nosed mouse, the woodland rat is here,
> The sightless mole, with nicely-pointed ear;
> The timid rabbit hails th' impervious gloom,
> Eludes the dog's keen scent, and shuns her doom.
> Various the tenants of this tangled wood,
> Who skulk all day, all night review the flood,
> Chew the wash'd weed driven by the beating wave,
> Or feast on dreadful food, which hop'd a milder grave. (ll. 157–81)

Now part of the National Trust and considered a Site of Special Scientific Interest on account of its rich biodiversity, Leigh Woods was in Yearsley's time pasture woodland with old pollards,⁴³ like 'the useful feeding oak', whose branches were harvested for at least a hundred years to keep homes warm. Most of the oldest surviving trees in Britain were pollards, which, unlike their brethren on the enclosed park reservations, were not felled to build ships nor allowed to grow so large and top-heavy that they were blown down by a storm. According to the late Oliver Rackham, '[a] tree needs to be at least 300 years old and preferably a pollard before it will harbour many of the more distinctive wood-pasture organisms.'[44] Moreover, the rotational felling of smaller trees practised in a coppiced wood like Leigh, as Rackham's work on ecology has revealed, was tremendously beneficial for plant diversity. The rabbit seeking shelter, the mole, the woodland rat, the long-nosed mouse, snail, caterpillar and vipers are 'tenants' because of the 'axe relentless', having to keep moving or die, but they would not be there in such diversity and numbers if not for it.[45] It is truly a 'tangled wood': not only in how the lives of plant, animal and human entangle in networks of utility and predation, but also in their fundamental interchangeability – 'if transmigration should prevail'.

Nature in 'Clifton Hill' is not property, or the preserve of the propertied, like the hunting grounds of Pope's *Windsor Forest*, where the gaze belongs to one who 'is master of all he surveys'.[46] Neither is Yearsley's nature the playground apprehended by Joachim Ritter, disentangled from work in order to free people to appreciate it aesthetically.[47] In the engagement with suffering, her nature has some similarities admittedly to the conception of Smith and other gentlewomen of the time as a landscape of feeling. But the similarity she shares with Clare, Bloomfield and other rural labouring poets, as practical user and 'tenant' of nature, is greater. There are differences still between them, however. Yearsley was a woman labouring poet, and it was to female suffering that she was most attuned. In 'Clifton Hill', it is her 'fav'rite cow' she first attends to at work; in the natural world, the limelight falls first on a robin mourning 'her brothers of the wood'. This is clearly the case as well with respect to the human world: the persona stands with the 'screaming milk-maids' near the beginning of the poem, and towards the end, with 'the fair Maniac', Louisa (l. 207). To her, this homeless woman 'confessed . . . that she had escaped from a Convent, in which she had been confined by her father, on refusing a marriage of his proposing, her affections being engaged to another man'.[48] Louisa and Yearsley's mother are the only two people commemorated by 'Clifton Hill', and both of them suffered a tragically premature death.[49]

Romantic Afterlives

Ecocriticism, according to Scott Slovic, is in its fourth wave.[50] This is Serenella Iovino's explanation of its materialist worldview:

> Taking matter as a text, material ecocriticism broadens and enhances the narrative potentialities of reality in terms of an intrinsic performativity of elements. At the same time, it broadens the range of narrative agencies, making

it a 'posthuman performativity,' where the 'posthuman' replaces the human/non-human dualism and overcomes it in a more dialectic complex dimension. Material ecocriticism is posthuman performativity in its narrative disclosures. It sees this performativity at work in the thick of things: stories, bodies, landscapes, bacteria, electric grids, quantum entanglements, waste dumps, animal testing, cyborgs, cheese, nuclear sites, oceanic plastic, art, time, nature.[51]

While it characterises much of what I've tried to do with Yearsley's 'Clifton Hill', I am a little wary of completely endorsing a discourse that traces its origins to the greening of the humanities in the 1990s at the US universities. Given my position as a woman academic at a Japanese university trying to understand the perspective of a woman labouring poet from England more than 200 years ago, I would like to suggest an alternative provenance with a longer history: the literary tradition of imposing upon an urban reading public the idea that we have something to learn from the people of the countryside.

It was, after all, in 1798 that Coleridge and Wordsworth first published their seminal *Lyrical Ballads, with a few other Poems*, on the presumption that 'the language of conversation in the middle and lower classes of society' might be 'adapted to the purposes of poetic pleasure'.[52] Wordsworth was more emphatic about who exactly were his models in the second edition, after he wrested control over the entire project from Coleridge:[53]

> Low and rustic life was generally chosen because in that situation the essential passions of the heart find a better soil in which they can attain their maturity, are less under restraint, and speak a plainer and more emphatic language; because in that situation our elementary feelings exist in a state of greater simplicity and consequently may be more accurately contemplated and more forcibly communicated; because the manners of rural life germinate from those elementary feelings; and from the necessary character of rural occupations are more easily comprehended; and more durable; and lastly, because in that situation the passions of men are incorporated with the beautiful and permanent forms of nature.[54]

It does seem paradoxical that a member of an emergent class, from a country on the cusp of world imperial domination, would be turning to people of a menial and provincial one for inspiration. Far from unique, it was a trend with the Romantics, English or otherwise.

During my nation's own phase of empire-building, the Romantic poet, naturalist novelist and university academic Tōson Shimazaki (aka Haruki Shimazaki) published *Chikuma River Sketches* (1911), a collection of short essays on village life in the mountainous prefecture of Nagano. Shimazaki had moved from Tokyo to Komoro, a small town at the foot of Mount Asama, then and still now an active volcano, where he taught Japanese and English at a private school for six years. 'Rain, wind, sunlight, birds, insects, weeds, soil, climate – these are all things that have to be,' he wrote, 'and yet they are also enemies against which the farmers must do battle.'[55] Before the modernisation of Japan in the nineteenth century, milk was regarded as an unclean animal fluid. Buddhists believed cow's milk to be 'white blood', which would bring down divine retribution if it was drunk.[56] While dairy farming was established by Shimazaki's time, it was mainly carried out further north, where the climate was too cold and dry for rice-growing. Thus it was probably owing to the rarity of the practice that *Chikuma River Sketches* carries numerous observations of the animal and the people connected with it. Visiting a student whose family had recently taken up dairying, the persona learns that 'some cows take kindly to being milked while others do not. Some are wild, some quiet; there are all kinds. Cows have very sensitive ears and can recognize their master's footsteps' (p. 8). Going to a breeding pasture, he meets an old cowherd there and is 'struck by the way in which the lives of human beings and of cattle are all blended together' (p. 11). He takes advantage when an opportunity arises in winter to visit a slaughterhouse, the proceedings of which he describes with great particularity: one cow, two bulls, a pig and ten butchers (who belong to an outcast caste) in 'white coveralls', their bare feet looking 'cold in their straw sandals' (p. 82). A veterinarian in a billed cap and black overcoat, overseeing the operation, tells the butchers to put on their best clothes for the New Year, saying 'you all look as though you've been boiled in soy sauce' (p. 85). *Nishime*, vegetables boiled in soy sauce, is a dish traditionally eaten on New Year's day. The food imagery draws the butchers and the animals they slaughter together to emphasise their exploitation by a society demanding more meat, yet growing increasingly squeamish of the animal death that this demand necessitates.

The Romantic interest in the nature of rural labouring-class people was maintained in the 1970s by British Marxist writers. It was in 1972 that John Barrell published his seminal work on labouring-class nature poetry, *The Idea of Landscape and the Sense of Place 1730–1840: An Approach to the Poetry of John Clare*. Barrell is regarded as one of the founders of cultural materialism, the prototype of Slovic and Iovino's materialist ecocriticism. By the end of the decade came *Pig Earth* (1979), the first of John Berger's *Into Their Labours* trilogy on labouring life in the French Alps, in which the London art critic, poet and novelist declares, 'it is such women and men who have taught me the little I know'.[57] 'A Question of Place', the first story, begins with the sentence: 'Over the cow's brow the son places a black leather mask and ties it to the horns' (p. 3). The cow is going to be slaughtered and the mask not only blocks its view but also 'protects the executioner from [its] last look' (p. 3). In 'Addressed to Survivors', a cow which has given the best milk in the village for four years, but whose time is up because it cannot continue doing so, is carried onto the lorry, its flanks cushioned with straw so that its skin might not be chafed (pp. 52–64). Affection and instrumentality were utterly entangled in the lives of these animals and the people who tended to them, which the evidence suggests characterised early modern farm life in England as well.[58] Cow, sheep, chicken or pig, they were killed by the very people who loved them: as Berger succinctly put it in his essay collection *About Looking* (1980), 'a peasant becomes fond of his pig and is glad to salt away its pork'.[59]

One of the best reasons for studying people in a different situation is to critique a direction we have taken in our own society. Berger's evocation of a disappearing lifeworld in *Pig Earth* and 'Why Look at Animals', the essay which I have quoted from *About Looking*, was part and parcel of his opposition to the factory farming system in his own country. It proved remarkably prescient, with the outbreak of BSE in the UK in the 1980s and 1990s, which shone a harsh light on an industry that turned cows into cannibals, and the only solution to which was mass animal slaughter.[60] However, when there is a steep power difference between the people doing the representing and the people being represented, there are dangers. First and foremost, the orientalism of a gaze that renders them as objects of anthropological curiosity. This was the case with Shimazaki and Yearsley, with the latter, doubly as novelty – the milkmaid who can write poetry – and as beholder writing in a bourgeois literary culture.[61] Second, the Marxist temptation to reify the proletariat, as in Berger seeing them as a font of wisdom. There are no noble savages: they are us under different circumstances. While there is much to learn from Yearsley's environmental sensibility, and from the smaller burden poorer people generally place on the environment, it should also never be forgotten that their choices are inextricably bound with a situation most of them would exchange away, if they could. Yearsley did not want to remain a milkmaid all her life. She aspired to be a poet, a dramatist, a novelist – in other words, one of the literati. This is the tragic irony of the ongoing environmental apocalypse: given the choice, most of us would not choose to lead an environmentally friendly life, because we have to be poor in order to truly live for the earth.

Notes

1. This essay has benefited tremendously from the funding extended to me through the Grant-in-Aid for Scientific Research (C) for the 2019 academic year.
2. 'History of Milk', a summary of Maria Rollinger's *Milch besser nicht: Ein kritisches Lesebuch* [Better not Milk: A Critical Reader], 2nd edn (Erfurt: JOU-Verlag, 2007), <http://www.eps1.comlink.ne.jp/~mayus/eng/> (accessed 30 August 2020).
3. Deborah Valenze, *Milk: A Local and Global History* (New Haven, CT: Yale University Press, 2011).
4. Simon Schama, *A History of Britain: The Fate of Empire 1776–2000*, Chapter 5, 'The Empire of Good Intentions' (London: BBC Worldwide, 2002), p. 262.
5. Elmer Verner McCollum, *The Newer Knowledge of Nutrition: The Use of Food for the Preservation of Vitality and Health* (New York: Macmillan, 1918), p. 151.
6. 'In southern Europe, lactase persistence is relatively rare – less than 40% in Greece and Turkey. In Britain and Scandinavia, by contrast, more than 90% of adults can digest milk'; Andrew Curry, 'Archaeology: The Milk Revolution', *Nature* 500, no. 7460 (2013): 22.
7. Amy Harmon, 'Why White Supremacists Are Chugging Milk (and Why Geneticists Are Alarmed)', *The New York Times*, 17 October 2018, <https://www.nytimes.com/2018/10/17/us/white-supremacists-science-dna.html> (accessed 2 October 2020).
8. Hannah More, 'A Prefatory Letter to Mrs. Montagu', in *Poems, on Several Occasions. By Ann Yearsley, a Milkwoman of Bristol* (London: Cadell, 1785), pp. iv–v.
9. Paula R. Feldman (ed.), *British Women Poets of the Romantic Era: An Anthology* (Baltimore: The Johns Hopkins University Press, [1997] 2000), pp. 832–3.
10. Ian Webster, '£350 in 1785 à 2020', *UK Inflation Calculator*, <https://www.officialdata.org/uk/inflation/1785?amount=350> (accessed 11 September 2020>
11. Feldman, *British Women Poets*, p. 833.
12. As Ivy Pinchbeck pointed out in *Women Workers and the Industrial Revolution 1750–1850* (London: Virago, [1930] 1981), p. 12.
13. According to More, 'a copy of [Yearsley's] verses was shewn [to her, and] said to be written by a poor illiterate woman', *Poems, on Several Occasions*, p. iv.
14. For example, in Yearsley's prefatory narrative to *Poems, on Several Occasions*, 4th edn (London: Robinson, 1786), in which after rebutting More's 'Prefatory Letter', she insisted her poetry was entirely her own work and had not been improved in any way by More; see p. xxx.
15. Feldman, *British Women Poets*, p. 834.
16. See Mary Waldron, 'Ann Yearsley and the Clifton Records', in Paul J. Korshin (ed.), *The Age of Johnson: A Scholarly Annual* 3 (1990): 301–29.

17. I am with Julie Cairnie who argues that the complexity of Yearsley's class identification is really the result of 'negotiati[ng] her awkward position as a laboring woman writer in literary culture'; in 'The Ambivalence of Ann Yearsley: Laboring and Writing, Submission and Resistance', *Nineteenth-Century Contexts: An Interdisciplinary Journal* 27, no. 4 (2005): 354.
18. Mary Waldron, *Lactilla, Milkwoman of Clifton: The Life and Writings of Ann Yearsley, 1753–1806* (Athens: The University of Georgia Press, 1996), p. 14.
19. As Steve Roud points out, milkmaids sang to their cows because it 'kept the beasts calm and helped the milk flow', in *Folk Song in England* (London: Faber, 2017), p. 539.
20. Refer to Erica Fudge, *Quick Cattle and Dying Wishes: People and Their Animals in Early Modern England* (Ithaca, NY: Cornell University Press, 2018), p. 217. I thank Adam Bridgen for drawing my attention to the extraordinary work of Erica Fudge.
21. William Cobbett, *Cottage Economy Containing Information Relative to the Brewing of Beer, Making of Bread, Keeping of Cows, [. . .] a Defence of the Rights of Those Who Do the Work* (New York: John Doyle, [1821] 1833), pp. 78–9.
22. Ann Yearsley, 'On the Remembrance of a Mother', *A Second Book of Poems on Various Subjects* (London: Robinson, 1787), pp. 161 and 164.
23. European pedestrian literature originates with Rousseau's *Reveries of the Solitary Walker*, in which he assesses the interaction between thinking and walking. William Wordsworth and a fellow student from Cambridge crossed the Alps on foot, which only vagrants and footpads did at that time. Among the places they visited was Neuchâtel, where Rousseau's 'Fifth Walk' considering walking and writing is set. See Jean-Jacques Rousseau, *The Confessions of J. J. Rousseau: With the Reveries of the Solitary Walker*, 2 vols (London: Printed for J. Bew, 1783), 2: 219–23. Refer also to Kenneth R. Johnston, *The Hidden Wordsworth: Poet, Lover, Rebel, Spy* (New York: Norton, 1998), p. 231.
24. Cairnie, 'The Ambivalence of Ann Yearsley', pp. 354, 357 and 363 n. 10.
25. Ann Yearsley, *Poems, on Several Occasions*, 4th edn (London: Robinson, [1785] 1786), p. 86. Quotations from 'Clifton Hill' are hereafter from this edition with line references in parentheses.
26. Fudge, *Quick Cattle and Dying Wishes*, p. 81.
27. Moira Ferguson considers these lines as a representation of female solidarity against patriarchal acts and attitudes, in 'Resistance and Power in the Life and Writings of Ann Yearsley', *The Eighteenth Century* 27, no. 3 (1986): 250.
28. Henry Kirke White, *Clifton Grove, a Sketch in Verse, with Other Poems* (London: Vernor and Hood, 1803), pp. 4–5.
29. Ibid. p. 19.
30. Donna Landry, *The Muses of Resistance: Laboring-Class Women's Poetry in Britain, 1739–1796* (Cambridge: Cambridge University Press, 1990), p. 26.
31. White, *Clifton Grove*, p. 25.
32. Patricia A. Griffin, *A Critical Edition of William Sampson's the Vow Breaker (1636)* (PhD thesis, Sheffield Hallam University, 2009), p. 77.

33. Catherine Keohane, 'Ann Yearsley's "Clifton Hill" and its Lessons in Reading', *Studies in Eighteenth-Century Culture* 41 (2012): 240–3.
34. Waldron, *Lactilla*, p. 110.
35. For other examples of Yearsley's criticism of systemic discrimination, see Cairnie, 'The Ambivalence of Ann Yearsley', p. 362.
36. Jeremy Bentham, *An Introduction to the Principles of Morals and Legislation* (London: Payne, 1789), p. 309.
37. Charlotte Smith, *Conversations Introducing Poetry: Chiefly on Subjects of Natural History. For the Use of Children and Young Persons*, 2 vols (London: Johnson, 1804), 1: 46–7.
38. Claire Knowles detects in Yearsley active attempts to blend in with bourgeois literary culture; see 'Ann Yearsley, Biography and the "Pow'rs of Sensibility Untaught!"', *Women's Writing* 17, no. 1 (2010): 168.
39. Katey Castellano, 'Moles, Molehills, and Common Rights in John Clare's Poetry', *Studies in Romanticism* 56, no. 2 (2017): 165 and 160.
40. John Clare, *Poems of the Middle Period: 1822–1837*, volume 4, ed. Eric Robinson, David Powell and P. M. S. Dawson (Oxford: Clarendon Press, 1998), p. 295.
41. Castellano, 'Moles, Molehills, and Common Rights', p. 159.
42. I am quoting Simon White from Chapter 12 of this volume.
43. Natural England, 'Wood pasture restoration in Leigh Woods', *The National Trust*, <https://www.nationaltrust.org.uk/leigh-woods/features/conservation-grazing-in-leigh-woods-> (accessed September 20, 2020).
44. Oliver Rackham, *Ancient Woodland: Its History, Vegetation and Uses in England* (Kirkcudbrightshire: Castlepoint Press, 2003), p. 202.
45. To quote Rackham, 'wood-pasture is an essential environment for the lichens and invertebrate animals which inhabit pollards and other trees'; ibid. p. 199. And, of course, it was because these were plentiful that the vertebrates came.
46. Landry, *The Muses of Resistance*, pp. 130–1.
47. Joachim Ritter, 'Landschaft: zur Funktion des Ästhetischen in der modernen Gesellschaft', *Schriften der Gesellschaft zur Förderung der Westfälischen Wilhelms-Universität zu Münster* 54 (Münster: Aschendorff, 1963): 18–9.
48. Yearsley, *Poems, on Several Occasions*, p. 98.
49. After the particularly harsh winter of 1783–4, Yearsley, her family and her mother were found almost starved to death, from which her mother did not recover. The mother's death is noted in the passage on Clifton Church.
50. Scott Slovic, 'Editor's Note', *Interdisciplinary Studies in Literature and Environment* 19, no. 4 (2012): 619–21.
51. Serenella Iovino, 'Theorizing Material Ecocriticism: A Diptych', *Interdisciplinary Studies in Literature and Environment* 19, no. 3 (2012), p. 459. Yearsley's molecular, materialist worldview is evident in her earlier poems as well as her later poems. See, Daniel P. Watkins, 'History and Vision in Ann Yearsley's Rural Lyre', in *The Age of Johnson: A Scholarly Annual* 20 (New York: AMS Press, 2010), pp. 262–4.
52. [William Wordsworth and Samuel Taylor Coleridge,] *Lyrical Ballads, with a few other Poems* (London: Arch, 1798), p. i.
53. For more on this power struggle between Wordsworth and Coleridge, refer

to Ve-Yin Tee, *Coleridge, Revision and Romanticism: After the Revolution, 1793–1818* (London: Continuum, 2009), pp. 59–63.
54. William Wordsworth, *Lyrical Ballads, with other Poems*, 2 vols (London: Longman, 1800), 1: xi.
55. Tōson Shimazaki, *Chikuma River Sketches*, trans. William E. Naff (Honolulu: University of Hawaii Press, 1991), p. 60. Quotations from the book are hereafter from this edition with the page references in parentheses.
56. Valenze, *Milk*, p. 3.
57. John Berger, *Pig Earth*, first published by Writers and Readers in 1979 (New York: Vintage International, 1992), p. xxvii. Quotations from the book are hereafter from this edition with the page references in parentheses.
58. According to Fudge, the 4,000 seventeenth-century wills she studied reveal 'a world of ongoing negotiation and tentative collaboration, a world, indeed, that was alive with individual wills (both human and animal) that were utterly entangled with each other; that was messy and uncomfortable, full of affection and instrumentality, life and death'. See *Quick Cattle and Dying Wishes*, p. 223.
59. John Berger, *About Looking*, first published by Writers and Readers in 1980 (London: Bloomsbury, 2009), p. 7.
60. The discovery that cows were fed products from the slaughter of other cattle was even more shocking to the British public than the fact that over four million of the animals were killed in order to contain the crisis. See Claire Ainsworth and Damian Carrington, 'BSE Disaster: The History', *New Scientist*, 25 October 2000, <https://www.newscientist.com/article/dn91-bse-disaster-the-history/> (accessed 3 October 2020).
61. Landry detects even in Yearsley's representations of other labouring women the deployment of a gaze that belongs to someone to whom they seem novel curiosities; see *The Muses of Resistance*, p. 133.

Chapter 11

Blake and the Pastoral-Georgic Tradition

Steve Clark

As often with handbooks, one of the points of interest with *William Blake in Context*[1] from Cambridge University Press (CUP) is what it omits. The section on 'Form, Genre, and Mode' includes essays on Comedy, Prophecy, Rhythm, Songs, Sound, Sublimity and System, Myth and Symbol.[2] There is nothing, however, on the poetry of sensibility from the eighteenth century: the didactic-encyclopaedic, the mock-heroic, the topographic, as well as the pastoral and georgic. In the section on 'Creative Cross-Currents',[3] David Duff's entry on 'The Eighteenth Century and Romanticism' restricts itself to Blake's slim volume of juvenilia *Poetical Sketches* (1783).[4] There are also no index entries for John Barrell and Raymond Williams, still probably the most influential British commentators on the ideological representation of landscape. This is indicative perhaps of the waning interest in Marxist historiography: E. P. Thompson gets three passing mentions, and solely on Blake's possible connections to the Muggletonians rather than his more influential account of the formation of working-class consciousness. Somewhat disappointing as well is the fact that there is not a single reference to Marilyn Butler's *Mapping Mythologies*,[5] despite her clear investment in the eighteenth-century genealogies of Blake's work,[6] and despite the blurb CUP endorsed in 2015 depicting her as a 'towering presence'.

Certainly, several aspects of Butler's posthumous volume deserve closer consideration.[7] While her argument is explicitly directed against American idealist-philosophical critics (primarily Frye, Bloom and Hartman), whom she indicts for their ahistoricism, she also takes aim at the British Marxist narrative of eighteenth-century pastoral and georgic verse as simply an occlusion of class oppression. To rehabilitate the pastoral-georgic tradition, Butler reinstates a 'Country' party, whose perspective she argues was most fully articulated in the poetry of sensibility running from Thomson, via Akenside, Collins, Macpherson and

Chatterton, through to Blake. She defines this group of writers in three ways. First, a 'strong provincial ideology' addresses a newly emergent readership excluded from high politics still centred on life at court.[8] Secondly, a physical environment set in the regional periphery is often depicted in primitivist terms. Thirdly, it is a backdrop that is supplemented by an alternative antiquarian genealogy of national culture (most vividly exemplified in the bardic persona of Iolo Morganwg adopted by Edward Williams). In other words, mythological speculation underpins transfiguration of landscape, a perspective that fairly resonates with the quasi-theosophical revolution radical environmentalists have been calling for.[9]

Admittedly, as Butler's argument was originally formulated in the 1970s, it lacks the perspectives we now have on 'every Species of Earth, Metal, Tree, Fish, Bird & Beast' (*Milton*, 24, l. 41, E122) in the work of Blake and other writers.[10] In recent ecocriticism, assumptions of human dominance over the natural environment are now routinely challenged. Even in 2002, it is perhaps inevitable that Kevin Hutchings sees the need in *Imagining Nature: Blake's Environmental Poetics* to caution against citing such aphorisms as 'Where Man is Not, Nature is Barren' (E38), or 'Natural Objects always did & do now Weaken deaden & obliterate Imagination in me' (E665), as support for readings of Blake's absolutist vision of imagination, or assuming he must necessarily be regarded as an exclusively urban writer.[11] The fact is Blake produced a large body of work over more than three decades of which some would clearly reinforce these conceptions better than others. This is not the case with respect to the late epic *Milton*, which he probably started writing in 1804 after his residence at Felpham in Sussex (the only time he ever lived outside London).[12] It is not only less anthropocentric than many of the shorter poems his readers today are more familiar with, but this essay wishes to argue that it can also be read ecologically within an eighteenth-century georgic-pastoral tradition. Finally, as one of the aims of this essay collection is to show how Romantic environmental sensibility is bound up with class, it should be pointed out that Blake's shifting economic circumstances are a further complication. At times quite wealthy, owning his own shop from the late 1780s to the early 1790s and then, during the war with France, forced back to basic engraving and accepting a patronage relation with William Hayley, Blake can be regarded both as a proletarian and as intermittently accepted by elite culture.

With these caveats in mind, I would like to re-examine Blake's *Milton* from the perspective of a more historically engaged environmental poetics, drawing on its indebtedness to the tradition of sensibility and focusing in particular on James Thomson, Mark Akenside and Iolo Morganwg (none of whom, incidentally, are even indexed by Hutchings). The poem relates the return to earth from heaven of Milton as a great redeeming figure, which climaxes in a confrontation between him, Los (Blake's avatar for the imagination), Milton, Ololon (Milton's emanation or female counterpart) and Satan when they all converge on Blake's 'Cottage Garden' (36, l. 26, E137). However, balanced against its cosmic dimensions, the poem features a relativistic phenomenology, hospitality to local environment, celebration of biodiversity, and an insistence on the value of transformative labour which also situates it firmly within the pastoral-georgic genre. *Milton* is set in the 'breathing fields' of Felpham (5, l. 2, E98), and the opening bardic song that calls Milton back, 'like Arthur from Avalon, in the hour of England's need',[13] centres on the dispute over 'the instruments of Harvest: the Plow & Harrow' (6, ll. 12–13, E99). In this essay I wish to explore the influence of James Thomson's Lucretian animism in *The Seasons* (1726–30), Blake's reworking of the theme of redemptive descent in Mark Akenside's *The Pleasures of Imagination* (1744) and his use of the phenomenology of place as expounded in Iolo Morganwg's *Poems, Lyric and Pastoral* (1794).

Blake and Thomson

Modern conceptions of rural beauty owe a considerable debt to James Thomson's poetical reflections in *The Seasons*, which inspired landscape painters from William Kent (1685–1748) to J. M. W. Turner (1775–1851).[14] Moreover Thomson's position on biodiversity, for example, as expressed in *Spring* (1728) on 'all [of creation being] so fine adjusted, that the loss / Of the least species would disturb the whole' (157–8),[15] is virtually de rigueur in environmental discourse today. Nevertheless, due to influential readings by John Barrell indicting the tradition of eighteenth-century pastoral-georgic for concealing actual relationships of power, ownership and control,[16] even critics who might have been expected to be sympathetic have been inclined to undervalue *The Seasons*. The work is not indexed even when frequently referred to by Hutchings,[17] and Butler clearly prefers *Liberty* (1735), Thomson's somewhat turgid historical pageant, to the most notable exemplar of the pastoral-georgic in the eighteenth century.[18] Yet its impact on Blake, to whom Marxist historians have generally been favourable, has been downplayed.

Structurally, Thomson's recounting of the decline of human civilisation from a prelapsarian ideal and its progress towards a new commercial golden age is broadly shared by Blake's retelling in his mythic poetry of the Biblical fall and the eventual restoration of humankind. *The Four Zoas: The Torments of Love and Jealousy in the Death and Judgement of Albion the Ancient Man*, the poetic prophecy that Blake worked on for a decade but never published, whose narrative of a 'golden feast' (13, l. 18, E308) that disintegrates into 'iron Times' of 'wedges', 'furnaces' and 'dire anvils' (16, ll. 1–4, E309), echoes that in *Spring* of the 'golden Age ... found no more amid these iron Times' (ll. 273–4). The division of Blake's primeval man (Albion) into four separate personalities (the Zoas) riven by recrimination and conflict corresponds to the post-lapsarian psyche portrayed by Thomson, in which Anger, Revenge, Envy and Fear continually contend for supremacy, with the result that

> Even Love itself is Bitterness of Soul,
> A pensive Anguish pining at the Heart:
> Or, sunk to sordid Interest, feels no more
> That noble Wish, that never-cloy'd Desire,
> Which, selfish Joy disdaining, seeks, alone,
> To bless the dearer Object of its Flame.
> Hope sickens with Extravagance; and Grief,
> Of Life impatient, into Madness swells;
> Or in dead Silence wastes the weeping Hours.
> Those, and a thousand mix'd Emotions more,
> From ever-changing Views of Good and Ill,
> Form'd infinitely various, vex the Mind
> With endless Storm. Whence, deeply rankling, grows,
> The partial Thought, a listless Unconcern,
> Cold, and averting from our Neighbour's Good;
> Then dark Disgust, and Hatred, winding Wiles,
> Coward Deceit, and ruffian Violence,
> At last, extinct, each social Feeling, fell
> And joyless Inhumanity pervades,
> And petrifies the Heart. Nature disturb'd
> Is deem'd, vindictive, to have chang'd her Course. (ll. 288–308)

Love decomposes into 'Bitterness of Soul', which overwhelms Desire, leaving only Extravagance and Madness; the tableau of Grief who 'in dead Silence wastes the weeping Hours' prefigures Enion in *The Four Zoas*, the emanation abandoned by her counterpart Tharmas, who 'wails from the dark deep' (34, l. 100, E324): 'What is the price of Experience' (35, l. 11, E325)? The 'ever-changing Views of Good and Ill' offered by Thomson's gallery of prosopopeia seem less the attributes of the human psyche than autonomous energies. Apart from the reference to 'Our Neighbour's good', from which 'listless Unconcern' is averting, this is a self-perpetuating universe in which human agency is hopelessly attenuated if not irrelevant. While there are animistic elements in the classical tradition from which the pastoral-georgic originates, Thomson could also be drawing from the empiricist philosophers, for whom thoughts and feelings being derived from sense impressions have an almost independent existence. His perspective on the emotions anticipates David Hume's *A Treatise of Human Nature* (1739) who accorded 'original existence' to the passions, which he insisted govern human behaviour.[19] As for 'Nature disturb'd', who has 'chang'd her Course', while she might be 'deem'd, vindictive' by those subject to her vengeance, this could be understood too in this day and age as the inevitable consequence of an environmentally destructive lifestyle.[20]

Blake's epistemology, at least in the more widely read short poems, may appear uncompromisingly personalised and idealist, but his mythopoeia customarily takes place in a non-anthropocentric universe. So even in the *Songs of Experience*, which Blake started printing in 1794, though the earth is personified as captive maiden in 'Earth's Answer' (31, ll. 1-6, E18), in 'Introduction' – the first poem in the section – she belongs to the 'slumberous mass' of 'dewy grass' (11, ll. 14-15, E18). This animistic stanza recalls the following lines from Thomson's allegorical poem *The Castle of Indolence* (1748):

> Is not the field, with lively culture green,
> A sight more joyous than the dead morass?
> Do not the skies, with active ether clean
> And fanned by sprightly zephyrs, far surpass
> The foul November fogs and slumbrous mass
> With which sad Nature veils her drooping face?[21]

It is easy to assume that Blake must be implacably hostile to Thomson's physico-theological view of the material world as 'dead morass' animated by non-human forces. One might even expect Blake to treat 'mass' negatively, as a technical term coined by Newton to refer to '[a] body; a lump; a continuous quantity' (Johnson 1).[22] Instead, Blake's famous image of Newton now with the London Tate Gallery depicts a youthful figure of immense if self-absorbed power.[23] Moreover, when Los first reveals himself to Blake in *Milton*, his claim that though 'generations of men run on in the tide of Time' he remembers everything of them 'for ever & ever' (22, ll. 24-5, E117) is actually taken from Thomson's tribute in *A Poem sacred to the Memory of Sir Isaac Newton* (1727): 'The noiseless tide of time, all bearing down / To vast eternity's unbounded sea, / Where the green islands of the happy shine, / He stemmed alone'.[24]

The well-known axiom 'Energy is Eternal Delight' from *The Marriage of Heaven and Hell* (E34) is compatible with the exuberant celebration of natural fertility in *The Seasons*, which in turn can be traced back to

Venus Genetrix, the 'Parent Power' of nature in Lucretius's *De Rerum Natura* (or, as translated by Thomas Creech, *Of the Nature of Things* (1682)).[25] In the *Summer* (1727) volume of *The Seasons*, Thomson had asserted that all human and creaturely life spring '[f]rom the same PARENT-POWER' (543). Blake applies the phrase to Tharmas, the male counterpart of Enion in *The Four Zoas* (4, l. 6, E301) and in *Milton* itself to Satan (11, l. 36, E105). Blake's only direct reference to Lucretius occurs in his annotations to the 1798 edition of Bacon's *Essays*, 'Every Body Knows that this is Epi[c]urus and Lucretius' (E620), who were regarded as the primary exponents of the materialist view of the universe depicted in *The Four Zoas* as 'fortuitous concourse' of atoms (27, l. 12, E318).[26] However, the abstract beings in *Milton*, referred to as 'Eternals' in the prophetic *Book of Urizen* (1794), are indebted to the indifference of Epicurean gods to humanity in Lucretius (5, ll. 169–85), who also locates the origin of religion in superstition and fear. (As *The Marriage of Heaven and Hell* states: 'All deities reside in the human breast' (E38).) More contentiously, I would argue that both Lucretius and Blake envision the world as a self-regulating system whose end may be imminent and in which the human presence is comparatively recent and eminently dispensable. In Lucretius, Epicurus is elevated to the role of sublime prophet whose mission, like Blake's Milton, is 'to teach Men to despise death' (38, l. 40, E139) through the contemplation of personal mortality and planetary extinction (5, ll. 1–59).[27]

Blake's depiction of the natural world in *Milton* draws heavily on Thomson's *Seasons*. The description of the garden of his cottage in Felpham mirrors the style of Thomson's catalogue of flowers in the prosopopoeia and in its Lucretian celebration of the power of generation:

> Thou perceivest the Flowers put forth their precious Odours!
> And none can tell how from so small a center comes such sweets
> Forgetting that within that Center Eternity expands
> Its ever during doors, that Og & Anak fiercely guard
> First eer the morning breaks joy opens in the flowery bosoms
> Joy even to tears, which the Sun rising dries; first the Wild Thyme
> And Meadow-sweet downy & soft waving among the reeds.
> Light springing on the air lead the sweet Dance: they wake
> The Honeysuckle sleeping on the Oak: the flaunting beauty
> Revels along the wind; the White-thorn lovely May
> Opens her many lovely eyes: listening the Rose still sleeps
> None dare to wake her. Soon she bursts her crimson curtain bed
> And comes forth in the majesty of beauty; every Flower:
> The Pink, the Jessamine, the Wall-flower, the Carnation
> The Jonquil, the mild Lilly opes her heavens! every Tree,
> And Flower & Herb soon fill the air with an innumerable Dance

Yet all in order sweet & lovely. Men are sick with Love!
Such is a Vision of the lamentation of Beulah over Ololon (31, ll. 46–63,
   E131)[28]

The perspective it offers is of a world where human beings are dominated by nature and natural urges: 'Men are sick with Love' seemingly because of 'the sweet Dance' of flowers. 'Thou', which signifies the human presence, is curiously disembodied. In Thomson, the flower garden is indicated as the pride of 'th'exulting Florist' (541), but the second-person pronoun is left unidentified in Blake. Rather revealing in terms of provenance is 'ever during doors', taken from Milton's 'ever during Gates' of heaven in *Paradise Lost* (7, l. 206),[29] which can in turn be traced to Lucretius's 'portarum claustra' (1, l. 70), 'the bolts of the gates' of nature.[30] Though the flower catalogue is a staple of pastoral elegy as an expression of 'lamentation', here the 'order sweet & lovely' of the 'innumerable Dance' seems impervious to any such intimations of mortality.

Immediately preceding the catalogue of flowers in Blake's *Milton* is a parade of birds:

Thou hearest the Nightingale begin the Song of Spring;
The Lark sitting upon his earthy bed: just as the morn
Appears; listens silent; then springing from the waving Corn-field! loud
He leads the Choir of Day! trill, trill, trill, trill,
Mounting upon the wings of light into the Great Expanse:
Reechoing against the lovely blue & shining heavenly Shell:
His little throat labours with inspiration; every feather
On throat & breast & wings vibrates with the effluence Divine
All Nature listens silent to him & the awful Sun
Stands still upon the Mountain looking on this little Bird
With eyes of soft humility, & wonder love & awe.
Then loud from their green covert all the Birds begin their Song
The Thrush, the Linnet & the Goldfinch, Robin & the Wren
Awake the Sun from his sweet reverie upon the Mountain:
The Nightingale again assays his son, & thro the day,
And thro the night warbles luxuriant; every Bird of Song
Attending his loud harmony with admiration & love.
This is a Vision of the lamentation of Beulah over Ololon! (31, ll. 28–45,
   E130–1)

As with the flowers, Blake follows Thomson closely: in *Spring*, it is a lark as well who initiates the chorus of birdsong (582–613). In both, there is a capacious sensibility which accommodates every species rather than compel them to compete among themselves for partners or for scarce and finite resources: all – to quote Thomson – 'the tuneful Nations ... / Are prodigal of Harmony'. Blake's catalogue of flowers ends on a near refrain of the line concluding his parade of birds, which seems as equally shorn of melancholic associations. If this is 'lamentation', what is celebration? 'All Nature ... & the awful Sun' venerates this 'little Bird'. Its solo performance 'trill, trill, trill, trill' not only suggests 'thrill', but also 'drill', the chick trying to release itself from within 'the lovely blue & shining heavenly Shell'. It is no longer 'the poor bird within the shell' which 'Hears its impatient parent bird ... / for the blue Mundane Shell inclosd them in' (21, ll. 28–30, E116). Confinement 'finishes where the lark mounts' (17, l. 27, E111), which becomes 'a mighty, Angel' (36, l. 12, E136) soaring into 'effluence Divine', where Blake slightly alters Milton's 'divine effulgence' (*Paradise Lost* (5, l. 458)).

While Blake has clearly taken on aspects of Thomson's 'philosophic eye', a viewpoint characteristic of the socially elevated, which regularly gestures to a collective, even global consciousness,[31] there are affinities between him and the labouring-class writers who took up the pastoral-georgic. They have, for example, a similar tendency to allude to their arduous physical task load and resentment at patronage relationships. Moreover, with respect to his own writing, though Blake asserts the very inspiration and spontaneity aspired to by middle-class Romantic poets (in his Felpham correspondence, he claims to have written *Milton* 'from immediate Dictation ... without Premeditation & even against my Will', E729), in continuing to insist that the lark 'labours with inspiration' he displays an attitude that is actually closer to Ann Yearsley's.[32] Indeed, Blake qualifies 'the Time it has taken in writing' seemingly 'producd without Labour or Study' by leaving no doubt as to it being inseparably connected with 'the Labour of a long Life' (E729).

Blake and Akenside

Mark Akenside's didactic poem *The Pleasures of the Imagination* (1744) is customarily regarded as a point of transition between the focus on the association of ideas in the early eighteenth century (as expounded in Joseph Addison's essays for *The Spectator*) and the more active conception developed during the Romantic period (as articulated, for example, by Samuel Taylor Coleridge).[33] Marilyn Butler also emphasises Blake and Akenside's proclivity for Creation myths and arcane cosmology.[34] Indeed, Akenside's work offers not only a generic precedent for Blake's prophetic books in its arcane intellectual eclecticism, but, in the dream vision of the goddess Euphrosyne and the demonic son of Nemesis (2, ll. 146–668),[35] also a template for the final showdown with Satan in Blake's 'Cottage Garden' in *Milton*.

First, for all their apparent power and malevolence, both the son of Nemesis and Satan are surprisingly easy to deal with. Harmodius – an elder, statesmanlike figure – grown cynical over the lot of humankind because of the death of his young lover Parthenia, has turned away from virtue,[36] having eyes only for Euphrosyne, the 'nymph' of good cheer, joy and mirth. The son of Nemesis is sent by the lord of creation as a rebuke for his self-absorption:

> Looking up, I view'd
> A vast gigantic spectre striding on
> Thro' murm'ring thunders and a waste of clouds,
> With dreadful action. (2, ll. 506–9)

However, the monster only needs to be confronted for him to be 'with ease / Disarm'd and quell'd, his fierceness he resigns / To bondage and to scorn' (2, ll. 584–6). Similarly, at Blake's garden in Felpham, Satan is so frightened by Milton that he is completely unable to attack: 'He trembled with exceeding great trembling & astonishment / Howling in his Spectre round his Body hungring to devour / But fearing for the pain for if he touched a Vital' (39, ll. 17–19, E140). Second, the 'spectre' in Akenside recurs in Blake. Third, Akenside's Euphrosyne and Blake's Ololon manifest themselves on earth in a similar way:

> Swift as the ligh'ning flash; the melting clouds
> Flew diverse, and amid the blue serene
> Euphrosyne appear'd. (2, ll. 636–41)

> And as one Female, Ololon and all its mighty Hosts
> Appear'd: a Virgin of twelve years nor time nor space was
> To the perception of the Virgin Ololon but as the
> Flash of lightning but more quick the Virgin in my Garden
> Before my Cottage stood (36, ll. 16–20, E137)

The militant stance of Euphrosyne and Ololon compels awestruck humility in both narrators.

Finally, with both episodes, there is a transformation of the landscape by radiant, otherworldly powers. When Euphrosyne ascends to heaven, 'the clouds / ...withdrew / Their airy veil, and left a bright expanse / Of empyrean flame' (2, ll. 438–41) too bright for human eyes to bear. As Milton descends on Blake's garden, 'my Path became a solid fire, as bright / As the clear Sun' (39, ll. 4–5, E140). At the end of the trial of Harmodius, Euphrosyne 'and the whole romantic scene / Immediate vanish'd; rocks, and woods, and rills, / The mantling tent, and each mysterious form / Flew like the pictures of a morning dream / When sun-shine fills the bed' (2, ll. 660–4). The 'tent' ('temporary habitation',

Johnson 2) is revealed as 'mantling' ('froth', Johnson 4), suggesting 'form' may also be no more than foam. While 'bed' suggests Harmodius wakes from sleep, he may have experienced his vision out of doors since the word could also refer to a '[b]ank of earth raised in a garden' (Johnson 4). In Blake, when Satan is vanished, Milton reunites with Ololon precipitating a vision so astounding it literally blows his mind: he 'fell outstretchd upon the path' (42, l. 25, E143). The risk of bathos by the climactic dispelling of illusion in Akenside is mitigated in Blake by the reinstatement of the tangible phenomena of the natural world:

> A moment, & my Soul returnd into its mortal state
> [. . .]
> Immediately the Lark mounted with a loud trill from Felphams Vale
> And the Wild Thyme from Wimbletons green & impurpled Hills
> And Los & Enitharmon rose over the Hills of Surrey
> Their clouds roll over London with a south wind . . . (42, ll. 26 and 29–32, E143)

A lark sings as Blake regains consciousness to a world precisely localised in Wimbledon (or Wimbleton, as it was known in the Romantic period) and 'the Hills of Surrey', familiar yet curiously transfigured. This is a modification of *The Pleasures of Imagination*, where a similar union of the divine and the natural does not take place until the next book (more than six hundred lines later) under the very different framework of the human imagination:

> Lo! she appeals to nature, to the winds
> And rowling waves, the sun's unwearied course,
> The elements and seasons: all declare
> For what th' eternal maker has ordain'd
> The pow'rs of man: we feel within ourselves
> His energy divine: he tells the heart,
> He meant, he made us to behold and love
> What he beholds and loves, the general orb
> Of life and being; to be great like him,
> Beneficent and active. Thus the men
> Whom nature's works can charm, with God himself
> Hold converse; grow familiar, day by day,
> With his conceptions; act upon his plan;
> And form to his the relish of their souls. (3, ll. 620–33)

The mind, in contrast to God, is feminised as 'she'. The 'elements and seasons' suggest a Lucretian world whose processes pre-exist and surpass the interference of the 'pow'rs of man'. Akenside's perspective is similar to Thomson's and other socially elevated writers in the range of its excursions: in Akenside's case, not only temporally, into the distant past, but spatially as well into extra-terrestrial realms. The 'general orb / Of being' suggests an enlarged sensory horizon, but also planetary orbits.[37] The 'sun's unwearied course' re-emerges in Blake's *Milton* as 'the unwearied Sun by Los created / To measure Time and Space to mortal Men (29, ll. 23–4, E127). In other words, the universe humankind inhabits is designed to be meaningful and intelligible.

Blake and Iolo

Of the three precursors to Blake discussed here, Edward Williams – aka Iolo Morganwg (Edward of Glamorgan) – is closest socially as a hybrid of proletarian and elite culture. The son of a stonemason and a woman with a genteel upbringing, Iolo, like Blake, was a craftsman with literary pretensions. Blake's *Milton*, as suggested by my discussion of the ending, is corporeally located in its phenomenology of place, which is at least analogous to if not directly derived from Iolo's *Poems, Lyric and Pastoral*.

A distinctive characteristic of labouring-class poetical expression is the important role played by the poet's habitation, a consequence perhaps of their lack of geographical mobility.[38] Iolo's cottage in the village of Flemingston becomes a kind of radial node. It represented 'home and my family, where all my little portion of happiness was centered' (1: xii).[39] As a dwelling which he himself built and maintained, not only is it comparable to his verse in being one of 'the real unsophisticated productions of the *self-tutored Journeyman Mason*' (1: xiii),[40] but also the physical evidence of his claim to a poetics that 'always refers its origin to *Divine communications*, and never talked of . . . *Religion of Nature*' (2: 199):

> My house is convenient, and whiten'd all o'er,
> An arbour of jessamine fronting the door;
> My flourishing orchard abundantly bears
> Fine plumbs, golden pippins and bergamot pears;
> The rose, the sweet pink, in my garden are found,
> Where dainties of health for my table abound (1: 170)

Blake's *Milton* could only be composed after a residence at Felpham, as the following lines make amply clear:

> For when Los joind with me he took me in his firy whirlwind
> My Vegetated portion was hurried from Lambeths shades
> He set me down in Felphams Vale and prepared a beautiful
> Cottage for me that in three years I might write all these Visions
> To display Natures cruel holiness: the deceits of Natural Religion[.] (36,
>   ll. 21–5, E137)

The celebration of his flight from Lambeth in London to the Felpham countryside echoes Iolo's joyful exit from the same city to 'DAVONA'S VALE' (1: 209) in Glamorgan.

The distrust of the capital, celebration of rural domesticity and an alternative provincial mythology are motifs that conform to the country tradition as defined by Butler. Blake's idyllic cottage is an opportunity to reclaim his 'Vegetated portion'[41] as well as write his searing visions of 'Natures cruel holiness', of which the following exposition in *Milton* is perhaps the most memorable in the entire work:

> The nature of infinity is this: That every thing has its
> Own Vortex; and when once a traveller thro Eternity.
> Has passd that Vortex, he perceives it roll backward behind
> His path, into a globe itself infolding; like a sun:
> Or like a moon, or like a universe of starry majesty,
> While he keeps onwards in his wondrous journey on the earth
> Or like a human form, a friend with who he livd benevolent.
> As the eye of man views both the east & west encompassing
> Its vortex; and the north & south, with all their starry host;
> Also the rising sun & setting moon he views surrounding
> His corn-fields and his valleys of five hundred acres square.
> Thus is the earth one infinite plane, and not as apparent
> To the weak traveller confin'd beneath the moony shade.
> Thus is the heaven a vortex passd already, and the earth
> A vortex not yet pass'd by the traveller thro' Eternity. (15, ll. 21–35, E109)

This splendid passage communicates with considerable force how the local and the universal, the transient and the eternal, the small and the infinite, rather than being absolute divisions are simply matters of perspective. To a person in a valley, the sun and moon do not seem any further than the edge of a 500-acre cornfield which stretches as far as the eye can see. The 'earth' only seems an 'infinite plane' to those living on it, but it is an effect of perspective no different from the cornfield: 'plane' after all recalls 'plain'. In this sense, contraction and expansion are merely two different perspectives because scale is purely relational, as Blake communicated a few pages earlier in his perception of 'Female Space': 'it shrinks the Organs / Of Life till they become Finite & Itself seems Infinite' (10, ll. 6–7, E104). If it is regarded as imprisonment by those outside, it is 'Infinite to those within' (10, l. 9, E104). It is as potentially evil as it is potentially redemptive: 'Satan vibrated in the immensity of the Space' (10, l. 8, E104) just as the unhatched lark may vibrate within an egg. In a universe where the local opens into the universal, the transient passes into the eternal, the very small and the very great merely relative, earthly experience situated in 'place' ceases to be limiting of selfhood, 'an Incrustation' as it were 'over . . . immortal / Spirit' (40, ll. 35–6, E142), as it is possible to take up 'abode / In Chasms of the Mundane Shell' (34, ll. 40–1, E134).

Butler locates the influence of Iolo Morganwg upon Blake's concept of reincarnation as an ascension through a hierarchy of states to a new identity.[42] Blake attended druidic ceremonies Iolo initiated on Primrose Hill in the early 1790s, employed the triad form in his own poetry and fervently espoused a Bardocentric national history.[43] In *Milton*, the pivotal moment of Blake assuming the status of prophet occurs when he merges with Los.

> Los descended to me:
> And Los behind me stood; a terrible flaming Sun: just close
> Behind my back; I turned round in terror, and behold.
> Los stood in that fierce glowing fire; & he also stoop'd down
> And bound my sandals on in Udan-Adan; trembling I stood
> Exceedingly with fear & terror, standing in the Vale
> Of Lambeth: but he kissed me and wishd me health.
> And I became One Man with his arising in my strength:
> Twas too late to recede. Los had enterd into my soul:
> His terrors now posses'd me whole! I arose in fury & strength. (22, ll. 5–14, E116–17)

Instead of being incinerated by the creative force, he is paid obeisance: Los wishing him 'health' poignantly echoes his own concern for his wife's rheumatism.[44] In the accompanying full-plate illustration, Los, hunched within a 'fierce glowing fire', tentatively places his foot outside the confining circle onto the bounded horizon-line of a green earth.[45] This gesture of stooping down recalls not only the previous page where Blake 'stooped down & bound' his sandal, perceived as a microcosm of 'this Vegetable World' (21, ll. 12–14, E115), but also of the remoulding of Milton two pages prior to that by Urizen, Blake's embodiment of reason and law, who 'stoop'd down / And took up water from the river Jordan: pouring on / To Milton's brain the icy fluid from his broad cold palm' (19, ll. 7–9, E112).

There are many suggestive textual parallels between Iolo and Blake. The paean to the sun opening Iolo's 'Ode on the Mythology of the Ancient British Bards' would have served as part of the elaborate solar rituals of a druidic ceremony:

> I saw yon orb, yon source of light,
> Give to this world its new-born ray,
> When first arose in fulgence bright
> The glories of primeval day. (2: 203)[46]

This seems comparable in tenor with the paean to 'ancient time' when the Son of God walked on 'Englands pleasant pastures' opening *Milton*

(1, ll. 1–4, E95). Iolo's fervent anti-militarism in 'The Horrors of War, a Pastoral', in which he asserts that '*swords* have long since been *beat into ploughshares*, and *spears into pruning-hooks* by all, except our still *unchristianized* RULERS and their *minions*' (2: 143), prefigures Blake's rebuke to 'silly Greek & Latin slaves of the Sword' (E95). Blake's 'I will not cease from Mental Fight, / Nor shall my Sword sleep in my hand' (1, ll. 11–12, E95) invites comparison with Iolo's 'FELL weapon, that in ruthless hand / Of warrior fierce, of despot king' (2: 160) opening 'Ode on Converting a Sword into a Pruning-Hook'. 'I soar'd a *Lark* and hymn'd the morn' so that 'The *Bardic song* shall now resound / Trill through these *templed hills* around' (2: 206 and 215), declares Iolo's 'Ode on the Mythology of the Ancient British Bards'.[47] In *Milton*, Blake offers a similar phenomenology of place where the larks 'descend / To their respective Earths' (36, ll. 3–4, E136): the '*templed hills*' refer to druidic stone circles, 'Earths' to the eastern gates of the city built by Los, Golgonooza.

'Places Remember Events', James Joyce wrote in his preparatory draft to *Ulysses*. As Paul Ricoeur notes in *Memory, History, Forgetting*, his classic discussion of the lived body and phenomenology of place:

> If [this] suggests something like a nostalgia desirous of 'putting things back in their place,' it has to do with the adventure of a being of flesh and bones who, like Ulysses, is in his place as much as the places visited as upon his return to Ithaca. The navigator's wanderings demand their right no less than does the residence of the sedentary person.[48]

The 'residence of the sedentary person' counterbalances the 'navigator's wanderings'. The eponymous hero of *Milton*, reduced by death to a 'mournful shade' (14, l. 35, E108), is released as the 'traveller thro Eternity' (15, l. 35, E109) and learns to see his life on earth as a 'bright pilgrimage of sixty years' (15, l. 52, E110). It may be an imaginary perspective; nevertheless, whether real or not, the characters in *Milton* have a very material presence. The work opens with an invocation to the Muses to 'descen[d] down the Nerves of my right arm / From out the Portals of my Brain' (2, ll. 6–7, E96). The heavenly Eternals here are greatly concerned with the grosser matters of the material world: 'Generation & the Vegetative Power' (14, l. 5, E108). Every experience is a seemingly necessary part of development; even a tiny ocean polyp mentioned in passing in the first half of the work (15, l. 8, E109) is revealed in the latter half as significant: 'For Golgonooza cannot be seen till having passd the Polypus', 'Or till you become Mortal & Vegetable in Sexuality' (35, ll. 22–4, E135). Golgonooza, as a place where all human activity is redeemed, cannot be reached without dissolving the boundaries between not only soul and body but also 'Mortal & Vegetable'. Also interesting is Ricoeur's assertion that '[t]o these alternatives of rest and movement is grafted the act of inhabiting, which has its own polarities: reside and displace, take shelter under a roof, cross a threshold and go out',[49] which is almost a gloss on the ideal of 'ordered Space' in *Milton*:

> The Sky is an immortal Tent built by the Sons of Los
> And every Space that a Man views around his dwelling-place:
> Standing on his own roof, or in his garden on a mount
> Of twenty-five cubits in height, such space is his Universe;
> And on its verge the Sun rises & sets. the Clouds bow
> To meet the flat Earth & the Sea in such an ordered Space:
> The starry heavens reach no further but here bend and set
> On all sides & the two Poles turn on their valves of gold:
> And if he move his dwelling-place, his heavens also move
> Wher'eer he goes & all his neighbourhood bewail his loss:
> Such are the Spaces called Earth & such its dimension: (29, ll. 4–14, E127)

The 'immortal Tent', reminiscent of Akenside's 'mantling tent', is supported by 'two Poles', both axes of the earth and long wooden staves.[50] The 'dimension' of Earth is mapped as 'dwelling place', 'abode', 'neighbourhood' and 'region'.

T. S. Eliot remarked of Blake that '[with him o]ne feels that the form is not well chosen. The borrowed philosophy of Dante and Lucretius is perhaps not so interesting, but it injures their form less.'[51] *Milton* might be seen as pilgrimage or prophecy, but it also has affinities with the pastoral-georgic tradition. The imperatives of casting off and self-annihilation are contained and absorbed within contextual ironies and continuous narrative retardation. Milton and Satan are doubles as well as opponents. Albion never finally rises. Instead the poem closes on an anticipated final 'Harvest' which is to still to come. Rather than the prospect of creaturely vengeance as envisaged in 'Auguries of Innocence',[52] it contains an inclusive catalogue of living species. 'Wild Thyme' – alternately 'downy & soft waving among the reeds' (31, ll. 51–2, E131), then 'a mighty Demon / Terrible deadly & poisonous', or 'appear[ing] only a small Root creeping in grass' (31, ll. 54–6, E136) – allows the 'Vegetable Body' to be located both inside and outside the 'Mundane Shell', which renews and redeems the world as dwelling place (42, l. 30, E143). As vantage points are potentially infinite, so 'more extensive / Than any earthly things, are Mans earthly lineaments' (21, ll. 10–11, E115).

Notes

1. Sarah Haggerty (ed.), *William Blake in Context* (Cambridge: Cambridge University Press, 2019).
2. Ibid. pp. 103–62.
3. Ibid. pp. 163–234.
4. Ibid. pp. 192–9.
5. Marilyn Butler, *Mapping Mythologies: Countercurrents in Eighteenth-Century British Poetry and Cultural History* (Cambridge: Cambridge University Press, 2015).
6. 'Antiquarianism' by Noah Heringman (Ibid. pp. 245–53) does contain an (unindexed) entry to Butler's 'Antiquarianism (Popular)', in Iain McCalman (ed.), *Companion to the Romantic Age* (Oxford: Oxford University Press, 1999), pp. 328–37.
7. The decision by CUP not even to update the bibliography to include relevant scholarship after the 1970s is surely deplorable in imparting to this intervention of hers the aura of a cryogenic time warp.
8. Butler, *Mapping Mythologies*, p. 8.
9. For example, according to Sea Shepherd founder Paul Watson, 'What we need if we are to survive is a new story, a new myth, a new religion. We need to replace anthropocentrism with biocentrism. We need to construct a religion that incorporates all species and establishes nature as sacred and deserving of respect'; in 'Biocentric Religion – A Call For', in Bron Taylor (ed.), *Encyclopedia of Religion and Nature* (New York: Continuum, 2005), pp. 176–9.
10. Quotations from Blake's poetry are from David V. Erdman (ed.), *The Complete Poetry and Prose of William Blake* (Berkeley and Los Angeles: University of California Press, 1982), with plate and line numbers followed by the page in Erdman's edition (E).
11. Kevin Hutchings, *Imagining Nature: Blake's Environmental Poetics* (Toronto: McGill University Press, 2002).
12. It may even have been among the 'immense number of verses on One Grand Theme' (E728) that he produced at Felpham between 1800 and 1803, though he may be referring here to *The Four Zoas*.
13. Frederick E. Pierce, 'The Genesis and General Meaning of Blake's "Milton"', *Modern Philology* 25, no. 2 (1927): 178.
14. The classic study of this is Ralph Cohen's *The Art of Discrimination: Thomson's The Seasons and the Language of Criticism* (Berkeley: University of California Press, 1964).
15. James Thomson, *The Seasons*, ed. James Sambrook (Oxford: Clarendon Press, 1981), p. 9. These lines are printed as an inset note, as Thomson removed them for the 1746 edition on which Sambrook's edition is based. Quotations from the poem hereafter are from this edition with line numbers in parentheses.
16. *The Idea of Landscape and the Sense of Place 1730–1840: An Approach to the Poetry of John Clare* (Cambridge: Cambridge University Press, 1972); *The Dark Side of the Landscape: The Rural Poor in English Painting, 1740–1830* (Cambridge: Cambridge University Press, 1983); and *English*

Literature in History 1730–80: An Equal, Wide Survey (New York: St Martins, 1983).
17. As previously noted, Hutchings, *Imagining Nature*, p. 120. Haggerty makes the same omission in *William Blake in Context*, p. 192.
18. See Butler, *Mapping Mythologies*, p. 28.
19. David Hume, *A Treatise on Human Nature: Being an Attempt to Introduce the Experimental Method of Reasoning into Moral Subjects*, 3 vols (London: Noon, 1739), 2: 253. The language of sentiment however derives from Lord Shaftesbury's *Characteristics of Men, Manners, Opinion and Times* (1711).
20. Environmental guilt is a theme shared by Christian and secular works. For example, it is in both Roger S. Gottlieb's *A Greener Faith: Religious Environmentalism and our Planet's Future* (Oxford: Oxford University Press, 2006) and James Lovelock's *The Revenge of Gaia: Why the Earth is Fighting Back – and How We Can Still Save Humanity* (London: Penguin, 2007).
21. James Logie Robertson (ed.), *The Complete Poetical Works of James Thomson* (Oxford: Oxford University Press, 1908), p. 295.
22. See Samuel Johnson, *A Dictionary of the English Language: In Which the Words are Deduced from the Originals*, 2nd edn, 2 vols (London: Collins, 1760).
23. See *The Large Colour Printed Drawings*, 'Object 24', in *The William Blake Archive*, <www.blakearchive.org/work/cpd> (accessed 1 May 2020).
24. Robertson, *The Collected Poetical Works of James Thomson*, p. 440.
25. Book 2, lines 612–20. See Titus Lucretius Carus, *Of the Nature of Things, in Six Books*, trans. Thomas Creech, 2 vols (London: Sawbridge, [1682] 1714), 1: 146–7. Quotations from the poem hereafter are from this edition with book and line numbers in parentheses.
26. As a more specific example, 'the youth shut up from / The lustful joy. Shall forget to generate & create an amorous image / In the shadows of his curtains and in the folds of his silent pillow' (*Visions of the Daughters of Albion*, 7, ll. 5–7, E50) seems directly borrowed from *De Rerum Natura*, 'Nay oft, as in the Fury of the Joy / The flowing SEED pollutes the am'rous BOY' (4, ll. 1028–9).
27. Note the insistence on the transience of the world in Book 5 (ll. 99–266) and also the catastrophic demise of humanity implied by the plague scenes that close Book 6 (ll. 1101–257). Thomson's *Winter* in its first edition finishes with a closing apocalyptic vision of how 'Dread WINTER has subdu'd the Year' (l. 359).
28. Compare the passage with Thomson's *Spring* (535–55).
29. John Milton, *Paradise Lost*, ed. Barbara K. Lewalski (Oxford: Blackwell, 2007), p. 207. Quotations from the poem hereafter are from this edition with book and line numbers in parentheses.
30. This is Creech's translation: 'As when the hind'ring Door / Imprisons up the longing Eye no more; / But, open'd wide, permits the eager Sight' (4, ll. 281–3).
31. Barrell notes that the georgic poet often displaces and usurps any posited divine viewpoint: *An Equal, Wide Survey*, pp. 74–8. On shifting scale of viewpoints, see Kevis Goodman, *Georgic Modernity and British*

Romanticism: Poetry and the Mediation of History (Cambridge: Cambridge University Press, 2004), pp. 38–66.
32. For parallels to Blake's reluctant dependence and reliance on Hayley, see Kerri Andrews, *Ann Yearsley and Hannah More, Patronage and Poetry: The Story of a Literary Relationship* (London: Pickering & Chatto, 2013).
33. This is the genealogy expounded in M. H. Abrams, *The Mirror and the Lamp: Romantic Theory and the Critical Tradition* (Oxford: Oxford University Press, 1953).
34. Butler, *Mapping Mythologies*, pp. 50–3.
35. Robin Dix (ed.), *The Poetical Works of Mark Akenside* (London: Associated University Presses, 1996). Quotations from the poem hereafter are from this edition with book and line numbers in parentheses.
36. The 'stately' goddess accompanying Euphrosyne is unnamed, but Robert D. Stock's understanding of her as 'Virtue' does make sense; see *The Holy and the Daemonic from Sir Thomas Browne to William Blake* (Princeton: Princeton University Press, 1982), pp. 174–5.
37. As in the 'heav'nly orbs' providing 'the glad abodes of life' (2, l. 316).
38. Yes, Iolo went to London, which Blake left for a few years, but they did not move as often nor did they have the same opportunities to tour Europe as their middle- and upper-class counterparts.
39. Edward Williams, *Poems, Lyric and Pastoral*, 2 vols (London: Johnson, 1794). Quotations from the poem hereafter are from this edition with volume and page numbers in parentheses.
40. 'My lot in life, nor blame I fate, / Unborn to title or estate, / Was to procure a slender stock, / By building *houses* on the *rock*' ('Castles in the Air', 1: 24).
41. For the details of Blake's residence, see Mark Crosby, '"The Sweetest Spot on Earth": Reconstructing William Blake's Cottage in Felpham, Sussex', *British Art Journal* 7, no. 3 (2006/7): 46–53.
42. In Iolo's words, 'Taliesin[, the sixth-century Celtic bard,] places this probational, divestigating or purifying *Metempsychosis* in the *Hell* of *Christianity*, whence the soul gradually rises again to *Felicity*' (1: xxi).
43. Butler, *Mapping Mythologies*, pp. 174–6.
44. As a less than paradisal aspect of Felpham: 'My Wife has bad Agues & Rheumatisms almost ever since she has been here' (letter to James Blake, dated 30 January 1803, E725).
45. See *Milton a Poem Copy C*, 'Object 46', in *The William Blake Archive*, <www.blakearchive.org/copy/milton.c?descld=milton.c.illbk.46> (accessed 7 May 2020).
46. Iolo defines 'LIGHT' as 'The emblem of purity, and holiness, the source of good, and by which all truths should be illumined. Every act by the Bard must be done *in the face of the sun, and the eye of the light*': in the preface to *The Heroic Elegies and Other Pieces* (London: Owen, 1792), p. lv.
47. The line 'To strike a *peaceful brother* dead' (2: 163) also anticipates the illustrations of Robert and William Blake as mirror images in *Milton a Poem Copy C*, 'Object 31' and 'Object 36' in *The William Blake Archive*.
48. Paul Ricoeur, *Memory, History, Forgetting*, trans. Kathleen Blamey and David Pellauer (Chicago: Chicago University Press, 2004), p. 149.
49. Ibid. pp. 149–50.

50. 'Poles' also recall the date of Iolo's ceremony: 'Sept 22, 1793, being the Day whereon the Autumnal Equinox occurred, and one of the four grand solemn Bardic Days' (2: 160).
51. T. S. Eliot, 'William Blake', in *Selected Essays* (London: Faber, 1951), pp. 320.
52. Olga Tokarczuk's *Drive Your Plow over the Bones of the Dead* (London: Penguin Random House, 2018) develops this into a concerted campaign of retaliation by the natural world against human encroachment.

Chapter 12

Untidying the Landscape: Romantic Poetics, Class and Non-Human Nature

Simon J. White

This essay revisits the contested relationship between Romantic environmental aesthetics and the development of the modern environmental movement to focus on the wild non-human animals that have often been marginalised in the various turns taken in the debate since the publication of Jonathan Bate's *Romantic Ecology* (1991). Under examination here are two significant writers in this context: William Wordsworth and John Clare. The former arguably contributed most to the aesthetics of wilderness management during the nineteenth and twentieth centuries (although, as will become clear, the extent to which Britain's upland landscapes were wild even in Wordsworth's day is questionable), while the latter is increasingly seen as the most important British poet of natural history. The point of departure for my intervention is to return to the actual places that formed the nature aesthetics of Wordsworth and Clare to consider how they had been and continue to be shaped by history. More information on these places through time is gradually becoming available within the disciplines of historical environmentalism and historical ecology. The perspective from which the two poets viewed the landscape, in terms of their respective social position or class, is also important because this impacted on how they interacted with the landscape and what they saw in the landscape. These are not insignificant comparisons because today Romantic nature aesthetics continues to influence the way many British people look at rural spaces around them, and how they think about questions of environmental preservation or restoration. For many people, expansive green spaces, particularly national parks like the Lake District, constitute nature at its best and most abundant, despite the 2016 *State of Nature* report finding that in terms of biodiversity and wildlife decline Britain is now 'among the most nature-depleted countries in the world.'[1] To say at the time of writing that Britain's natural heritage has been all but destroyed generally provokes an incredulous response when so much of the landscape is still green (as of 2011 only 7 per cent of the British landscape was urban, and there are many green spaces within most urban environments too[2]), even amongst academic colleagues.

The continuing influence of Romantic nature aesthetics is illustrated by a somewhat fraught conversation I recently had with a friend about plans for a solar farm on a greenfield site near the village where we both live. My friend explained that, being a nature lover, he could not support such a development. I asked of the large monoculture fields ploughed and planted right up to the thin, hacked-back hedges, where is the nature there? (Indeed, as was the case for most of the twentieth century, there is often more nature and biodiversity in older, lower-density middle-class suburban areas – those areas where houses have decent gardens – than in the agricultural landscape.[3]) This conversation made me think of a passage from *Romantic Ecology*: 'the "Romantic ecology" reverences the green earth because it recognizes that neither physically nor psychologically can we live without *green* things; it proclaims that there is "one life" within us and abroad, and that the earth is a single vast ecosystem which we destabilize at our peril' (my emphasis).[4] Bate sees the nature aesthetic of Wordsworth (and Ralph Waldo Emerson) as the foundation of the modern environmental movement. His reading of Wordsworth has been critiqued on the grounds that there was no agreed definition of nature during the Romantic period and that it is anachronistic to read recent developments in the science of ecology (for example, 'ecosystem' science) into Romantic writings. Second-wave ecocriticism has focused on the way literary texts represent relationships between humans and non-human nature(s), and third-wave Romantic ecocriticism has taken this re-historicisation further in endeavouring to identify connections between Romantic writing and developments in eighteenth- and nineteenth-century natural science (and natural philosophy).[5] For me these responses to *Romantic Ecology* miss the point because Bate's broader claim that Wordsworth's Romantic nature aesthetic inspired, and continues to inspire, mainstream environmentalism in Britain is undeniably correct. My friend has a very Wordsworthian 'reverence' for 'green' spaces, like that felt by many British people. (The farmland on which a development is planned is valuable because it is green; according to this way of seeing the land, farm buildings are an acceptable part of the green landscape, whereas land that is developed for housing or non-farming purposes, such as the production of solar energy, is not.) The question is whether the influence of the Wordsworthian Romantic nature aesthetic has been a positive one.

For Wordsworth the presence of humans working the land is central to the nature that he represents in his poetry. While Timothy Morton's conceptualisation of Wordsworth's nature as 'ambient' (or ambient-green) is persuasive, the idea that 'the human species' does not feature in it is debatable.[6] It might be true regarding the transformational crossing of the Alps or Snowden moments in 'The Prelude' (1805), but in several other important poems, smallholder protagonists are subsumed into the agricultural landscape around them; this is the case, for example, in 'Michael' (1798) and 'The Ruined Cottage' (1797–1804). In the latter poem the reclamation of the cottage by non-human nature is represented as a reflection of the protagonist's gradual decline. Wordsworth's *Guide to the Lakes* (1810) shapes Bate's reading of the poet as 'an exemplar of Romantic ecology' because it celebrates small-scale farming and a symbiosis between nature and the farmers and shepherds who work the land.[7] The problem is that it is not at all clear that the typical upland farming model, whether small-scale or otherwise (and upland farming in Britain was and remains predominantly small-scale), preserved or preserves biodiversity and broader ecosystem health. Wordsworth's Lake District was never the timeless place implied in many of his poems; virtually all environments are a product of continual, often rapid, change once inhabited by humans. In a study of the impact of human activity on the Lake District, Ian Whyte finds that 'there have been a number of earlier times (beginning in Neolithic Britain) characterized by rapid landscape and environmental change[, but] each period was roughly an order of magnitude worse [in terms of the impact on non-human nature] than its predecessor'.[8] During the immediate 'post-medieval' period there was some regeneration (or rewilding) of the landscape, but from the eighteenth century increased grazing pressure from cattle and then sheep turned upland Cumbria into the ecologically impoverished or, in George Monbiot's words, 'sheepwrecked' place it is today.[9] Overgrazing reached crisis point in parts of the Lake District as early as the mid-eighteenth century due to a weakening of the manorial courts, which had previously exercised control over common grazing rights.[10] Parliamentary enclosure did not affect the landscape of upland Cumbria as much as other parts of Britain,[11] and where enclosure took place this did not lead to more careful management of pasture and a consequent reduction in overgrazing. In fact grazing density only increased through the nineteenth and twentieth centuries to the extent that it often exceeded the 'ecological or even agricultural carrying capacity' of the land.[12] As Tom Williamson observes, 'sheep tend to be selective grazers and, at high densities, suppress the growth of more palatable plants and grasses, and of heather, leading to the development of a more uniform, species-poor acidic grassland characterized by *Nardus stricta*, *Molinia caerula* and reeds'.[13] This is the environment that most informed Wordsworth's concept of nature, and, through the development of national parks in the nineteenth and twentieth centuries,[14] shaped the still prevalent British view of that which constitutes a valuable natural (or green) place. In turn this dominant aesthetic has contributed to the production of a rural environment in which human activities are always central; especially sheep farming (we tend to romanticise the upland pastoral in ways that we do not the lowland arable or mixed farming landscape; indeed, Wordsworth's legacy is partly responsible for this situation too) of the kind that can be found in so many of Britain's best-known national parks, for example the Lake District, the Peak District and the Yorkshire Dales.[15] (One of the two most biodiverse parts of Britain today is in Cumbria, but it is not upland Cumbria (the Lake District) as celebrated in Wordsworth's poetry, but the much less fashionable and less well-known lowland Northeast Cumbria. The other is in Mid-Wales.[16])[17] In other parts of the world, national parks are devoted to wild non-human species (although, even in such parks or reserves, there is often human incursion; for example, through wildlife tourism).

Morton is correct in his assessment that the nature represented in Wordsworth's poetry is distinguished by a relative absence of wild non-human animals.[18] This is partly a product of the open upland landscapes that often inspired the poet, including those that initiated the crossing of the Alps and ascent of Snowden moments in 'The Prelude'. Most of these environments were not particularly species-rich during the late eighteenth and early nineteenth centuries (and there is even less biodiversity in many of them today).[19] Moreover, Wordsworth's nature poetry represents imaginary landscapes that have little to do with direct observation of a specific location at a specific moment in time. In literary-historical terms, 'Michael' and 'The Ruined Cottage' are important poems; they are not about the ecological health or (bio) diversity of the land represented in them. Even the occasional poems that do prominently feature wild non-human beings in the landscape, such as 'Hart-Leap Well' (1800), 'To a Butterfly' (1807) or 'To a Cuckoo' (1815), do not focus on the (suffering) non-human subject. 'To a Butterfly' and 'To a Cuckoo' are primarily about the speaker, and 'Hart-Leap Well' is more concerned with the impact of the hunt described in the narrative on the human protagonist, and then the way the story of the hunt shapes local human popular culture. The titular hart is explicitly and unapologetically anthropomorphised; represented as being irresistibly drawn, when in extremis, to a place that had profound meaning for him. As is often the case in Wordsworth's writing, an equivocally represented wild non-human nature is conceptually and poetically tidied up and then presented as being inextricably bound up with the moral and spiritual development of the human subject, and human culture more generally.

As Wordsworth sensed, our imaginative relationship with the other forms of life that share the earth with us (or 'nature', however one defines it) is important. When confronted by a new environment, we humans can employ our common sense (something that is almost always limited by received opinion and the prevailing ideology) to reconfigure our surroundings to fit our immediate cultural needs (I am using the word 'cultural' in its broadest sense, to include, for example, economic systems). In a world dominated by capitalism, these needs must be ever-changing (to drive economic development). This results in constant transformations of the landscape; something that often involves the destruction of other forms of life. Or we can employ our adaptability and intelligence to adjust our culture to our surroundings. Recently, in the Westernised world, we have generally chosen the first option because it is easier, requiring less imagination and effort; it is the unthinking thing to do because it conforms to the prevailing capitalist ideology and involves reducing the complexity (or biodiversity) of a place to make way for a much simpler (in terms of biological complexity) and tidier environment. The second option is what many supposedly uncivilised Indigenous or First Peoples did in Australasia and North America, and what remaining Indigenous hunter-gatherer tribes in the Amazon continue to do today in the face of the desire of many Westernised South Americans to 'develop' the region. This is not to say that early human migration had no impact on other species; the geological record suggests that the disappearance of many species of megafauna coincided with the appearance of humans. The fact remains, though, that in terms of the impact it has on other life forms, human culture(s) can be heavy- or light-touch. Wordsworth's poetic response to landscapes that have already been repeatedly transformed by humans throughout history, including the non-human beings that inhabit those landscapes, is to further envelop them within human culture. This is what happens in 'Michael', 'The Prelude' and 'Hart-Leap Well', where the titular hart becomes a vector for human moral development. Aspects of this development may tangentially benefit other species and the ecosystems they inhabit. Like animal poems by Anna Letitia Barbauld, Charlotte Smith, Joanna Baillie and Mary Robinson, 'Hart-Leap Well' draws upon the genteel, and later, middle-class cult of sensibility to promote a more considerate and empathetic treatment of non-human beings, even if it has not always been seen this way in studies of the poem.[20] Such a reading does not alter the fact that the non-human represented in 'Hart-Leap Well' is a palimpsest for all non-human species, and is ontologically transformed as it is adopted (tidied) into human culture.

The English impulse to render non-human nature tidy, to adapt it to the contours of human culture, is a product of class-based attitudes that filtered down from the aristocracy and the gentry to the burgeoning middle classes in the eighteenth and nineteenth centuries. The neat middle-class garden is an echo of the ornamental flower garden or the Brownian park designed to blend in with the countryside beyond, but cleansed of untidy biodiversity, including, as was sometimes the case, human settlements. (When labouring-/working-class families seek neatness and tidiness in their gardens, this is often a manifestation of their aspiration to middle-class status.) A perception of this very English desire for order in the natural environment is clear from a letter that the Scottish novelist Mary Brunton wrote to her mother during her 1809 tour of the northern counties of England: 'Kirkby Lonsdale [. . .] is the most rural, pretty, interesting place imaginable. It is a true English village – English in its *neatness* [. . .] – and English, above all, in its Church Yard – smooth as velvet – *green* as emeralds – *clean*, even to the exclusion of a fallen leaf from one of the tall trees that surround it' (my italics).[21] Today there is an extensive market in the various chemicals that keep lawns green, clean and weed-free. Some gardeners are installing artificial turf which is consistently green, and, for obvious reasons, renders the desired monoculture appearance much easier to maintain. Others are switching to artificial plants and shrubs or removing potential food sources such as invertebrates and berries as they appear because the larger non-human beings that they attract create mess and disorder.[22] I am not suggesting for a moment that Wordsworth would have approved of such trends in garden taste and design, rather that his cerebrally sanitised 'ambient-green' poetics of nature is a progenitor of this desire for a similarly sanitised corporeal or 'real-world' nature. There is, however, an alternative Romantic poetics of nature; one that focuses both on wild non-human beings as independent suffering subjects with their own interests, and on the messy, decaying, variegated and abandoned margins of the agricultural landscape. This very different way of seeing the non-human can be glimpsed in the work of some eighteenth- and early nineteenth-century labouring-class poets. For example, Mary Leapor's 'Crumble Hall' (1751) constructs an equivalence (in terms of precarity, intrepidity, etc.) between human- and non-human-animal subjects.[23] Unarguably, though, it is most consistently and strikingly present in the poetry of John Clare.

Clare wrote hundreds of poems exclusively or primarily devoted to wild non-human beings. Yet he receives only two passing references in

Christine Kenyon-Jones's *Kindred Brutes: Animals in Romantic-Period Writing* (2001), the only book-length study that focuses on representations of living non-human animals in Romantic writing (and it is an interesting study despite the sidelining of Clare), in comparison to the fifty-odd pages and sixty-odd references devoted to Wordsworth. This is an omission that reflects the dominance of Wordsworth's nature poetics in Romantic literary studies, even in an age of historicist revisionism (alongside his indirect but continuing influence on the everyday British idea of a flourishing, as in biodiverse, natural landscape). In Clare's representations of the pre- and the post-enclosure landscape there is often a tension between human interests and those of non-human beings. This is something that we do not see anything like as often in Wordsworth's nature poetry. In 'The Moorehen's Nest' (*c.* 1825–6), a personified 'poesy' is associated with an imaginative and empathetic response to the land, including the non-human beings who inhabit it. The speaker expresses a general disdain for humans 'working' the soil: 'I hate the plough that comes to disarray / Her [poesy's] holiday delights – and labours toil / Seems vulgar curses on the sunny soil / And man the only object that disdains / Earth's gardens into deserts for his gains'.[24] This passage reveals a modern sense of the wanton destruction generally involved in the relationship between humankind and wild non-human nature, especially when driven by capitalist societies' dependence on constant 'gain' or growth at a time (the beginning of the nineteenth century) when most regarded the earth's natural resources as limitless and inexhaustible.[25] (The warnings of individuals such as Thomas Malthus about the dangers of unchecked human population growth were not concerned with the risk to the earth's ecosystems.[26]) There is also an awareness of the homogenising effect, and tendency towards monoculture, of so-called agricultural improvement. The association of wild nature with 'gardens' reflects the return to nature in eighteenth-century elite taste; the Brownian idea that the best landscape gardens were those that appeared the most natural, and what is more natural than wild nature itself? Similarly, the idea that the farmed landscape resembles a 'desert' reflects both the prevalent belief that deserts are devoid of life, and the growing realisation that certain kinds of agriculture, particularly in Britain's colonies, could turn previously 'Edenic' places into 'arid desert wastes'.[27] Given that the majority of Clare's poetry was inspired by the agricultural landscape, these lines suggest two questions: what is the reason for Clare's conflicted response to the farming landscape, and, perhaps more importantly, what kind of environment shaped Clare's response to non-human nature?

Before enclosure, Clare's Northamptonshire was part of the central open-field champion belt of lowland England in which the main activity was three-field rotation arable farming. Folded village livestock grazed fallow fields, the dung from which 'replenished some of the nutrients depleted by repeated cropping'.[28] The mixed farming woodland areas to the south, east and west of the champion belt provided more abundant habitats for flora and fauna. Copses and larger wooded areas, linked by networks of hedges around assarted fields (hedges that generally contained numerous species of flora and could be 10–15 metres wide, unlike today's comparatively thin, hacked-back hedges) provided a 'wide range of niches, [as well as] a variety of food sources' for non-human species of fauna, and regular coppicing offered a 'rich succession of habitats' for those species as trees and hedges regrew.[29] As Tom Williamson notes, though, the 'broad distinction between "woodland" and "champion" [was] never as clear-cut as historians sometimes imply'. The central champion areas also 'boasted diverse environments, and [significantly] this was increasingly the case as enclosure [of open fields] proceeded'. It is true that when humans began to cultivate the land, apex predators such as the bear, wolf and lynx were hunted to extinction. Paradoxically, the kind of environment that farming produced in lowland Britain also increased overall biodiversity, and by the seventeenth and eighteenth centuries it 'boasted a vast range of wildlife'.[30] Early eco-critical writing on Clare tended to equate open fields with the ecological health of the land,[31] but it must be remembered that Clare's response to enclosure was heavily inflected by an emotional attachment to the landscape of his childhood. The impact of parliamentary enclosure on non-human species was not as clear-cut as some have suggested.

The persecution of non-human beings by humans began long before parliamentary enclosure, and in some respects continues to this day. The list of non-human species perceived as pests for which parishes offered a bounty (this only ended in the nineteenth century), or which landowners saw as a threat to their 'sport' and strove to eliminate (this still goes on, sometimes illegally), is almost endless.[32] Enclosure did involve the erection of the fences that Clare hated, and the loss or degradation of some local wildlife habitats, but the process was also accompanied by significant hedge and tree planting and the creation of some new ponds (critical wildlife habitats). It is true that many of the new hedges were of less ecological value than older established hedges in woodland regions, generally being comprised of just one species and regularly trimmed rather than coppiced or laid. ('Effort and investment' were also expended in 'simplifying and tidying' – in other words, ecologically degrading – the species-rich hedges in woodland regions.[33] As coal became the main domestic fuel and hedges ceased to be managed as a fuel source, for humans they became simply barriers; and it is this, rather than enclosure per se, which probably drove the ecological degradation that continues to this day.[34]) Nevertheless, the open-field landscape of champion districts was a particularly poor environment for small songbirds and most mammals, apart from a few open-ground specialists such as the brown hare.[35] Because enclosure created more of the edge habitats that so many non-human beings had evolved to favour, the process often increased overall biodiversity in the farmed landscape, even if some species fared better than others.[36] The improvement of so-called wastes (such as heaths, moors and wetland) was a very different matter and, especially in the case of wetlands, often had a devastating impact upon flora and fauna. (Williamson distinguishes between enclosure and improvement, such as the conversion of moorland into pasture, or the draining of wetlands.[37]) Clare's apparent angst regarding the social consequences of enclosure for labouring-class humans is well documented, and, although the process evidently generated some employment, when other associated social and economic trends that particularly affected the lives of labouring people in the countryside are taken into account, his sense that the lives of the rural poor were becoming more difficult in the early nineteenth century is justified.[38] Likewise, Clare's oft-expressed view that agricultural improvers had little interest in non-human nature, and that the motivation behind enclosure and agricultural improvement in general was increased 'gain' or profit, is broadly correct. The idea that the enclosure of open fields diminished the overall ecological health of the farmed landscape is, as I have suggested, much less certain; indeed, the evidence points to the contrary being the case in many places.

Whether journeying through an open field or an enclosed landscape, the observer would have been required to expend some effort to find these previously mentioned habitat 'niche[s]' to view wild nature. Pre-enclosure, there would have been fewer of them,[39] and, although the young Clare had occasionally indulged the temptation to trespass onto estate land, post-enclosure it would have been necessary to trespass onto newly enclosed fields to find the wild species he loved, the presence of, and unhindered access to which, was so integral to his very being.[40] For obvious reasons, many of the small birds that feature prominently in Clare's poetry build their nests in covert and thus safer marginal and peripheral places, and Clare's bird-nest poems provide an encyclopaedic account of their innovation and creativity. From the humble 'hedge sparrow' (dunnock) that 'Near the hedge bottom weaves [a nest] of homely stuff / Dead grasses and mosses green' ('Birds Nests' (*c.* 1832), MP 4, ll. 10–11), to the firetail (redstart) and the wryneck that seek out holes in 'rotten' or 'hollow tree[s]' (MP 4, 'The Firetails Nest' (*c.* 1832), l. 9; 'The Wrynecks Nest' (*c.* 1819–32), l. 7), to the 'Sand Martin' (*c.* 1832) 'Drilling small holes' in banks within 'rude waste landscapes far away from men' (MP 4, ll. 3–6), or the yellow wagtail that nests beneath an abandoned broken plough 'Upon an edding [headland] in a quiet nook [. . .] among grass and flowers' ('The Yellow Wagtails Nest' (*c.* 1825–6), MP 3, ll. 2–7), all are seeking sites for their nests away from the human-dominated centres of the farmed landscape. Several poems represent the speaker's struggle to find these hidden marginal or peripheral places. In 'The Yellow Hammer's Nest' (*c.* 1825–6), the speaker commences: 'let us stoop [. . .] – Aye here it is stuck close beside the bank / Beneath the bunch of grass that spindles rank / Its husk seeds tall and high – tis rudely planned / Of bleached stubbles and the withered fare / That last year's harvest left upon the land' (MP 3, ll. 3–11). In 'The Nightingale's Nest' (1832) we are given an extended account of the bird's desire to remain hidden, and the effort required of the human speaker to find her: 'There I have hunted like a very boy / Creeping on hands and knees through matted thorns / To find her nest and see her feed her young / & vainly did I many hours employ / All seemed hidden as a thought unborn / & where these crimping fern leaves ramp among / The hazel under boughs – I've nested down / & watched her while she sung' (MP 3, ll. 12–19). Nor would it have been easy to find larger mammals such as the fox, badger, polecat or pine marten either (all of which feature in Clare's poems), most of which tend to shun open spaces, especially in daylight. A desire to get down and close to the land, to root around in the undergrowth, to stoop or go on hands and knees, would be necessary to observe the smaller mammals and invertebrates that also appear in Clare's poems.

Many of the kind of marginal or peripheral places that provided habitats for wild non-human nature were also the kind of places that labouring-class humans took advantage of for moments of rest or social interaction, on the way to and from work, or during the interstices between periods of work. In 'The Yellow Hammer's Nest', Clare's speaker makes an explicit connection between the way both wild non-human species and human labourers rely on such hidden 'quiet nook[s]' to escape from the 'toil' or human processing of the land for 'gain' that grinds down the human labourer as much as non-human beings (in the case of the latter, often to death), or forces them into peripheral or edge habitats. Some of Clare's poems memorialise or lament the loss of incongruous, untidy or marginal features in the landscape because they were important to individual humans, or to local human communities, or to the development and maintenance of local popular human culture. In 'To a Fallen Elm' (1830), the tree that, before the 'ruin' of 'enclosure', was home to the nesting 'mavis' (song thrush) (MP 3, ll. 25 and 57) was also a playground for young children and a shelter from sun and rain for travelling humans. In 'The Lamentations of Round-Oak Waters' (1818), the *genius loci* of the stream laments that (again, pre-enclosure) his once vegetated banks (now razed by the 'plough') had provided habitats for the wildlife that would 'court the curious eye' of the human speaker, and a place to rest for labouring humans such as the 'shepherd with his sheep / And with his lovely maid' or the 'Cowboy'.[41] Some of these places were used by groups whom even most of the labouring poor would shun and marginalise. The old hawthorn memorialised in 'Langley Bush' (*c*. 1819–20) – lost to old age rather than to enclosure – was not only an important focus for the development of local popular culture, it also attracted gypsies; a persecuted group who led a precarious life at the untidy margins of a landscape rationalised as resource and property, and who continued to fascinate Clare throughout his life: 'thy spots a favourite wi the smutty crew / and soon thou must depend on gipsy fame' (EP 2, ll. 14–15).[42]

Most of the landscape features whose disappearance Clare laments were of little economic value to the large-scale farmer, and they also got in the way of the technological transformation of agriculture. The process of enclosure and of improvement more generally was about the rationalisation of farming and facilitating the application of technology, whether new processes (such as the application of marl or quicklime) or new kinds of machinery (such as the threshing machine). In some cases, the zeal to improve became an end in itself, which meant that even land that could never be made to turn a profit during normal times (e.g. when prices began to fall after the Napoleonic wars) was drained or spread with marl or quicklime to increase fertility, only to be abandoned soon after.[43] This technological transformation intensified during the period of Victorian 'high farming', when artificial fertilisers such as superphosphates were introduced, leading ultimately to the kind of scorched-earth farming we have today. Under the predominant rationale of modern farming, incongruous, untidy features and marginal spaces (understood as unproductive) should be removed or cut back to create ever larger fields that can accommodate ever larger machinery. Clare 'hate[s] the plough' because it is the technology that in his day most represented the destruction of biodiversity and the creation of a homogenised monoculture farming landscape. This anger is expressed in many of his poems, most explicitly in the previously cited passage from 'The Moorehen's Nest'. Clare's sense that the technologisation of the farming landscape was something monstrous anticipates Martin Heidegger's mid-twentieth-century view that the modern worship of science and technology (STEM subjects are still venerated today as more 'useful' than other ways of seeing / interacting with the world) was perverting the relationship humans have with their environment. In his analysis of Heidegger's disparate writings on nature, David Cooper remarks: 'in the technological way of revealing, specifically, the natural world is experienced or encountered as so much "standing-reserve" – something "on tap" for us, to be drawn on and from so as to serve our practical needs'.[44] For Heidegger, 'technology is monstrous, [. . .] in that it "drives out every other possibility of revealing", to such a degree that it is no longer appreciated as just one possibility'.[45] In his view, the veneration of technology has stifled the human imagination with destructive consequences for countless other forms of life on earth.

It can be argued that, even in Clare's day, no part of the British landscape was pristine or unchanged by human activity; but this is beside the point. When we do get glimpses of healthy, interconnected ecosystems in Clare's poetry, it is in places that he believed had been left alone or were rarely frequented by human beings.[46] These places are 'reveal[ed]' in very different ways from landscapes dominated by the 'plough' (or human technology), which, in Heidegger's terms, are defined by 'the modern urge to "order it" [nature] and "challenge it" [. . .] to produce "maximum yield at minimum [financial] expense"'.[47] (Of course there are real, as opposed to monetary, 'expense[s]' involved in the technologisation of the landscape, such as the loss of non-human nature, or the physical and social impact on human labourers and their communities; but these costs are not borne by landowners and farmers.) In 'The Robin's Nest' (*c.* 1832), for example, Clare's speaker celebrates a place so rarely visited by humankind that '[human] footmarks seem like miracles' (MP 3, l. 61). The old wood described in the poem is a secret haven where various wild non-human species, from the 'moss as green as silk' (MP 3, l. 13) to the 'wood robin' (MP 3, l. 68), have the freedom (from the destructive 'mercenary sprit' (MP 3, l. 36) of humans) and, crucially, the time, to flourish: 'nought lends / a hand to injure – root up or disturb / the things of this old place – there is no curb / of [human] interest industry or slavish gain / to war with nature' (MP 3, ll. 51–5). For Clare, unlike Wordsworth, the only way that non-human nature can prosper in any meaningful way is if it is left alone by humans. As W. John Coletta notes, because Clare's old wood has been left alone to flourish for a long period of time, in modern terms, it displays the resilience of 'old growth' woodland ecosystems: 'an ability to adapt to circumstance or even to adapt circumstance to itself'.[48] Again, Clare anticipates Heidegger's advocacy for 'that stance towards the [non-human] natural world which "lets beings be"'.[49] Even though we are not told exactly where the speaker is situated during his observations, it is evident that he does not 'disturb' the various non-human beings who inhabit the wood.[50] Rather, unlike most humans within so-called civilised societies, he adjusts to his surroundings in a 'culturally light-touch' way and allows the wonder of the place to be revealed to him.[51] The speaker notices extraordinary (for those in the right mindset) details that would be destroyed without a thought by advocates of so-called agricultural 'improvement', from the unique textures and colours on the trunk of an old oak tree, to the amazing variety of moss and lichen, the 'crimping uncurling ferns' (MP 3, l. 11) and the abundance of bird and wildflower species that sing and bloom 'as if for [him]' (MP 3, l. 19). There is a wonderous complexity and beauty which Clare's speaker contrasts with the dull, homogeneous, technologised human world that he has left behind him.

In a world dominated by just one species, an old wood like Clare's cannot subsist without a willingness on the part of humankind to leave parts of the landscape free from technological 'interfer[ence]', and the human impulse to 'tidy' non-human nature, over a long period of time. The important habitats for non-human fauna remain, within nooks and crannies in, around and underneath the abundant flora and the detritus left behind by the seasonal cycle of life and death. Detritus is especially important for invertebrates at the base of the food chain, and therefore for species of fauna further up the food chain. The old wood is a fecund place precisely because of the presence of organic matter that most humans see as unsightly, or as clutter, or as a nuisance, or as barriers to profit. From dead trees to fallen leaves and weeds (or native plants), to the invertebrate species that we dismiss as pests, we strive to expunge them all – whether from gardens or from the agricultural landscape – because they detract from the biologically cleansed environment to which so many of us increasingly aspire. At the beginning of the twenty-first century we are just beginning to learn about the value of dead and decaying organic matter, for some of which we have an especial dislike. A recent study indicates that the presence of large animal carcasses within an ecosystem, particularly in significant numbers following a mass mortality event, can increase biodiversity; but leaving large carcasses to lie when they could be removed is taboo.[52] Clare's old wood is a haven for non-human nature because it displays what he calls 'old neglect' (MP 3, l. 50), which simply means that all of the immensely valuable (in ecological if not financial terms) products of 'neglect', for example dead and decaying organic matter, have been left to accumulate, and then be recycled, over a long period of time. These products would have been regularly tidied away had the place been subject to conventional human aesthetic and economic standards. Unlike most humans (and this is still true today), Clare can see that the categories of living and dead flora and fauna that we strive to expunge from the environment wherever we can are, in many respects, foundational to the health of an ecosystem. In Clare's healthy, wondrous wood, the 'very weeds as patriarchs appear' (MP 3, l. 63).

The larger the area of what, in 'The Robin's Nest', Clare calls 'safety's wildness' (MP 3, l. 51), the better for non-human nature. Scattered small patches of land given over to wild nature, such as the wildlife havens that still exist in some older and less manicured gardens (there are very few such gardens in typical high-density new-build housing estates), will not be enough to save many non-human species if our compulsive tidying up of the landscape persists. Rather, what is also needed is a transformation of popular landscape aesthetics: in what we see and value in our environment. As this essay has revealed, during the Romantic period there was a class inflection to landscape aesthetics in Britain. Wordsworth's homogenised 'ambient-[green]' landscapes, devoid of untidy wildness, were in many respects a product of genteel landscape aesthetics which, through the nineteenth and twentieth centuries, fed into developing middle-class ideas about nature. Whereas Clare's celebration of a more varied and variegated landscape, one in which there was space for wild non-human nature, was shaped by his immersion within rural labouring-class culture. In Clare's landscape vision, the untidy margins of the landscape were often as important for labouring-class humans as they were for wild non-human species. Of course, it is Wordsworth's aesthetic, through the 'visioning of rural areas by hegemonic middle-class culture', that dominates the way many British people see the landscape today.[53] In this way of seeing, where villages are chocolate-box-tidy, verges cut back and fields green, it doesn't matter whether there is very much 'nature' in the countryside beyond domesticated animals and monoculture agricultural crops. Clare's poetry offers an alternative way of seeing the land. Indeed, even today there is a class-based tension between country people from a labouring- or working-class background, who are often open to a little more ecologically productive untidiness in the landscape, and the majority who share the dominant land aesthetic (including most of those within hunting and shooting communities that tend to be at least upper middle class). I have seen this tension in my own small village within a very Wordsworthian Area of Outstanding Natural Beauty (AONB) in rural Oxfordshire, which has not yet been completely colonised by middle-class incomers. Ultimately, if we want a world with a greater variety and complexity of non-human life, we must embrace the best (for there are negative aspects too in the relationship between labouring-/working-class people and the land) of the labouring-/working-class toleration for more untidy variety in the landscape. Remember Britain is one of the most denatured countries in the world (non-human nature in the British countryside is continuing to disappear at an exponential rate), and 96 per cent of the biomass of all the mammals that inhabit the earth is now made up of us and our domesticated animals.[54]

It is extremely unlikely that humans in the supposedly developed world (or in many parts of the developing world) could ever acquire the ethical bandwidth required to share the land with other species in the way imagined by communitarian or so-called deep ecologists, such as Aldo Leopold. Leopold's 'land ethic [. . .] enlarges the boundaries of the community to include soils, waters, plants, and animals, or collectively: the land [. . .and transforms] the role of homo sapiens from conqueror of the land-community to plain member and citizen of it'.[55] In the end – and I accept that this idea also presents some (not insoluble) problems – the best compromise would be for humankind to finally take on board the view of forward-thinking individuals like Clare, and a number of modern ecologists and environmental thinkers, that non-human nature needs to be left alone – or, on Heidegger's terms, 'let be' – to prosper in all its untidy variety, and give it more space to do so. Clare's 'neglected' old wood shows how, if allowed a little bit of room, non-human nature could still survive and flourish in an intensively technologised country like Britain, even when humans have been farming adjacent land for many centuries. Think of the wondrous and enchanting (albeit untidy) ways in which nature might reveal itself again were humans to return to non-human beings the kind of space advocated by proponents of rewilding such as George Monbiot, or even better, half the planet, as suggested by E. O. Wilson.[56] Of course, it shouldn't just be the poor and marginalised (in other words, those without power and influence) who are made to bear the burden of reviving wild non-human nature. This is not such a problem in the developed world because the vast majority of those at the lower end of the social hierarchy have been displaced from the land. A recent study by Guy Shrubsole indicates that in England roughly 50 per cent of the land is 'owned' by just 1 per cent of the population.[57] While in the developing world, poor and marginalised people are often at the vanguard of the struggle to defend some of the few remaining hotspots of biodiversity on earth from the predations of rich and powerful people. As I write, in the central Indian state of Chhattisgarh, the Indigenous (or Adivasi) Gond people are trying to save the Hasdeo Arand forest – one of the largest remaining fragments of India's ancient forest – from destruction, in response to the plans of the mining giant Adani, with federal government support, to further 'develop' the area for open-cast coal mining.[58] Poor and marginalised people will risk their lives to protect the wild non-human nature that is such an important part of their identity, and upon which they depend for their survival. The Indigenous tribes and their defenders struggling to hold back the destruction of the Amazon rainforest are being routinely attacked and killed with impunity, and in increasing numbers, by illegal loggers or miners and by 'land-grabbers' with influential connections.[59] These two examples forcefully illustrate the way that those humans at the very bottom of the pile in terms of wealth, power and influence (like Clare) are often the most willing to live with the untidy variety of non-human nature rather than seek to control, appropriate and culturally or technologically dominate non-human flora and fauna.

Notes

1. D. B. Heyhow et al., *The State of Nature 2016* (Nottingham: The National Biodiversity Network, 2016), p. 6.
2. Robert Watson et al., *UK National Ecosystem Assessment: Synthesis of Key Findings* (Cambridge: UNEP-WCMC, 2011), p. 60.
3. See Tom Williamson, *An Environmental History of Wildlife in England, 1650–1950* (London: Bloomsbury, 2013), pp. 165–74.
4. Jonathan Bate, *Romantic Ecology: Wordsworth and the Environmental Tradition* (London: Routledge, 1991), p. 40.
5. Lisa Ottum and Seth T. Reno, 'Recovering Ecology's Affects', in Lisa Ottum and Seth T. Reno (eds), *Wordsworth and the Green Romantics: Affect and Ecology in the Nineteenth Century* (Durham: University of New Hampshire Press, 2016), p. 5.
6. Timothy Morton, *Ecology Without Nature: Rethinking Environmental Aesthetics* (Cambridge, MA: Harvard University Press, 2007), p. 164.
7. Bate, *Romantic Ecology*, p. 45.
8. Ian Whyte, 'Upland Britain: Cultural Processes and Landscape Change through Time', *The International Journal of Biodiversity Science and Management* 2, no. 3 (2006): 138–9.
9. See George Monbiot, *Feral: Searching for Enchantment on the Frontiers of Rewilding* (London: Allen Lane, 2013), pp. 153–66.
10. See Christopher P. Rogers, Eleanor A. Straughton, Angus J. L. Winchester and Margherita Pieraccini, *Contested Common Land: Environmental Governance Past and Present* (New York: Earthscan, 2011), p. 38.
11. David Simpson, *Wordsworth's Historical Imagination: The Poetry of Displacement* (New York: Methuen, 1987), p. 90.
12. See Louis Mansfield, 'Upland Farming and Wilding', *ECOS* 35, nos 3–4 (2014): 15. See also Williamson, *An Environmental History of Wildlife in England, 1650–1850*, p. 100.
13. Williamson, *An Environmental History of Wildlife in England*, p. 100.
14. Dewey W. Hall, *Romantic Naturalists, Early Environmentalists: An Ecocritical Study* (Farnham: Ashgate, 2014), pp. 115–46. See also Jonathan Bate, *The Song of the Earth* (London: Picador, 2000), p. 23.

15. Hall, *Romantic Naturalists, Early Environmentalists*, pp. 115–46.
16. Heyhow, *The State of Nature 2016*, p. 70.
17. For an account of Wordsworth's influence on the development of national parks, see Scott Hess, *William Wordsworth and the Ecology of Authorship: The Roots of Environmentalism in Nineteenth-Century Culture* (Charlottesville: University of Virginia Press, 2012), pp. 68–115.
18. Morton, *Ecology Without Nature*, p. 164.
19. Mansfield, 'Upland Farming and Wilding', p. 15.
20. See David Perkins, *Romanticism and Animal Rights* (Cambridge: Cambridge University Press, 2003), pp. 77–88.
21. Mary Brunton, *Emmeline, with Some Other Pieces, to which is prefixed A Memoir of Her Life, including Some Extracts from Her Correspondence* (Edinburgh: Manners and Miller, 1819), p. xii.
22. *Costing the Earth*, 'Plastic Gardens', produced by Emma Campbell, aired 23 October 2019 on BBC Radio 4 <https://www.bbc.co.uk/programmes/m0009jl4> (last accessed 24 August 2020).
23. See Barbara K. Seeber, 'Animals and the Country-House Tradition in Mary Leapor's "Crumble Hall" and Jane Austen's *Mansfield Park*', in Katherine Quinsey (ed.), *Animals and Humans: Sensibility and Representation, 1650–1820* (Oxford: Voltaire Foundation, 2017), pp. 276–8.
24. Eric Robinson, David Powell and P. M. S. Dawson (eds), *John Clare: Poems of the Middle Period, 1822–1837*, 5 vols (Oxford: Clarendon Press, 1996–2003), 3, ll. 32–6. All future references will be to this edition and will be indicated by the abbreviation MP followed by volume and line numbers in parentheses.
25. Robert Dyball and Barry Newel, *Understanding Human Ecology: A Systems Approach to Sustainability* (New York: Routledge, 2015), p. 165.
26. Robert J. Mayhew, 'The Publication Bomb: The Birth of Modern Environmentalism and the Editing of Malthus's *Essay*', in Robert J. Mayhew (ed.), *New Perspectives on Malthus* (Cambridge: Cambridge University Press, 2016), p. 240.
27. Diana K. Davis, 'Deserts', in Andrew C. Isenberg (ed.), *The Oxford Handbook of Environmental History* (Oxford and New York: Oxford University Press, 2014), pp. 114–15.
28. Williamson, *An Environmental History of Wildlife in England*, p. 5.
29. Ibid. pp. 48–9.
30. Ibid. pp. 7 and 57.
31. See, for example, James C. McKusick, *Green Writing: Romanticism and Ecology* (Basingstoke: Macmillan, 2000), pp. 85 and 90.
32. See Roger Lovegrove, *Silent Fields: The Long Decline of a Nation's Wildlife* (Oxford: Oxford University Press, 2007), pp. 1–16. See also Briony McDonagh and Stephen Daniels, 'Enclosure Stories: Narratives from Northamptonshire', *Cultural Geographies* 19, no. 1 (2012): 112–13.
33. Williamson, *An Environmental History of Wildlife in England*, p. 106.
34. G. Barnes and T. Williamson, *Hedgerow History: Ecology, History and Landscape Character* (Oxford: Windgather Press, 2006), pp. 130–2.
35. Eric L. Jones, *Revealed Biodiversity: An Economic History of the Human Impact* (Singapore: World Scientific Publishing, 2014), p. 62.
36. Lovegrove, *Silent Fields*, p. 40.

37. See Williamson, *An Environmental History of Wildlife in England*, pp. 101–3.
38. See Simon J. White, *Romanticism and the Rural Community* (Basingstoke: Palgrave Macmillan, 2013), p. 8. Enclosure on its own did not have a negative impact on the quality of life of the rural labouring poor in Clare's Northamptonshire (see McDonagh and Daniels, 'Enclosure Stories', pp. 107–21) but enclosure was by no means the only social and economic trend affecting their lives.
39. Lovegrove, *Silent Fields*, p. 40.
40. See John Goodridge and Kelsey Thornton, 'John Clare: The Trespasser', in Hugh Haughton, Adam Phillips and Geoffrey Summerfield (eds), *John Clare in Context* (Cambridge: Cambridge University Press, 1994), pp. 87–129.
41. Eric Robinson and David Powell (eds), *The Early Poems of John Clare, 1804–1822*, 2 vols (Oxford: Clarendon Press, 1989), 1, ll. 61–2, 65, 90 and 105. All future references will be to this edition and will be indicated by the abbreviation EP followed by the volume and line numbers in parentheses.
42. See Simon J. White, 'Landscape Icons and the Community: A Reading of John Clare's "Langley Bush"', *John Clare Society Journal* 26 (2007): 21–2.
43. Williamson, *An Environmental History of Wildlife in England*, p. 100.
44. David E. Cooper, 'Heidegger on Nature', *Environmental Values* 14, no. 3 (2005): 345.
45. Ibid. p. 346.
46. Katey Castallano suggests that 'Clare conceives of human neglect as the last patron of the wild natural world's uninhibited unfolding life', in *The Ecology of British Romantic Conservatism, 1790–1837* (New York: Palgrave Macmillan, 2013), p. 160.
47. Cooper, 'Heidegger and Nature', 346.
48. John W. Coletta, 'Ecological Aesthetics and the Natural History Poetry of John Clare', *John Clare Society Journal* 14 (1995): 30.
49. Cooper, 'Heidegger and Nature', p. 346.
50. See John Goodridge, *John Clare and Community* (Cambridge: Cambridge University Press, 2013), pp. 134–8.
51. For an account of Clare's sense of himself as 'just another mammal', see McKusick, *Green Writing*, p. 81.
52. S. C. Frank, R. Blaalid, M. Mayer, A. Zedrosser and S. M. J. G. Steyaert, 'Fear the Reaper: Ungulate Carcasses May Generate an Ephemeral Landscape of Fear for Rodents', *Royal Society Open Science* 7, no. 6 (2020), part 4, para. 1–6, <https://doi.org/10.1098/rsos.191644> (accessed 24 August 2020).
53. Mark Shucksmith, 'Re-Imagining the Rural: From Rural Idyll to Good Countryside', *Journal of Rural Studies* 59 (2018): 163.
54. Vaclav Smil, *Harvesting the Biosphere: What We Have Taken from Nature* (Cambridge: The MIT Press, 2013), pp. 234–5.
55. Aldo Leopold, 'Land Ethic', in *A Sand County Almanac: And Sketches Here and There* (Oxford: Oxford University Press, 1989), p. 204.
56. See Monbiot, *Feral* and E. O. Wilson, *Half-Earth: Our Planet's Fight for Life* (New York and London: Liveright, 2016).
57. See Guy Shrubsole, *Who Owns England? How We Lost Our Green and*

Pleasant Land, and How to Take It Back (London: Harper Collins, 2019), p. 7.
58. See Brian Cassey, 'India's Ancient Tribes Battle to Save their Forest Home from Mining', *The Guardian*, 10 February 2020, <https://www.theguardian.com/environment/2020/feb/10/indias-ancient-tribes-battle-to-save-their-forest-home-from-mining> (accessed 24 August 2020).
59. See Scott Wallace, 'Death Stalks the Amazon as Tribes and Their Defenders Come under Attack', *National Geographic*, 15 November 2019, <https://www.nationalgeographic.com/history/2019/11/defenders-threatened-tribes-warn-mounting-hostility-amazon/> (last accessed 24 August 2020). See also Alexander Zaitchick, 'Rainforest on Fire', *The Intercept*, 6 July 2019, <https://theintercept.com/2019/07/06/brazil-amazon-rainforest-indigenous-conservation-agribusiness-ranching/> (accessed 24 August 2020) and Scott Wallace, *The Unconquered: In Search of the Amazon's Last Uncontacted Tribes* (New York: Crown Publishers, 2011), pp. 47–66.

Chapter 13

Sensing the Population Debate: Poverty, Ecology and the Senses in Malthus and his Critics

Peter Denney

In his 1807 critique of *An Essay on the Principle of Population*, William Hazlitt compared the conclusions of its author, Thomas Robert Malthus, to the observations of city-dwellers who liked to ramble through the country in pursuit of a reinvigorating experience of nature. Actually, Malthus's *Essay* deliberately eschewed the rural escapism that influenced picturesque tourists and readers of pastoral poetry. Instead, the book privileged economic over aesthetic concerns, while upholding a new pessimism regarding the capacity of the earth to sustain human life. Far from searching for objects of rural beauty, Malthus's work on population drew on the senses to elaborate a range of social and ecological issues. The problem, according to Hazlitt, was that 'his attempts at philosophy' were like the 'exploits' of urban tourists, who sought to 'taste the fresh air' in the country, but who got 'no further than Paddington, White Conduithouse, or Bagnigge-wells, unable to leave the smoke, the noise and dust, to which they [had] so long been used!'[1] Hazlitt acknowledged, then, that Malthus's *Essay* was neither a picturesque nor a realistic description. On the contrary, in Hazlitt's opinion, Malthus rejected idealistic visions only to embrace a negative fantasy of nature as the embodiment of the disfigured sensory environment created by commercial modernity.

First published in 1798, Malthus's *Essay* ushered in a new ecological perspective in which scarce environmental resources placed limits on economic development and population growth.[2] This ecological view overturned many Enlightenment ideas of improvement, notably the belief that a large, expanding population was a laudable goal attainable through a perpetual increase in the productivity of the land. Malthus articulated his alternative pessimistic view in scientific terms. And yet, there was a social ideology underpinning this ecological outlook. Malthus argued that an important means of curtailing population growth involved restricting the right of the poor to parish relief, an entitlement deemed to foster idleness and irresponsible breeding. Along with this reframing of poverty, Malthus's dour, utilitarian attitude to nature came into conflict with a rival Romantic sensibility, leading to a bitter population debate. Anticipating more recent discussions of Malthusian ideas, which returned to popularity in the 1960s but caused heated disagreement in ensuing decades,[3] a crucial feature of this debate was the vexed link between social justice and environmental sustainability.

This essay examines the significance of the senses in the population debate, with particular emphasis on the meanings Malthus and some of his Romantic critics attributed to sight, sound, eating, smell and touch in their discussions of poverty, ecology and rural society. References to the senses abounded in the population debate, and yet this debate has never been examined from a sensory perspective. To some extent, the sensory focus in Malthus's *Essay* can be associated with its role as a contribution to the French Revolution controversy, a propaganda war which politicised the senses in myriad ways, from a loyalist insistence on plebeian neatness to a radical attack on patrician gluttony.[4] The sensory values and practices of the poor also featured in Malthus's writing. Most famously, the notorious culinary metaphor of 'Nature's mighty feast', included in the expanded 1803 edition, drew on a seasonal celebration such as took place during the long holiday of Christmas, in which social distinctions were temporarily relaxed through the licensed gratification of heightened senses, singing no less than drinking. But this form of hospitality, so crucial to the myth of 'Merry England', was depicted by Malthus as a misguided form of benevolence. In the *Essay*, poverty was related to noise, hunger, stench, coarseness and visual disgust, with such sensory dysfunction being regarded as a sign of the disequilibrium between nature and society. Accordingly, ecological scarcity was often imagined in terms of the undesirable sensory expressions of the labouring classes, who were thus expected to regulate their senses in an attempt to forestall social disorder and environmental crisis. Many Romantic critics of Malthus focused on the immorality and cold-heartedness of the principle of population, repudiating his demonisation of the sensory habits of the poor. And yet some critics also argued that the poor needed to regulate their senses in ways consistent with Malthus's recommendations. By exploring the role of the senses in Malthus as well as his early opponents, Robert Southey and William Hazlitt, this essay will analyse the population debate to show how emerging ecological attitudes were shaped by a broader dispute about the propriety of sensory experiences and their attendant social relations.

From the first edition onwards, Malthus's *Essay* made the senses central to his thesis that population increased more quickly than food supply. Such a claim attributed enormous significance to eating and sexual activity. Moreover, these biological needs constituted the basis of sensory experiences, taste and touch, which drove social, economic and ecological forces on a local, national and even global scale. Malthus regarded humans, in 'quasi-materialistic' fashion, as essentially eating, touching beings.[5] And such basic needs for food and sex generated unsustainable population growth, since the power of reproduction was 'infinitely greater' than the capacity of the 'earth to produce subsistence'.[6] By associating people with these corporeal sensory experiences, Malthus earned the indignation of many critics. For in both natural history and moral philosophy, humans were distinguished from animals by the capacity to use reason to control their proximate bodily senses.

In large part, the importance assigned to the senses by Malthus derived from his concern with improvement. Building on the psychological theories of John Locke, Enlightenment intellectuals conceived improvement as a fundamentally sensory affair.[7] This had two main aspects. First, Locke argued that all knowledge originated in the senses, meaning that people could enhance their mind and moral character through education or manipulation of their environment. Second, people were motivated, according to Locke, by the pursuit of pleasure and the avoidance of pain, emotional states triggered by sensory inputs. From this insight emerged a utilitarian position in which the regulation of the senses was regarded as crucial to maximising the happiness of individuals within a polity. Accordingly, sensory management was linked to cultural refinement, political and social change, and economic progress.

To demonstrate the impossibility of unlimited improvement, Malthus addressed the role of the senses in a range of contexts, including connections between poverty and environment. Revealingly, his conception of the relationship between humans and the natural world was indebted to the optimistic Christian utilitarianism propounded by William Paley in *The Principles of Moral and Political Philosophy* (1785). Combining utilitarian morality with natural theology, Paley argued that the study of Creation revealed the benevolence of God, who designed life to facilitate the attainment of happiness. This was evidenced by the positive feelings generated by many sensory experiences. As Paley attested, if misery was meant to be a dominant feature of life, the senses would be 'sores and pains' rather than 'instruments of gratification and enjoyment', while external objects would occasion offence rather than delight. But God did not make 'every thing we tasted, bitter; every thing we saw loathsome; every thing we touched, a sting; every smell a stench; and every sound a discord'. Quite the opposite, for happiness had a divine sanction, as indicated by 'both the capacity of our senses to receive pleasure, and the supply of external objects fitted to receive it'.[8] Although Paley came to share Malthus's view of the threat of overpopulation after reading the *Essay*, at this time, in 1785, his Christian utilitarianism posited that a large, burgeoning population fulfilled a key purpose of God by increasing the 'quantity of happiness in a given district'.[9] According to Paley, the fecundity of humans and animals meant their population would eventually be constrained by food supply. But in Britain there was still such scope for agricultural improvement that overpopulation did not pose a danger in the foreseeable future. For Malthus, this optimistic interpretation of population growth, if translated into state policy, would lead to certain misery, especially among the labouring classes. And such misery was often registered in sensory terms, not just as the pains of hunger, but also as dirtiness, stench and other unpleasant experiences. In the second edition of the *Essay*, for example, Malthus portrayed the Scottish Highlands as experiencing perilous demographic stress,[10] with biophysical limits contributing to moral shortcomings, as revealed by the senses of the poor. Population pressure in this region of Scotland was construed to result from a mixture of meagre soil fertility, defective agriculture and weak personal character, ensuring low living standards among cottagers, who lived in 'damp and stinking houses'.[11]

In the first edition of the *Essay*, Malthus modified the Christian utilitarianism of Paley to argue that the principle of population comprised a set of fixed natural laws, which doomed society to a 'perpetual oscillation between happiness and misery'.[12] Varying across social boundaries and geographical locations, this was an uneven but ultimately beneficial process designed by God to advance civilisation. For Malthus, population increased until it was constrained by 'positive' checks such as famine, war or disease, or 'preventive' checks such as delayed marriage or reduced offspring. All these checks entailed misery or vice, orchestrated by God to deal with the problem of scarcity, which accompanied population growth in a world of finite resources. While scarcity generated suffering, Malthus regarded it as a necessary evil, since the fear of hunger, deprivation and pain was a divine means to induce people to work.[13]

The resulting theodicy valorised misery, leading Malthus to focus on negative sensory experiences in his consideration of human interactions with the natural environment. Placing the theories of Locke in a religious framework, the senses were crucial to his claim that God formed 'mind out of matter'.[14] Scarcity brought on by population pressure, asserted Malthus, was the spur to labour and intellectual activity. This was imagined as a sensory phenomenon in which the 'cravings of hunger' or the 'pinchings of cold' stimulated 'exertions'. Such exertions banished idle habits and aroused the mental faculties, facilitating a progression from savagery to civilisation. Establishing a materialist foundation for his theodicy, Malthus formulated a unique perspective on the mind-body problem,[15] as the senses generated ideas through conflict with a niggardly, resistant environment:

> The first great awakeners of the mind seem to be the wants of the body. [. . .] They are the first stimulants that rouse the brain of infant man into sentient activity, and such seems to be the sluggishness of original matter that ... these stimulants seem, even afterwards, to be necessary to continue that activity[.] Some of the noblest exertions of the human mind have been set in motion by the necessity of satisfying the wants of the body.[16]

Without these stimulants, these sensory impressions of hunger, cold or some other form of physical discomfort, Malthus added, humans would sink to the 'level of brutes'. It was evil that created effort, effort that created mind, and mind that created civilisation. This proposition was supported by Locke's notion that the avoidance of pain was a more powerful motivation than the pursuit of pleasure. In consequence, undesirable sensory experiences came to be associated by Malthus with ecological limits, the scarcity which drove labour, prosperity and the production of knowledge. Following this logic, the misery occasioned by scarcity was crucial to ensure that people fulfilled the divine injunction to cultivate the earth.

By linking the principle of population to this largely corporeal understanding of life, Malthus strengthened his refutation of the utopian schemes of William Godwin, who was a primary target of the *Essay*. Godwin's *Enquiry Concerning Political Justice* (1793) constituted a major contribution, on the radical side, to the debate about the French Revolution in Britain. As a result, it had a substantial influence on political discussions of the senses.[17] Godwin posited the inferiority of sensory as opposed to intellectual experiences, with the prioritisation of the former leading variously to despotism, ignorance and decadence. Thus, kings were accused of using visual display to 'dazzle' their subjects, while landowners were derided for being addicted to the 'pleasures of the palate' or the 'gratifications of neatness, elegance, and splendour'.[18] Godwin speculated that, in the reformed society of the future, it would be possible for the mind to control the body, enabling people to approach a state of human perfectibility marked by the equalisation of property and an increase in leisure. Such a situation would reduce the pursuit of sensory pleasures, which were thought to predominate in commercial modernity. As Godwin noted towards the end of his treatise: 'One tendency of a cultivated and virtuous mind is to diminish our eagerness for the gratifications of the senses.'[19] In this enlightened society, there would be no war, no disease, no crime and no scarcity, and with no need for sex, the population would always be sustainable by the earth.

Central to Malthus's critique of Godwin was the contention that people were unable to entirely subordinate their senses to reason. Sensory experiences connected the body to the mind, and in doing so produced a self shaped, if not governed, by its physical environment. Godwin's suggestion that sexual passion might one day become defunct was countered by Malthus on the basis that the 'pleasures of the senses' were fundamental impulses conducive to utilitarian morality.[20] According to Malthus, the 'body has more effect upon the mind than the mind upon the body'.[21] And since the body was porous and vulnerable to environmental conditions, it followed that environmental circumstances influenced the mind. This insight was probably derived from contemporary ideas about the effects of the physical environment, notably climate, on identity and health.[22] The proponents of these ideas assumed that people were unable to completely divorce themselves from their surroundings, because the senses were always open to external stimuli. In analogous fashion, Malthus claimed that 'reason' could prevent the 'abuse of sensual pleasures', but it could not 'extinguish' them.[23] The 'lower classes' were regarded as particularly incapable of cultivating reason, since their persistent 'want' and unrelenting labour resulted in them remaining governed by the senses, which functioned mostly as inlets of suffering.[24]

To reinforce the corporeal aspects of intellectual activity, Malthus described walking through the rural environment as being a bodily as well as an aesthetic affair, with picturesque vision, if over-indulged, terminating in tactile discomfort. 'A walk in the finest day through the most beautiful country,' he remarked, 'if pursued too far, ends in pain and fatigue.'[25] This passage was one of the few instances in the *Essay* in which land was attributed an aesthetic value. Due to the rise of picturesque taste in the late eighteenth century, the dominant aesthetic attitude to the land tended to privilege remote, visual perceptions of the natural and social world at the expense of other sensory experiences.[26] The pursuit of such disembodied, aestheticised views, for instance, was a marked feature of Malthus's tour of the Lake District in the summer of 1795. In his diary of this tour, Malthus recorded himself, guidebook in hand, obsessively searching for the best viewing stations from which to appreciate picturesque scenes. Intriguingly, however, he also remarked, after a day sailing around Lake Windermere, that his attempt to see all the best sights left him feeling 'cold hungry & tired'.[27]

Besides searching out picturesque views, Malthus was attentive also to the economic and social aspects of rural life. Throughout his tour, he commented on wages, markets, food prices, agricultural practices and the conditions of the poor.[28] Discerning signs of scarcity in Ambleside despite the solid wages of harvest time, Malthus learnt from a local landlord of the redundancy of handloom weavers brought about by the introduction of the spinning jenny. He communicated too his observations on plebeian diet, noting regional variations in taste for different food items. These were concerns which Malthus would examine in the *Essay* as factors either mitigating or exacerbating the disparity between population and resources. Unlike his travel diary, however, the *Essay* eschewed aesthetic interpretations of the rural environment. In fact, when Malthus used the word 'beautiful', it was not to describe landscape, but to satirise the ideal society imagined by Godwin. The purpose was to suggest that Godwin's utopian plans were coloured by aesthetic considerations, which did not correspond to the 'true and genuine situation of man on earth'.[29] Thus, Malthus emphasised the factual basis of his own focus on the niggardliness of nature. And this account was demonstrated by the negative sensory experiences of the labouring classes, whose insufficient nourishment and 'stunted' growth testified to the bodily effects of ecological limits.

In some sections of the *Essay*, Malthus did adopt a predominantly visual attitude to the natural and social world to lend authority to his apocalyptic visions, but this was represented as part of a scientific approach. The principle of population was underpinned by an insistent empiricism in which observed facts about the physical environment revealed the universal laws of nature. Combining natural history with natural philosophy, these laws were demonstrable by mathematics, while remaining consistent with 'actual observations'.[30] Global travel journals, agricultural surveys and works of conjectural history were cited to show that the causes of scarcity varied across time and space. Nevertheless, the tension between population and resources could be inferred in every one of these instances through straightforward ratio computations. Without checks, Malthus pronounced, population increased in a geometrical ratio, while food production only increased in an arithmetical ratio. These calculations were drawn from observations in natural history on the tendency of reproductive rates in plants and animals to exceed limits of land and subsistence, which Malthus simply extended to humans.[31] Unlike Malthus, works of natural history had assumed, following Linnaeus, that the plenitude of life on earth was a visual confirmation of the goodness of God.[32] The argument of the principle of population, however, was that a conception of the 'earth' as a site of struggle, always prone to scarcity, was 'more consistent with the various phenomena of nature which we observe around us and more consonant to our ideas of the power, goodness, and foreknowledge of the Deity'.[33]

In addition to making scarcity due to population pressure central to discussions of poverty, Malthus also envisaged the *Essay* as contributing to the loyalist response to the French Revolution debate. Anti-Jacobin propaganda argued that the popular reform movement promised to undermine the sensory order of commercial modernity by agitating for equality of property. Such equality was held to be incompatible with civility, peace and prosperity.[34] Accordingly, reformers were charged with attempting to bring about universal poverty in Britain, or, worse still, seeking a reversion to a state of nature, imagined in negative terms as a situation of savage primitivism in which people were beset by lawlessness, brutality, ignorance and deprivation. In his attack on Godwin, Malthus reinforced this conservative argument by foregrounding the effects of equality on the senses. It was impossible, he asserted, that all members of society could 'share alike the bounties of nature'; for, if there was 'no established administration of property, every man would be obliged to guard with force his little store', causing 'triumphant' 'selfishness' and 'perpetual' 'contention'.[35] Put simply, the result of equality was sensory anarchy, characterised by noise, hunger and physical violence.

Even modest forms of equality were futile, Malthus alleged. If the labouring classes improved their living conditions and attained a higher proportion of the means of subsistence, population would grow until poverty or starvation returned. According to Malthus, the creation of a 'terrestrial paradise', with no extraneous luxuries in order to maximise food production, would entail the complete conversion of pastoral to arable land.[36] And if corn was cultivated at the expense of cattle – Malthus made the strategic observation – everyone would have to adopt a vegetarian diet,[37] undermining the taste for roast beef, which loyalists often alluded to as evidence of the liberty, vigour and good fortune of the rural people.[38]

Of course, Malthus did not believe that anyone had a right to roast beef, or any food for that matter, unless they earned it through gainful labour. Although he recognised that arable rather than pastoral farming could support a larger population, this was ultimately an unsustainable situation: while scarcity might be postponed it could never truly be eradicated.[39] In addition, livestock produced dung, which helped maintain optimal soil fertility. For Malthus, almost the only, if temporary, solution to the problem of overpopulation was the abolition of the poor laws, a system of parish relief which provided financial assistance to labourers in the event of unemployment, dearth or disablement. In a world of limited resources, the poor laws were unjust – Malthus posited – since the recipients of relief obtained food without producing any, diminishing its availability for other more deserving people. Worse, by increasing prices, this could in turn put the remaining workers at greater risk of destitution and dependence on parish assistance. As a result, the poor laws were held to intensify rather than alleviate poverty. They were also immoral, because the guaranteed subsistence removed 'one of the strongest incentives to sobriety and industry', the fear of hunger, a feeling God designed to ensure the cultivation of the land.[40] With the poor laws as security, labourers spent rather than saved any surplus wages, most likely at the alehouse, where they indulged in 'drunkenness and dissipation'.[41] All these issues compounded Malthus's main problem with the poor laws, which was that they enabled recipients to have children without being in a position to support them, hastening population growth while shrinking food supply. As a major source of idleness, depravity and pending ecological crisis, 'dependent poverty', concluded Malthus, 'ought to be held disgraceful'.[42]

Malthus published the *Essay* towards the end of a tumultuous decade, when the debate about the French Revolution in Britain politicised the question of poverty. This debate combined with harvest failures, food riots and depressed economic circumstances in the countryside to shine a spotlight on the plight of the rural labouring classes, especially their struggle to meet basic subsistence needs. The war with republican France, declared in early 1793, inflated food prices and disrupted European markets for the rest of the decade and beyond.[43] Worse still, war broke out when agricultural workers were suffering the effects of the deficient harvest of the previous year.[44] Another bad harvest in 1794 was followed by a severe winter, and that in turn by an inclement, unstable summer. The result was an even more dreadful harvest in 1795. These successive crop failures caused a sharp spike in wheat prices, decreasing the real wages of the labouring classes, who experienced almost famine-like conditions.[45] A good yield in 1796 did provide a brief respite, but the situation of food scarcity brought about by crop failures returned again from 1799 to 1801.

Since bread was not only a crucial component of the diet of the labouring classes but also a status symbol for them, the shortages triggered riots throughout England and Wales.[46] While the rioters aimed to lower the price of bread, or stop the export of grain to more lucrative markets, the government and the propertied elite worried that more radical sentiments might be at play.[47] Gripped by fears of revolution in the early

Autumn of 1795, Elizabeth Montagu distributed loyalist tracts to her poor 'Country Neighbours' in a bid to stifle their 'Rioting' disposition.[48] Nevertheless, she could do nothing about their preference for white bread. Reviewing the same circumstances, Frederick Eden went as far as to argue that the 'distress' of rural labourers was due not to 'inadequate wages' but to their diet, their refusal to give up white bread for other 'cheap and agreeable substitutes'.[49] In *The Wealth of Nations*, Adam Smith had proposed that potatoes produced strong, healthy plebeian bodies, and their cultivation across Britain would enhance agricultural productivity and facilitate sustainable population growth.[50] Drawing on Smith, the potato was regularly recommended as a substitute for bread by loyalist supporters and philanthropists during the revolutionary decade.[51] For William Buchan, in 1797, potatoes promised an end to famine, while also discouraging the labouring classes from visiting the alehouse, since, unlike bread, cheese and bacon, they were not a 'parching food'.[52] The poor could improve their health, income and morality, he concluded, by switching from bread to potatoes and from roast beef to broths, soups or stews. Likewise, Hannah More published loyalist tracts to convince the poor that protest was futile and sinful, and that an adjustment of diet was sufficient to guarantee subsistence even during conditions of scarcity. Referring to the 'famous cold winter' of 1795, More noted that bad weather always had the potential to destroy crops, but potatoes being more resistant would be a more stable supply of nourishing food.[53] By contrast, radical writers rejected idle conduct and an extravagant diet as causes for the hunger and suffering of the labouring classes.[54] They refused to see the subsistence crises as merely environmental events caused by bad weather. Rather, from a radical perspective, they were manifestations of injustice which could be alleviated through political reform. As William Frend asserted in 1795, 'war' rather than climate was the 'chief' reason for the 'distress' of the poor, since it raised unequal taxes, exacerbating the problem of high food prices.[55]

Malthus published the first edition of the *Essay* between these food crises, and his pessimistic analysis of poverty was informed by the desperate conditions of the labouring classes. On the topic of food substitutes, he initially said very little. But he did acknowledge the potential of Smith's suggestion that, if English labourers developed a taste for potatoes and more land was devoted to cultivating them, Britain could support a larger population.[56] In response to the scarcity of 1799–1800, the leading exponent of agricultural improvement, Arthur Young, emphatically promoted the cultivation of potatoes. Young recognised that the enclosure of the countryside had made agricultural labourers more vulnerable to food shortages by reducing their access to common land, which correspondingly increased the importance of the variable wages they received. In common with loyalist critics, he insisted that the recent high food prices arose 'entirely' 'from the seasons', while submitting a social and economic solution to this environmental problem.[57] Specifically, Young proposed as an antidote to food shortages the allocation of small plots of land for cottagers, who could, by growing potatoes and keeping a cow for milk, enjoy 'wholesome and nourishing' alternatives to bread regardless of any future scarcity.[58] He also floated the idea of reforming the poor laws to exclude from the relief proffered all food except potatoes, rice and soups. This would, Young claimed, expand the cultivation of potatoes across Britain, as the poor became 'habituated' to a 'cheaper way of satisfying their hunger', diminishing their 'taste' for 'bread'.[59]

In the second edition of the *Essay*, published in 1803, Malthus expressed approval for restricting parish relief to potatoes, rice and soups, but mainly because the measure would harden the distinction between the deserving and undeserving poor. These food substitutes were held in disdain by the labouring classes. Accordingly, their adoption would create a disincentive to apply for assistance by making it a source of shame. Malthus proposed that the only food to be given to the poor should be the 'brownest bread', with clothing also being restricted to the 'coarsest and scantiest apparel'.[60] In this way, shame was treated as a sensory affair, which could be internalised by taste and touch, by everyday acts of eating inferior meals and wearing uncomfortable clothes. Elsewhere, the poor laws were regarded by Malthus as the primary reason for the high bread prices during the 1799–1800 scarcity, since they artificially inflated the cost of commodities. Although he was still in principle opposed to parish relief, he believed its inflation of food prices enforced a 'strict economy' on labourers, which had proved positive in the recent food shortages.[61] While Malthus agreed that recipients of relief should only receive food they considered inferior to white bread, he rejected Young's assumption that the widespread cultivation of potatoes could eliminate scarcity in Britain. Cheap, prolific and easy to grow, potatoes might enable the labouring classes to live in relative 'plenty' (at least for a time).[62] But, as the case of Ireland demonstrated, these conditions would encourage early marriage and generate a surplus population for whom there would be no employment, potatoes being less labour-intensive than other crops.[63] A shift from bread to potatoes, then, would result in mass idleness and abject poverty. If this cheap food became universal among the poor, Malthus concluded, scarcity, and even famine, would eventuate when bad weather or other environmental circumstances compromised it, since there would be no more affordable alternatives to eat.

To some extent, Malthus moderated his pessimism in the second edition of the *Essay* by placing more emphasis on 'moral restraint', a preventive check involving sexual abstinence and delayed marriage, as a means of facilitating an improvement in the conditions of the poor. The inculcation of moral restraint was partly to be achieved by reforming the sensory habits of the labouring classes through a process of popular education.[64] According to Malthus, by understanding the principle of population and thus the 'true and permanent' causes of poverty, labourers could be motivated to postpone sexual passion.[65] But far from entailing misery, as represented in the first edition, this would promote happiness, because delayed marriage increased the 'sum of pleasurable sensations', being characterised by genuine love rather than youthful lust.[66] In addition, for Malthus, properly directed knowledge generated an aversion to squalidness, which in turn encouraged labourers to develop 'habits of sobriety, industry, independence, and prudence' along with higher standards of 'cleanliness and comfort'.[67] Cleanliness became a key concept in the expanded 1803 version of the *Essay*, and it assumed a heightened concern with sensory management, namely the appearance, feel and health of the body. Moreover, Malthus argued that education was also important to dissuade the poor from noisy protest. Without understanding that poverty was a personal failure, the 'cries of hunger' would become 'blended' with 'political discontents', as the labouring classes attributed circumstances of scarcity to government or society as opposed to nature.[68]

In the second edition of the *Essay*, Malthus suggested that a shift in the sensory behaviour of the poor, from dirty to clean, noisy to quiet, and indignant to patient in response to hunger, signified progress towards a culture of moral restraint. In this way, popular education was construed as crucial to the maintenance of political stability and social control as well as environmental sustainability. Evidently, the regulation of the senses worked in concert with the control of sexual appetites to establish an equilibrium between population growth and food production in a world of finite resources.

Nevertheless, this advancement of the labouring classes remained dependent on the abolition of the poor laws. Indeed, in the 1803 revision of the *Essay*, Malthus espoused a harsher attitude to the rights of the poor, any redress of which he conceived as a violation of the laws of nature detrimental to industry, sobriety and forbearance.[69] He criticised Thomas Paine's *Rights of Man* (1791–2) for championing the eradication of poverty through redistributive schemes such as social insurance programmes and lower, fairer taxes. Among the 'mischiefs' occasioned by Paine's book, Malthus asserted with reference to the food riots, was the tendency to blame 'human institutions' and 'government proceedings' for various social ills when the causes were actually personal and environmental.[70] Both customary practice and natural jurisprudence upheld a God-given right to subsistence, as enshrined in the poor laws. Paine took this right a step further with the redistributive plans he conceived to replace the poor laws, which were guided by the notion that, in a civilised society, not only subsistence, but also a decent level of comfort, was a matter of justice rather than charity.[71] For Malthus, however, such radical proposals threatened to exacerbate the disaffection of the poor by encouraging them to see their distress as a rationale for revolution.

A concern to counter Paine prompted Malthus to formulate his notorious metaphor of 'nature's mighty feast' to illustrate that anyone whose labour was not required by society had 'no claim of *right* to the smallest portion of food', or even to exist at all.[72] In representations of rural life, the image of the feast had long evoked ideas of social harmony and natural abundance, with rich and poor alike apparently benefiting from the prosperity of a populous, productive nation, as symbolised by excessive eating, joyful noise and vibrant colour. By contrast, Malthus depicted the feast of nature as an event demanding the exclusion of the poor, whose unregulated senses affronted the rich. If unemployed labourers were permitted to share in the wealth of the nation, even when the market did not need them, this would result in social conflict and sensory disorder. For Malthus, it was not hunger, but the belief in 'provision for all', which made the poor 'clamorous', furious and deranged in their senses. In an apocalyptic scenario, the rights of the poor were represented as incompatible with the 'happiness' of the propertied elite, whose pleasurable consumption was destroyed by exposure to the noise and offensive 'spectacle of suffering'. Guaranteed subsistence turned 'nature's mighty feast' into a scene of universal privation, with unsustainable population growth transforming 'plenty' into 'scarcity'.[73]

For his Romantic critics, the metaphor of 'nature's mighty feast' became the supreme illustration of the inhumanity of the principle of population. As Robert Southey noted in his review of the *Essay* in 1804, the passage implied that continued economic growth required starving 'the poor into celibacy', while urging the rich to 'harden their hearts'.[74] Moreover, because this passage depicted scarcity as a sensory phenomenon, the Romantic detractors of Malthus often addressed the senses in imagining an alternative relationship between population, poverty and environmental resources. Southey described the *Essay* as the 'political bible of the rich, the selfish, and the sensual'.[75] This notion that the principle of population licensed the sensual gratifications of the rich, while restricting the senses of the poor to negative stimulants such as hunger or tactile discomfort, became a common claim among Romantic critics of Malthus. Because of the adverse reception, Malthus withdrew the passage from the third edition of 1806. Nevertheless, the exclusion of the poor from the feast of nature continued to be cited by Romantic writers as proof that the concept of ecological scarcity functioned to justify social injustice and extreme economic inequality in violation of Christian ideas of charity, humanity and the fecundity of the earth.

In his review of Malthus's *Essay*, written in consultation with Samuel Taylor Coleridge, Southey argued that the metaphor of 'nature's mighty feast' invoked an image of society in which British liberty was replaced by Oriental despotism, with the poor reduced to the status of cattle. To require the unemployed poor to starve in order to control population growth weakened the moral basis of society, adding emotional sterility to sensory deficiency. As he wrote in a later essay on poverty, if the labouring classes experienced too much 'misery', their feelings would become deadened as surely as 'coarse' manual work hardened their skin and destroyed their 'finer sense of touch'.[76] Making Britain resemble an 'Oriental monarchy', the rich could satisfy, unchecked, their taste for luxury, while political resistance would be eliminated by transforming the 'refractory' John Bull into the 'tractable' John Ox.[77]

By 1804, when Southey wrote his review of Malthus's *Essay*, he had already begun to soften his earlier radicalism. In a critical response to an essay on Helvetius by Mary Hays, Southey had previously attacked the radical materialist model of improvement on the grounds that the manipulation of sensory inputs was insufficient to create virtue or ability.[78] This rejection of social engineering was predicated on the belief that humans were not merely bundles of senses shaped by environmental settings. In addition, Southey was concerned about the role of materialism in promoting atheism. Despite differing from Hays in political outlook, Malthus also espoused a variant of materialism, which gave prominence to the senses. But this theory was developed to justify a conservative position, favourable to religion. In his quasi-materialist model of conservatism, undesirable sensory experiences, especially hunger, were the means by which God motivated humans to work. Southey denounced this conflation of theology and utilitarian psychology as inimical to Christianity. Ignoring Malthus's emphasis on moral restraint in the second edition of the *Essay*, he was repelled by the way in which motivation was conceived to be a matter of bodily impulses rather than ethical decisions. In similar fashion, many critics noted that the principle of population reduced labourers to animals, eating, fornicating beings with no capacity to control their passions. As Southey remarked, quoting Coleridge,[79] Malthus assumed that 'lust and hunger' were 'alike passions of physical necessity', with both being 'independent of the reason and the will'.[80]

Southey's review repudiated the notion that the main cause of poverty was the perpetual discrepancy between population growth and food supply. For Malthus, as interpreted by Southey, such a looming catastrophe could only be averted by denying charity to – and suppressing the fertility of – the labouring classes. This proposition conflicted with Southey's Christian conception of nature as a perfect, harmonious system designed by God to meet human needs. As he complained to John Rickman, the principle of population cast Malthus 'against God Almighty'.[81] According to Southey, a beneficent, fecund nature had to be part of the divine plan, for otherwise people would be unable to obey the 'first great' Christian commandment: 'Be fruitful, and multiply, and replenish the earth and subdue it.'[82] In a later review of the *Essay*, published in 1812, Southey used this commandment to provide a theological justification for the expansion of empire. Overpopulation could never be a problem in Britain, he claimed, unless some global disaster destroyed the entire planet. This was because colonisation provided an effective means to manage any so-called surplus population, with British naval power establishing control over spacious lands across the world.[83] Even within Britain itself, Southey argued that the presence of untapped waste lands indicated that poverty caused by ecological scarcity was a result of unjust social policies and practices rather than inexorable environmental circumstances. 'If a country be overpeopled, and crowded, and distressed, in regard to its system of society', he professed, 'the fault lies in that system of society, not in the system of nature.'[84] By 1804 Southey had rejected the ideas of Godwin, but he still retained the radical conviction that human distress had political and social dimensions.

For Southey, the debate about population focused attention not just on the conditions of the poor, but on the effects of social and economic change on their senses. This consideration of adjustments in the sensory experiences, habits and values of the labouring classes was particularly important in relation to the expansion of mechanised industrial production, which Southey regarded as a major cause of poverty.[85] Employment tended to be more lucrative and regular in the new manufacturing towns of northern England than in rural villages in the southern counties. But Southey argued that factory workers were worse off than agricultural labourers, not least because their senses became deranged, impaired or deadened in crowded urban locations. In his 1812 review of Malthus's

Essay, he commented on the 'filth' and depravity which resulted from 'crowding human beings together', while suggesting that poor children should be prepared for the army or navy rather than be exposed to the 'stench and moral contagion of cotton mills'.[86] Evidently, population growth was only positive in the countryside, where dispersed settlements prevented the pollution of the atmosphere characteristic of crowded places. Moreover, as Southey made clear, undesirable sensory experiences were associated with immorality as well as disease. One contributor to the population debate, the physician Thomas Jarrold, rebutted this notion that agricultural labour was more conducive to health than factory work on the grounds that the heat of cotton mills created an 'artificial atmosphere', which resembled the kind of 'warm climate' deemed to rejuvenate individuals with delicate constitutions. By contrast, there was no 'process ... more dusty than the threshing or grinding of corn'.[87] It was inevitable that Southey would disagree with this postulation, even though he believed that the cold climate in England made the situation of both the rural and urban poor more conducive to suffering and disease than anywhere else in Europe.[88] Clearly, though, nothing was less favourable to 'physical and moral' wellbeing than factory work, of which the 'impure atmosphere of crowded rooms' caused disease, while the prospect of unremitting 'misery' undermined hope and religion.[89] Although Southey implied that Malthus's *Essay* justified the manufacturing system, it was equally concerned about the effects of industrial towns on the health and morality of the labouring classes.[90] Indeed, Malthus stressed the problem of overcrowding, seeing it as a metonym for overpopulation. Drawing on John Aikin's observations in and around Manchester, he echoed Southey in condemning the 'foulness of the air' in crowded locations.[91] In addition, by perverting the senses, manufacturing districts operated as a check on population growth, as the debilitation of plebeian bodies elevated mortality rates.

Intriguingly, too, Southey shared with Malthus the belief that the establishment of a system of national education was the key to improving the situation of poor.[92] Through such a system, plebeian sensory habits and practices could be transformed. Instead of them getting drunk in a tavern while their families starved, education could teach the labouring classes self-control. They might then be incentivised to regulate their senses if they understood that by doing so they could raise their living standards and achieve a more comfortable existence.

A number of issues raised by Southey were reiterated in William Hazlitt's critique of Malthus's *Essay*, published in 1807, shortly after the Whitbread Bill made the principle of population the basis for a new campaign to reform the poor laws. Like Southey, Hazlitt denied that poverty resulted from any discrepancy between agricultural production and population growth. On the contrary, food scarcity was caused by 'moral and political circumstances' rather than environmental factors.[93] For Hazlitt, neither overpopulation nor nature was the issue, but the unfair and unequal distribution of resources. 'While there is waste among the rich, or neglect of lands, or while the breed of horses is encouraged so as to put a stop to the breed of men', Hazlitt asserted, 'the distresses of the poor, or the restraints on population' could not be attributed to the 'necessary effects of the laws of nature, of the unavoidable disproportion between the increase of mankind and the capacity of the earth to produce good for a greater number'.[94] Elsewhere, Hazlitt condemned Malthus for regarding the labouring classes as 'so many animals *in season*'.[95] Here, however, he alleged that they were treated worse than the horses which filled the stables of the spacious grounds of the rich. In consequence, it was absurd to link poverty to ecological scarcity, when there were ample resources for such animals, kept purely to satisfy the pleasure of their patrician owners.

In his *Essay*, Malthus supported patrician superfluous consumption, reasoning that luxuries could be retrenched during times of need. Grain grown for 'horses kept for pleasure', for example, could be redirected to the 'lower classes' during food shortages.[96] Clearly, Hazlitt disagreed. So, too, in 1808, did the clergyman Robert Ingram, who did not believe this was something 'luxurious people' would ever do as he very much doubted if any of them had parted with their 'supernumerary horses' during the grain crises.[97] It should be noted at this point that Malthus was ambivalent towards luxury. While he believed a luxurious society that prioritised manufacturing over agriculture was undesirable, he could still endorse the acquisition of consumer goods by the labouring classes so long as it promoted prudence and moral restraint.[98]

The significance of the senses in the understanding of poverty was a prominent theme in Hazlitt's critique of Malthus. To some extent, this sensory focus derived from the way in which Hazlitt interpreted the principle of population as an apology for the luxury of the landed classes. As evidenced throughout his *Reply*, Hazlitt imagined luxury as a matter of the senses, or more precisely, of the 'sensual passions'.[99] In the ancient Roman empire, he recorded, luxury encompassed an elite proclivity for 'feasting' on exotic animals, reclining on 'silken couches', scenting the air with perfumes, viewing 'lewd exhibitions', listening to 'lascivious songs' and participating in 'wanton dances'.[100] A similar situation, according to Hazlitt, was transpiring among the affluent classes in contemporary Britain, where luxury was creating a distorted, segregated sensory environment.

Malthus denigrated the poor for their filth, stench and ragged clothing, attributing these negative sensory experiences to moral shortcomings which exacerbated population pressure by encouraging vice. And yet he was approving, Hazlitt implied, of the vice associated with the luxury of the rich. In response to Malthus's alleged imputation of immorality against the poor, Hazlitt observed that their 'filth' was comparable to the 'rouge' worn by women of fashion. 'The poor grovel in disagreeable sensations', he conceded, but 'the rich wanton in voluptuous ones'.[101] Moreover, insofar as the 'disagreeable sensations' of the poor were a consequence of privation, this state was ultimately brought about by the 'sensual passions' of the rich. As Hazlitt explained, 'luxury in some classes may produce want in others, but poverty is in this case the effect of the unequal distribution of the produce of the earth, not of its real deficiency'.[102] The affluent classes may have been able to provide for their own children, but they consumed much more than even large plebeian families, and it was for this reason that their luxury, rather than the idleness or irresponsible breeding of under-employed and under-remunerated labourers, depleted environmental resources, causing scarcity and poverty. For Hazlitt, the principle of population required that the labouring classes be 'ready to perish of want except as they are kept from it by severe and unremitting exertion', while their polite superiors were expected to enjoy perpetual 'ease and luxury for no other purpose than to keep the good things of this life to themselves'.[103] The sensory deprivation or discomfort, which accompanied so much manual labour, contrasted with the pleasurable, over-stimulating quality of patrician leisure. And yet, much to the ire of Hazlitt, Malthus also aimed to stop the 'coarse enjoyments' of the poor, treating them as mere 'brutes'. Factory workers had an excellent reason to escape to a pot-house, where they could 'hide their greasy clothes and smutched faces' from the contemptuous gaze of polite onlookers.[104] Likewise, only the most cold-hearted would deny agricultural workers their respite from 'severe labour', even if they chose to drown their cares in a 'mug of ale, in noise, and mirth, and laughter'.[105]

In an attempt to refute Malthus's fatalistic environmental determinism, which stressed the futility of political change, Hazlitt highlighted the deleterious sensory effects of a corrupt, oppressive government. Citing the window tax and candle tax, he noted that these unjust revenue-raising measures eliminated light from plebeian cottages.[106] Meanwhile, the 'higher classes' tended not even to encounter the 'sight of misery', as they were 'unwilling to descend from the highest pitch of luxury', remaining within the confines of their bright, airy mansions and expansive, solitary parks.[107] This division between rich and poor, as suggested by both Hazlitt and Southey, was imagined as a sensory as well as social division. For Malthus, as we have seen, the senses functioned in the labouring classes as inlets of misery, registering painful or unpleasant experiences, which motivated industrious behaviour and sexual prudence, thereby relieving pressure on food supply. It was perhaps not surprising, then, that Hazlitt would deride Malthus for the delight he took in the 'dearth' of nature, or for his pessimistic sensory assessment of rural life, filtered through the smoke, noise and dust of a disorienting, industrialising nation.

Notes

1. William Hazlitt, *A Reply to the Essay on Population* (London: Longman, 1807), p. 241.
2. See Fredrik Albritton Jonsson, 'Island, Nation, Planet: Malthus in the Enlightenment', in Robert J. Mayhew (ed.), *New Perspectives on Malthus* (Cambridge: Cambridge University Press, 2016), pp. 128–51.
3. Since concerns about overpopulation became prominent in the 1960s, there has been much debate about how to reconcile issues of environmental sustainability and social justice on a global scale. From the beginning, there has been considerable suspicion of neo-Malthusian arguments, which attribute environmental problems to the high fertility of developing countries rather than to the excessive consumption of developed countries. Relatedly, people in the Global South are understandably reluctant to curtail their own economic development in response to the demographic sensitivities, aesthetic preferences and consumer habits of people in the global North. Nevertheless, current views of population stabilisation as essential for avoiding chronic ecological disruption continue to emphasise fertility more than overconsumption or the unequal distribution of resources. For issues of social justice and environmental sustainability in recent discussions of overpopulation, see Diana Coole, 'Population, Environmental Discourse, and Sustainability', in Teena Gabrielson, Cheryl Hall, John M. Meyer and David Schlosberg (eds), *The Oxford Handbook of Environmental Political Theory* (Oxford: Oxford University Press, 2016), pp. 279–87.
4. See Peter Denney, 'The Emotions, the Senses and Popular Radical Print Culture in the 1790s: The Case of the *Moral and Political Magazine*', in Jock Macleod, William Christie and Peter Denney (eds), *Politics and Emotions in Romantic Periodicals* (Cham: Palgrave Macmillan, 2019), pp. 49–72.
5. Roy Porter, 'The Malthusian Moment', in Brian Dolan (ed.), *Malthus, Medicine, and Morality: 'Malthusianism' after 1798* (Amsterdam: Rodopi, 2000), p. 61.
6. Thomas Robert Malthus, *An Essay on the Principle of Population* (1798), ed. Antony Flew (London: Penguin, 1970), p. 71.
7. See Carolyn Purnell, *The Sensational Past: How the Enlightenment*

Changed the Way We Use Our Senses (New York: Norton, 2017), pp. 27–8 and 40–1.
8. William Paley, *The Principles of Moral and Political Philosophy* (1785), ed. D. L. Le Mahieu (Indianapolis: Liberty Fund, 2002), p. 40.
9. Ibid. p. 420.
10. Fredrik Albritton Jonsson, *Enlightenment's Frontier: The Scottish Highlands and the Origins of Environmentalism* (New Haven, CT: Yale University Press, 2013), p. 194.
11. Thomas Robert Malthus, *An Essay on the Principle of Population*, 2nd edn (London: Johnson, 1803), p. 323.
12. Malthus, *Essay* (1798), p. 67.
13. On the theological aspects of the *Essay* of 1798, see D. L. LeMahieu, 'Malthus and the Theology of Scarcity', *Journal of the History of Ideas* 40, no. 3 (1979): 467–74; J. M. Pullen, 'Malthus's Theological Ideas and Their Influence on His Principle of Population', *History of Political Economy* 13, no. 1 (1981): 40–7.
14. Malthus, *Essay* (1798), p. 202.
15. For Malthus's perspective on the mind-body problem, see Donald Winch, *Malthus* (Oxford: Oxford University Press, 1987), pp. 33–4.
16. Malthus, *Essay* (1798), p. 203.
17. See Denney, 'Emotions, Senses and Popular Radical Print Culture', pp. 61–4.
18. William Godwin, *Enquiry Concerning Political Justice, and its Influence on Morals and Happiness*, 3rd edn, 2 vols (London: J. Johnson, 1798), 1: 44 and 2: 50.
19. Godwin, *Enquiry*, 2: 527.
20. Malthus, *Essay* (1798), p. 147.
21. Ibid. p. 153.
22. Charles J. Withers, *Placing the Enlightenment: Thinking Geographically about the Age of Reason* (Chicago: University of Chicago Press, 2007), pp. 139–48.
23. Malthus, *Essay* (1798), p. 148.
24. Ibid. p. 149.
25. Ibid. p. 147.
26. Peter Denney, '"The Sounds of Population Fail": Changing Perceptions of Rural Poverty and Plebeian Noise in Eighteenth-Century Britain', in Anne M. Scott (ed.), *Experiences of Poverty in Late Medieval and Early Modern England and France* (Farnham: Ashgate, 2012), pp. 305–7.
27. T. R. Malthus, 'Diary of a Tour of the Lake District', in John Pullen and Trevor Hughes Parry (eds), *The Unpublished Papers in the Collection of Kanto Gakuen University*, 2 vols (Cambridge: Cambridge University Press, 2004), 2: 35.
28. On Malthus's interest in these matters, see Robert J. Mayhew, *Malthus: The Life and Legacies of an Untimely Prophet* (Cambridge, MA: Harvard University Press, 2014), pp. 52–3.
29. Malthus, *Essay* (1798), p. 133.
30. Ibid. p. 163.
31. For the influence of natural history on Malthus, see Margaret Schabas,

The Natural Origins of Economics (Chicago: University of Chicago Press, 2006), pp. 107–8.
32. Peter Harrison, 'Natural History', in Peter Harrison, Ronald L. Numbers and Michael H. Shank (eds), *Wrestling with Nature: From Omens to Science* (Chicago: University of Chicago Press, 2011), pp. 130–1.
33. Malthus, *Essay* (1798), p. 200.
34. Gregory Claeys, *The French Revolution Debate in Britain* (Basingstoke: Palgrave Macmillan, 2007), pp. 80–92.
35. Malthus, *Essay* (1798), p. 134.
36. Ibid. p. 135.
37. See Tristram Stuart, *The Bloodless Revolution: A Cultural History of Vegetarianism from 1600 to Modern Times* (New York: Norton, 2006), pp. 408–10.
38. See, for example, Arthur Young, *The Example of France, A Warning to Britain*, 4th edn (London: Richardson, 1794), pp. 113–14.
39. Malthus, *Essay* (1798), pp. 187–9.
40. Ibid. p. 98.
41. Ibid. p. 99.
42. Ibid. p. 98.
43. Chris Evans, *Debating the Revolution: Britain in the 1790s* (London: Tauris, 2006), pp. 86–7; Jennifer Mori, *Britain in the Age of the French Revolution, 1785–1820* (Harlow: Pearson, 2000), pp. 154–5.
44. T. C. W. Blanning, *The Origins of the French Revolutionary Wars* (London: Longman, 1986), p. 145.
45. Roger Wells, *Wretched Faces: Famine in Wartime England, 1793–1801* (London: Breviary Stuff, [1986] 2011), pp. 40–1.
46. Andrew Charlesworth, *An Atlas of Rural Protest in Britain, 1548–1900* (London: Croom Helm, 1983), pp. 97–9.
47. Wells, *Wretched Faces*, pp. 136–7.
48. Elizabeth Montagu to Elizabeth Carter, 9 September 1795, Huntington Library MS, MO 3751.
49. Frederick Morton Eden, *The State of the Poor: A History of the Labouring Classes in England*, 3 vols (London: Davis, 1797), 1: 492.
50. Jonsson, *Enlightenment's Frontier*, pp. 132–3.
51. Sandra Sherman, *Imagining Poverty: Quantification and the Decline of Paternalism* (Columbus: Ohio State University Press, 2001), pp. 41–52 and 177–89.
52. William Buchan, *Observations Concerning the Diet of the Common People* (London: Strahan and Cadell, 1797), p. 28.
53. Hannah More, *The Way to Plenty* (London: Marshall, 1795), pp. 22–6.
54. See, for example, John Thelwall, *The Tribune* (1795–6), in Gregory Claeys (ed.), *The Politics of English Jacobinism: Writings of John Thelwall* (University Park: Pennsylvania State University Press, 1995), p. 253.
55. William Frend, *Scarcity of Bread* (London: 1795), p. 2.
56. Malthus, *Essay* (1798), pp. 117–18.
57. Arthur Young, *The Question of Scarcity Plainly Stated and Remedies Considered* (London: McMillan, 1800), p. 71.
58. Ibid. p. 79.
59. Ibid. p. 80.

60. Malthus, *Essay* (1803), p. 565.
61. T. R. Malthus, *An Investigation of the Cause of the Present High Price of Provisions* (London: Johnson, 1800), pp. 18–20.
62. Malthus, *Essay* (1803), p. 576.
63. For Malthus and the potato debate, see Catherine Gallagher and Stephen Greenblatt, 'The Potato in the Materialist Imagination', in *Practicing New Historicism* (Chicago: University of Chicago Press, 2000), pp. 128–32.
64. Philip Connell, *Romanticism, Economics and the Question of 'Culture'* (Oxford: Oxford University Press, 2001), pp. 65–6.
65. Malthus, *Essay* (1803), p. 506.
66. Ibid. p. 500.
67. Ibid. p. 557.
68. Ibid. p. 527.
69. Gareth Stedman Jones, *An End to Poverty? A Historical Debate* (London: Profile Books, 2004), pp. 103–4.
70. Malthus, *Essay* (1803), p. 534.
71. Thomas Paine, *Rights of Man* (1791–2), in Bruce Kuklick (ed.), *Political Writings* (Cambridge: Cambridge University Press, 2000), p. 235.
72. Malthus, *Essay* (1803), p. 531.
73. Ibid. p. 531.
74. Robert Southey, 'Malthus's Essay on Population', *Annual Review* 2 (1804): 300.
75. Ibid. p. 298.
76. Robert Southey, 'The Poor', *Quarterly Review* 15, no. 29 (1816): 209.
77. Southey, 'Malthus's Essay', p. 301.
78. David Craig, *Robert Southey and Romantic Apostasy: Political Argument in Britain, 1780–1840* (Woodbridge: Boydell Press, 2007), pp. 37–8.
79. Samuel Taylor Coleridge, *Marginalia*, ed. H. J. Jackson and George Whalley, 6 vols (Princeton: Princeton University Press, 1980–2001), 3: 806.
80. Southey, 'Malthus's Essay on Population', p. 296.
81. Robert Southey to John Rickman, 8 February 1804, in Kenneth Curry (ed.), *New Letters of Robert Southey*, 2 vols (New York: Columbia University Press, 1965), 1: 351.
82. Robert Southey, 'Inquiry into the Poor Laws,' *Quarterly Review* 8, no. 16 (1812): 355.
83. Connell, *Romanticism*, p. 165.
84. Southey, 'Malthus's Essay on Population', p. 297.
85. Craig, *Robert Southey*, pp. 73–5.
86. Southey, 'Inquiry into the Poor Laws', pp. 338 and 353.
87. Thomas Jarrold, *Dissertations on Man, Philosophical, Physiological, and Political* (London: Cadell and Davis, 1806), pp. 61–2.
88. Robert Southey, *Letters from England* (1807), ed. Jack Simmons (Gloucester: Alan Sutton, 1984), pp. 145–6.
89. Ibid. p. 210.
90. Donald Winch, *Riches and Poverty: An Intellectual History of Political Economy in Britain, 1750–1834* (Cambridge: Cambridge University Press, 1996), pp. 271–2.
91. Malthus, *Essay* (1803), p. 308.

92. Craig, *Robert Southey*, pp. 77–8.
93. Hazlitt, *Reply*, p. 74.
94. Ibid. p. 349.
95. Ibid. p. 127.
96. Malthus, *Essay* (1803), p. 478.
97. Robert Ingram, *Disquisitions on Population* (London: Hatchard, 1808), p. 54.
98. Winch, *Riches and Poverty*, pp. 272–3.
99. Hazlitt, *Reply*, p. 195.
100. Ibid. pp. 199–200.
101. Ibid. p. 230.
102. Ibid. pp. 192–3.
103. Ibid. p. 272.
104. Ibid. p. 332.
105. Ibid. p. 330.
106. Ibid. p. 210.
107. Ibid. p. 263.

Afterword: 'A tear to Nature's tawny sons is due': Alexander Wilson's *The Foresters* and Romantic Period Uprootings

Bridget Keegan

In 1804, Alexander Wilson set off with two companions to make a journey through what is now Pennsylvania and New York to visit Niagara Falls. The expedition is described in his extended 2,219-line loco-descriptive poem, *The Foresters*.[1] It was not a strictly touristic excursion. His purpose was professional: to seek new species of birds to describe, draw and add to the inventory that would bring him renown as the 'Father of American Ornithology'. Earlier that year, in June, Wilson had become a citizen of the recently established nation of the United States of America. He had emigrated to the young country from Scotland in 1794. In his native town of Paisley, Scotland, Wilson had been apprenticed as a weaver at the age of thirteen. However, like so many of the inhabitants of that region, he was also a poet.[2] Upon the publication of his first volume in 1790, he abandoned his work as a weaver to become a peddler and chapman, wandering the Scottish countryside selling his wares and observing the Scottish landscape. Wilson is one of the few labouring-class poets of the era who dared publish work containing explicit political protest.[3] Briefly imprisoned and fined for these works, he sought to evade further prosecution by emigrating to America. In America, Wilson reinvented himself, became a protégé of the founding American naturalist, William Bartram, and pursued his interests as a natural historian and editor, eventually publishing his nine-volume *American Ornithology* (1808–14).[4]

Wilson's biography is exemplary of many other narratives of early American self-invention (or reinvention) popularised by near contemporaries like Benjamin Franklin. Such narratives continue to lure immigrants to the United States even today. However, just as with many of the works and artists explored by the preceding chapters in this collection, Wilson's life and art illustrate the complications and compromises of colonial mobility. Further demonstrating a point that is made in different ways, forms, times and places by the essays included in this volume, an analysis of Wilson's poem underscores the intersectionalities of environment, race, class and gender in the Romantic period. As the essays all suggest, by reading texts through these lenses we are able to call out larger ideological trends while emphasising the unique improvisations of individual artists within (and sometimes against) those trends. Simply put: one person's or one group's intentional or chosen placement (necessarily) means another person's or another group's forced displacement. One person's or group's choice to place themselves in a particular relation to the natural environment (necessarily) means another person or group is displaced in relation to the natural environment. Whether the opportunity to impose a particular ideal of nature occurs in India, the English countryside or California, and whether the writer is an agricultural labourer, an urban artisan or a suburban gentleman, through the compelling essays of this volume we are able to remark upon how geographical mobility and socio-economic mobility are linked in new and powerful ways in the Romantic period. These essays illustrate the manifold opportunities, risks and ravages of mobility, for humans and the environment, that come into focus during this period. Collectively, the essays suggest how the diverse cultural and environmental interactions and interventions continue to shape current conversations about humanity's responsibility for that environment.

There is much in *The Foresters* that replicates the conventions of English prospect poetry (and the problematic environmental politics that prospect poetry underwrites, as critics like John Barrell and Tim Fulford have argued).[5] However, for Wilson, the American landscape offered an array of possibilities – both aesthetic and social – to a poet now far less constrained by the confines of his rank or occupation. In the opening stanzas of the poem, Wilson reflected upon the boundless vistas of his new home in comparison with his native land:

> While bare bleak heaths and brooks of half a mile
> Can rouse the thousand bards of Britain's Isle.
> *There* scarce a stream creeps down its narrow bed,
> There scarce a hillock lifts its little head,
> Or humble hamlet peeps their glades among
> But lives and murmurs in immortal song.
> Our western world, with all its matchless floods,
> Our vast transparent lakes and boundless woods,
> Stamped with the traits of majesty sublime,
> Unhonored weep the silent lapse of time [. . .] (p. 6)[6]

The American landscape and American democracy created promising opportunities for Wilson as a person and a poet. The possibilities and limits of self-fashioning, shaped by one's race, class, gender, nationality and one's natural environment, and the ways in which these multiple categories reinforce and conflict with one another, particularly on a global scale, becomes possible for men like Wilson on a wide scale only during the late eighteenth century. How each of these categories can at once empower but also impede identity and the artistic expressions of that identity are thoughtfully and varyingly explored in the previous chapters of this collection. While Wilson's ability to relocate was not yet typical, it was nonetheless increasingly feasible even for those of working-class backgrounds – and certainly for those in the emerging middle classes. More significantly, Wilson's delight in the ability to roam freely through a landscape was, as is well known, a distinctly Romantic phenomenon but one that was not equally distributed. In England and Scotland, the freedom to wander, to roam, was not accessible to all classes. Strict vagrancy laws, which were enforced with greater rigour from the 1780s forward, would have rendered a working man out on the open road suspect. And, as the experience of James Woodhouse attests, access for those of the labouring classes to particular kinds of environments, such as private gardens or estates, meant equally serious accusations of trespass. Colonial spaces, whether in America or Asia, provided potentially greater access, even though such access was not without costs and risks, including the threat of tiger attacks, or in Wilson's case, an encounter with a rattlesnake, described in a lengthy passage near the conclusion of the poem.

According to Wilson's biographer, Edward Burtt, Jr, between 1803 and 1810 Wilson 'traveled ... through fifteen of our eighteen states and all four territories, over twelve thousand miles'.[7] Wilson's mobility, then, was remarkable for a man of any class. His poem describing one of his earliest journeys represents, moreover, a significant contribution to the mythologising of the American frontier. While Wilson's interest in the American wilderness was from the perspective of an Enlightenment scientist, his poetry integrates key Romantic tropes including sublime encounters with natural wonders, most notably with the destination of the trek, Niagara Falls. On his travels, Wilson encountered immigrants from many regions of Europe, hardworking settlers, humbly making their livelihoods and carving settlements in the seemingly untouched valleys and forests. He praised their georgic virtues and their imposition of agriculture as an improvement upon uncultivated nature. But Wilson did not merely transpose English literary expectations and aesthetic values upon the American environment. He demonstrated an affective ambivalence towards what had been erased from the scene, whether trees or Native peoples. While the clearing of forests to make way for agriculture is celebrated in the title of the poem as well as in key scenes, elsewhere, Wilson lamented the destruction of old-growth trees, devastated in this case not by men but by the natural disaster of a tornado:

> Huge pines that towered for centuries on high,
> Crushed by each others ruins prostrate lie,
> Black with devouring flames, of branches bare,
> Their ragged roots high tilted frown in air; (p. 19)

Displacing the responsibility for this ruin to the destructive powers of nature itself (rather than the acquisitive settlers) potentially resolves the possible contradictions of Wilson's distinct aesthetic responses to the felling of trees. When it is a natural phenomenon, it can be mourned. When it is intentional human intervention, inspired by Enlightenment notions of improving upon nature, it is celebrated. Passing through the forest, Wilson extolled the results of European industriousness:

> And sudden opening on the ravished eye,
> Green fields, green meadows, gardens, orchards, lie
> In rich profusion round the cottage neat,
> Log-built; but Peace and Industry's retreat.
> Here down green glades the glittering streams descend;
> Here loaded peach trees o'er fences bend;
> [. . .]
> And all around that meets the eye or ear,
> Proclaims the power that spreads its influence here.
> Hail, Rural Industry! man's sturdiest friend,
> To thee each virtue must with reverence bend,
> To thee what heart denies spontaneous praise,
> From gloomy woods such glorious scenes to raise!
> Great giver of God's gifts to man below! (pp. 40–1)

The resolution Wilson arrives at in several places throughout the poem to the uprooting of Native peoples is far less neat, however.

Unlike many early American cultural works contributing to the myth of Manifest Destiny, Wilson did not depict a wilderness that was completely uninhabited before the arrival of Europeans. He acknowledged the traces of the displaced Indigenous peoples whose settlements were destroyed, even as he portrayed their eradication from the scene as contributing to 'improvement'. We see in these passages that while British class distinctions may be fluid in the new nation, presumed racial distinctions are reinforced. Wilson's Enlightenment optimism about human or natural improvement has its limits, as is evident in his description of the transformation of an Indian settlement:

> We pause to mark amid this valley green
> How changed the tenants, how improved the scene!
> Where wretched wigwams late like kennels stood,
> Where bark canoes stole skulking o'er the flood,
> Where mangled prisoners groaned, and hatchets glared,
> And blood-stained savages the fire prepared.
> There glittering towns and villages extend,
> There floating granaries in fleets descend,
> There ploughmen chant, and mowers sweep the soil,
> And taverns shine, and rosy damsels smile. (pp. 42–3)

Wilson is not alone among Romantic poets in depicting Native Americans.[8] He is, however, one of the few poets who wrote about them based upon direct personal experience, and, to my knowledge, the only poet of labouring-class origins to have done so. Perhaps due to his own experiences of social marginalisation and resultant displacement, he is able to offer more sympathetic portrayals of Indigenous individuals. For example, in a lengthy passage late in the poem, Wilson imagines a lone Indian mourning the loss of his village (p. 49). The scene opens with Wilson looking down upon a valley that has been cleared for the settlers to pasture livestock. From a prospect view, it is a 'scene of sheltered sweet repose'. Yet simultaneously, Wilson introduces another spectator, one for whom such prospects are far less benign. The 'poor Indian haply wandering here' serves as a double to the poet. For him, and his 'eye forlorn', it is a scene of loss and devastation, as he 'Beholds the spot where once his wigwam stood, / Where warrior's huts in smoky pride were seen'. But the loss is not merely personal as he bemoans the devastation of 'His nation's residence! his native green!' While a lone Indian is a less threatening presence, there is no question that he stands in for the totality of his people. The warrior's elegiac soliloquy sounds a good deal like something out of Oliver Goldsmith, except that the village the Indian describes is not so much deserted as utterly erased from the landscape. In those 'happy days! For ever, ever gone!'

> When these deep woods to white men were unknown;
> Then the Great Spirit gave us from on high,
> A plain broad path, and unclouded sky;
> Then herds of deer in every thicket lay;
> Peace blest our nights, and Plenty crowned our day; (p. 49)

With the arrival of the Europeans, 'dark clouds around our nation roar'. The warrior is surrounded by darkness and the graves of his ancestors, the traces of his people on the land obliterated. In the following stanza he describes a detailed inventory of loss. Parts of the landscape remain, but their significance is permanently altered: the tree under which 'Our aged chiefs the nation's welfare weighed', or the creek where the warrior fished. The tribe's collective activities, whether festive or martial, are gone and, worse, desecrated by European agriculture:

> Now all is lost! and sacrilege is spread!
> Curst ploughs profane the mansions of the dead!
> Our warriors wander on a distant shore,
> And strangers triumphed where they begged before. (pp. 49–50)

On the one hand such mournful, nostalgic figures are staples in the literature of sensibility. We see such figures in Wordsworth, for instance, although they are typically labouring-class or marginalised figures, like the Leech Gatherer, rather than a Native American. More significantly, Wilson's choice of language is telling. The warrior insistently signals the losses to his nation, not merely to himself. What he describes is the forced uprooting of a whole people, an uprooting that extends to the ploughing through of their gravesites. As Tim Fulford and others have noted, the imagery used to depict Native Americans in the Romantic period often recalls the representation of Scottish Highlanders. Thus, while Wilson's description may seem a rehearsal of familiar tropes, his experience of a partially forced displacement may inform his ambivalent depiction of the Indigenous man's condition. Wilson stops short of identifying with the experience of this figure, but he concludes the passage by pointing to the culpability of his own culture:

> Howe'er stern Prejudice these woes may view,
> A tear to Nature's tawny sons is due;
> The same false virtue and ambitious fire,
> Which nations idolize, and kings admire,
> Provoke the white man to the bloody strife,
> And bid the Indian draw his deadly knife; (p. 50)

Whatever savagery Native peoples might be guilty of, Wilson provides a more sympathetic context by ennobling the warrior's perspective and extolling his 'manly heart'. As this passage makes clear, one man's Eden is another man's Hell, even when it is the same scene viewed from the same prospect. The class, race and nationality of the viewer irrevocably inflect the perception of the natural environment.

There is much that a modern reader might critique as politically problematic in Wilson's poem. However, scenes such as this underscore the complexity of positions articulated – on a global scale – by individuals who are empowered, destroyed or otherwise affected by the increased scale and scope of social and resultant environmental change occurring during the Romantic period. The critical perspectives represented by the contributors to this volume emphasise the depth of the archive still to be plumbed and the continued relevance of intersectional examinations of writers from across the class spectrum. The 1816 global 'year without a summer' that was memorialised in much great literature of the Romantic period was an early reminder that our environment is and has always been global. In that global context, we continue to witness the localised impact of transnational capitalism made possible by colonial expansion. Wilson's warrior anticipates today's climate refugees, driven from their homes not by Europeans seeking to impose agricultural 'improvement', but by the manifold crises resulting from economic 'improvements' promised by industrial capitalism and made possible by massive exploitation of fossil fuels. We would do well to heed the important lessons available when cultural and environmental history are put in dialogue and to which the contributions to the collection offer rich testimony.

Notes

1. The poem was first published serially in 1809–10. There are no modern editions of Wilson's poetry, but an 1818 edition of the poem is available on Google Books which is the version referred to in this essay. The poem is also included in the 1876 two-volume collection *The Poems and Literary Prose of Alexander Wilson*, edited by Alexander Grosart.
2. It was noted by Robert Brown, editor of the two-volume late Victorian collection of Paisley Poets: 'The poetic fervour thus so long, fully, and enthusiastically manifested by many of the inhabitants of Paisley, continues unabated down to the present day. These circumstances have given rise to the exaggerated statements of humorists, that every fifth person in Paisley is a poet,' in *Paisley Poets with Brief Memoirs of them and Sections from their Poetry*, 2 vols (Paisley: Cook, 1890), 1: ix.
3. For an account of Wilson's political poetry, see Gerard Carruthers, 'Alexander Wilson: The Rise and Fall and Rise of a Laboring Class Writer', in John Goodridge and Bridget Keegan (eds), *A History of British Working Class Literature* (Cambridge: Cambridge University Press, 2018), pp. 70–84. See also Gerard Carruthers, 'Alexander Wilson: Scots Poet', in Edward H. Burtt, Jr (ed.), *Alexander Wilson: Enlightened Naturalist* (Lewisburg, PA: Bucknell University Press, 2016), pp. 1–21.
4. As part of the bicentennial of Wilson's death, Edward H. Burtt, Jr and William E. Davis, Jr published a well-illustrated biography, *Alexander Wilson: The Scot Who Founded American Ornithology* (Cambridge, MA: Harvard University Press, 2013).
5. John Barrell, *The Idea of Landscape and the Sense of Place, 1730–1840: An Approach to the Poetry of John Clare* (Cambridge: Cambridge University Press, 1972); Tim Fulford, *Landscape, Liberty and Authority: Poetry, Criticism and Politics from Thomson to Wordsworth* (Cambridge: Cambridge University Press, 1996).
6. Alexander Wilson, *The Foresters: A Poem, Descriptive of a Pedestrian*

Journey to the Falls of Niagara (Newtown: Siegfried and Wilson, 1818). Quotations from *The Foresters* are hereafter from this edition with the page number in parentheses.
7. Edward H. Burtt, Jr, 'Biographical Sketch', in Burtt, *Alexander Wilson: Enlightened Naturalist*, p. xxx.
8. For an excellent overview see Tim Fulford, *Romantic Indians: Native Americans, British Literature and Transatlantic Culture, 1756–1830* (Oxford: Oxford University Press, 2006).

Index

Poem and book titles are filed under the author's name. Page numbers in *italics* refer to illustrations, and those with the suffix 'n' refer to notes.

agricultural 'improvement', 10, 29–30, 149, 249, 252, 258, 274–5, 278
   Clare's response, 236, 238, 240, 242
   EIC land management, 8, 99, 103, 114, 115
   Woodhouse's response, 175, 177, 180–2, 186, 187
agriculture
   Chinese peasant farmer, 23
   cows/dairy farming, 195, 196, 197, 199, 203, 205–6, 240, 259
   ferme orné (ornamental farm), 161–2
   food supply, 252, 255, 256–9, 265
   monoculture, 231, 235, 236, 240, 243
   nature's productivity limits, 174, 177, 180–2, 186–7, 232, 238, 240, 241
   rotational farming, 202–3, 237
   sheep farming, 98, 161, 167, 197, 199, 206, 232–3, 240
Akenside, Mark, *The Pleasures of Imagination*, 213, 218–21, 225
Alayric-Fielding, Vanessa, 46
Alipur, 97, 99–100, 104–5, *132*
Alps, 80, 83, 205, 208n, 232, 233
Amazon rainforest, 234, 244
anarchism, 157–8, 256, 261
ancestral worship, 63–4
Anderson, Aeneas, *A Narrative of the British Embassy to China*, 18, 19–20, 22–3, 26

animals
   animal rights, 200–1, 206, 234
   death of, 113–14, 115, 116–17, 119–24, 205–6, 239
   see also birds; cows (human-bovine relationships); deer (harts); human-animal relationships; hunting; sheep; tigers; wild animals
animism, 117, 213, 214–15
Anson, George, 53
Anthropocene, 78–9, 86–7, 89, 187
anthropocentrism
   vs biocentrism, 10, 145, 212, 244
   in *The Last Man*, 84–5, 86
   non-anthropocentric universe, 215–16, 220
anthropomorphism, 233–4
Arabian Nights, 66, 69, 70
architecture
   in China, 39–40, 43, 44–7, *131*
   Ionic, 104
   Palladian, 25, 43, 44, 95, 97, 102, 104, *134*
   Roman, 104–5
aristocracy *see* upper class
Armitage, Edward, *Retribution*, 116
Arnold, David, 101, 115
Assam, 113–15, 117–19, 123, 124, *135*, *136*
Assam Forest Regulation Act (1931), 119

Atkinson, James, *City of Palaces*, 103, 105
Attiret, Father Jean-Denis, 28, 50
Augusta of Saxe-Gotha-Altenburg, Princess, 45, 49

Barrell, John, 3, 211
  The Dark Side of the Landscape, 151, 213
  The Idea of Landscape and the Sense of Place, 205, 273
Barrow, John, *Travels in China*, 18, 20–1, 24–6
Bate, Jonathan, *Romantic Ecology*, 145, 172, 230, 231, 232
beauty
  chinoiserie/Chinese style, 41, 44
  estates/landscapes, 24–8, 150, 157, 160–1
  nature as, 9, 10, 27, 48, 185
  picturesque as, 19, 21, 149–50
  Thomson's influence, 213
  wilderness/wildness, 4, 8
Beijing, 17, 19, 50
Bending, Stephen, 183
Bengal
  famine, 100–4, 108
  garden houses (*bagan bari*), 94–9, 102–6
  Munro killed by tiger, 116
Bentham, Jeremy, *An Introduction to the Principles of Morals and Legislation*, 200–1
Bentinck, Lord William Henry Cavendish, 118
Berg, Maxine, 35
Berger, John
  About Looking, 206
  Pig Earth, 205–6
Berque, Augustin, 157
Bertram, Aldous, 46
biocentrism, 10, 145, 212, 244
biodiversity
  capitalism and, 7, 157, 234, 236, 240, 241, 242, 244–5
  enclosure movement and, 201, 232, 237–40
  environmental aesthetics and, 230–3, 243–4
  rotational farming and, 202–3, 237
  Sea Shepherd Society/ELF, 10, 157
  social class and, 231, 234–5, 243
  Thomson and Blake, 213
bioempathy, 144–5
birds, 217–18, 238–9, 242, 272, 274
Bishu Shanzhuang (Leng), *130*
Bishu Shanzhuang (Mountain Resort to Escape the Heat), 22–3, 29, 42, *130*
Blake, William, 211–25
  Akenside's influence, 213, 218–21, 225
  Book of Urizen, 216
  The Four Zoas, 214, 216
  The Marriage of Heaven and Hell, 215, 216
  Milton, 212–13, 215–25
  Morganwg's influence, 212, 213, 221–5
  Poetical Sketches, 211
  Songs of Experience, 215
  Thomson's influence, 213–18
  'The Tyger', 116, 161
Blakely, Kara, 53
Bloomfield, Robert, 167, 173, 198, 201, 203
  The Farmer's Boy, 201
botany, 47, 102–3, 106, 114, 115, 117, 118
Brassier, Raymond, 80–1
bread, 257–9
Breakthrough Institute, 86, 87
Brewer, John, 149
Brighton, Royal Pavilion, 53
Bristol, 42, 47
Britain
  biodiversity of, 230–3, 237–8, 243–4
  chinoiserie fashion, 17–18, 19, 27, 34–6, 38, 42–53, 141
  EIC regulation, 102, 107, 108
  EIC returnees, 93–4, 95, 96, 106
  exotica imports, 117
  food shortages, 257–9
  riots, 257–8, 261
  war with France, 46, 158, 212, 240, 257

British empire, 93–109, 113–24
  Assam tea plantations, 113–15, 117, 118–24, *135*
  Bengal famine, 100–4, 108
  colonial capitalist economy, 94, 96, 98–9, 101–3, 107–8, 114, 118
  country houses (garden houses, India), 94–9, 102–6
  postcolonialism, 2–3, 4, 7–8
  theological justification, 263
Brower, Matthew, 123
Brown, John, *An Estimate of Manners and Principles of the Times*, 35
Brown, Lancelot 'Capability'
  and Chinese landscapes/gardens, 26–7, 37, 49–51
  landscape aesthetic, 50–1, 174, 175, 178, 183, 235, 236
Brunton, Mary, 235
Buchan, William, 258
Burckhardt, Lucius, 157
Burke, Edmund
  on East India Company, 93–101, 106–7
  'Speech on Fox's India Bill', 93, 99, 100–1
  on the sublime, 27, 48
Burlingame, Anson, 64
Burtt, Edward, Jr, 274
Butler, Marilyn, *Mapping Mythologies*, 211–12, 213, 218, 222, 223
Byron, Lord George Gordon, 'Darkness', 79, 80–3, 84, 89

Calcutta, 95, 97–8, 100, 102–5, *134*
Calcutta Botanic Gardens, 102–4, *134*
California, 60–2, 64, 66, 69–70
Callicott, J. Baird, 144
Calvert, Frederick, *137*
Camberwell, 152
Canton (Guangzhou), 17, 38–41, 44–7, 52–3, *131*
capitalism
  and biodiversity, 7, 157, 234, 236, 240, 241, 242, 244–5
  British landowners' profit motive, 174–5, 177–87, 238, 240, 241
  carbon capitalism, 78, 79, 182–3, 244–5, 278

  colonial capitalist economy, 94, 96, 98–9, 101–3, 107–8, 114, 118
Castellano, Katey, 201–2
Castiglione, Giuseppe, (aka Shining Lang), *130*
catastrophe/*katastrophē*, 79–82, 86, 88–9
Cathcart, Charles Allan, 17
Chakrabarty, Dipesh, 'The Climate of History', 78, 79
Chambers, Sir William, 20–1, 28, 37–41, 43–53
  'Of the Art of Laying Out Gardens Among the Chinese', 37, 43, 47
  Designs of Chinese Buildings, Furniture, Dresses, Machines, and Utensils, 37, 39, 41, 43–7, 50, *131*
  Dissertation on Oriental Gardening, 21, 37–8, 49–52, 53
  'Explanatory Discourse by Tan Chet-qua', 52
  Kew Gardens, 37, 45–7, 49, 52, 53, *131*
Champion, Frederic, 122
Chang, Elizabeth Hope, 30n, 34, 37
Changchun Yuan (the Garden of Eternal Spring), 29
charity, 148, 184, 201, 250, 258, 261, 262, 263
Chattopadhyay, Swati, 95
Chen, Jeng-Guo S., 36
Chhattisgarh, India, 244
China, 17–30, 34–54
  architecture, 39–40, 43, 44–7, *131*
  British embassy (1792), 17–29, 53
  EIC links, 17, 37, 38, 39, 42
  eremitical tradition, 159–60
  European access restrictions, 17, 38–41
  imperial semiotics, 4, 19, 21, 24–5, 28–9, 42, 46–7
  population, 11, 22–3, 61
Chinatowns, 60–72
  California, 60–2, 64, 66, 69–70
  Stevenson's depictions, 66–72
  Twain's depictions, 63–4, 69, 70–2
Chinese Exclusion Act (1882), 61
Chinese gardens, 18–30

Anderson's descriptions, 18, 19–20, 22–3, 26
Barrow's descriptions, 20–1, 24–6
Chambers's descriptions and designs, 20–1, 28, 37–41, 43–53, *131*
class-based access, 18–19, 22–3, 24, 26–8, 29
Holmes' descriptions, 18–19, 22
Macartney's descriptions, 18, 21–2, 24, 25–8
Staunton's descriptions, 18, 21, 25, 26
Wordsworth's knowledge and evocations of, 18, 21, 23, 25
chinoiserie in Britain, 17–18, 19, 27, 34–6, 38, 42–53, 141
Chipko movement, 1, 10
Christian environmentalism
  Blake and his influences, 10, 213–14, 218, 220–5
  Cowper, 10, 141–3, 144–6, 148, 152
  Evangelicalism, 141–2, 148–9, 151, 152
  Woodhouse (Christian stewardship), 174, 177
Christian utilitarianism, 251–2, 262
Christianity, 10, 63, 65, 115, 262–3
Christmas, William, 174
cities as loci of corruption
  British cities, 141, 142, 144, 148, 151, 152, 263–4
  Chinatowns, 60–72
  colonial cities, 104
Clapham, 142, 148–9, 150–1, 152
Clare, John, 167, 172, 230, 235–43
  'Birds Nests', 238
  The Early Poems of John Clare, 240
  'To a Fallen Elm', 239
  'The Firetails Nest', 238
  John Clare: Poems of the Middle Period, 238–9, 241–3
  'The Lamentations of Round-Oak Waters', 240
  'Langley Bush', 240
  'The Mole', 201–2
  'The Moorehen's Nest', 236, 240
  'The Nightingale's Nest', 239
  'The Robin's Nest', 241–3
  'Sand Martin', 238–9
  'The Wrynecks Nest', 238
  'The Yellow Hammer's Nest', 239
  'The Yellow Wagtails Nest', 239
Clark, Timothy, 85
class *see* social class
classicism *see* neoclassicism
Clifton, 196
  'Clifton Grove' (White), 198–9
  'Clifton Hill' (Yearsley), 195, 196–203
  'Fair Maid of Clifton', 199
climate change, 78–90, 278
  ecomodernism, 86–7, 89
  as emergency, 2–3, 83, 84
Closterman, John, 104, *135*
coal
  as fuel, 178, 237
  mining, 175, 180, 182–3, 186, 244–5
Cohen-Vrignaud, Gerard, 36
Coleridge, Samuel Taylor, 158–60, 162–4, 168, 204, 218, 262–3
  'Christabel', 163
  Greta Hall, 159, 160
  'Kubla Khan', 25, 32n, 53
  Lyrical Ballads (with Wordsworth), 176, 204
  'The Nightingale', 162–3
  'The Picture; or, the Lover's Resolution', 164
  'Reflections on Having Left a Place of Retirement', 168
  'Religious Musings', 143
  review of Malthus's *Essay*, 262–3
  'The Rime of the Ancyent Marinere', 163
Coletta, W. John, 241
colonialism *see* British empire; empire
common land, 149, 158, 232, 259
Connor, Patrick, 46
consumer culture, 35, 42, 43, 108, 265
Cook, Catherine, 60
Cooper, David, 241
Corfield, Penelope, 96
country houses (garden houses, India), 94–9, 102–6
Cowper, William, 141–7, 148, 152
  'Retirement', 141, 146, 148
  The Task, 141, 142–3, 144–5, 145–6, 147, 151

284 Index

cows (human-bovine relationships), 196, 197, 199, 203, 205–6, 240, 259
Crispinus Scriblerus, 174–9, 181–2, 183–8
Crutzen, Paul, 79
Cumbria, 8, 28, 232–3
Curzon of Keddleston, George Nathaniel, Marquis, 195

Daniell, Thomas and William, 109
Davies, Jeremy, 172
De Bolla, Peter, 163–4
deep ecology, 145, 244
deer (harts), 233–4
Dejung, Christof, 96
Denton Hall, 182
depopulation, 48, 85, 101, 157
Designs of Chinese Buildings, Furniture, Dresses, Machines, and Utensils (Chambers), 37, 39, 41, 43–7, 50, *131*
despotism, 18, 24–5, 36, 50, 52, 89, 253, 262
Dickens, Charles, *Sketches of Boz*, 152
Dickinson, Emily, 9
Dinas Bran from Llangollen (Wilson), 98, *133*
disease, 60, 66, 67, 84–6, 115, 118, 151
disgust, discourse of
  decaying matter, 242–3
  human bodily cleanliness, 65, 67, 260, 266
  human bodily remains, 63–4, 82, 101, 103
  poverty, 82, 83, 250, 252, 266
  social class and race, 72, 85–6
Dissertation on Oriental Gardening (Chambers), 21, 37–8, 49–52, 53
Dodsley, Robert, *136*, 165, 166
  'Description of the Leasowes', 160
drought, 100, 103, 175, 178, 187
Du Halde, Jean-Baptiste, *Description of the Empire of China*, 40
'Dudley, Worcestershire' (Turner), 79
Duff, David, 211

Earth Liberation Front, 2, 157
East India Bill (1783), 93, 99, 100–1
East India Company (EIC), 93–109
  British state regulation of, 102, 107, 108
  Burke's critique, 93–101, 106–7
  land management, 95, 96–7, 98–104, 106–8
  links to China, 17, 37, 39, 42
  social class, 37, 38, 93–4, 95, 96, 106
ecocriticism
  biocentrism, 212
  labouring-class writing, 172–3, 187, 237
  materialism, 203, 205
  overview of, 3–4, 5, 7, 231
ecofeminism, 145, 154n
ecogothic
  Stevenson, 60, 62, 63, 66–72
  Twain, 62, 63–6, 69, 71–2
ecological 'other', 61–3, 65–6, 67, 69–72
ecology
  ecosocial sensibility, 175, 177–8, 183, 185, 186–7
  nature's productivity limits, 174, 177, 180–2, 186–7, 232, 238, 240, 241
  scarcity and population, 250, 252–61, 263, 265, 266
ecomodernism, 86–7, 89
Eden *see* Garden of Eden
Eden, Frederick, 258
education
  distanced elites, 78, 82, 90
  EIC officials, 5–6, 37
  labouring class poets, lack of, 19, 165, 198
  for moral/social improvement, 251, 260, 264
Eliot, T. S., 225
Emmet, Robert, 159
empire
  Chinese imperial semiotics, 4, 19, 21, 24–5, 28–9, 42, 46–7
  Japanese empire, 204–5
  Roman empire, 101, 104–5, *135*, 265
  see also British empire
Enclosure Act (1773), 51

enclosure movement
  and biodiversity, 201, 232, 237–40
  in *Crispinus Scriblerus*, 174–5, 177, 185
  drought, 178, 187
  food supply, 177, 258–9
  labouring class loss of land, 7, 51, 158, 164, 167–9, 238, 258–9
  middle class influenced by, 158, 164, 168–9
  upper class control of, 7–8, 149, 158, 160, 168, 174–5, 178
Enmore Castle, 163
Enville, 160, 162
environmental aesthetics *see* Romantic environmental aesthetics
environmental catastrophes, 78–90; *see also* drought; famine
environmental ethics
  bioempathy, 144–5
  Leopold's land ethics, 8, 11, 244
  see also Christian environmentalism; stewardship
environmentalism, 1–10, 107–9, 168, 231, 244–5; *see also* Christian environmentalism; stewardship
eremitical tradition *see* hermits/ hermitages
An Essay on the Principle of Population (Malthus)
  1st edition, 249–50, 252–3, 254–7, 258
  2nd edition, 259–67
Evangelicalism, 141–2, 148–9, 151, 152
Everett, Nigel, 99

famine
  Bengal, 100–4, 108
  Britain, 178, 257–8
  Byron, 82
  Malthus, 11, 23, 252, 257
Fay, Eliza, 102
Felpham, Sussex, 212, 213, 216, 219, 221–2
females
  the 'female' in Blake's *Milton*, 213, 219–20, 222
  objectification of, 199
  status of, 36
  suffering of, 197, 200–1, 203
feminisation, 35, 43, 220
ferme orné (ornamental farm), 161–2
Fishman, Robert, 147–8, 149
Flemingston, Glamorgan, 221–2
flowers, 143, 147, 161, 166, 184–5, 216–17, 235
follies, 38, 42–3, 45, 46, 161
food supply, 249–52, 255, 256–9, 261, 263, 265
forests
  deforestation protests, 1, 10, 244–5
  India, 8, 98, 113–15, 118–19, 121, 124, 244
  USA, 70, 274–5
  wildness, 48, 115, 118, 121
France
  factor in British/Chinese talks, 17
  French Alps, 205
  French Revolution, 250, 253, 256, 257
  war with Britain, 46, 158, 212, 240, 257
Francis, Philip, 104–5
Fraser, James Baillie, 102–3, 108, *134*
Frederick, Prince of Wales, 43, 45, 49
Frend, William, 258
Frykman, Jonas and Maja Povrzanović, 117
Fulford, Tim, 273, 277

garden houses (country houses, India), 94–9, 102–6
Garden of Eden
  Bengal as, 100, 101–2, 103–4, 106, 107
  intersectionality, 277
  pre-colonised spaces, 236
  suburbs as, 142, 146
Gee, Edward Pritchard, 117
gender
  the 'female' in Blake's *Milton*, 213, 219–20, 222
  and intersectionality, 36, 201, 273–4
  see also ecofeminism; females; feminisation; masculine identity
George III, King, 49, 52

georgic mode
  Bloomfield, 167, 173
  Burke, 107
  Wilson, 274
  Woodhouse, 174–7, 186, 187–8
  Yearsley, 197
georgic-pastoral mode *see* pastoral-georgic mode
Gilpin, William, 25, 149, 164
Gissing, George, 152
Global South, 2, 78, 244–5
God
  benevolence of, 107, 251–2, 255–6
  and environmental responsibility, 86, 100–1
  Malthus on, 252–3, 257, 262
  in nature, 142–3, 144–5, 146, 149, 152, 220–1
Godwin, William, 87, 253–4, 255, 256
  Enquiry Concerning Political Justice (Godwin), 253–4
  Malthus's opposition to, 253–4, 255, 256
Gold, John, 179
Goldsmith, Oliver
  The Citizen of the World, 34, 37, 42
  The Deserted Village, 51
Gond people, 244
gongshi (scholar's stones), 40–1, 47
Gopal, Priyamvada, *Insurgent Empire*, 2–3
gothic mode, 38, 48, 50–1, 161; *see also* ecogothic
Gray, Thomas, 149
Green Imperialism (Grove), 11n, 101, 106
green spaces, 144, 145, 230–2, 233, 235, 243
greenwashing, 108–9
Greta Hall, 159, 160
Griffith, William, 118
Grove, Richard, *Green Imperialism*, 11n, 101, 106
guns, 120–1, 122, 200

Haggerty, Sarah, *William Blake in Context*, 211
Hagley, 160, 162

Halfpenny, William, 43, 46
  Architecture in the Chinese Taste, 43
Hamilton, Charles, 27
Hampstead, 150, 151, 158
Harris, John, 44
harts (deer), 233–4
Hasdeo Arand forest, 244
Hassell, John, 148–9
Hastings, Warren, 97–8, 99–100, 102
Hayot, Eric, 50
Hazlitt, William, 11, 249, 264–7
  A Reply to the Essay on Population, 249, 264–7
health
  nature beneficial for, 141–5, 150–2, 223
  suburbs beneficial for, 141–2, 145–7, 150–2
Heber, Bishop Reginald, 103
Heidegger, Martin, 240–1, 244
Hellman, Lisa, 41
hermits/hermitages, 48–9, 159–60, 163, 164, 167–8
Hester Williams, Kim D., 71
Heyman, Peter, 5
Hill, Octavia, 152
Himley, 176–7, 178
Hinduism, 10, 100–1, 103, 106, 121
Hirschfeld, Christian, 38
Hodges, William, 97–100, 102, 108
  Natives drawing Water from a Pond with Warren Hastings' House at Alipur in the Distance, 97, 98, 102, *132*
  Travels in India, 102
  View of an Indian Village with a Man Seated in the Foreground, *133*
  A View of Marmalong Bridge with a Sepoy and Natives in the Foreground, 98
  View of Warren Hastings' House at Alipur and Two Figures in the Foreground, 97, *132*
Hogarth, William, 35, 44, 49
  Marriage A-la-Mode series, 35
Holcroft, Thomas, *Anna St Ives*, 188
Holmes, Samuel, *Journal by One of the Guard on Lord Macartney's Embassy to China*, 18–19, 22

Hooghly, river, 102, 103, 105
Hsu, Hsuan L., 66
Hudson, Nicholas, 36
human and non-human agency, 79–80, 83, 87–8
human-animal relationships
  animals eat human remains, 101, 103
  Clare's depictions of, 201–2, 235–41
  distinction (use of reason), 251
  fellow suffering beings, 9, 200–1, 203, 235
  in gardens, 41, 45, 48, 161
  health benefits of, 143–4, 147
  see also animals; birds; cows (human-bovine relationships); hunting; sheep; tigers
human bodies
  cannibalism, 64, 82
  cemeteries/graves, 63–4, 69, 160
  dirt and cleanliness, 65, 67, 260, 266
  disease, 60, 66, 67, 84–6, 115, 118, 151
  eaten by animals, 101, 103
  extinction imagined, 80–3, 85, 88
  fragility vis-à-vis tiger, 115–16, 117, 119, 121–2
  see also health; senses (Malthus)
human-plant relationships
  bioempathy, 143–4, 147
  botany, 47, 102–3, 106, 114, 115, 117, 118
  Chinatown food cultivation, 64
  Chinese peasant farmer, 23
  deforestation protests, 1, 10, 244–5
  flowers, 143, 147, 161, 166, 184–5, 216–17, 235
  profit-motive, impact of, 174, 177, 181–2, 184–5, 186–8
  see also forests; jungle (*jungli*); trees
humanness
  animalistic and brutish, 64, 66, 71–2, 84, 253, 266
  degrees of (relates to race), 85–6
  possibility of 'improvement', 86–7, 251, 253–4, 260, 262, 264
Hume, David
  'Of the Standard of Taste', 45

A Treatise of Human Nature, 215
hunter-gatherers, 234
hunting
  in British countryside, 121, 146, 200, 233, 237, 243
  in Indian jungle, 113–14, 115, 116–17, 119–24
Hutchings, Kevin, *Imagining Nature*, 212, 213

'improvement'
  human mind and morals, 86–7, 251, 253–4, 260, 262, 264
  to landscape aesthetic, 24, 25, 164, 178–9, 185, 187–8, 275
  see also agricultural 'improvement'
India, 93–109, 113–24
  art, Indian people in, 95, 97, 99, 102, 105–6, 107, *132*, *133*, *134*
  Chipko movement, 1, 10
  country houses, 94–9, 102–6
  famine, 100–4, 108
  Indian Rebellion (1857), 116
  labouring class, 94–5, 97, 99, 100–8, 114, 119–20, 122, 244
  'otherness' of Indians, 105, 115, 116, 122, 124
  tea plantations, 113–15, 117, 118–24, *135*
Indian Forest Act (1878), 119
Indigenous people, 5, 8, 65, 106, 234, 244–5, 275–7
industrialisation
  carbon capitalism, 78, 79, 182–3, 244–5, 278
  industrial aesthetic, 47, 161
  and poverty, 255, 263, 264
  and Romantic aesthetic, 30, 172
  technology effects, 61, 69, 86–9, 120, 179, 187, 240–2
  Woodhouse's experience of, 178–9, 182–3
Ingram, Robert, 265
intersectionality, 36, 62, 96, 201, 273, 278
Ionic architecture, 104
Iovino, Serenella, 203–4, 205
Ireland, 24, 259
  Irish Rebellion (1803), 159

Jamieson, Dale, 89
Japan, 2, 204–5
Jarrold, Thomas, 264
Jesuit Order, 28, 29, 38, 42, 44, 48, 50
Johnson, Samuel, *A Dictionary of the English Language*, 215, 219–20
Jonsson, Frederik Albritton, 1
Joyce, James, *Ulysses*, 224
jungle (*jungli*), 101, 113–15, 117–19, 121–4

Kangxi Emperor, 29
Kanpur, 116
Keegan, Bridget, 173, 174, 177, 184, 272–8
Keetley, Dawn, 62–3, 72
Kelley, Theresa, 114
Kent, William, 48, 49, 213
Kenyon-Jones, Christine, *Kindred Brutes*, 236
Keohan, Catherine, 200
Kew Gardens, 37, 45–7, 49, 52, 53, *131*
Kirkby Lonsdale, 235
Kitson, Peter, 37, 51, 54
Kobilka, Brian K., 144
Kyd, Thomas, 103

labouring class
  in British cities, 147, 151, 152
  in China, 11, 22–3, 48–9
  definition, 5–6
  ecosocial sensibility, 175, 177–8, 183, 185, 186–7
  education/the 'unlearned', 18–19, 165, 195–6, 198
  embassy to China, access and exclusion, 18–19, 22–3
  enclosure movement, loss of land, 7, 51, 158, 164, 167–9, 238, 258–9
  in India, 94–5, 97, 99, 100–8, 114, 119–20, 122, 244
  Marxist writers interest in, 205, 206
  orientalisation of class, 36
  representations of, 83, 98, 166, 167, 198–9, 204, 277
  in Switzerland, 82, 83
  tidying wild nature, 235, 239–40, 243

labouring-class poets
  Blake, 212, 218, 221
  Clare, 167, 172, 205, 235, 237–9
  ecocriticism, 172–3, 187, 237
  geographical mobility, 9–10, 196
  Wilson, 272, 274
  Woodhouse, 173, 186–8
  Yearsley, 195–7, 201
Laird, Mark, 166
Lake District
  biodiversity, 168, 230, 232–3
  Chambers, 28
  Coleridge, 159
  Gray, 149
  Malthus, 254
  national park, 8, 30, 230
  Wordsworth, 8, 25, 30, 142, 232–3
land ethics
  'land' and 'landscape' defined, 158–9, 164, 166–7, 178
  Leopold, 8, 11, 244
land management
  EIC in India, 95, 96–7, 98–104, 106–8
  Hampstead Heath byelaws, 158
  Indian tea plantations, 114–15, 118, 119
  productive vs ornamental, 168–9, 174, 187
  see also agricultural 'improvement'; agriculture; enclosure movement; stewardship
Landry, Donna, 183, 199
landscape gardens (in Britain)
  and adjoining landscape, 94–5, 99, 105–6, 149–50, 161, 183, 235
  Brownian aesthetic, 50–1, 174, 175, 178, 183, 235, 236
  Chinese gardens, compared with, 20–1, 24–5, 26–7, 28
  Chinese influence, 17–18, 26–7, 42–53
  enclosure aesthetic, 158, 160, 168, 174–5, 178
  melancholia, 159, 160, 162–3, 165–6, 167, 217–18
landscape painting
  of Chinese gardens, 23, 29, *130*
  country houses/India, 94, 95, 97–8

picturesque, 19, 98, 149
  Thomson's influence, 213
  Woodhouse's critique, 178
landscapes
  desolate, 88, 159
  georgic vs pastoral, 166–7
  tidiness aesthetic, 234–5, 239–43
  see also enclosure movement
larks, 217–18, 220, 224
Latour, Bruno, 86
Leapor, Mary, 'Crumble Hall', 188, 235
The Leasowes, 20, 158, 160–3, 164–6, 173, 179
  map, 136, 160, 161, 164, 166, 169n
Lefkowitz, Robert J., 144
Lei, Daphne Pi-Wei, 62
Leigh Woods, 196, 202–3
Leng, Mei, *Bishu Shanzhuang*, 130
Leopold, Aldo, *A Sand County Almanac*, 8, 11, 244
The Life and Lucubrations of Crispinus Scriblerus (Woodhouse), 174–9, 181–2, 183–8
Lissanoure castle, Antrim, 24
Liu, Yu, 37, 42, 49
Lloyd, Robert, 141, 146
  'The Cit's Country Box', 141
Lloyd Smith, Allan, 62
Locke, John, 251, 252–3
Lofft, Capel, 198
London
  Blake, 212, 220, 221–2
  Goldsmith, 34
  middle class, 42, 141
  Montagu, 183
  Morganwg, 223
  Woodhouse, 174
  see also Clapham; Hampstead; Kew Gardens
Lowe, Lisa, *Immigrant Acts*, 62
Lowther Hall, Westmorland, 28
Lucretius, Titus Lucretius Carus, 216–17, 220, 225
Lyttelton, George, Baron, 160, 168, 173

Macartney, George, 1st Earl, 17, 18, 21–9, 53

An Embassy to China, 18, 21–2, 24, 25–8
McCollum, Elmer, 195
MacKenzie, John M., 3
Makdisi, Saree, 36
Malm, Andreas, 79
Malthus, Thomas Robert, 249–67
  An Essay on the Principle of Population, 249–50, 252–3, 254–7, 258, 259–67
  vs Godwin's utopianism, 253–4, 255, 256
  Hazlitt's response, 11, 249, 264–7
  Malthusianism in culture, 10–11, 61, 64, 250
  vs Paine, 260–1
  Paley and Locke, influence of, 251–3
  Southey's response, 11, 261–4
  vs Young's utopianism, 187, 258–9
Marlow, William, *View of the Wilderness at Kew*, 46, 131
Marx, Karl, 167
Marxist criticism, 3–4, 5, 36, 177, 205, 206, 211, 213
Masaki, Taizo, 77n
masculine identity, 83, 113, 120–2, 123–4, 182
Mason, William
  The English Garden, 51
  An Heroic Epistle to William Chambers, 52
Maurice Ashley-Cooper and Antony Ashley-Cooper, 3rd Earl of Shaftesbury (Closterman), 104, 135
Mays, J. C. C., 163
Mee, Benjamin, 97–8
melancholia, 159, 160, 162–3, 165–6, 167, 217–18
middle class
  and Chinatown's ecological 'other', 8, 62, 65
  chinoiserie as marker of, 34–6, 38, 42–4, 53, 141
  commerce celebrated in gardens, 47, 50
  definition, 5
  education, 5–6, 37, 196

middle class (*cont.*)
   and EIC employees, 37, 38, 93–4, 95, 96, 106
   embassy to China, access and exclusion, 18–21, 24, 26, 37–8
   enclosure movement, 158, 164, 168–9
   Indian tea plantations class structure, 121, 122–3
   picturesque aesthetics, 8, 19, 142, 148–52, 198–9, 249
   relocation/reinvention, 274
   sensibility cult, 201, 234
   in suburbs, 141–2, 145–52, 231
   tidying wild nature, 235, 243
   visitors to The Leasowes, 162
milk, 195, 205
milkmaids, 195–9, 203
Milton (Blake), 212–13, 215–25
Milton, John
   'Il Penseroso', 163
   Paradise Lost, 217, 218
Mitchell, W. J. T., 116–17
moles, 201–2
Monbiot, George, 232, 244
Montagu, Elizabeth, 173–4, 175, 180–7, 258
More, Hannah, 195–6, 258
Morganwg, Iolo (Edward Williams), 212, 213, 221–4
   'Horrors of War, a Pastoral', 224
   'Ode on Converting a Sword into a Pruning-Hook', 224
   'Ode on the Mythology of the Ancient British Bards', 223–4
   Poems, Lyric and Pastoral, 213, 221–4
Morton, Timothy, *Ecology without Nature*, 3–4, 10, 172, 231–2, 233
Munro, Hugo, 115–16

'nabobs', 93–4, 95
Nagano, Japan, 204–5
Nash, John, 151
national parks, 8, 30, 178, 230, 233
National Trust, 152, 202
Native Americans, 65, 275–7
Natives drawing Water from a Pond with Warren Hastings' House at Alipur in the Distance (Hodges), 97, 98, 102, *132*
nature
   aestheticisation of, 3–10, 25, 27, 29–30
   agricultural productivity limits, 174, 177, 180–2, 186–7, 232, 238, 240, 241
   Brownian aesthetic, 50–1, 174, 175, 178, 183, 235, 236
   destructive power, 275
   God found in, 142–3, 144–5, 146, 149, 152, 220–1
   harmony, 145, 172, 176, 263
   health benefits of, 141–5, 150–2, 223
   melancholia, 159, 160, 162–3, 165–6, 167, 217–18
   'nature's mighty feast' (Malthus), 250, 261–2, 265
   in the suburbs, 147, 149, 152
   Thomson and Blake, 213, 215–17
   Wordsworth's concept of, 231–3
   see also wild nature
neoclassicism
   architecture in China, 25, 43, 44
   architecture in India, 95, 97, 102, 104–5
   The Leasowes, 161, 165
   origin of pastoral-georgic, 173, 214–15
   vs portrayals of China, 35, 42, 43, 44–5, 47
Newman, Lance, 72
Newton, John, 141, 144, 148
Niagara Falls, 272, 274
Nicholls, Frank, 119, 121–3, *136*
Nishime, Leilani, 71
Nixon, Rob, 71, 106
Noble, Charles, 39–40
non-human agency *see* human and non-human agency
North America, 234; *see also* USA
Northamptonshire, 236–7

opium dens, 65
orientalism, 36, 60, 62, 66, 69–72
Orkney islands, 88
'otherness'
   of Chinese immigrants (ecological

'other'), 8, 61–3, 65–6, 67, 69–72
EIC returnees to Britain ('nabobs'), 93–4, 95
of Indian people, 105, 115, 116, 122, 124
of the tiger, 115, 123
use of viewpoint of, 87
overpopulation *see* population; senses (Malthus)
Oxfam, 78
Oxfordshire, 243

pagodas, 39, 45–7, 53, *131*
Paine, Thomas, *Rights of Man*, 260–1
Painshill, Surrey, 27
Paley, William
  Christian utilitarianism, 251–2
  The Principles of Moral and Political Philosophy, 251
Palladian architecture, 25, 43, 44, 95, 97, 102, 104, *134*
Palladian Garden House in a Wooded Park (Porter), 104, 105–6, *134*
Palumbo-Liu, David, 61
Park Village, London, 151
pastoral-georgic mode
  Blake, 212–13, 218, 225
  Butler, 211
  Thomson, 213, 214–15
  Yearsley, 197
  see also georgic mode
pastoral mode
  Blake, 217
  farming methods, 233, 249, 256
  Hodges, 99
  Morganwg, 221, 224
  Porter, 105
  Shenstone, 160
  suburbs, 148
  Woodhouse, 162, 167
  see also sheep
paternalism, 98–100, 104
pathos, 159, 163, 165–6
patronage, 18, 19
  Blake, 212, 218
  Chambers, 6, 37, 49
  Hodges, 97, 98, 108
  White, 198

Woodhouse, 165, 173
Yearsley, 195–6
Perdue, Peter, 39
performativity, 113, 184, 203–4
Pevsner, Nicholas, 151
Peyrefitte, Alain, 17
philanthropy, 148, 184, 201, 250, 258, 261, 262, 263
photography, tigers, 114, 122, 123
physiognomy, 85–6
picturesque aesthetics
  Chinese garden as model of, 21, 22, 24–8, 48, 50
  Christian environmentalism, 142–3, 148–9, 151, 152
  vs corporeal/senses (Malthus), 254–5
  desolation/wilderness/wildness, 4, 8, 29–30, 48, 85
  landscape painting, 19, 98, 149
  and social class, 8, 19, 142, 148–52, 198–9, 249
Pielak, Chase, 116, 121
plantations *see* tea plantations
Poe, Edgar Allan, 'The Raven', 65–6
'Poetical Shoemaker', 158, 165
Pollok, Fitz William Thomas, 119–20
poor laws, 249–50, 256, 257, 259, 260–1, 264–5
Pope, Alexander, 48, 196–7
  Windsor Forest, 196, 203
population
  Chinatowns, 60, 64
  control of (China), 11
  depopulation, 48, 85, 101, 157
  ecological scarcity, 250, 252–61, 263, 265, 266
  growth benefits, 22–3, 249, 252
  as mob, 39–40, 61, 64
  see also cities as loci of corruption
Porter, David, 30n, 35, 37–8, 39, 41, 42
Porter, John Young, 104, 105–6, 108, *134*
  Palladian Garden House in a Wooded Park, 104, 105–6, *134*
postcolonialism, 2–3, 4, 5, 7–8
potatoes, 258–9
poverty
  and industrialisation, 255, 263, 264

poverty (*cont.*)
　'nature's mighty feast' (Malthus), 250, 261–2
　poor laws/parish relief, 249–50, 256, 257, 259, 260–1, 264–5
　and social justice, 250, 261–3, 265, 266–7
　Woodhouse's experience of, 176, 178
Pratt, Mary Louise, 110n
primitivism, 87, 173, 212, 256
Prinsep, William, 118–19
Pumpelly, Raphael, *Across America and Asia*, 61, 64

Qianlong Emperor, 22, 27, 28, 29
Qing Dynasty, 22, 29

race
　in Canton, 39
　in Chinatowns, 60–72
　hierarchy of, 85–6, 122
　Indigenous people, 234, 275–7
　and intersectionality, 273
　milk linked to white supremacism, 195
　'otherness' and Indian people, 105, 115, 116, 122, 124
　and social class, 2–3, 4–5, 8, 36, 72, 85–6
Rackham, Oliver, 202–3
Radclyffe, T, *Wolverhampton from the Penn Road*, 137
Ramsden, A. R., *Assam Planter*, 113, 135
Ray, Sarah Jaquette, 63, 65
Raynal, Abbé, 100, 101, 107
Regulating Act (1773), 102
religious environmentalism
　ancestral worship, 63–4
　Hinduism, 10, 100–1, 106, 121
　paganism, 223–5
　see also Christian environmentalism
Repton, Humphry, 47, 48, 149–50
Retribution (Armitage), 116
Revill, George, 179
Ricoeur, Paul, *Memory, History, Forgetting*, 224–5
Rigby, Kate, 7, 83, 115
riots, 257–8, 261

Ripa, Matteo, 42, 47
Risse, Guenter B., 71
Ritter, Joachim, 203
Ritvo, Harriet, 123
Rizzo, Betty, 180
Rollinger, Maria, 195
Roman empire
　architecture and culture, 104–5, *135*, 265
　civil law (usufruct), 101
Romantic environmental aesthetics
　as Anthropocene aesthetic, 79
　and biodiversity, 230–3, 243–4
　Brownian aesthetic, 50–1, 174, 175, 178, 183, 235, 236
　China as an aestheticised space, 35–6, 50, 52–3
　Chinatowns, 60, 62, 71
　and race, 8, 18
　and social class, 7–9, 18, 19, 23, 97
　see also beauty; enclosure movement; picturesque aesthetics; sublime
Rooker, Edward, *131*
Rousseau, Jean-Jacques, 87, 143
　Les Reveries du Promeneur Solitaire, 196–7
Rowe, Nicholas, *The Biter*, 35
Roxborough, William, 103
Royal Academy of Arts, 49, 108
Royal Military Academy, Woolwich, 108

Samson, Miles David, 49
San Francisco, 60, 62, 64, 66, 69–70
Sandleford Priory, *137*, 173–4, 175, 180–2, 183–7
satires, 34, 35, 37, 42–3, 52, 141
scarcity and population *see* population, ecological scarcity
scholar's stones (*gongshi*), 40–1, 47
science
　biology and exotica, 117
　botany, 47, 102–3, 106, 114, 115, 117, 118
　language, 1, 4
　Malthus's use of, 249, 255
　technology effects, 61, 69, 86–9, 120, 179, 187, 240–2
Scotland, 1, 68, 88, 252, 272, 274, 277

Sea Shepherd Society, 10, 157
senses (Malthus), 249–57, 259–67
   equality of property effects, 253–4, 256
   Hazlitt's critique, 11, 249, 264–7
   negative sensations, 252–4, 255, 257, 259–61
   and reason, 251, 253–4, 262–3
   Southey's critique, 11, 261–4
Shaftesbury, Anthony Ashley Cooper, 3rd Earl of, 43, 104, *135*
Shah, Nayan, 60
sheep, 98, 161, 167, 197, 199, 206, 232–3, 240
Shelley, Mary, 79–80, 83–90
   Frankenstein, 79, 83, 86–9, 90
   History of a Six Weeks' Tour (with P. B. Shelley), 83
   The Last Man, 79, 80, 83–6, 89
Shelley, Percy Bysshe, 79–80, 83, 86, 87, 89–90
   History of a Six Weeks' Tour (with M. Shelley), 83
   'Mont Blanc', 84–5
   Prometheus Unbound, 79, 80, 86, 89
Shenstone, William, 158, 160–9, 173, 179
   The Judgment of Hercules, 167–8
   'A Pastoral Ballad, in Four Parts', 160
Shimazaki, Tōson, *Chikuma River Sketchbooks*, 204–5, 206
Shrubsole, Guy, 244
Shugborough, 53
Sinology, 37, 52, 53–4
Sivaramakrishnan, K., 118
Sivils, Matthew Wynn, 62–3, 72
slavery, 42, 60, 66, 72, 88, 105, 108
   abolition movement, 148, 201
Slovic, Scott, 203, 205
Smith, Adam
   The Theory of Moral Sentiments, 143, 178
   The Wealth of Nations, 258
Smith, Charlotte, *Conversations Introducing Poetry*, 201, 203
Smith, Samuel, 51
Snow, John, 151
social class
   China's class structure, 11, 21–3, 48–9
   chinoiserie as marker of, 17–18, 19, 27, 34–6, 38, 42–53, 141
   of EIC employees, 37, 38, 93–4, 95, 96, 106
   embassy to China, access and exclusion, 18–29, 37–8
   and environmentalism/climate crises, 1–10, 78–85, 89–90
   Indian tea plantations class structure, 113, 114, 119, 120, 121–3, 124
   and race, 2–3, 4–5, 8, 36, 72, 85–6
   and suburbs, 141–2, 145–52
   and transport, 148, 150, 196–7, 221
   see also labouring class; labouring-class poets; middle class; upper class
social justice, 250, 261–3, 265, 266–7
solar power, 231
Somerset, 163
South America, 87–8, 234, 244
Southey, Robert, 11, 261–4
Springwood, Charles Fruehling, 120
Stallybrass, Peter, 151
Staunton, Sir George Leonard, 17
   An Authentic Account of an Embassy, 18, 21, 25, 26
Stevenson, Robert Louis, 60, 62, 63, 66–72
   'Across the Plains', 67, 76n
   The Amateur Emigrant, 70
   'Despised Races', 67
   'A Gossip on Romance', 60
   The New and Old Capitals, 66
stewardship
   Christian, 174, 177
   in colonial India, 100–7
   ecomodernism, 86–7, 89
   ongoing, 273
   Woodhouse as land steward, 173–4, 175, 177, 180–1, 182, 184–7
   see also Christian environmentalism
Stoermer, Eugene F., 79
Stone, Lauwrence, 149
Strange, Sir Thomas, 104, 106

sublime
- Alps, 80
- awe, 149
- in Chinese gardens, 21, 27–8, 48, 50
- industrial aesthetic, 47, 161
- Niagara Falls, 274
- reaction to agriculture/industrialisation, 29–30
- Shenstone, 160, 161

suburbs
- in Britain, 141–2, 145–51, 231
- in India, 104, 106

Surrey, 27, 151–2, 220
Suzhou gardens, 22
Swedish East India Company, 37, 38
Switzerland, 79, 82–3, 208n, 232, 233

Tambora eruption, 79–80
Taussig, Michael, 121
taxation, 63, 100, 258, 260, 266
tea plantations, 113–15, 117, 118–24, 135
technology, effects of, 61, 69, 86–9, 120, 179, 187, 240–2
Teltscher, Kate, 102
Temple, William, 48
Thompson, E. P., 211
Thomson, James, 200, 213–18
- *The Castle of Indolence*, 215
- *Liberty*, 213
- *A Poem sacred to the Memory of Sir Isaac Newton*, 215
- *The Seasons*, 200, 213–15, 215–17
- *Spring*, 213–15, 215–17
- *Summer*, 216

Thornton, John, Henry and Marianne, 148
Thunberg, Greta, 2
Thurow, Lester, 1
tigers, 113–24
- bodies as hunting trophies, 113–14, 115, 116–17, 119–24
- visual representations, 116, 121–2, 135, 136

Tory motifs/perspective, 25, 38, 51–3, 99
transport, and social class, 148, 150, 196–7, 221

trees
- in art, 97, 99, 105
- felled by settlers, USA, 275, 276–7
- pollards, 202–3
- in suburbs, 147, 148–9, 150, 151–2
- tree root house/hermitage, 160
- woodlands, 202–3, 237, 241–3, 244

Tuana, Nancy, 2
Turner, J. M. W., 148, 213
- 'Dudley, Worcestershire', 179

Twain, Mark, 62, 63–6, 69, 70–2
- 'The Mysterious Chinaman', 65–6
- *Roughing It*, 63, 69, 72

Ulrich, Roger S., 144
UNESCO, 29–30
United States of America (USA), 1–2, 8, 147, 234, 272–7; *see also* Chinatowns

upper class
- chinoiserie as marker of, 35–6, 38, 42–53
- climate crises and privilege, 78–85, 89–90
- in colonial India, 93–7, 99, 107
- definition, 5
- education, 78, 82, 90, 196
- and EIC employees, 37, 38, 93–4, 95, 96, 106
- embassy to China, access and exclusion, 18, 21–2, 24–8, 29
- enclosure movement, 7–8, 149, 158, 160, 168, 174–5, 178, 238
- hunting, 121, 146, 243
- landowners' profit motive, 174–5, 177–87, 238, 240, 241
- 'nature's mighty feast' benefits (Malthus), 250, 261–2, 265
- revolution fears, 258, 261
- tidying wild nature, 235
- Twain's depiction, 72

urban spaces, 60, 62, 68, 70, 149 *see also* cities as loci of corruption; suburbs
USA *see* United States of America (USA)
utilitarianism, 251–2, 262
utopianism
- Godwin, 87, 253–4, 255, 256

Percy and Mary Shelley, 83, 86–8
Young, 187, 258–9

Valenze, Deborah, *Milk: A Local and Global History*, 195
Van-Hagen, Steve, 174
'A View of the Botanic Garden House and Reach' (Fraser), 102–3, *134*
View of the Wilderness at Kew (Marlow), 46, *131*
villa urbana, 104–5
villages
  in Britain, 148, 151, 243
  in India, 99, 101–2, 119
villas, 95, 97, 104–5, 147, 148, 152
Virginia, Chinese quarter, 65

Waldron, Mary, 200
Walpole, Horace, 42–3
  'On Modern Gardening', 51
Wanshu Yuan (the Garden of Ten Thousand Trees), 18, 22–8, 29
Ward, John, 1st Viscount Dudley and Ward, 173, 177
Warde, Paul, 107, 108
Washington, Chris, 83
Watson, Paul, 10
Whale, John, 149
Whig motifs/perspective, 24, 42, 47, 50–3, 99–100, 160, 172
Whitbread Bill (1807), 264
White, Allon, 151
White, Henry Kirke, 'Clifton Grove', 198–9
White, Richard, 168
Whitman, Walt, 9
Whyte, Ian, 232
wild animals
  Clare's depictions, 201–2, 235–41
  see also birds; deer (harts); tigers
wild nature
  aestheticisation of, 4, 8, 23, 27, 29–30, 51
  desolate/empty of people, 87–8, 159
  forests, 48, 115, 118, 121
  human tidying of, 235, 239–40
  jungle, 101, 113–15, 117–19, 121–4
wilderness
  American frontier, 274–5
  city returned to, 69–70
  flower garden, 184–5
  pleasure garden, 25
  tamed into productiveness, 177, 181
  and tigers, 48, 113–14, 120, 121–4
  Wordsworth's influence, 8, 30, 230
'The Wilderness Walk', *137*, 184
William-Wynn, Sir Watkin, 98
Williams, Edward *see* Morganwg, Iolo (Edward Williams)
Williams, Raymond, 4, 211
  The Country and the City, 4, 11n
  Culture and Materialism, 4
  Keywords, 4
Williamson, Tom, 232, 237, 238
Wilson, Alexander, 272–8
  American Ornithology, 272
  The Foresters, 272, 273–7
Wilson, E. O., 14n, 244
Wilson, Richard, *Dinas Bran from Llangollen*, 98, *133*
Wimbledon, 220
wind power, 231
Windsor Castle, 84
Wolverhampton, *137*, 178
Wood, Frances, 17
Wood, Gillen D'Arcy, 82
Woodhouse, James, 158, 165–7, 173–88, 274
  'An Elegy to William Shenstone', 165, 167
  'The Lessowes', 165, 166, 167
  'The Lessowes, after Shenstone's Death', 165
  The Life and Lucubrations of Crispinus Scriblerus, 174–9, 181–2, 183–8
  Life and Poetical Works of James Woodhouse, 174
  Poems on Sundry Occasions, 165–6, 173
  'Spring', 165–6
Woodland Cottage, Clapham, 148–9
woodlands, 9, 202–3, 237, 241–3, 244
Wordsworth, William, 142–3, 145, 204, 230–6, 243
  'To a Butterfly', 233
  Chinese gardens, knowledge and evocations of, 18, 21, 23, 25, 53

Wordsworth, William (*cont.*)
   'To a Cuckoo', 233
   dominance and legacy, 9, 172, 230–3, 236, 243
   The Excursion, 161
   'green' language and spaces, 145, 230–2, 233, 235, 243
   Guide to the Lakes, 232
   'Hart-Leap Well', 233, 234–5
   Lyrical Ballads (with Coleridge), 176, 204
   'Michael', 232, 233, 234
   national parks, 8, 30
   The Prelude, 18, 25, 53, 142, 174, 232, 233, 234
   'Resolution and Independence', 23
   'The Ruined Cottage', 232, 233
   'Tintern Abbey', 143

working class *see* labouring class; labouring-class poets
World Heritage Sites, 29–30
Wunderkammer, 44, 46

'Year without a Summer' (1816), 79, 80, 278
Yearsley, Ann, 195–203, 206
   'Clifton Hill', 196–203
   Poems on Several Occasions, 195–6
Yorkshire Dales, 157, 168, 233
Yoshida, Shoin, 77n
Young, Arthur, 187, 258–9
Yuanming Yuan (the Garden of Perfect Brightness), 19–22, 27, 28–9

Zuroski Jenkins, Eugenia, 30n, 35

EU representative:
Easy Access System Europe
Mustamäe tee 50, 10621 Tallinn, Estonia
Gpsr.requests@easproject.com

www.ingramcontent.com/pod-product-compliance
Lightning Source LLC
Chambersburg PA
CBHW052046220426
43663CB00012B/2458